Praise for *The Asianization of Christianity*

This book offers theological reflections that provide a fresh perspective on God's mission, showcasing the unique contributions of leaders from various parts of Asia. A notable feature of the book is its precise contextual-theological framework, which delves into God's salvation plan, the incarnation of Christ, the inspiration of the Bible, and the evolution of mission from Jewish to non-Jewish contexts. Furthermore, *The Asianization of Christianity* goes beyond traditional approaches to cultural adaptation. It proposes a theological paradigm that fosters a Christlike community practicing contextualized faith. Dr. Jonathan James adeptly weaves together diverse experiences and multifaceted theological reflections, transcending the limitations of conventional contextual theology. This is a masterful work that will inspire and challenge readers in the coming decades about the authentic expression and sharing of the Christian faith in the diverse cultural settings of Asia.

—Rev. Dr. Clement Chia, principal and director of community ministry, Singapore Bible College

The Asianization of Christianity: New Models for Mission is written by practitioners, not ivory-tower scholars removed from daily realities. The authors seek to appropriately *baptize* the cultural practices with biblical meaning, instead of *burying* or *burning* them. They offer proven principles and strategies for effective church-planting among the unreached peoples of Asia. All these occur without the spirit of imperialism, superiority, colonialism, or an imposition of false guilt. This gives believers the freedom to live biblically in their own context, to sing and dance to their own tunes for the glory of our Master. By reading the captivating examples of indigenization shared in the book, readers see the matchless creativity of God, and at the same time, acknowledge that different cultural groups are becoming acquainted with the unchanging gospel. I would highly recommend this book as a required text for all missionaries. Read, then adapt these amazing insights to your mission field.

—Dr. Alvin Low, president, Assisting Churches and Theological Schools (ACTS International), Colorado Springs, Colorado

Global mission has been a recurring theme over the last two millennia. The face of the globe changed with the preaching of the gospel, beginning from the early apostles. In the last two centuries, as the gospel was preached in Africa and Asia, it was largely through notable missionaries who were either American or European. Consequently, Christians were mainly aware of the Western approach to the gospel. But then missiologists introduced the term "contextualization," and this was a turning point. So the gospel progressed from globalization to contextualization. Now we see in this book by Dr. Jonathan James a new phrase, "the Asianization of Christianity." *Asianization* is a broad term that encompasses outreach activities to different Asian nations, according to their values, practices, and thought patterns. This is not just a fashionable term but an apt one, because the book outlines a new paradigm of mission that goes beyond contextualization. This book may be one of the best things that could happen to the church in the twenty-first century. It is a compelling mission handbook backed up by solid research to build bridges to the cultures of Asia without compromising the essence of the gospel. I highly recommend this book to church leaders, students, and missionaries in Asia and throughout the world.

—Dr. Emmanuel Damara, senior pastor, Grace Community Baptist Church, Telangana, India

I am thrilled with the publication of *The Asianization of Christianity: New Models for Mission*, edited by Dr. Jonathan D. James. I see it as a fulfillment of the prophetic utterances by global researchers and missiologists that the church in the Global South would play a significant role in facilitating global mission in the twenty-first century. This is a book by Asian missional practitioners disseminating theological and methodological insights to effectively reach and disciple Asia through indigenous and contextual ways. It is a significant compendium of mission research that will empower Christian leaders and churches in the Global South communities in the praxis of *missio Dei*.

—Rev. Dr. Isac Soundararaja, general secretary, Indian Missions Association, and former principal of Hindustan Bible Institute, India

The Asianization of Christianity: New Models for Mission has great relevance to the indigenization of the gospel message, with a special focus on interacting with the varieties of Asian cultures and religions. The three sections ("Core Issues," "Mission and Church," and "Training and Discipleship") are written in a convincing manner to wean away the remnants of Western theological grids and undertones that are still lurking in many circles within the Asian church context. I heartily endorse this comprehensive volume for study in theological colleges and churches in Asia. This will help indigenous churches to overcome the myriads of challenges and the waves of persecution faced in contemporary mission contexts.

—Rev. Dr. Raja Singh Elias, general secretary,
Indian Evangelical Mission, Bengaluru, India

THE ASIANIZATION OF CHRISTIANITY

THE ASIANIZATION OF CHRISTIANITY

NEW MODELS FOR MISSION

Edited by

Jonathan D. James

FORTRESS PRESS

MINNEAPOLIS

THE ASIANIZATION OF CHRISTIANITY
New Models for Mission

29 28 27 26 25 24 1 2 3 4 5 6 7 8 9

Library of Congress Cataloging-in-Publication Data

Names: James, Jonathan D., editor. | Johnson, Todd M. (Todd Michael), writer of foreword.
Title: The Asianization of Christianity : new models for mission / edited by Jonathan D. James.
Description: Minneapolis : Fortress Press, [2024] | Includes bibliographical references.
Identifiers: LCCN 2023059591 (print) | LCCN 2023059592 (ebook) | ISBN 9781506494661 (paperback) | ISBN 9781506494678 (ebook)
Subjects: LCSH: Christianity and culture--Asia. | Christianity and other religions--Asian. | Intercultural communication--Asia. | Intercultural communication--Religious aspects--Christianity.
Classification: LCC BR115.C8 A85 2024 (print) | LCC BR115.C8 (ebook) | DDC 266.0095--dc23/eng/20240226
LC record available at https://lccn.loc.gov/2023059591
LC ebook record available at https://lccn.loc.gov/2023059592

Cover design: Alisha Lofgren
Cover image: General View of Inner Geumgang by Sin Hak-gwon. Purchase, Friends of Asian Art Gifts, Gift of Dr. Mortimer D. Sackler, Theresa Sackler and Family, and Brooke Russell Astor Bequest, 2017; Wikimedia commons: Creative Commons CC0 1.0 Universal Public Domain Dedication and donated by The Metropolitan Museum of Art.

Print ISBN: 978-1-5064-9466-1
eBook ISBN: 978-1-5064-9467-8

CONTENTS

FOREWORD

I was on a sabbatical in Thailand in 2010 when a friend of mine, a Thai Buddhist professor at Chiang Mai University, asked, "Christianity is a Western religion, isn't it?" Having often heard this refrain, I explained that Christianity in fact began in Asia, and as Exhibit A, I gifted him a copy of our new *Atlas of Global Christianity* (Edinburgh University Press). After a few days of studying the book, the professor returned and said, "These maps and charts certainly convinced me that Christianity is a global religion." As they say, pictures are worth a thousand words.

And yet, more words are necessary. Christianity was, is, and will always be an Asian religion. The first and most obvious fact related to this is that Christianity began in Palestine and Israel, western Asia by today's United Nations boundaries. Africans and Asians constituted the majority of the world's Christians until the year 923 CE, when they were eclipsed by Europeans as Christianity declined in Asia. Years later, when Christianity was reintroduced to Asia, it was as a Western religion. This is, of course, profoundly different from what most of our history books portray.

It is in this context that Jonathan D. James aptly titles his book *The Asianization of Christianity*. James uses the term "Asianization" as a synonym for "indigenization," applied authentically within the context of each Asian theology and culture. With thousands of cultures in Asia, restoring the Asian roots of the Gospel is not conceived as a one-size-fits-all methodology. For this task, James brings together a formidable group of missionaries, pastors, scholars, NGO executives and other practitioners, to spotlight the rich heritage of ancient civilizations while remaining true to the unchanging Gospel. This is the core concept of the Asianization of Christianity. It should be recognizably Asian, certainly not Western as it is so often perceived. While several contributors still grapple with the perception of Christianity as a "foreign potted plant," this book is an appeal for the global nature of Christianity, but especially for its historical Asian roots and its current cultural relevance to global Christianity.

While Asia is also the most religiously diverse continent in the world, most of its resident population has never heard the Gospel. Considering this fact, the contributors offer contextualized approaches presenting the Gospel to people in other religions: namely Hindus, Muslims, Buddhists, and animists. With our research showing that 87 percent of all Muslims, Hindus, and Buddhists do not personally know a Christian, such embodied applications are critical to global mission. The case studies throughout this volume show how to build bridges, not only across cultures, but across religions.

James synthesizes the many threads offered by contributors into a "New Model" for mission, addressing the most pressing issues of Asianization while giving credit for this new paradigm to the myriads of Asian Christians spreading the Gospel in the region. He has reimaged Christian mission as a global endeavor, with Asian perspectives best suited for Asian contexts.

Perhaps fittingly, in another volume, Nigerian theologian Victor Ezigbo and Black American ethics professor Reggie Williams captured the need for Asianization well when they wrote, "Christianity is not truly global by its mere presence in many countries of the world. It is truly global when two criteria are met. First, the local communities of the world's nations are given the freedom to rethink and re-express Christianity's teaching about God's relationship with the world through Jesus Christ. And second, the local communities see themselves as equals, conversing and critiquing each other and contributing theologically to Christianity's long tradition."[1] These two criteria are precisely what makes this book so urgent. It

1 Victor Ifeanyi Ezigbo and Reggie L. Williams, "Converting a Colonialist Christ: Toward an African Postcolonial Christology," in *Evangelical Postcolonial Conversations: Global Awakenings in Theology and Praxis*, ed. Kay Higuera Smith, Jayachitra Lalitha, and L. Daniel Hawk (Westmont, IL: InterVarsity Press, 2014), 88–101.

provides a more authentic faith for those already in the Christian churches while offering a more compelling gospel for those found in other religious communities. In this way, *The Asianization of Christianity* is an excellent guide to the future of Christianity in Asia and beyond.

Todd M. Johnson

The Eva B. and Paul E. Toms Distinguished Professor of Mission and Global Christianity, Gordon-Conwell Theological Seminary, USA.

PREFACE

During my visits to teach missiology and evangelism in Asia, I noticed that my students would come alive whenever I asked the class to make informed observations about their cultures. I learned so much about culture from my students, but when it came to the issue of contextualization, I sensed that there were real struggles in integrating culture with Christianity. However, when given the proper tools and encouragement, these theological students became confident to reflect on and see their cultures with new eyes.

My prayer is that theological thinkers from every corner of Asia will be encouraged to collaborate with other theological thinkers from Asia and beyond—"with one mind striving side-by-side for the faith of the gospel" (Phil 1:27). This will result in dynamic churches that accept full responsibility in fulfilling all the components of the Great Commission and seek culture-specific theological solutions for the progress of the gospel in Asia.

I am indebted to Dr. John Hall for his outstanding editorial support. I also want to thank Arville Wasserman for her prompt and capable help in the arduous task of copy editing, and Dr. Jesudas Athyal and the team at Fortress Press for their great encouragement. I am also most appreciative of the board of directors of the Sheridan Institute of Higher Education for their support in this project. I say a big thank you to all the contributors for their time and effort in sharing their research and ministry efforts. Finally, I thank my wife Elizabeth and my children Ben and Mel for their constant encouragement. I also thank all my siblings and their families, as well as the board of Asia Evangelistic Fellowship International (AEFI) for supporting me and this project in prayer.

Jonathan D. James

TABLES AND FIGURES

Tables

Figures

INTRODUCTION
The Asianization of Christianity

by Jonathan D. James

Introduction

In 1992, I met a missionary from Myanmar who had been sent to the United States for a six-month training stint in Christian mission. I asked him whether, after his training, he was ready to pass on the skills and concepts he had acquired to church leaders in Myanmar. His reply, "I'm ready, but I don't have an overhead projector to do the training in my country," staggered me. Those were the days when overhead projectors were in vogue (before PowerPoint), but I had not seen a single overhead projector in my prior visits to Myanmar. While it troubled me that such a training program had been provided without consideration of the trainee's home culture, more concerning was the fact that the Myanmar trainee equated biblical training with Western technology. From this and many other observations, I have formed the opinion that the expansion and establishment of Christianity in Asia has been too Eurocentric.

In this introduction, I expand on this opinion, using examples of how Westernization has caused a disjunction with people of other cultures. I then introduce and define the term "Asianization" as a possible corrective in the church's missionary outreach.[1] Next, I broach the notion of an

---

1 I use the term "church" in a broad sense (not individual houses of worship) and refer mostly to the collective body of churches within the Protestant denomination of Christianity. Also, in this book, the writers and I use the

appropriate biblical basis for the Asianization of Christianity and outline its three challenges. Finally, I provide an overview of the chapters in the book and identify its readership.

The Disconnect in a Westernized Gospel

In the history of Christianity, we note how the faith underwent several cultural transformations, starting with Hellenization,[2] when the Hebrew scriptures were translated into Greek using Greek literary forms.[3] Also, in this period, the early church leader Justin Martyr helped situate Christianity in Greco-Roman thought forms.[4] The Romanization of Christianity occurred almost simultaneously with Hellenization, with Emperor Constantine's political influence helping the process. Later, the most significant change took place when the Europeanization of the faith reached its height during the eighteenth and nineteenth centuries, and European missionaries were sent in great numbers to Africa, Asia, and the rest of the world. The American missionaries came to Asia soon after their European counterparts. What I heard in the Philippines (a nation largely evangelized by US missionaries) summed up the sentiment of many Filipino Christians: "The Spaniards Hispanized us while the Americans denominationalized us."[5]

Asian and African pastors trained by Western missionaries often dressed in Western attire, wearing coats and ties in sweltering temperatures

---

word "mission" as a term that encompasses the work of the church. The word "missions" (in the plural, which was previously used specifically in relation to the outreach of people with little or no Christian exposure) was replaced by the word "mission" in the twentieth century.

2 "Hellenization" is a term used in reference to the influence of Greek culture, especially in the ancient world.

3 Harold W. Atteridge, "Hellenistic Culture," Frontline PBS, 1998, https://www.pbs.org/wgbh/pages/frontline/shows/religion/portrait/hellenisticculture.html.

4 Atteridge, "Hellenistic Culture."

5 Field notes, 2009. Some of the information for this chapter is from my field notes taken in the Philippines and Myanmar during the years 2008–2011.

because that was how the Western missionaries dressed.[6] Japanese Christians wondered why they could not participate in the eucharist with rice and sake instead of bread and red wine,[7] bemoaning the church's slowness in adapting Christian liturgy to the common cultural realities of Asia. Ledogar expressed their sentiments of "Why should our brothers in the East be shackled with what, after all, are the traditions of the West? Why not throw out the old Roman liturgy that no one understands and start over with a radically new and adapted one?"[8] The late Asian evangelist G. D. James, in his humorous way, drew attention to the singing in Asia of Western hymns that contain lyrics such as "Let the blessed sunshine in," a practice that has some relevance in the United Kingdom but certainly not in countries where there are "four seasons: hot and hotter, wet and wetter!"[9]

It is generally acknowledged that one of the most prolific and far-reaching missionary enterprises of the eighteenth century was the Moravian mission movement, shaped by the pietistic teaching of its founder, Count Nicolaus Ludwig von Zinzendorf (1700–1760).[10] However, contemporary scholars have criticized its "Eurocentric leadership style and role" in the mission field.[11]

In summary, technology, liturgy, dress code, and leadership are just some of the European mores embedded in and potentially counterproductive to teaching the gospel in Christian mission.

---

6 Paul Ayokunle, "A Call for the Africanisation of Christianity," *Moya Chronicles* 32, no. 4 (2022): 1–2.

7 Robert Ledogar, "Liturgy, Asian Style," *Commonweal*, April, 2, 1965, https://www.commonwealmagazine.org/liturgy-asian-style.

8 Ledogar, "Liturgy, Asian Style."

9 G. D. James, *G. D. James in Australia* (Sydney, Australia: Asia Evangelistic Fellowship, 1999), 50.

10 A. J. Lewis, *Zinzendorf the Ecumenical Pioneer: A Study in the Moravian Contribution to Christian Mission and Unity* (Philadelphia, PA: The Westminster Press, 1962), 12.

11 John Mark Terry and Robert L. Gallagher, *Encountering the History of Missions: From the Early Church to Today* (Grand Rapids, MI: Baker Academic, 2017), 130–139.

Taking a different but related tack, I draw your attention to historians of mission who have examined why some countries have been more resistant to the gospel than others. For example, Sng[12] found that resistance to introducing new ideas and ways of thinking was stronger in nations with rich and ancient civilizations. Culbertson[13] supported this hypothesis and demonstrated that today, "the northern half of Africa, the Middle East, the areas once ruled by the ancient Babylonian and Persian empires, and much of Asia, including India and China" (both with rich and ancient cultures), remain largely resistant to the gospel.

Sng also found that in parts of Africa and Latin America, the absence of written languages was viewed by missionaries as an invitation to impose their (European) literary traditions in conjunction with their gospel teachings.[14] For example, when Spanish missionaries entered the Philippines in the sixteenth century, they regarded its tribal nature and lack of a strong literary foundation with contempt; without hesitation, they proceeded to establish their (Spanish) language and religion.[15] In Myanmar, Christians converted by the early missionaries were predominantly Karen and Chin people (from animistic backgrounds). Only 2 percent of the Bhama (Buddhists, the majority ethnic group) became Christians, and this trend has continued[16] because Christian missionaries do not understand the rich and ancient culture of Theravada Buddhism, which the Bhama people practice.

One assumes that there would have been less resistance to the gospel if the missionaries had respected and sought to communicate with the local culture and frame of mind. It follows that the scenario in Asia could be turned around if intercultural engagement is instituted. These

---

12 Bobby Sng, "Gospel and Culture," in *Changing Times, Unchanging Word*, ed. Bobby. Sng (Singapore: The Bible Society of Singapore, 2014), 63–74.

13 Howard Culbertson, "10/40 Window: Do you need to be stirred to action?", accessed July 12, 2022, http://home.snu.edu/~hculbert/1040.htm.

14 Sng, "Gospel and Culture."

15 "The Spanish Period," Encyclopedia Britannica, accessed July 19, 2022, https://www.britannica.com/place/Philippines/The-Spanish-period.

16 "Ethnic Groups of Myanmar: An Ethnological Guide to Burmese Tribes," Rainforest Cruises, accessed July 10, 2022, https://www.rainforestcruises.com/guides/ethic-groups-of-myanmar.

propositions will be addressed in the book in some detail, as indicated by the following chapters. But first, I define in simple terms what "Asianization" means.

Asianization and Culture

Asianization, simply put, is the process of valuing and acquiring Asian culture as a bridge or conduit for making the gospel understandable and, hopefully, acceptable in Asian terms.[17] Asianization recognizes, first, that the Bible was written in the culture of its day; second, that its message must be conveyed in a language and method that is appropriate for the recipient; and third, that the missionary entering the frame of reference of the learner is engaging in a bicultural medium of communication, which could be a form of pidgin or creole language. Thus three cultures could be at play.

I use the term "Asianization" as a synonym for "indigenization," which has often been used in mission literature. But Asianization is not conceived as a one-size-fits-all methodology; it is to be envisaged and applied authentically within the context of each Asian theology and culture. Moreover, it is assumed that Asianization is compatible with the essence of the gospel message (more on this below).

"Culture" is used in various ways. For example, some people restrict their usage of the term to so-called high cultural items, such as music, arts, and etiquette. The Willowbank Report on Gospel and Culture[18] defined culture more broadly: "an integrated system of beliefs (about God or reality or ultimate meaning) of values (about what is true, good, beautiful, and normative), of customs (how to behave, relate to others, talk, pray, dress, work, play, trade, farm, eat, and so on), and of institutions which express these beliefs, values, and customs (government, law courts, temples or

---

17 Laray M. Barna, "Stumbling Blocks in Intercultural Communication," in *Intercultural Communication: A Current Perspective*, ed. M. Bennett, (Yarmouth, ME: Intercultural Press, 1998), 100–111.

18 The Lausanne Occasional Paper: The Willowbank Report—Consultation on Gospel and Culture. *Lausanne Committee for World Evangelization* (Orlando, FL: Lausanne Committee for World Evangelization, 1978), 7.

churches, family, schools, hospitals, factories, shops, unions, clubs), which bind a society together and give it a sense of identity, dignity, security, and continuity." What follows is a commentary on three aspects of culture mentioned in the above definition.

First, culture implies a set of shared key beliefs and ideologies, which may be religious or secular. Typically, these beliefs and concepts are transmitted from generation to generation, permeating people's actions and intentions. For instance, in Muslim countries, the concept *tawhid* (God's unitarian nature) is pervasive; in Hindu society, *karma* (the law of cause and effect) underpins Hindu thinking and actions; in Buddhist societies, *anatta* (no permanent self or soul) consumes their thoughts and actions;[19] and for secularists, the ethic of self-improvement is an integrating idea.

Second, culture is practiced by groups of people in institutions, communities, and villages, and it is fundamental to their collective identities. Furthermore, group norms contribute to the sustainability and survival of groups. According to Kroeber and Kluckhohn,[20] "Culture consists of patterns, explicit and implicit, of and for behavior acquired and transmitted by symbols, constituting the distinctive achievement of human groups, including their embodiments in artifacts."

Third, whereas culture is essential for the survival of its constituents, it is also subject to change. The whirlwinds of globalization and postmodernism have changed world religions; Christianity, Islam, Hinduism, and Buddhism have all redefined themselves in some shape or form. This phenomenon is both challenging and exciting in the context of the mission of the church.

How the Church Has Responded

Arguably, the church has undertaken three main missionary approaches to culture.[21]

19 Sng, "Gospel and Culture."

20 Alfred L. Kroebar and Clyde Kluckhohn, *Culture: A Critical Review of Concepts and Definitions* (New York: Vintage Books, 1963), 181.

21 These three approaches are adapted from Richard Niebuhr's famous categorization of Christianity and culture: Christ against culture, the Christ of

Cultural Negation

This approach occurs when a missionary repudiates the receiving culture and imposes the missionary's culture in its stead. This act implies that the receiving culture is considered unworthy and should be shunned. The missionary discourse from the late eighteenth to the early nineteenth century implied that missionaries had twin responsibilities, namely, to evangelize and civilize (according to the missionaries' culture).[22]

Cultural Appropriation

This approach occurs when the missionary admires (or pretends to admire) aspects of the receiving culture and adopts them without seeking to know or follow the protocols for the adoption, which may be motivated by a wish to win favor, including as a device to "sell" the Christian gospel, or it may be arbitrary or whimsical.

Intercultural Engagement

This approach is taken deliberately when the missionary genuinely respects the receiving culture and seeks to become conversant. This was exemplified by Bartholomeus Ziegenbalg, the German missionary who spent a decade in Tranquebar, India (now known as Tharagambadi, Tamil Nadu) during the early eighteenth century and wrote two voluminous books on Hindu religion and culture.[23] This approach will be described and discussed in our book through various case studies. Intercultural engagement is based on the premise that the God of the Bible is both a transcendent God and an immanent God who cares for humanity and is present in the suffering of people. Intercultural engagement seeks common ground for communication between people of different cultures.

---

culture, Christ above culture, Christ and culture in paradox, and Christ the transformer of culture.

22 James I. H Macdonald, *The Redeemer's Reign: Foreign Missions and the Second Advent* (London: Marshall and Scott, 1910).

23 William Sweetman, "The Prehistory of Orientalism: Colonialism and the Textual Basis for Bartholomeus Ziegenbalg's Account of Hinduism," *New Zealand Journal of Asian Studies* 6, no. 2 (2004): 12–38.

A Biblical Basis for Asianization

In the first book of the Bible, Genesis 12:2–3, the promise given to Abraham is the first revelation of God's plan for the nations, which I take to be an advocation for intercultural engagement between nations: "I will make you into a great nation, and I will bless you; I will make your name great, and you will be a blessing. I will bless those who bless you, and whoever curses you I will curse; and all peoples on earth will be blessed through you."

Thus the underlying principle for the Asianization of Christianity is that Christian mission should strive to perpetuate God's universal blessing of all people in Asia. Abraham's mandate was to be a blessing to the whole world as a medium for God's mercy and saving grace. The election of Israel did not imply the rejection of nations; it was intended as the vehicle through which God's saving grace would be transmitted to the wider world. Three further principles follow.

Incarnation

The most palpable basis for indigenization/Asianization in Christianity is the incarnation, when God became man some two thousand years ago in the person of Jesus Christ. Jesus did not come as an angel, a heavenly being, or a foreigner.[24] The writer of Hebrews 2:17 said of Jesus, "For this reason he had to be made like them, fully human in every way, in order that he might become a merciful and faithful high priest in service to God, and that he might make atonement for the sins of the people." Thus God became man so that he could identify fully with humankind and show us the way to eternal life.

Moreover, Jesus came into a specific religious-cultural group: Judaism. He did not come as a "generalized human being" without cultural attachment.[25] Jesus was brought up in the Jewish culture, spoke

24 Jonathan D. James, "Christianity and Culture: How Asian Missions Can Be Modelled According to the Indigenous Principle," *BIJAK—Basileia Indonesian Journal of Kadesi* 2, no. 2 (2019).

25 Andrew F. Walls, *The Missionary Movement in Christian History: Studies in the Transmission of Faith* (Maryknoll, NY: Orbis Books, 1996), 26–36.

the Jewish language, and showed remarkable respect for the norms and practices of that culture.[26] After Jesus died, rose, and ascended to heaven, the first Christians were Jewish people, but Jesus gave these Jewish disciples the Commission to share the gospel with all nations (Matt 8:18–20; Acts 1:8).

Inspiration of the Bible

Christians believe that the Bible is the inspired word of God. The Bible, therefore, is God's means of communicating to us in a literal form. In doing so, God accommodates human language. He communicates to us using words, phrases, and concepts with which we are familiar. For example, God has used anthropomorphisms, and so we read of God's "face," "hands," "arm," "eyes," and "ears" (Lev 20:6; Isa 23:11; Ps 89:10; Ps 34:15; Neh 1:6). God spoke to several men who wrote the Bible over different periods according to their personalities and literary styles. The apostle John used the unique Hebrew style of symbolism in his writings, whereas Paul resorted to the Greco-Roman sequential, logical style.

Paul's Missionary Pattern

Paul practiced cultural engagement in his missionary travels to non-Jewish communities, and he resorted to quotations from secular Greek thinkers when speaking to the Greek philosophers in Mars Hill, as recorded in Acts 17. In each congregation Paul founded, he appointed local or indigenous elders to nurture and shepherd the new churches.

Jerusalem was the capital or headquarters of Christianity for a brief time.[27] However, after the historic meeting of church leaders recorded in Acts 15, the apostolic leaders concluded that "no group of Christians had the right to impose" cultural practices about life and faith on another group of Christians.[28] This brought about the great expansion of Christianity from Jerusalem to Rome and later to the rest of Europe, reaching the entire world.

---

26 James, "Christianity and Culture."

27 Walls, *The Missionary Movement*, 16–18.

28 Walls, *The Missionary Movement*, 16–18.

The Threefold Challenges of Asianizing Christianity

First, consideration must be given to how best to communicate the gospel to the people of Asia. As indicated above, effective communication entails respecting and engaging with the receiving culture. The gospel must be communicated clearly and accurately through the lenses of the recipients' languages and worldviews. The goal is not necessarily to make Asians *understand* the gospel (in terms of our acceptable models), but to make it understandable in their contexts. In this way, our communication is akin to building bridges to understanding. Theological terms and concepts must be explained in ways that make sense to the recipients. The theologian Tillich's[29] popular slogan, "Religion is the substance of culture, and culture is the form of religion," is a clever attempt to close the gap between theology and culture. In other words, since religion and culture are intertwined, religious ideas and concepts will be better understood if they are framed in the culturally appropriate aspects of the receiving culture, such as folklore, songs, proverbs, symbols, images, and idioms.

Besides the focus on content, the presentation of the gospel must also reflect local formats and conventions. So, in reaching Muslims, who have much respect for Scripture, the way the missionary or preacher handles the Bible is of utmost importance. For example, I have noticed that in congregations of Muslim converts, the Bible is placed on a small rostrum, and the preacher sits on the floor and turns the pages of the Bible. In reaching Hindus in Indian villages, who are primarily oral learners, missionaries would find that storytelling about the narratives of Christ is suitable and effective.

Second, the missionary needs to consider how the new churches of converts should be organized physically and spiritually. Presumably, Western architectural artifacts, such as the steeple, church bells, and gigantic crosses, would not be appropriate. So what should the worship center look like? What would be the basis of the liturgy? Would women and men be seated in separate sections of the church (as in the case of church life in South Asia)?

29 Paul Tillich, *Theology and Culture* (New York: Oxford University Press, 1959), 41–42.

Related to the issues of church structure and architecture is the issue of the lifestyles and customs of new believers. For instance, what would be the role of festivals, such as Diwali or the Mooncake Festival, for those who become Christians in India, Malaysia, and Singapore? Should Sikh converts shave their beards and trim their hair?

Third, there must be a discussion on how new believers will be nurtured as disciples and trained to carry out the Great Commission. Scholars such as Bryson[30] and Kim and Bonk[31] suggested that learning styles must be culturally based. For example, most Asians living in villages are oral learners who are event-oriented. This means that unlike most Westerners, who are time-oriented, oral learners in Asia focus on the ever-present now. Therefore, for the latter, time is measured in rich and meaningful activities and dialogue.[32]

Western degree-based theological education may be good for the West and Asian countries influenced by the West. In this book, we consider alternative models for Asia that are more culturally appropriate, such as training courses based on relational learning.

Overview of the Book's Content and Focus

The book is organized into three sections: core issues, mission and church models, and training and discipleship models.

Under core issues (chapters 1–4), the major theoretical constructs of indigenization and contextualization are explored. Alongside this, the historical perspective of the gospel's expansion is investigated. Finally, the role of biblical communication in mission is introduced, together with a discussion of the role that worldview plays in reading the Bible in Asia.

---

30 Joy Eilisha Bryson, "Effectiveness of Working Individually Versus Cooperative Groups: A Classroom-Based Research Project," University of Pennsylvania, 2007, http://www.sas.upenn.edu/~jbryson/.

31 Kyong-Jee Kim and Curtis J. Bonk, "Cross-Cultural Comparisons of Online Collaboration," *Journal of Computer-mediated Communication* 8, no. 1 (2002), https://academic.oup.com/jcmc/article/8/1/JCMC814/4080404.

32 Harry Box, *Don't Throw the Book at Them* (Pasadena, California: William Carey Library, 2014), 8.

The mission and church section (chapters 5–12) contains useful material and case studies of evangelism and church planting in selected countries in Asia. The thrust is on addressing the issues surrounding the three world religions in Asia, namely, Buddhism, Islam, and Hinduism, while the world of animism is also explored.

In the training and discipleship section (chapters 13–17), mission practitioners offer cases and insights on training and discipling Christians in Thailand, China, the Philippines, and Indonesia. The discipling of the Filipino diaspora community in Singapore is also addressed.

A new model of mission emanating from the chapters in the book is outlined in the concluding chapter based on the following: people, principles, structures, and scope and praxis.

An international team of missiologists, academics, and mission practitioners (all from Asian backgrounds) have written relevant chapters based on their decades of mission experience. Mission work in China, India, Indonesia, Malaysia, Nepal, Pakistan, the Philippines, and Thailand is discussed, while diaspora ministries to Asians in Singapore, the UK, and the US are considered.

Readership

The book will have general appeal, but it is most likely to appeal to the following:

- practitioners of mission and evangelism, such as missionaries, Bible translators, and church planters
- students at Bible colleges, seminaries, and secular institutions specializing in religious studies, Asian studies, and cultural anthropology
- researchers in Asian culture, religious studies, and world Christianity
- pastors of churches with diaspora congregations and mission committee members
- leaders of mission boards and missionary-sending agencies.

Conclusion

I began the introduction with the argument that Western culture embodied by missionaries has affronted Asians and created confusion about and resistance to the true nature of the gospel. Next, I introduced the term "Asianization," which is synonymous with "indigenization," and explained the importance of its key ingredient, intercultural engagement, in Christian mission. I provided an overview of how the church has sought to address the issue of culture in its missionary outreach. Then I invoked the biblical basis for the Asianization of Christianity and envisaged three challenges for the Asianization of the gospel. Finally, I listed the chapters in the book and identified its readership.

In articulating the need for the Indian Church to be "Indianized," the American missionary E. Stanley Jones[33] invoked a traditional Indian marriage custom. After the pomp and ceremony, the female friends of the bride, surrounded by a band of musicians, accompany the bride to the bridegroom's home. Then the bride is ushered into the bridegroom's home, and the bride's women friends quietly leave. This is as far as they go, according to Jones,[34] who then said, "That is our [the church's] joyous task in India—to know Jesus is to introduce Him to India and then retire . . . to trust India with Christ and to trust Christ with India."[35] These words written in the 1920s are a poignant reminder of what this book aspires to do for Asia in the twenty-first century and beyond.

Bibliography

Atteridge, Harold. W. "Hellenistic Culture." Frontline PBS, 1998. https://www.pbs.org/wgbh/pages/frontline/shows/religion/portrait/hellenisticculture.html.

Ayokunle, P. "A Call for the Africanisation of Christianity." *Moya Chronicles* 32, no. 4 (2022): 1–2.

Barna, Laray M. "Stumbling Blocks in Intercultural Communication." In *Intercultural Communication: A Current Perspective,* edited by M. Bennett, 100–111, Yarmouth, ME: Intercultural Press, 1998.

33 Eli Stanley Jones, *The Christ of the Indian Road* (New York: Abingdon, 1925).

34 Jones, *The Christ of the Indian Road.*

35 Jones, *The Christ of the Indian Road*, 160.

Bryson, Joy Eilisha. "Effectiveness of Working Individually Versus Cooperative Groups: A Classroom-Based Research Project." *University of Pennsylvania*, 2007. http://www.sas.upenn.edu/~jbryson/.

Box, Harry. *Don't Throw the Book at Them*. Pasadena, California: William Carey Library, 2014.

Culbertson, Howard. "10/40 Window: Do you need to be stirred to action?" Accessed July 3, 2022. http://home.snu.edu/~hculbert/1040.htm.

Encyclopedia Britannica. "The Spanish Period." Accessed July10, 2022. https://www.britannica.com/place/Philippines/The-Spanish-period.

Rainforest Cruises. "Ethnic Groups of Myanmar: An Ethnological Guide to Burmese Tribes." Accessed July10, 2022. https://www.rainforestcruises.com/guides/ethnic-groups-of-myanmar.

James, G. D. *G. D. James in Australia*. Sydney, Australia: Asia Evangelistic Fellowship, 1999.

James, Jonathan D. "Christianity and Culture: How Asian Missions Can Be Modelled According to the Indigenous Principle." *BIJAK—Basileia Indonesian Journal of Kadesi* 2, no. 2 (2019): 45–52.

Jones, Eli Stanley. *The Christ of the Indian Road*. New York: Abingdon, 1925.

Kim, Kyong-Jee and Curtis J. Bonk. "Cross-Cultural Comparisons of Online Collaboration." *Journal of Computer-Mediated Communication* 8, no. 1 (2002). https://academic.oup.com/jcmc/article/8/1/JCMC814/4080404.

Kroeber, A. L., and Clyde Kluckhohn. *Culture: A Critical Review of Concepts and Definitions*. New York: Vintage Books, 1963.

Lausanne Occasional Paper: The Willowbank Report—Consultation on Gospel and Culture. *Lausanne Committee for World Evangelization*. Orlando, FL: Lausanne. 1978. 2: 1–15.

Ledogar Robert J. "Liturgy, Asian Style." *Commonweal*, April, 2, 1965. https://www.commonwealmagazine.org/liturgy-asian-style.

Lewis, A.J. *Zinzendorf the Ecumenical Pioneer: A Study in the Moravian Contribution to Christian Mission and Unity.* Philadelphia, PA: The Westminster Press, 1962.

Macdonald, J.I. *The Redeemer's Reign: Foreign Missions and the Second Advent*. London: Marshall and Scott, 1910.

Niebuhr, Helmut Richard. *Christ and Culture*. New York: Harper and Row, 1961.

Sng, Bobby. "Gospel and Culture." In *Changing Times, Unchanging Word,* edited by Bobby Sng, 63–74. Singapore: The Bible Society of Singapore, 2014.

Sweetman, William. "The Prehistory of Orientalism: Colonialism and the Textual Basis for Bartholomeus Ziegenbalg's Account of Hinduism." *New Zealand Journal of Asian Studies* 6, no. 2 (2004): 12–38.

Terry, John M., and Robert L. Gallagher. *Encountering the History of Missions: From the Early Church to Today*. Grand Rapids, MI: Baker Academic, 2017.

The Holy Bible. New International Version. Grand Rapids, MI: Zondervan Publishing House, 1984.

The Willowbank Report on Gospel and Culture: Lausanne Occasional Paper. *Lausanne Committee for World Evangelization*. Orlando, FL: Lausanne. 1978. 2: 1–15.

Tillich, Paul. *Theology and Culture*. Oxford: Oxford University Press, 1959.

Walls, Andrew F. *The Missionary Movement in Christian History: Studies in the Transmission of Faith*. Maryknoll, NY: Orbis Books, 1996.

SECTION ONE

CORE ISSUES

1

BRIDGING THE GOSPEL—A CONTEXTUALIZATION FRAMEWORK

by Jonathan D. James

Introduction

In his important chapter on "Evangelism in an Asian Context," Keith Hinton presented an account of an apparently devout Christian woman in Singapore who, at her sister's funeral, called on the spirits to haunt her sister's husband who had caused her sister much grief in life.[1] The Christian community was shocked that this Christian person would do such a thing. It was later revealed that although this woman was a Christian, she also believed in Chinese spirits and the doctrine of revenge in the afterlife. Sadly, like this woman, many Christians are not fully converted because their inner core is still based on past belief systems.[2] One's religion (or culture) goes beyond emotions and feelings to the will, intellect, and heart.[3] Therefore, the gospel must penetrate deeper to the "heart holds" of that culture.[4]

---

1 Keith W. Hinton, "Missions and Church Growth: Evangelism in an Asian context," in *World Missions: The Asian Challenge, A Compendium of the Asia Missions Congress '90*, ed. Asia Missions Congress (Manila: The Asia Missions Congress, 1990), 388–401.

2 Hinton, "Missions and Church Growth."

3 Louis Berkhof, *Systematic Theology* (Grand Rapids, MI: Eerdmans,1988), 233.

4 Lit Sen Chang, *Strategy of Missions in the Orient* (Hong Kong: Presbyterian and Reformed Press, 1969), 77.

In this chapter, I argue that real growth and fruitfulness in the church in Asia will only be achieved when the gospel is indigenized and contextualized, and I reinforce my argument with a six-part framework of contextualization that I have developed. The framework is an attempt to help Christian leaders who want to embark on contextualization but are either doubtful or confused about the process.

However, before embarking on my framework, I share three observations on the relationship between culture and Christianity. Then I proceed to define and discuss indigenization and contextualization for mission work in Asia. I conclude the chapter by noting challenges in contextualization.

Culture and Christianity

First, culture is an integral part of the Bible. God chose to reveal Himself through Middle Eastern culture, and Jesus was born into Jewish culture. Therefore, God speaks in and through culture. We cannot stop being Asian, African, or Australian; our cultural identity (even though tainted by sin) is a gift from God. Therefore, culture and the Bible are necessarily interrelated. As disciples of Christ, we are called to embody the gospel within cultures—our own and the culture of those with whom we seek to share the gospel. The nature of the gospel and of the church's mission means that the Christian missionary must translate the gospel into the thought patterns and idioms of the receiving culture.[5]

Second, culture was subject to the fall of humankind; therefore, all cultures need redemption. The apostle Paul taught that the world and its cultures are the object of God's love: "God was reconciling the world to Himself in Christ" (2 Cor 5:19, *New International Version*). Thus the mission practitioner must discern the aspects of culture espoused in the Bible. In line with this, Richard Niebuhr advocated that "Christ is the transformer of culture."[6]

---

5 Marcus Dean, "The Missionary as a Cultural pilgrim," Evangelical Missions Quarterly 48, no. 4 (2012):10–14.

6 Richard Niebuhr, *Christ and Culture* (New Haven: Yale University Press, 1951), 195.

Third, culture is alluded to in the Bible as both temporal and eternal. We are called to interact with the cultures of the world (1 Cor 9:20–22),[7] and we must do so as pilgrims (Heb 11:9–10).[8] In our human frailty and finiteness, we cannot reach perfection in the contextualization of the gospel. None of us comes from a culture that perfectly reflects the identity of Christ that Scripture prescribes. However, the scene in Revelation 7:9, when the believers from "every nation, tribe, people and language" stand before Jesus, depicts the resilience of cultures. It is intriguing and mysterious that God, at the end of time, would be concerned about the cultures of the world. John the apostle described his vision of the coming heavenly city and vividly portrayed how the "glory and honour of the nations will be brought into it" and that "nothing impure will ever enter into it."[9] Therefore, all cultures will somehow be renewed by God at the end of the age. Hence whatever we invest as mission practitioners in contextualizing the gospel is not a waste.

Indigenization and Contextualization

In this section, I define the terms "indigenization" and "contextualization" and note the differences and common elements in the two concepts.

The word "indigenous" comes from two Latin words, *indu* (within) and *gignere* (to beget or give birth to),[10] so it refers to something that is birthed in

7 "To the Jews I became like a Jew, to win the Jews. To those under the law I became like one under the law (though I myself am not under the law), so as to win those under the law. To those not having the law I became like one not having the law (though I am not free from God's law but am under Christ's law), so as to win those not having the law. To the weak I became weak, to win the weak. I have become all things to all people so that by all possible means I might save some."

8 "By faith he made his home in the promised land like a stranger in a foreign country; he lived in tents, as did Isaac and Jacob, who were heirs with him of the same promise. For he was looking forward to the city with foundations, whose architect and builder is God."

9 Rev 21:26–27.

10 "Indigenous," Merriam-Webster Dictionary, accessed April 2, 2023, https://www.merriam-webster.com/dictionary/indigenous.

the country in which it is found. In mission, the term "indigenous" refers to the gospel being planted and rooted in the native soil so that it can blossom in its unique culture and situation. An indigenous missionary is one who seeks to take the gospel to their people group.

John Nevius (1829–1893) introduced the concept of indigenous mission.[11] As a Presbyterian missionary to China in the late 1800s, Nevius strongly rejected the traditional mission approach and introduced a different path to initiate an independent, self-supporting local church. He also disliked the missionaries' practice of supporting national workers from foreign mission funds, contending that local churches should pay local workers from local funding.[12] Nevius stipulated three ways to measure the indigenization of a church planted by a foreign missionary: It must be self-governing (as to leadership), self-supporting (as to manpower and finance), and self-propagating (as to evangelism and church reproduction).[13] Cardinal Stephen Kim echoed Nevius's mission principle when declaring that, unless indigenization takes place, "the Christian message will remain an idiom foreign" to the new culture.[14]

The word "contextualization" originated from the Latin word *contextus,* which means *weaving together.*[15] When an idea or practice from one culture relates to and is woven into another culture, contextualization occurs. The word was first used in Christian theology by Shoki Coe, who looked for new ways to understand the gospel in his native Taiwan.[16] While this term stemmed from and was popularized by the liberal school

11 R. Pierce Beaver, "The History of Mission Strategy," in *Perspectives: On the World Christian Movement,* ed. Ralph D Winter and Steven C Hawthorne (Pasadena, CA: William Carey Library, 1999), 247–300.

12 Beaver, "History of Mission Strategy."

13 Beaver, "History of Mission Strategy."

14 Lit-sen Chang. 1969. *Strategy of Missions in the Orient,* 10.

15 Daniel R. Sanchez, "Contextualization and the Missionary Endeavor," in *Missiology: An Introduction to the Foundations, History, and Strategy of World Missions,* ed. John Mark Terry, Ebbie Smith, and Justice Anderson (Nashville: Broadman and Holman, 1998), 318.

16 Shoki Coe, "In Search of Renewal in Theological Education," *Theological Education* 9, no. 4 (1973): 233–243.

of Christian theology, it is now widely used by evangelical missiologists and scholars.[17]

Kraft's two metaphors of tree and seed are apt in shedding light on contextualization: A grown tree taken from one country and transplanted in another country is not contextualization.[18] But taking a seed from one country (the gospel) and planting it in another country is contextualization because the seed absorbs the soil's minerals and grows into a tree that looks different from trees grown in the original country.

Although the two words, contextualization and indigenization, are often used interchangeably, there are subtle differences. Whereas indigenization is "making something more native," contextualization is "putting information into a context, or making sense of information from the situation or location in which the information was found."[19]

Today, scholars accept that the two words can be used interchangeably; however, contextualization is deemed more suited to the practice of mission work because it takes account of emerging contexts.[20] Bevans favored the term contextualization because it emphasizes that new contexts must be addressed in our ever-changing world: "Theology needs to interact and dialogue not only with traditional culture value, but with social change, new ethnic identities, and the conflicts that are present as the contemporary phenomenon of globalization encounters the various peoples of the world."[21]

In short, both words are useful, but contextualization[22]—the weaving-together process by which missionaries interpret, communicate,

---

17 Jackson Wu, *One Gospel for All Nations: A Practical Approach to Biblical Contextualization* (Pasadena, CA: William Carey Library, 2015).

18 Charles H. Kraft, "Culture, Worldview and Contextualization," *in Perspectives on the World Christian Movement*, ed. Ralph D Winer and Steven C Hawthorne (Pasadena: William Carey, 1999), 389.

19 "Contextualization vs. Indigenization," WikiDiff, accessed April 2, 2023, https://wikidiff.com/indigenization/contextualization

20 Simon Shui-Man Kwan, "From Indigenization to Contextualization: A Change in Discursive Practice rather than a Shift in Paradigm," *Studies in World Christianity* 11 (2005): 236–250.

21 Bevans, *Models of Contextual Theology*, 21.

22 In the introduction I used the word "indigenization" but, in this chapter, I use "contextualization."

and apply the Bible in new cultures—is the preferred term in missionizing, as implied by Wu,[23] Bevans,[24] and Sanchez.[25]

Six-Part Contextualization Framework

Contextualization cannot be done in a hurry. It is a cyclical process where people from a culture interact with Scripture culturally, live out their understanding of the Bible within their context, and reengage with culture to find more insights that reshape their practices. To guide the implementation of this process, I have developed a framework with the following six stages: understand the gospel, understand the culture's worldview, frame the gospel, emphasize what fits, discern what does not fit, and redeem the marginal/neutral elements of the culture.

Understand the Gospel

To contextualize the gospel message, a mission practitioner must first understand the essence of the gospel. The word gospel is derived from the Greek word *euangelion*, meaning *good news*.[26] The gospel contains the message of God's salvation of the world through his son Jesus Christ. Jesus is God's solution to the sin problem that humankind experienced after the fall in Genesis chapters 1–3. Dodson made the case that unlike other religions, "Christianity is rooted . . . in history—namely, the life, death, and resurrection of Jesus."[27] The coming of Christ is part of the good news that began in the Old Testament and continued in the New Testament in four parts (or acts): creation, the fall, redemption, and restoration. A brief review of these parts follows.

Creation: "In the beginning God . . ." (Gen 1:1) is the affirmation of God as creator of heaven and earth. Creation points to the origin of life

23 Wu, *One Gospel for All Nations*.

24 Bevans, *Models of Contextual Theology*.

25 Sanchez, "Contextualization and the Missionary Endeavor."

26 Linda Woodhead, *An Introduction to Christianity* (Cambridge, UK: Cambridge University Press, 2004).

27 Jonathan Dodson, *Unbelievable Gospel: Sharing a Gospel Worth Believing* (Grand Rapids: Zondervan, 2014), 112.

but also to a creator whose "love led Him to share . . . one of the greatest gifts . . . existence."[28] Consequently, everything he created was "good" (Gen 1:31). God's creation of Adam and Eve introduced the theological concept of *imago Dei* (image of God) because humankind was made in God's image.

The fall of man: Adam and Eve's sin (also recorded in the context of Satan and his act of temptation leading to the fall) was an act of disobedience against God, which is referred to as the fall. Adam and Eve's sin introduced humankind's subjection to Satan, conflict, and death: "Personal, interpersonal, and social breakdowns abound because life is severed from its source."[29]

Redemption: God revealed his plan for ending the problem of sin and pain with the promise of a deliverer in the Old Testament—his son Jesus Christ. The New Testament then records the life, death, and resurrection of Jesus as the centerpiece of the gospel. Because Jesus's death is substitutionary (he died in place of the world) and his resurrection is the guarantee of the final resurrection of all those who believe in Him, the gospel is good news for the world. Those who believe in Christ's death and resurrection are made new ("born again") through the Holy Spirit (John 3:3; 2 Cor 5:17), and through the power of the Holy Spirit, believers of Christ experience the freedom and dynamics to live meaningfully for the glory of God.

Restoration/glorification: The second coming of Christ promises ultimate hope for Christians in terms of restoration (the glorification of believers and healing of creation), as "creation itself will be set free from its bondage to decay and obtain the glorious liberty of the children of God" (Rom 8:21).

Understand the Worldview of the Culture

Because culture pertains to the entire gamut of a person's life, Christians' intercultural engagement must take on a holistic approach. Luzbetak's characterization of culture as an onion with multiple layers is a useful

28 Ministerial Association of Seventh-Day Adventists, *Seventh-day Adventists Believe: A Biblical Exposition of 27 Fundamental Doctrines* (Washington, D.C.: Ministerial Association, 1988), 73.

29 Brian J. Walsh, and J. Richard Middleton, *The Transforming Vision: Shaping a Christian World View* (Westmont, IL: InterVarsity Press, 1984), 70.

metaphor.[30] The most important and deepest layers of culture, according to Luzbetak, are "ideology, cosmology, and worldview." Worldview is the semiconscious way we look at life or the lenses we use to see reality.[31] Worldview is followed by values, and the surface layer is made up of "artifacts and observable behavior."[32]

Moon and Simon categorized three representative worldviews, and the latter two resonate with Asia: guilt/innocence, shame/honor, and fear/power.[33] The first word in each pair identifies the problem, while the second word suggests its solution.[34]

The guilt/innocence worldview is representative of the West.[35] Western culture is based on individualism, underpinned by rights (to one's beliefs, opinions, etc.). Morality in this worldview is based on right and wrong: "Central values include individual responsibility, an internalized code of conduct, and individualism."[36] Those who break the law are served a punishment proportionate to the crime. Hence people who live under this worldview spend time finding solutions to the problem of guilt.

The shame/honor worldview is upheld not only in Asia but also in the Middle East and parts of Africa. In this worldview, family, community, and social status are valued above everything else. If one does not practice the norms of society or family, they will be considered dishonorable. A dishonorable act would bring shame. Therefore, people who live in the shame/honor worldview spend time trying to be free from shame.

The fear/power worldview is common among tribal and folk communities in Asia, Africa, and Latin America. Reality for people under this worldview is based on the unseen spiritual realm of spirits, ghosts,

---

30 Louis Luzbetak, *The Church and Cultures: New Perspectives in Missiological Anthropology* (Maryknoll, NY: Orbis Books, 1988).

31 Luzbetak, *The Church and Cultures*, 11.

32 Luzbetak, *The Church and Cultures*.

33 W. Jay Moon, and W. Bud Simon, *Effective Intercultural Evangelism: Good News in a Diverse World* (Downers Grove, IL: IVP, 2021).

34 Moon and Simon (2021) explore four worldviews in their book, but I only list the three pertinent to my chapter.

35 Moon and Simon call it the "guilt/justice worldview," but I have called it the "guilt/innocence worldview."

36 Moon and Simon, *Effective Intercultural Evangelism*.

and otherworldly beings. People make decisions based on the spirit world, resulting in the belief/practice of superstition, spells, and sacrifices to appease spirits: "The spiritual and physical world intermingle through nature, matter, rituals, ancestors, and other forms. In this worldview, people fear that these powers will act capriciously."[37] People who live under this worldview spend their time overcoming fear.

If people in Asia read the Bible through the Western worldview, they do so because they have been taught to see the gospel through Western eyes. Moon and Simon drew our attention to the account in Genesis 3 known as the fall of humankind, a fundamental teaching in Christianity.[38] Moon and Simon contended that the Genesis story is about all three worldviews: Adam and Eve were guilty, they were ashamed, and they hid from God out of fear.[39] Hence the Bible can be read across cultures in a way that relates to all the worldviews.

Beyond a threefold reading of the Genesis passage, the Bible has specific passages that address each of the three worldviews. In John 8:1–11, a woman caught committing adultery is brought before Jesus and receives forgiveness as Jesus says to her, "Go and leave your life of sin" (John 8:11). This account deals with the guilt/justice worldview.

In Luke 15, the prodigal son who took his father's inheritance and squandered it on worldly pleasures returns home and is met by his father, who covers his son's shame with robes, a ring, and a feast. This passage addresses the shame/honor worldview.

Additionally, the numerous instances in the Bible of Jesus's miraculous works, such as calming the storm, feeding five thousand hungry people, and delivering people from demons, address the fear/power worldview.

Frame Gospel Terms to the Culture

The gospel must make sense in the receiver's culture. To illustrate why the gospel must be interpreted through the receiver's cultural vocabulary, I appeal to the most well-known verse in the Bible: John 3:16 (a concise summary of the gospel). However, it is unrealistic to expect people in Asia

37 Moon and Simon, *Effective Intercultural Evangelism*, 55.

38 Moon and Simon, *Effective Intercultural Evangelism*.

39 Moon and Simon, *Effective Intercultural Evangelism*.

to hear and sufficiently understand the gospel from John 3:16 and put their faith in Christ. John 3:16 reads, "For God so loved the world that he gave his one and only son, that whoever believes in him shall not perish but have eternal life." I single out three concepts from this verse that warrant exploration: God, love, and eternal life.

First, the concept of God does not exist in Buddhist cultures. Spirits exist in folk Buddhism. However, on hearing "God" in John 3:16, a Hindu may ask, "Which god?" because of the polytheistic nature of Hinduism. Furthermore, the conception of god in Hinduism is not the personal God of the Bible but an unknown force. The Muslim listener, on hearing "God gave his . . . son," would cry out, "Blasphemy!" because of two strong Muslim doctrines: God cannot beget a child (unlike a human being) and God has a unitarian nature.

Second, the term *love* needs explanation. Love in the Buddhist mind is merely "passion" or "erotic love."[40] In Buddhism, seeking something outside ourselves is useless because they believe that everything we need is within.[41] Seeking fulfillment in another is attachment, which will ultimately end in suffering.

Third, eternal life is not appealing to either Hindus or Buddhists because both want to escape the endless cycle of life and attain *moksha* or *nirvana/nibanna*.[42]

Therefore, the Christian communicator must be aware that Asians come from diverse cultural backgrounds, and so gospel words and concepts must be framed through the receiver's lens. It is also best to avoid Christian jargon, such as *new birth* and *redemption*. The challenge for the Christian communicator is to find alternative words and phrases that listeners can relate to. For the Buddhist, phrases such as "how to escape the endless suffering" or "gift of eternal good life without suffering" would make more

40 Field notes, 2004.

41 Carol Anderson, *Pain and Its Ending: The Four Noble Truths in the Theravada Buddhist Canon* (London: Routledge, 2013).

42 Moksha means release or liberation from the cycle of births and rebirths. Nirvana, also termed Nibanna, is the goal of Buddhism—the release from this world.

sense in explaining John 3:16. And for the Muslim, *Rasulu'llah* (apostle or messenger of God)[43] would be more suitable (at least initially) than son of God in reference to Jesus.[44]

Emphasize What Fits

While the receiving culture may have elements that distort the gospel, it may also have synonymous elements that express the gospel more adequately. For example, in South and East Asia, three values are upheld: strong families, respect for elders, and the collectivistic life—all taught and displayed in scriptures as the norm. Both the Old and New Testaments teach these values. Clearly, in South and East Asia, these three values resonate with the gospel far better than values expressed in Western culture. Therefore, this cultural trait should be "exploited" or used effectively for the gospel.

Table 1.1. Asian values and the Bible (adapted from Felipe Tan).[45]

Asian Values	Biblical Values
Strong family relationship	Christian church considered a family
Respect for elders	God is our father
Collectivism and group affinities	Christian fellowship

Table 1.1 above shows how strongly family relationships (and the other two values in Asian society) can resonate with the biblical teaching of the church as a family, God as father, and the significance of Christian fellowship.

43 Taken from the Qur'an, Surah 4:157.

44 This information is gathered from my conversations in India and Malaysia during the years 2012-2015.

45 Felipe Tan. "Contextualizing the Gospel Message in Asia: An Adventist Approach." Prepared for the International Faith Learning Seminar, Institute of Christian Teaching, Silver Springs, MD, September 1993. https://christintheclassroom.org/vol_11/11cc_211-226.htm.

Another important issue is that the world of Asia is a world of spirits and the supernatural. For example, for the Chinese and some other East Asians, the fifteenth day of the seventh month of the lunar calendar marks the Hungry Ghost Festival, when the gates of hell are flung open and ghosts roam the earth to visit their living relatives.

By contrast, the biblical world is a world where Christ, in announcing his kingdom, cast out demons and performed miracles. While the church needs to grapple with how Chinese Christians might deal with the Hungry Ghost Festival, it is positive that Asians can relate to the Bible's depiction of spiritual forces—good and evil. The Western world, broadly speaking, is a dualistic world that separates spirit and matter, body and soul.

The West is also informed by the Enlightenment, from which Western theology has adopted a rational, scientific worldview with little room for the miraculous, demonic power, and healing. So the biblical teaching about Christ who, after his resurrection, is said to have "disarmed the powers and authorities and made a public spectacle of them, triumphing over them" (Col 2:15) would read differently for Asian Christians than Christians influenced by Enlightenment philosophy. In the Muslim world and in countries like Thailand,[46] there are increasing reports that people are experiencing supernatural encounters with Christ through signs and wonders.[47]

Discern What Does Not Fit

The apostle Paul used the cultural norm of the city of Corinth to speak against incest to the church there: "It is actually reported that there is sexual immorality among you, and of a kind that even pagans do not tolerate" (1 Cor 5:1). This implies that the mission practitioner can invoke contemporary ethical systems when these systems agree with biblical standards. However, even when there are no ethical standards or common ground to draw from, the biblical norms must be respectfully introduced.

---

46 See chapters 9–11 and 13 in this volume.

47 James Stuart Bell, *Encountering Jesus* (Bloomington, MN: Bethany House, 2015).

In the history of mission, Western missionaries were discerning enough to point out to Hindus in India that the practice of *sati* (widow burning) was not biblical because it involved the murder/suicide of widows.[48] This practice was later outlawed by the British in the state of Bengal in 1829.[49] (Incidentally, the Mughal emperor Akbar tried to abolish this practice in 1582, without success).[50]

Similarly, the head-hunting practices of tribes in Northeast India,[51] East Malaysia, and Indonesia were outlawed mainly through the influence of Christian missionaries.[52]

John Sung (1901–1944), a famous Chinese evangelist, conducted evangelistic and teaching meetings throughout China and Southeast Asia. During his meetings, he called out the "cultural sins" of the Chinese in a dramatic way. For example, he often brought a black coffin to his meetings and drew out of it strips of red cloth with inscriptions of various sins—"concubines, opium smoking, cheating. . ."—specific to the people in China at that time.[53]

Whereas the Bible does not endorse any one culture (or call for uniformity in customs as Islam traditionally does), the biblical worldview is based on values, and the promise of the Bible is that Christ offers the power of the Holy Spirit to "actualize those values in the lives of His disciples."[54]

---

48 The issue here is not commonality between the receiver's culture and the messenger's culture, but common ground between the receiver's culture and biblical teachings and practices.

49 Although Christian missionary William Carey was one of the people who advocated against *sati*, Hindu reformers such as Ram Mohan Roy were also against this practice.

50 John C. Marshman, *History of India from the Earliest Period to the Close of the East India Company's Government* (Edinburgh: William Blackwood, 1876).

51 Frederick Downs, *History of Christianity in India. Vol. 5, Part 5* (Bangalore: The Church History Association of India, 1992).

52 Janet Hoskins, *The Play of Time: Kodi Perspectives on Calendars, History, and Exchange* (Berkeley: University of California Press, 1993).

53 Hinton, "Missions and Church Growth: Evangelism," 400.

54 Darrell L. Whiteman, "Contextualization: the Theory, the Gap, the Challenge," *International Bulletin of Missionary Research* 21, no.1 (Spring 1997): 4–7.

In the earlier example of the Chinese woman who called on spirits, clearly only the outer layer of her life had been converted. The core of her being (her worldview) needed conversion. In calling for a worldview conversion, Kraft cautioned, "When we speak of the conversion of a worldview, we are not talking of a complete conversion. A complete exchange of one worldview for another is as far as we know . . . impossible. We are, rather, looking at partial conversion in terms of the number of assumptions (sub-paradigms, paradigms, subthemes, etc.) that are changed."[55]

Nevertheless, mission practitioners can take solace in the biblical teaching that believers progressively transform in their faith journey until they are freed from the presence of sin (Phil 1:6; Col 3:4). In this respect, Mukuka, who cited Gaiser,[56] preferred the word transformation to conversion: "I believe the word transformation to be more comprehensive, inclusive, and altogether more wholistic than the word conversion. This wholistic understanding hails from the fact that, God's transformation of all things—the heavens and the earth, humans, and all creatures—is at the heart of biblical theology."[57]

Redeem the Marginal/Neutral Elements of the Culture

We must analyze the culture to recognize traces of biblical values, and we must interrogate the culture to carefully discern its parts that do not fit with Scripture. The author of Hebrews instructed us that "anyone who lives on milk, being still an infant, is not acquainted with the teaching about righteousness. But solid food is for the mature, who by constant use have trained themselves to distinguish good from evil" (Heb 5:13–14). The questions we must ask in dealing with cultural aspects on the margins are,

---

55 Charles H. Kraft, *Worldview for Christian Witness* (Pasadena, CA: William Carey Library, 2008), 60–108.

56 Frederick J. Gaiser, "A Biblical Theology of Conversion," in *Handbook of Religious Conversion*, ed. H. Newton Malony and Samuel Southard (Birmingham, AL: Religious Education Press, 1992), 94.

57 Christopher Mukuka, "Towards a Christ-transforming Culture: A Missiological Model," *Ministry: International Journal for Pastors* (2017, para 14), https://www.ministrymagazine.org/archive/2017/08/Towards-a-Christtransforming-culture-A-missiological-model

Can cultural elements be renewed or redeemed? That is, can new biblical content be added to make them acceptable?

In Chinese culture, a significant integrating value is present, called *guanxi* or *relationship*.[58] A person's social standing and interpersonal well-being is underpinned by *guanxi*—the quality of friendships built on trust and reciprocity. People make decisions based on how *guanxi* affects their network of relationships.[59] They also avoid friction in decision-making, so some decisions might entail personal loss for people. The downside of *guanxi* and its obligations is that some Chinese may even be reluctant to foster new friendships because a one-sided relationship would mean a loss of face.[60]

Although *guanxi* may lead to ideas and practices outside the scope of the Bible, it can be used by the Christian practitioner as a point of initial agreement, contact with the Bible's teachings on Christian fellowship, and an invitation for deeper exploration of the Bible. We can take *guanxi* and add to it the full implications of what Scripture teaches in 1 John 1:3—all Christian fellowship involves the Father and Jesus Christ, 1 Timothy 6:2—believing masters must be shown respect as fellow believers, and Hebrews 13:16—do good, share with others, and please God. In making these comparisons, we can help Chinese believers see the richness of Christian fellowship and add to the limitations of *guanxi*. Wendel Sun, a Chinese scholar, explained how this practice can add depth to *guanxi*: "To apply this to the contemporary church in China, the gospel creates a harmonious society (i.e., the church) in which one gains a new primary identity.[61] This new society includes all—rich and poor, Han and minority—in Christ.

58 Yadong Luo, Ying Huang, and Stephanie Lu Wang, "Guanxi and Organizational Performance: A Meta Analysis," *Management and Organization Review* 8, no.1 (2011):139–172.

59 Yadong Luo, Ying Huang, and Stephanie Lu Wang, "Guanxi and Organizational Performance."

60 Yadong Luo, Ying Huang, and Stephanie Lu Wang, "Guanxi and Organizational Performance."

61 Wendel Sun, "Union with Christ and Contextualization in China," *China Source Quarterly* 20, no.1 (Spring 2018): para 17, https://www.chinasource.org/resource-library/articles/union-with-christ-and-contextualization-in-china/

This body works together, each member serving the others for the good of the body (Eph 4:4–16). No longer do diverging groups need to battle one another for face or fortune. Rather, in Christ, believers together put on the armor of God and together battle the true enemy of peace.

Wherever Hindus are in the world, Diwali is celebrated.[62] It is also called the *Festival of Lights* because, at one point, some gods overcame lesser gods and brought hope to the people. Many Hindus who have become Christians stay away from this celebration because of its multiple Hindu gods and demons.[63] However, some Christian missionaries and pastors have tried to redeem this celebration by infusing it with new meaning.[64] They take the verse in John 1:9 that "Jesus is the true light that gives light to all men" and encourage former Hindus to celebrate Diwali with candles and lights within this new meaning. Hence the Hindu festival is redeemed.

Likewise, there are many festivals like the Mooncake Festival, celebrated among East Asians, where new meaning can be provided by studying the underlying historical and cultural issues in the light of biblical values. In this way, Asian identity is maintained while partaking in cultural festivals with a new meaning and focus.

Challenges of Contextualization

Practicing contextualization in mission is like walking on a tightrope. With insufficient contextualization, the gospel may sound obscure and foreign, while too much leads to another gospel (Gal 1:8), a form of heresy called syncretism or Christopaganism.[65] It is helpful to keep this principle in

62 Diwali is also known as *Deepavali*.

63 According to Hindu legend, Lord Rama defeated Ravana after Rama was in exile for fourteen years. After this victory over Ravana, the people of the Indian city Ayodhya welcomed Rama by lighting rows of clay lamps. So, Diwali became a celebration of Rama's victory and the victory of truth over evil.

64 See: https://standrewchurch.in/christian-reflections-for-diwali/

65 Dean S. Gilliland, "New Testament Contextualization: Continuity and Particularity in Paul's Theology," in *The Word Among Us: Contextualizing Theology for Mission Today*, ed. Dean Gilliland (Dallas, TX: Word Publishing, 1989).

mind and in view: Contextualization is a means to an end, and the end is evangelism (of nonbelievers), discipleship, and training of believers.

Hiebert provides helpful advice in tackling the challenges of contextualization.[66] He advocates that mission practitioners summon the help of informed members of the congregation to critically evaluate their traditions or beliefs and consider them in the light of their biblical understanding.

Conclusion

The main thrust of this chapter was my six-part contextualization framework: understand the gospel, understand the cultural worldview, frame gospel terms to the culture, emphasize what fits, discern what does not fit, and redeem the marginal/neutral elements of the culture.

The gospel can and should be made relevant in every culture. Mission practitioners must identify with the cultures they are reaching and make relevant adaptations, even though there may be discomfort. However, the gospel also interrogates every culture at some point. Where the Bible sets a limit, mission practitioners must set a limit. The goal of contextualization is growth and understanding. The gospel will always create some kind of discomfort in all societies (1 Cor 1:18). Our goal as mission practitioners is to ensure that we do not put any obstacles in the presentation and outworking of the gospel.

In sum, contextualization is the means of creating a local theology for the cultures in Asia. Contextualization is vital to the task of the church today, just as it was in the mission of God two thousand years ago, when God "became flesh" within the Jewish culture (John 1:14).

Bibliography

Anderson, Carol. *Pain and Its Ending: The Four Noble Truths in the Theravada Buddhist Canon*. London: Routledge, 2013.

Beaver, R. Pierce. "The History of Mission Strategy." In *Perspectives: On the World Christian Movement,* edited by Ralph D Winter and Steven C Hawthorne. Pasadena, CA: William Carey Library, 1999.

---

66 Paul G. Hiebert, *Anthropological Insights for Missionaries* (Ada, MI: Baker Academic, 1986).

Bell, James Stuart. *Encountering Jesus*. Bloomington, MN: Bethany House, 2015.

Berkhof, Louis. *Introduction to Systematic Theology*. Grand Rapids, MI: Eerdmans, 1988.

Bevans, Steven B. *Models of Contextual Theology*. Maryknoll, NY: Orbis Books, 2002.

Chang, Lit Sen. *Strategy of Missions in the Orient*. Hong Kong: Presbyterian and Reformed Press, 1969.

Coe, Shoki. "In Search of Renewal in Theological Education." *Theological Education* 9, no. 4 (1973): 233–243.

Dann, Rob B. *Father of Faith Missions: The Life and Times of Anthony Norris Groves*. Georgia: Authentic Media, 2004.

Dean, Marcus. "The Missionary as a Cultural Pilgrim." *Evangelical Missions Quarterly* 48, no. 4 (2012):10–14.

Dodson, Jonathan. *Unbelievable Gospel: Sharing a Gospel Worth Believing*. Grand Rapids, MI: Zondervan, 2014.

Downs, Frederick S. *History of Christianity in India Vol. 5, Part 5*. Bangalore: The Church History Association of India, 1992.

Doyle, Tom. *Dreams and Visions: Is God Awakening the Muslim World?* Nashville, Tennessee: Thomas Nelson, 2012.

Gaiser, Frederick J. "A Biblical Theology of Conversion." In *Handbook of Religious Conversion*, edited by H. Newton Malony and Samuel Southard. Birmingham, AL: Religious Education Press, 1992.

Gilliland, Dean S. "New Testament Contextualization: Continuity and Particularity in Paul's Theology." In *The Word Among Us: Contextualizing Theology for Mission Today,* edited by Dean Gilliland. Dallas, TX: Word Publishing, 1989.

Hiebert, Paul G. *Anthropological Insights for Missionaries*. Ada, MI: Baker Academic, 1986.

Hinton, Keith W. "Missions and Church Growth: Evangelism in an Asian context." In *World Missions: The Asian Challenge, A Compendium of the Asia Missions Congress '90,* edited by Asia Missions Congress, 388–401. Manila: The Asia Missions Congress, 1990.

Hoskins, Janet. *The Play of Time: Kodi Perspectives on Calendars, History, and Exchange.* Berkeley: University of California Press, 1993.

Kraft, Charles H. "Culture, Worldview and Contextualization." In *Perspectives on the World Christian Movement: A Reader*, edited by Ralph Winter and Steven C Hawthorne. Pasadena, CA: William Carey Library, 1999.

———. *Worldview for Christian Witness*. Pasadena, CA: William Carey Library, 2008.

Kwan, Simon Shui-Man. "From Indigenization to Contextualization: a Change in Discursive Practice Rather Than a Shift in Paradigm." *Studies in World Christianity* 11 (2005): 236–250.

Kwast, Lloyd E. "Understanding Culture". In *Perspectives on the World Christian Movement,* edited by Ralph D Winter and Steven C Hawthorne, Pasadena, CA: William Carey Library, 1999.

Luo, Yadong, Ying Huang, and Stephanie Lu Wang. "Guanxi and Organizational Performance: A Meta Analysis." *Management and Organization Review* 8, no.1 (2011):139–172.

Luzbetak, Louis. J. *The Church and Cultures: New Perspectives in Missiological Anthropology.* Maryknoll, NY: Orbis Books, 1988.

Marshman, John. C. *History of India from the Earliest Period to the Close of the East India Company's Government.* Edinburgh: William Blackwood, 1876.

Mead, Hunter. *Types and Problems of Philosophy.* New York: Henry Holt and Company, 1964.

Merriam-Webster Dictionary. "Indigenous." Accessed April 2, 2023. https://www.merriam-webster.com/dictionary/indigenous

Mukuka, Christopher K. "Towards a Christ-transforming Culture: A Missiological Model." *Ministry: International Journal for Pastors,* 2017. https://www.ministrymagazine.org/archive/2017/08/Towards-a-Christtransforming-culture-A-missiological-model

Moon, W. Jay and W. Bud Simon. *Effective Intercultural Evangelism: Good News in a Diverse World.* Downers Grove, IL: IVP, 2021.

Niebuhr, Richard. *Christ and Culture.* New Haven: Yale University Press, 1951.

Salamone, Frank A. *Encyclopedia of Religious Rites, Rituals, and Festivals.* New York: Routledge, 2004.

Sanchez, Daniel R. "Contextualization and the Missionary Endeavor." In *Missiology: An Introduction to the Foundations, History, and Strategy of World Missions,* edited by John Mark Terry, Ebbie Smith, and Justice Anderson. Nashville: Broadman and Holman, 1998.

Seventh-day Adventists. *A Biblical Exposition of 27 Fundamental Beliefs.* Washington, D.C.: Ministerial Association, 1988.

Sun, Wendel. 2018. "Union with Christ and Contextualization in China." *China Source Quarterly* 20, no.1, (Spring 2018). https://www.chinasource.org/resource-library/articles/union-with-christ-and-contextualization-in-china/

Tan, Felipe. "Contextualizing the Gospel Message in Asia: An Adventist Approach." International Faith Learning Seminar, September. *Institute of Christian Teaching.* Silver Springs, MD: Institute of Christian Teaching, 1993.

Tan, Justin. T. "You Have Made All Things Beautiful in Their Time: Reflections on the Spirit of Beauty" In *Spirit Wind: The Doctrine of the Holy Spirit in Global Theology –A Chinese Perspective,* edited by Peter L. Tie and Justin T. T. Tan, Eugene, OR: Wipf and Stock Publishers, 2021.

Whiteman, Darrell. L. "Contextualization: The Theory, the Gap, the Challenge." *International Bulletin of Missionary Research* 21, no.1 (1997): 2–7.

Walsh, Brian J and J. Richard Middleton, *The Transforming Vision: Shaping a Christian Worldview*. Westmont, IL: InterVarsity Press, 1984.

WikiDiff. "Contextualization vs. Indigenization." Accessed April 2, 2023. https://wikidiff.com/indigenization/contextualization

Woodhead, Linda. *An Introduction to Christianity*. Cambridge: Cambridge University Press, 2004.

Wu, Jackson. *One Gospel for All Nations: A Practical Approach to Biblical Contextualization*. Pasadena, CA: William Carey Library, 2015.

2

AN OVERVIEW OF CHRISTIANITY'S EXPANSION AND INDIGENIZATION IN ASIA

by Violet James

Introduction

For centuries, Southeast Asia was influenced by India and China's cultures and religions, which have significantly shaped the lives of the people. In the thirteenth century, the Arabs introduced Islam to the islands of Indonesia and the Philippines through Malacca. The Portuguese were the first Europeans to arrive in the sixteenth century, followed by the Spanish, Dutch, French, and British. The Portuguese, Spanish, and French introduced Roman Catholicism to the regions they penetrated, while the Dutch and British brought Protestantism. Spain colonized the Philippines in the sixteenth century, and France penetrated the Indochina region in the eighteenth century. The Dutch took possession of Indonesia at the time of the Spanish colonization in Asia, and both these powers were in control for more than three hundred years. The British occupied Myanmar, Malaysia, and Singapore in the nineteenth century. Thailand was spared colonization.

Colonialism has had a somewhat enigmatic reception in Southeast Asia.[1] Hence Christianity has been regarded as a European religion for

1 Violet James, "Christianity in South-eastern Asia, 1910–2010," in *ATLAS of Global Christianity*, ed. Todd Johnson and Kenneth R. Ross (Edinburgh: Edinburgh University, Press, 2010), 146–147.

most of its history due to its association with the European colonizing powers. Therefore, the corollary was that, being a non-Western world, Asia was a mission field ripe for evangelization. However, in the past two centuries, this premise has been challenged as mission bases have become mission fields because of the presence of many Christians in Asia, Africa, and Latin America. The percentage of Christians in Asia has increased significantly, yet in the light of a huge Asian population that embraces other religions or ideologies, the number of Christians is still very small.

For hundreds of years, Asian peoples have regarded Christianity as alien, associating it with the colonial masters who came to conquer, plunder, and inevitably impose their beliefs, customs, and languages. In the eyes of Asians, a Christian is one who embodies the religion and culture of the Western colonizers, be they Portuguese, Spanish, French, British, or American. The foreign missionaries who accompanied the colonial rulers into these Asian countries were compelled by their love for Jesus to propagate the gospel in these territories. However, the gospel was presented in such a way that the recipients saw the religion as a Western package. That is, to become a Christian meant that one must believe what the Westerner believes, worship their God, attend a place of worship that reflects their style of church, sing their songs, speak their language, and embrace a certain lifestyle that befits the new religion.

In this chapter, I provide a historical sketch of how Christianity entered Asia, the methods employed by Roman Catholic and Protestant missionaries, and the responses of those subjected to missionary endeavors. I also propose incarnational approaches for missionaries and evangelists to consider for the future.[2]

2 The incarnational approaches are patterned after Jesus Christ, who although he was God, took on human flesh and "incarnated" among mankind. He put aside his deity as it were, and identified with the least, the lost, and the marginalized, demonstrating humility and compelled with compassion as he saw the crowds, harassed and helpless. We must model after Jesus Christ, who guides us in how we do mission among different people, as we adapt to and accommodate various situations.

Birth of Christianity in Asia

Because most Asians have perceived it as a Western religion, Christianity has borne the brunt of negative responses in many parts of Asia. However, Christianity was birthed in Asia, as recorded in the book of Acts 2:5–11: "Now there were staying in Jerusalem God-fearing Jews, from every nation under heaven . . . Parthians and Medes and Elamites and residents from Mesopotamia, Judea and Cappadocia, Pontus and Asia, Phrygia and Pamphylia, Egypt and the parts of Libya near Cyrene; visitors from Rome (both Jews andconverts to Judaism, Cretans and Arabs."

Luke, the writer of the book of Acts, mentioned "devout men from every nation under heaven" (v. 5) to substantiate the diversity of founding groups at that time, which included both the Roman Empire and the world beyond. Thousands were impacted by the message that the apostle Peter preached on that Day of Pentecost in 30 BCE. This, presumably, identified the first Christian community in Jerusalem. They met in homes (Acts 2:42) and conducted "church," as mentioned in the passage. These people who were in Jerusalem for the Festival of Thanksgiving eventually returned to their respective towns and villages. The assumption is that they established Christian communities wherever they went.

While the book of Acts is silent on the establishment of these subsequent centers of Christianity, church history records traditions, myths, and factual stories about the existence of Christianity in Asia in the first few centuries. For example, Eusebius of Caesarea (died 339 or 340 BCE), the first church historian, recorded that the disciples of Jesus cast lots and went to different places of the then-known world.[3] In the document *The Acts of Thomas*,[4] there was an account of how Thomas Didymus, one of the twins and an apostle of Jesus Christ, was sent to India as early as the third century. Indeed, a church in India today traces its beginnings to St. Thomas.[5]

---

3 Tony Lane, *A Concise History of Christian Thought* (MI: Baker Academic, 2006).

4 F.A D' Cruz, *St Thomas the Apostle, in India* (Madras, India: Hoe, 1922), 25.

5 F.A.D' Cruz, *St Thomas.*

Clear historic evidence shows that the centers of Christianity in the first few decades were Edessa and Seleucia-Ctesiphon in the Central Asian and Mesopotamian regions, where the stories of Abraham and the nation of Israel emanated from.[6] The church was originally known as the Syrian Church or the Church of the East. Later, it was referred to as the Nestorian church, presumably because the Nestorians, when ousted from the Roman Empire, became part of this church. This church existed before the Christianization of the Roman Empire, which started with the conversion of Emperor Constantine the Great in 312 BCE. Thus the Syrian/Nestorian church was independent of the Roman Empire and possibly more faithful in carrying out the Great Commission given by Christ to his apostles. Due to persecution, its people traveled eastward from the Roman Empire, and wherever they went, they propagated the gospel of Jesus Christ.[7] The missionaries used Syrian, rather than Latin or Greek, to preach the gospel and disciple the people. In the seventh century, Syrian Christians entered China and established churches there.[8]

Characteristics of the Christian Church in Asia

No one knew of the existence of Christianity in China until the sixteenth century, when a stele (a huge monument, measuring nine by three feet tall, constructed as a celebration stone) was discovered by archaeologists in Xi'an, China. On this huge stele were the dates of its construction (781 BCE) and when Christianity first entered China under the leadership of Alopen (635 BCE). According to T.H. Ho, the stele commemorated the propagation of the Syrian faith in China. This "man of great virtue," Alopen, was received by the emperor in his royal court in Chang'an, the traditional name for Xi'an, and the emperor invited him to translate Syrian Scripture in the imperial library.[9]

6 Samuel H. Moffett, *A History of Christianity in Asia, 1* (Maryknoll: NY: Orbis Books, 1998), 46.

7 Moffett, *A History of Christianity in Asia*, 46–80.

8 T.H. Ho, "Ancient Stone Marks: China's First Encounter with Christianity," *Christianity Today* 66, no. 8, (April 2022): 25.

9 Ho, *Ancient Stone Marks*.

I take it that the Emperor of China, Tang Taizong, was a very liberal-minded and eager scholar who welcomed the Christians, studied their teachings, realized the similarities with the Confucian teachings that the Chinese people adhered to and allowed the Syrians to propagate this faith.[10] I also assume that the Syrians were aware of the ethical teachings of Confucius and saw how closely they were related to Christian teachings. If so, this was an early act of indigenizing the teachings of Jesus in a language and culture different from theirs but compatible with the recipient Chinese people.[11]

I infer that these Syrian Christians were evangelistic and missional wherever they went, even more so than the Christians within the Roman Empire. They tried their utmost to make the gospel understandable to the different peoples they encountered. I assume that the leadership was in the hands of the Syrians rather than the Chinese people, based on the list of Syrian names found on the stele.

Further evidence on the stele was a form of syncretism—that is, the fusion of other beliefs alongside that of Christianity, thus diluting the Christian faith—that may have taken place during the Syrian mission's 150 years in China (635–781 BCE). The three symbols on the stele were the cross, a lotus flower, and rolling clouds, representing the three religions in China: Christianity, Buddhism, and Taoism. Such syncretistic teachings probably led to the retardation of the church and its final demise in China, as the subsequent Roman Catholic missionaries who entered China (thirteenth to fourteenth centuries) could not find any trace of Nestorian Christianity.

Eventually, the Chinese automatically shunned anything Western, including the Christian faith. From the seventeenth to the twentieth centuries, the Chinese and other Asian peoples had a legitimate reason for their hostility toward Westerners because of colonialism and imperialism. In the eyes of the local peoples, the colonial powers and the missionaries were one and the same. The foreigners came with guns to colonize and

---

10 Ho, *Ancient Stone Marks*.

11 Andrew Walls from the Center of World Christianity, in his book entitled *The Missionary Movement in Christian History* (1996), used the phrase "making a person feel at home" frequently as he taught contextualization and indigenization as the gospel penetrated in the non-Western world.

Bibles to evangelize.[12] Thus the church of the East eventually disappeared from China but remained in parts of Central Asia that eventually became part of the Mongolian Empire under Genghis Khan. And, as mentioned above, there were traces of Nestorian presence in India and the Far East.

Coming of Western Missionaries to Asia

Those who came to be called "Western missionaries" first entered Asia in the latter part of the thirteenth century. Franciscan and Dominican friars, compelled by their love for Jesus, left the comforts of their own countries to enter Asia, typically in the wake of European traders and adventurers. For example, from the late sixteenth to the mid-seventeenth century, the Portuguese established trading posts along the coastal areas in Goa, Macao, Malacca, and Nagasaki. Their interest was solely commerce, but some of the traders married local women, thereby insinuating their Christian religion and lifestyle. Later, missionaries came to these trading posts and established mission centers in the ports.

In the sixteenth century, Spanish traders were accompanied by missionaries, and the latter Christianized the local peoples.[13] This was evident in the Philippines. The Spanish ruled the Philippines for over three hundred years, adding Roman Catholicism to the animism of the inhabitants.[14] However, the French Roman Catholic missionaries who went to Indochina in the seventeenth century were persecuted by the Confucian leaders. There were also internal wars and dynastic quarrels among the local leadership. It was a cry for help to re-establish a prince on his throne that triggered interferences by the French government, leading eventually to its colonization of the northern, central, and southern parts of Vietnam, Cambodia, and Laos. The French called this land mass "Indochina," even though the countries were distinct in language, religion, and culture[15].

---

12 Brian Stanley, in *The Bible and the Flag*, addresses this dilemma because of the close association of the missionaries with the colonial powers.

13 Robbie Goh, *Christianity in Southeast Asia: Series 7* (Singapore: Institute of Southeast Asian Studies, 2005), 25.

14 Goh, *Christianity in Southeast Asia*.

15 Violet James, "The Protestant American Response to the Vietnam War" (PhD diss., Aberdeen University, 1989).

The Protestant Dutch, who first came to Indonesia in the seventeenth century as traders, eventually colonialized Indonesia, ruling over the people for more than three hundred years. Like the Portuguese, the Dutch were concerned only with commerce; the accompanying clergy were there to provide pastoral care for their own people.

Missionaries in Europe were impacted by the religious revivals of the eighteenth and nineteenth centuries, when many churches were renewed, and Christians were compelled to carry out the Great Commission given by Christ to the disciples in the first century. One of the outcomes of the many revivals was the establishment of mission organizations, such as the Rhenish Missionary Society, which sent out missionaries from Europe to Indonesia to work among the tribal peoples, such as the Batak, who were known to be head-hunters and cannibals.[16] The apostle to the Bataks was Ludwig Nommensen (1834–1918), who studied the culture and religion of the people, served them for fifty-six years, and eventually saw a great breakthrough and transformation among them, resulting in the establishment of a thriving Batak church.[17] Nommensen's first convert to Christianity was Rajah Pontus Lumbantobing, a man of significant authority.[18] The strategy Nommensen employed was to use people in authority in the Batak villages, regarded as *rajas* (kings), as soon as they were converted, assigning them roles in the organized churches to provide vital support to the church's growth and expansion.[19]

The British East India Company (EIC) went to India in the seventeenth century. Thanks to its superior weapons and strategies and the internecine battles between local warring bodies, the EIC became the dominant force in the whole of India by the late eighteenth century.[20] With the support of the British government, the EIC continued to expand its

16 Ludwig Schreiner, "Nommensen Ingwer Ludwig," in *Biographical Dictionary of Christian Missions*, ed. Gerald H. Anderson (NY: Macmillan Reference, 1998), 499–500.

17 Schreiner, "Nommensen Ingwer Ludwig."

18 Schreiner, "Nommensen Ingwer Ludwig."

19 Samuel Moffett, *A History of Christianity in Asia* (Maryknoll, NY: Orbis Books, 2007), 623.

20 William Dalrymple, *The Anarchy: The Relentless Rise of the East India Company* (London: Bloomsbury, 2019).

empire to include Burma, Malaysia, and Singapore. Interestingly, like the Dutch, the British did not intend to transform Indian culture or religion; their focus was entirely on profit-making through trade and commerce, not proselytization. William Carey (1761–1834), the father of modern Protestant missions, was threatened with imprisonment many times by British EIC officers for preaching the gospel to Indians. It was only when Carey went to Serampore, then ruled by the Danish government, that he and his team of missionaries gained protection and were able to freely evangelize the Indians.[21]

The coming of the Western missionaries was inevitably associated with colonialism. Though the missionaries were distinct from the colonial powers and were motivated by different causes, they were typically perceived as partners in oppressing the local people and imposing their culture and religion.

A clash was inevitable between Christianity and high religions,[22] such as Hinduism, Buddhism, Islam, and Confucianism. Christianity, being an exclusive religion, clashed immediately with all these religions that were primarily inclusive religions, except for Islam. For example, in Vietnam, the French imposed Roman Catholicism upon a people for whom Confucianism had been deeply ingrained for over a thousand years, especially in North Vietnam. Both beliefs demanded exclusive allegiance: Christianity to the pope in Rome and Confucianism to the ruling emperor. The Vietnamese resented the French and the religion they represented.[23]

In the sixteenth century, the Jesuits successfully broke new ground in China. They understood the need for common ground for communicating effectively with the Chinese (and other Asians). The Franciscans and Dominican missionaries came to Asia with a mindset that all indigenous

---

21 Timothy George, *Faithful Witness: The Life and Mission of William Carey* (Westmont, IL: InterVarsity Press, 1991).

22 High religions are religions that are well established, having institutions, leadership, and sacred writings, as opposed to low religions, which are primal in nature and have none of the aforementioned elements.The low religions worship spirits and are often gripped by overwhelming fear of almost everything and anything. For further understanding, see Gailyn van Rheenen, 1991.

23 Violet James, "American Protestant Missions and the War in Vietnam."

cultures were pagan and sinful. They tried to replace the pagan cultures with the gospel of Christ and the teachings of the Roman church.

Some outstanding Jesuit missionaries identified with the Chinese culture and language and impressed the Chinese emperors and their leaders with new knowledge. Matteo Ricci, Adam Schall von Bell, and Ferdinand Verbiest were three outstanding scholars who accommodated the Chinese Confucian culture, spoke the Chinese language, and took on Chinese names.[24] They impressed the courts with their knowledge of mathematics, astronomy, cartography, and other sciences. The Jesuits identified with the Confucian culture and indigenized the Christian faith. They were well received both by the officials and the ordinary people. Ricci studied the practice of ancestor worship among the Chinese and concluded that it was not religious but social and political. Confucius taught the importance of the people's submission to their ruler through the practice of filial piety. Ricci concluded that ancestor worship taught the people to submit to those who ruled over them or were older than them, and that this helped cement the nation, resulting in harmony and unity, so they should not be hindered from doing it. Ricci also used the Chinese terms *tien* and *shang ti* for God in his writings. However, out of jealousy, some Franciscan and Dominican missionaries reported these unbiblical practices to the pope. This battle came to be known as the Chinese Rites controversy, which came to a head when the emperor and officials objected to the foreigners trying to determine the correct term for God in Chinese, together with other religious practices. These created great animosity toward the foreigners, who appeared audacious to debate on things that were Chinese. Subsequently, this resulted in the emperor's prohibition of foreign missionaries carrying on their work in China. The pope in Rome also recalled the Jesuits. This was especially unfortunate because the antagonism was precipitated by the European missionaries.[25]

The Americans, the last of the foreigners to rule and missionize the Asians, came to "liberate" the Filipinos from the Spanish in the late nineteenth century (1898 CE), but they remained to rule them and opened the

24 Violet James, "Why Christianity Failed to Take Roots in the Soil of China" (Master's thesis, Wheaton College, 1978).

25 James, "Why Christianity Failed to Take Roots."

doors for Protestantism to enter the country. Thus Protestantism in the Philippines is only a recent phenomenon.

Transplantation of Western Christianity in Asia

To what extent did Western missionaries superimpose their culture on the local people and regard indigenous culture as inferior? And, as reflected by Jonathan James in the introduction, how often did local churches, when established, resemble—aesthetically and functionally—the church in the missionaries' homelands?[26]

Some Roman Catholic missionaries, such as the Jesuits, and some Protestant missionaries saw the need to indigenize and accommodate the local peoples they served. Most of the missionaries, especially the British and American missionaries in the eighteenth and nineteenth centuries, had a predisposition characterized by a sense of superiority, called "the white man's burden," first mentioned by Rudyard Kipling (1865–1936) in his poems from 1897 and 1899.[27] That is, they saw it as their moral duty to transform indigenous cultures with Christianity, commerce, and civilization, but not necessarily in that order.[28]

Over time, Asian societies increasingly came to resent the insinuations and imprecations of Western missionaries. Anti-foreign feelings, hostility, and pride in their own cultures and religions increasingly manifested. One such example was China's Boxer Rebellion in 1900, in which hundreds of missionaries, their children, and local Chinese Christians were brutally massacred.[29] The missionaries were called "foreign devils," and

26 Many historians have written on the foreignness of Western churches and denominations replicated and transplanted into the local churches.

27 William Easterly, *The White Man's Burden* (London: Oxford University Press), 2007.

28 The missionaries believed that only Christianity could reform the nonbelievers, and this must be accompanied by changing their cultures and learning the missionaries' way of life, customs, practices, and language. Often converts were given Biblical names or "Christian" names.

29 Ruth Tucker, *From Jerusalem to Irian Jaya* (Grand Rapids, MI: Eerdmans, 2004), 203–204.

the local Chinese Christians were called "running dogs."[30] In this context, Chinese Christians saw the need to establish indigenous Chinese churches, not the mainline denominations transplanted by the European missionaries. Three churches are worthy of mention here: the True Jesus Church (1917) founded by Chang Lin Shen, which grew to about one hundred thousand members by 1949; the Assembly Hall started by Watchmen Nee (1922), better known as Little Flock, which had a membership of seventy to eighty thousand; and the Jesus Family, founded by a former Methodist evangelist, Ching Tien Ying, which had 140 communes in eight provinces, all characterized by simplicity, honesty, and communal living.[31]

When the communists took over China in 1949, all missionaries were repatriated or imprisoned, and the churches established by the missionaries were brought under the control of the communist government. This was known as the Three-Self Patriotic Movement (TSPM). Indigenous churches that decided against coming under the control of the state went underground; they were called "underground churches," today referred to as "house churches." Just before 1949, an estimated quarter of Chinese Christians were part of these churches. During Mao's Cultural Revolution (1966 onward), the Christians who suffered the brunt of persecution were from the TSPM and not the underground churches.

Open Doors, Hostility, Indigenization, and Syncretism

The Philippines and Indonesia were colonized by Europeans for more than three hundred years. The Spanish colonial power came and forced Roman Catholicism on the people. However, those who practiced animism merely added this new religion to their old beliefs, customs, and practices, creating a hybrid religion that was different from that of their ruling masters.

30 A "running dog" is one who blindly follows the missionary and panders to his whims and fancies. Any local person found with the missionaries was automatically guilty and incurred the wrath of the Boxers (fighters).

31 Read Delwyn Vaughn Rees's *The Jesus Family in Communist China* for this fascinating story.

The Dutch Protestants who ruled over Indonesia did not enforce their faith on the local people. As mentioned above, their main concern was commerce, and they did not want to provoke the people. They brought in pastors to serve their own community, not to evangelize the local people. Only later did the German Lutherans, under the Rhenish Missionary Society, intend to evangelize the local people. Nommensen learned the Batak culture and customs and impacted these people who were once cannibals, as the Christian faith transformed their lives and lifestyle. However, Islam posed a great threat to the missionary movement because Muslim traders had entered Indonesia centuries before the Europeans. Unlike the Spanish rulers who contained them in the south of the Philippines in Mindanao, the Dutch did not. Hence Indonesia has the largest number of Muslims of any nation today, and the Philippines has the largest number of Christians of any Asian nation today.[32]

Another interesting feature is the contrast between the churches of Japan and Korea. Both countries were impacted by American Protestant missionaries in the nineteenth century, yet the Korean church grew by leaps and bounds while the Japanese church was stymied. Shearer attributes this to the fact that indigenization took place very early in the Korean church, whereas local Japanese attempts to indigenize the church were pooh-poohed as being cult-like by the American missionaries.[33] In Korea, the term for God was not an import from the Chinese; it was their very own *hananim*, a local name for their God. When used in the translation of the Korean Bible and in the preaching of the gospel, *hananim* took off like wildfire.[34]

The other possible attribute in Korea came from the Nevius method, named after the American missionary, John Nevius, who visited Korea and taught the missionaries to implement this strategy of discipleship and church growth. Nevius believed that if every Christian is discipled

32 Goh, *Christianity in Southeast Asia.*

33 Roy Shearer, *Wildfire: Church Growth in Korea* (Grand Rapids, MI: Eerdmans, 1966), 39–40.

34 Roy Shearer, *Wildfire.*

by someone and every church is self-propagating, self-supporting, and self-governing, the church will grow strong and large.[35]

The church in Japan lost a golden opportunity for Asianization when the efforts of the Japanese Christian, Kanzo Uchimura (1861–1930), were rejected as cultic.[36] Uchimura grew up as a Shinto but was disillusioned with Shintoism. When he studied at Sapporo Agricultural College, he was exposed to Christianity and eventually became a Christian. He longed for a church that reflected Japanese culture and practice, and when he started a church, he called it the "non-church movement." He did not mean to deny its church-ness; rather, he wanted to emphasize the church's Japanese-ness, unlike the American church transplanted into Japan. The missionaries feared it as cultic, discouraged him, and even shunned him, but Uchimura persevered. He said, "The Japanese could easily be taught Christianity if they were properly instructed, that is, if they were directed to the teachings of the Bible and not instructed in the rites and formalities of church institutions."[37]

Challenges from High Asian Religions

As stated at the outset, many of the world's religions were birthed in Asia, such as Hinduism, Buddhism, and Islam. These religions, regarded as high religions by anthropologists, were already established with sacred writings, institutions, liturgies, and leadership. When Buddhism was promulgated in parts of Asia such as China, it was contextualized in such a way that the Buddha was not dark-skinned but yellow-skinned, and he was not skinny but large to identify with the worldview of the Chinese people, who believed in prosperity, happiness, good health, and longevity. This led the local people to feel right at home in this foreign faith. This was true also in Myanmar and Thailand, even though Buddhism was birthed in India (Nepal today). The Buddhist faith has been skillfully integrated into the

35 Kanzo Uchimura, "Can Americans Teach Japanese in Religion?" *Japan Christian Intelligencer* 1, (Spring 1926): 357–61.

36 This term is used by Jonathan James in the introduction of this book.

37 Tucker, *From Jerusalem to Irian Jaya*, 270.

Chinese, Japanese, Korean, Sri Lankan, Thai, Burmese, and Singaporean cultures because many people have adopted the faith as their very own.[38]

Today, India sees itself as a Hindu nation, although for a long period in the past, Islam was the dominant religion and is still practiced by a substantial minority. Despite the presence of the British in India for three hundred years, Christianity did not gain a strong following. Presumably, Christianity was and is regarded by many Indians as the religion of their imperialistic colonial masters. Unsurprisingly, within the Indian diaspora today, Hinduism is the predominant faith.[39]

From the seventh century onward, Islam was an aggressive conqueror worldwide. Muslim traders and missionaries brought with them their faith, especially to Southeast Asia. Today, Brunei, Indonesia, Malaysia, and southern Thailand are Muslim nations, largely resistant to the advancement of Christianity.[40]

Whereas Asian religions continue to pose major challenges to evangelization in Asia, missiologists such as Phil Parshall, Terry Muck, and Paul Hiebert claim that Asian high religions have learned and are still learning from Christianity to make their faiths more viable in the modern and postmodern world.[41] Hiebert quotes A. F. C. Wallace's theory of revitalization, which states that whenever traditional worldviews are challenged or threatened by external changes, and cultures and religions are overwhelmed by more powerful ones, people will make one of three choices: they convert to the new, adopt some things from the new while retaining the old, or reinterpret their beliefs and start new movements. These faiths realize that Christianity is a force to contend with, and it is imperative to adapt and make accommodations for their religions to survive and thrive.[42]

38 Terry Muck, "Missiological Issues in the Encounter with Emerging Buddhism," *Missiology: An International Review* 28, no. 1 (April 2000): 35–45.

39 Paul Hiebert, "Missiological Issues in the Encounter with Emerging Hinduism," *Missiology: An International Review* 28, no. 1 (April 2000): 47–63.

40 Dudley Woodberry, "Missiological Issues in the Encounter with Emerging Islam," *Missiology: An International Review* 28, no.1 (April 2000): 19–34.

41 Woodberry, Missiological Issues Islam.

42 Hiebert, Missiological Issues Hinduism.

Conclusion

In this chapter, I examined the concept of indigenization/Asianization in some of the early centers of Christianity in Asia, such as the St. Thomas church and the Syrian/Nestorian church in the first several hundred years. During this examination, I noticed that the early Christian missionaries were not Westerners but Asians. They communicated in the languages of the local peoples and gave them the Bible or catechism in the vernacular. However, other issues were not handled as well, and syncretism crept in, diluting the faith. Eventually, Christianity disappeared from some of these places, which are communist, Islamic, and Hindu countries today.

When Western foreigners entered Asia, the missionaries and colonizing powers generally did not know or understand the cultures, customs, and worldviews of these people. They looked upon them as inferior, with cultures and religions that were idolatrous and pagan. They also came with the white man's burden—the urge to civilize, commercialize, and Christianize the local people. When the nations came of age and nationalism was rife, resentment and hostility reached a climax that erupted in wars and bloodbaths, such as the Boxer Rebellion.

I contend that Asianization needs to be much more than indigenization. For missionaries to thrive in places where the gospel has not yet penetrated, they must recognize that one method does not fit all of Asia. Asia is complex, comprising numerous races, groups, worldviews, cultures, and languages. Therefore, one methodology or strategy will not enable missionaries to succeed in their endeavors. They need to understand the unique features, worldviews, and spiritual needs of each country. Their aim is to make every nation, tribe, and people feel at home in the Christian faith, but this can only be achieved with sensitivity, prayer, and understanding of the gospel to avoid syncretism.

The gospel is unchanging, but the methods for its teaching are variable. We must respect these ancient civilizations with their rich heritage, then incarnate the love and life of Christ through the proclamation of the gospel and through deeds that will make a difference in the lives of the people. We must allow the Holy Spirit to direct us as he did in the early church, and like the apostle Paul, be all things to all humankind so that we can save some of them (1 Cor 9:19–23).[43]

Bibliography

Blair, William and Bruce Hunt. *The Korean Pentecost and the Sufferings which Followed.* UK: Banner of Truth Trust, 1977.

Comby, Jean. *How to Understand the History of Christian Mission.* London: SCM Press, 1996.

Dalrymple, William. *The Anarchy: The Relentless Rise of the East India Company.* London: Bloomsbury, 2019.

D' Cruz, F. A. *St Thomas the Apostle, in India.* Madras, India: Hoe. Easterly, William. *The White Man's Burden.* Oxford: Oxford University Press, 2007.

George, Timothy. *Faithful Witness: The Life and Mission of William Carey.* Westmont, IL: InterVarsity Press, 1991.

Goh, Robbie. *Christianity in Southeast Asia: Series 7.* Singapore: Institute of Southeast Asian Studies 2005.

Halverson, Dean. *The Compact Guide to World Religions.* Bloomington, MN: Bethany House, 1996.

Hefley, James and Marti Hefley. *By Their Blood: Christian Martyrs of the Twentieth Century.* Ada, MI: Baker Publishing, 1979.

Hiebert, Paul. "Missiological Issues in the Encounter with Emerging Hinduism." *Missiology: An International Review* 28, no.1 (2000): 47–63.

———. "Indigenization." *Global Anabaptist Mennonite Encyclopedia*, http://www.gameo.org/encyclopedia/contents/I54ME.html.

Hoefer, Herbert E. "Why are Christians Persecuted in India?" *International Journal of Frontier Missions* 18, no. 1 (2001):7–13.

Hoke, Donald. *The Church in Asia.* Chicago, IL: Moody Press, 1975.

Ho, T. N. "Ancient Stone Marks: China's First Encounter with Christianity," *Christianity Today* 66 (8), 2022.

James, Violet. "Why Christianity Failed to Take Roots in the Soil of China." Master's thesis, Wheaton College, 1978.

---

43 Paul instructed the Corinthian Church with some missional principles that he and his associates undertook wherever God sent them on their missionary journeys. One of the key principles he underlined in this passage was to be all things to all people to bring some people to the faith: "I have become all things to all people, so that by all possible means I might save some" (1 Corinthians 9:22).

———. "American Protestant Missions and Their Response to the Vietnam War." PhD diss., Aberdeen University, 1989.

———. "Christianity in South-Eastern Asia, 1910–2010." In *ATLAS of Global Christianity*, edited by Todd Johnson and Kenneth R. Ross, 146–147. Edinburgh: Edinburgh University Press, 2010.

Johnson, Todd, and Kenneth Ross. *ATLAS of Global Christianity, 1910–2010*, Edinburgh Press, 2009.

Kane, Herbert J. *A Concise History of the Christian World Missions.* Ada, MI: Baker Academic, 1978.

Lane, Tony. *A Concise History of Christian Thought*. Ada, MI: Baker Academic, 2006.

McDermott, Gerald. R. *Can Evangelicals Learn from World Religions*. Westmont, IL: InterVarsity Press, 2000.

McDowell, Josh and Don Stewart. n.d. *Concise Guide to Today's Religions,* London, UK: Scripture Union Press.

Moffett, Samuel H. *The Christians of Korea.* NY: Friendship Press, 1962.

———. *A History of Christianity in Asia*, 1. Maryknoll: NY: Orbis Books, 1998.

———. *A History of Christianity in Asia*, 2. Maryknoll, NY: Orbis Books, 2007.

Muck, Terry. "Missiological Issues in the Encounter with Emerging Buddhism." *Missiology: An International Review* 28 (1): 35–45, 2000.

Neill, Stephen, Gerald Anderson, and John Goodwin. *Concise Dictionary of Christian World Mission*. Nashville: Abingdon Press, 1971.

Neill, Stephen. *The History of Missions*. New York: Penguin, 1964.

———. *A Story of the Christian Church in India and Pakistan*. Grand Rapids, MI Eerdmans, 1970.

Noll, Mark. *Turning Points: Decisive Moments in the History of Christianity*. MI: Baker Academic, 2012.

Pani, D. "Fatal Hindu Gospel Stumbling Blocks." *International Journal of Frontier Missions* 18, no. 1 (2001): 23–32.

Pickard, David. "Challenges Facing Asian Missions." In *Into the 21st Century: Asian Churches in Mission,* edited by Met Castillo and Katie Sisco, 110–128. New Delhi: Evangelical Fellowship of Asia, 1989.

Poon, Michael. *Christian Movements in Southeast Asia: A Theological Exploration.* Singapore: Armour Publishing, 2010.

———. *Engaging Society: The Christian in Tomorrow's Singapore*. Singapore: Trinity Theological College, 2013.

Rees, Vaughan. *The Jesus Family in Communist China*. Milton Keynes: Paternoster Press, 1959.

Richardson, Don. *Eternity in Their Hearts*, Ventura, CA: Regal Books, 1984.

Ridenour, Fritz. *So, What's the Difference? A Look at 20 Worldviews, Faiths and Religions and How They compare to Christianity*. Ventura, CA: Regal Press, 2001.

Schreiner, Ludwig. "Nommensen Ingwer Ludwig." In *Biographical Dictionary of Christian Missions,* edited by Gerald H. Anderson, 499–500. NY: Macmillan Reference, 1998.

Shearer Roy. *Wildfire: Church Growth in Korea.* Grand Rapids, MI: Eerdmans, 1966.

Sng, Bobby. *In His Good Time.* Singapore: Bible Society of Singapore, 2003.

Sng, Bobby, and Chee Pang Choong. *Church and Culture in the Singapore Context.* Singapore: Graduates Christian Fellowship, 1991.

Stanley, Brian. *The Bible and the Flag: Protestant Mission and British Imperialism in the 19th and 20th Centuries.* New York: Apollos, 1990.

Sunquist, Scott. *A Dictionary of the Asian Christianity.* Grand Rapids, MI: Eerdmans, 2001.

Tennent, Timothy. *Theology in the Content of World Christianity.* Grand Rapids, MI: Zondervan, 2007.

Tucker, Ruth. *From Jerusalem to Irian Jaya,* Grand Rapids, MI: Zondervan, 2004.

Van Rheenen, Gailyn. *Communicating Christ in Animistic Contexts.* Pasadena, CA: William Carey Library, 1991.

Varg, Paul V. "A Survey of Changing Mission Goals and Methods." In *Christian Missions in China,* edited by Jessie Lutz, Boston, MA: D. C. Heath and Company, 1959.

Walls, Andrew. F. *The Missionary Movement in Christian History: Studies in the Transmission of Faith.* Maryknoll, NY: Orbis Books, 1996.

Woodberry, Dudley. "Missiological Issues in the Encounter with Emerging Islam." In *Missiology: An International Review* 28 no.1 (2000): 19–34.

Uchimura, Kanzo. "Can Americans Teach Japanese in Religion?" *Japan Christian Intelligence* 1, (Spring 1926): 357–61.

3

MISSION AS COMMUNICATION

by Peter Thein Nyunt

Introduction

"Mission" is a term used in both religious and secular contexts. Literally, it refers to sending forth "a commission to carry out the will of a superior."[1] Theologically, it is deeply rooted in communicating the triune God and involving the whole church in the *missio Dei*, the mission of God.[2] In fact, mission is not a by-product of ecclesiology (the doctrine of the church) or of soteriology (the doctrine of salvation). Mission originates and anchors itself in a communicating God. Thus mission is at the very heart of the Gospel and the life of the church.

Arguably, God's actions in mission are manifested in the context in which people live and, of course, his mission always takes place in a specific social context.[3] David J. Bosch argued that to summarize God's actions in mission, "one of the best words available to us is the word communication."[4] Hence if the church and its mission are to be effective, communication is the primary focus. According to R. Daniel Shaw and Charles van

---

1 Walter C. Kaiser, *Mission in the Old Testament: Israel as a Light of the Nations* (Secunderabad, India: OM Books, 2006), 11.

2 German theologian—Karl Hartensein is attributed to have coined this term in the 1930s. The idea is that mission is the work of the church because it stems from God and is an attribute of God.

3 David J. Hesselgrave, *Communicating Christ Cross-Culturally* (Grand Rapids: Academic Books, 1978), 21.

4 David J. Bosch, "Reflections on Biblical Models of Mission," in *Toward the 21st Century in Christian Mission*, ed. James M. Phillips and Robert T. Coote (Grand Rapids, MI: Eerdmans, 1993), 188.

Engen, "communication as mission is a dynamic process of making God known in particular contexts."[5]

In this chapter, I structure my argument about the context in mission communication within three aspects: the biblical perspective of communication, the theological perspective of communication, and the principles of contextual communication.

Biblical Perspective of Communication

Communication within the Bible occurs in specific places and times, and its meaning and usefulness are derived from Scripture.[6] Indeed, without a biblical foundation, Christian communication would be inconceivable. A. D. Manuel stated that the Bible is the story of the communication of God with humankind and their communication with others.[7] Manuel's depiction emphasizes the centrality of communication in the Bible between God and his chosen people.[8] Likewise, Sundersingh claimed that "one of the central themes of the Bible is to describe the purpose of God's communication."[9]

However, the word "communication" is conspicuously absent in the Bible. Yet the Bible is essentially a book about *God speaks*. In this regard, Alex G. Smith stated:

> Significantly, in the Bible God "spoke" more than "wrote." . . . In creation God repeatedly "said" and it was done (Gen. 1:3f).

5 R. Daniel Shaw and Charles van Engen, *Communicating God's Word in a Complex World: God's Truth or Hocus Pocus?* (New York: Rowman and Littlefield Publishers, 2003), xiv.

6 Charles E. van Engen, *Mission on the Way: Issues in Mission Theology* (Ada, MI: Baker Academic, 1996), 37.

7 Albert Manuel, *Communication and the Church* (New Delhi: ISPCK, 1994).

8 Peter Thein Nyunt, *Missions amidst Pagodas: Contextual Communication of the Gospel in BurmeseBuddhist Context* (Carlise, UK: Langham Monograph, 2014), 20.

9 Julian Sundersingh, *Audio-Based Translation: Communicating Biblical Scripture to Nan-Literate* (Bangalore: SAIACS Press, 2001), 42.

> Throughout Genesis God spoke to Adam and Eve (3:9f); to Cain (4:6–10); to Noah (6:13); to Abram (12:1); to Abimelech (20:3); to Rebekah (25:23); to Isaac (26:2); to Jacob (31:3) and so forth. God spoke directly to Moses (Ex. 3:4f); Joshua (Josh. 3:7); Gideon (Judg. 6:14); Samuel (1Sam. 3:11); David (1Sam. 23:2); Solomon (1Kg. 3:11) and many others. God spoke to the prophets and through them as mouths to the nations. John the Baptist, Jesus, and the disciples spoke to individuals, families, and multitudes. . . . The Bible is replete with multiple accounts of dialogues between God and men, and amongst humankind themselves.[10]

The connotation of these words, "God speaks," is manifest in the expression "thus says the Lord," which appears more than four thousand times in the Bible and has become "the equivalent of God's self-communication in history."[11] Noticeably, God's first communication in the Bible appears in Genesis 1:3, where God says, "Let there be light." The last communication occurs in Revelation 22:20, where Jesus says, "Yes, I am coming soon." His spoken words to humankind have been kept alive until now through the testimony of Scripture. The above address of God takes place through the specific intervention of God in human history. In this intervention, "God speaks" means both the act and content of God's self-communication. Thus the centrality of the Bible is God's speaking to all peoples and nations in all possible languages, cultures, and media; and the variety of media is the hallmark of his communication.

The formal self-communication of God began with the first human and continued unabated despite the sin of humankind. In short, throughout the Bible, God showed Himself in a variety of ways. Lucien Legrand expressed it this way:

---

10 Alex G. Smith, "Communication and Continuity through Oral Transmission," *Communicating Christ Through Story and Song: Orality in Buddhist Context,* ed. Paul H. De Neui (Pasadena, CA: William Carey Library, 2008).

11 Joseph Palakeel, "God's Word in Human Words: Interfaces between the Bible and Communications," in *The Bible and the Technologies of the Word,* ed. Joseph Palakeel (Bangalore: Asian Trading Corporation, 2007), 17.

> The God of the Bible is a God who speaks. He speaks to the Patriarchs, sending Abraham on his foundational journey to the land beyond (Gen.12:1–3), accompanying him and his descendants with his blessings, promises (13:14–17; 15:1–21; 28:13–15), and challenges (22:2, 15–18; 18:10–15, 16–32). He reveals Himself to Moses and calls him (Ex. 3:4–14). Through his word, he leads his people into freedom. . . . God will continue to speak through the prophets whose essential identity is to be God's mouthpieces. Their basic utterance is the "pronouncement formula." Thus says the Lord Yahweh.[12]

God not only *speaks* to human beings; he also communicates through his actions, made explicit in the recurring formula "they will know that I am Yahweh" (Ezek 12:15). This statement occurs in the context of liberation from Egyptian captivity (Exod 7:5, 17; 14:18; 16:12) and in the Babylonian liberation (Ezek 5:13; 6:13f; 11:10, 12; 12:16, 20; 13:21; 14:8). Thus communication in the Bible is conveyed verbally and in actions. God's deeds, actions, and gestures are integral to his communication. God also employs various forms of communication, such as literature, drama, story, and poems, and he uses people, places, times, rulers, cultures, natural events, and historical events to communicate his plan of salvation.

As the foregoing analysis has revealed, the word "communication" embodies a multiplicity of ways in which two or more persons interact with one another, and every communicational event of God is a call and a commission. The Bible is the only existing record of God's communication to humankind and our responses to his initiatives. It is written in human languages under the inspiration of the Holy Spirit and takes place in particular contexts (2 Tim 3:16–17; 2 Pet 1:19–21; 3:15–16).

Kraft explained that the Bible is a written medium of communication "in terms of the perceptual categories of the cultural frame of reference."[13] This observation is apt because it notices that the Bible is

---

12 Lucien Legrand, "Communication and the Bible," *Indian Theological Studies* 40 no. 1 (2003): 9–10.

13 Charles H. Kraft, *Culture, Communication and Christianity: A Selection of Writings by Charles H. Kraft.* (Pasadena, CA: William Carey Library, 2001), 31.

recorded in human cultural contexts. Thus communication is always contextual. For example, in the Old Testament, God's communication to the Jewish people is in terms of Jewish thought patterns, and, arising from them, the Jewish responses to his message are necessarily in the Hebrew language and culture. Likewise, in the New Testament, the records of communicational events are written in terms of Greek, Aramaic, and Greco-Roman culture.[14] These exchanges demonstrate that God implemented his communication in the discourse of his recipients, thereby revealing his insights in a manner comprehensible to them. This medium enabled the respondents to respond in ways appropriate to their culture. Therefore, whereas first and foremost the Bible represents the self-communication of God, it is a rich source of human experiences and expressions of truth, goodness, and beauty that stand the test of time. In short, the Bible's communication is truly contextual.

Theological Perspective of Communication

Viewed from a theological perspective, God's communication reflects his trinitarian community of God the father, God the son, and God the Holy Spirit (Gen 1:26), and this relationship is ongoing. In the eternal mystery of the father, the son, and the Holy Spirit, we find that the father communicates Himself to the son (Matt 17:5) so that God's person remains intact as he is related eternally to the son he begot. The son, too, surrenders all to the Father in a communication of love (John 16:28). Jesus's person as son also remains intact and reveals the Holy Spirit (John 16:13–15). The intimate relationship among the three personas of the Trinity is based on complete equality, as noted in Genesis 1:26, Luke 3:21–22; and John 16:28. In this trinitarian perspective, God is seen as revealing Himself as father, son, and Holy Spirit and communicating relationally.

Theologians have intimated that the word "communication" is very much a theological expression.[15] Does this imply that Christianity is a faith

---

14 Kraft, *Culture, Communication and Christianity*, 33.

15 Franz-Josef Eilers, *Communicating in Ministry and Mission: An Introduction to Pastoral Evangelizing Communication* (Bangalore: Asian Trading Corporation, 2004). 24.

of communication? Johannes Heinrichs and Avery Dulles, among others, have proposed that it is.[16] Agreeing with them, Sogaard commented, "The Christian religion itself is a religion of communication with a communicator God who has utilized a wide variety of media. The Bible is a narrative of this communication of God to mankind: through creation, through the prophets, through his mighty acts, through his son Jesus Christ, through the Holy Spirit, and through his people, the Church. The message of Christ should be communicated to all people in the world."[17]

The point being made here is that since the creation of the world, God has been communicating with humanity, and the culmination of his communication is the incarnation as demonstrated by the life of Jesus Christ.

Kraft stated that incarnation is God's primary means of communication: "All divine communication is, in a way, incarnational, which comes not only in words but also in life."[18] God's words have no validity until they have been brought into human life, history, and culture. Jorgensen claimed that "the truth of God is never a Platonic idea, the reflections of which are visible only as shadows on a dark wall. Instead, it [the truth] becomes incarnate in the restrictions of the historical events, in a Hebrew or a Hellenistic thought pattern."[19] Thus incarnation is indeed contextual. God relates to us as persons, within our context, applicable to us—through other persons. Since the beginning of human existence, God has usually chosen this contextual approach to reaching people. In Jesus, he produced the supreme example of incarnation. In other words, Jesus was the full and ultimate communication of God to humanity and bound within space and time.

16 Johannes Heinrichs, "Theory of Practical Communication: A Christian Approach," *Media Development* 27, no. 1 (1981): 3–9; Avery Dulles, *The Survival of Dogma*. (Garden City, NY: Doubleday, 1971).

17 Viggo Sogaard, *Media In Church and Mission: Communicating the Gospel* (Pasadena, CA: William Carey Library, 1993).

18 Kraft, *Culture, Communication, and Christianity.*

19 Knud Jorgensen, "Models of Communication in the New Testament," *Missiology: An International Review* 4, no. 4 (October 1976), 466.

As pointed out by Nida,[20] the incarnation is both the crowning event of God's communication with humankind and the event in which all other forms of God's communication with people are embodied. That is why Nida stated that God always communicates with us where we are and as we are, immersed in life, within our historical circumstances.[21] Surely, the incarnation of God in Jesus Christ demonstrates God's concern for effective communication. Strictly speaking, it is the locus within and through which all thinking about effective communication takes place. Therefore, communication is intrinsically part of God's mission, and it must be contextual because it is always interactional.

Principles of Contextual Communication

Viewed from a Christian perspective, God communicates to make Himself known to human beings and to be understood so that human beings may accept his offer of salvation and affirm their relationship with God. The unique task entrusted to the church is to continue communicating his message to the world (John 20:21; Matt 28:18–20).

As stated above, communication is central to mission. In this section, I present eleven principles of effective contextual communication for missionizing. I developed these principles in my previous book, *Missions Amidst Pagodas*.[22] The principles that follow are the bare bones of the theory of effective communication. They are to be applied in specific situations, and they outline the relevant techniques and methods of communication.

Contextual communication occurs when the communicator has a clear purpose and goal for the message. Typically, the purpose of communication is for the communicator to convey an intended meaning in their message that is understood by the recipient. As Smith said, "The legitimate purpose of communication is to gain access to the mind through the

20 Eugene A. Nida, *Message and Mission* (Pasadena, CA: William Carey Library, 1972), 200–210.

21 Nida, *Message and Mission*, 222.

22 Peter Thein Nyunt, *Missions*, 2–8.

gate of understanding."[23] As for the goal of the message, from a Christian mission perspective, goals are framed by what we believe God wants to achieve through our (and his) communication of the gospel. For example, the purpose of evangelism is to communicate the gospel so that people may understand it and respond through conversion and membership in a local congregation.

Contextual communication is a personal interaction between the communicator and the recipient, but it is also social, even when conducted in a one-on-one interaction. This is why Smith quotes Augsburger, who said, "Communication is co-response-ability."[24] He emphasized that communication entails reciprocity, which presupposes a mutual responsibility for pulling off the exchange.[25] Charles H. Kraft pointed to the personal nature of God's communicational strategy, which characterizes all Christian communication: "Incarnation—personal participation in the lives of his recipients—is his constant method. And as in all life-changing communication, the person (whether God Himself in Christ or another person as God's representative) is a major component of the message conveyed."[26]

Thus the personal nature of Christian communication has to do with the relational nature of the message. Just as God wants to establish a relationship with human beings through his communication, Christian gospel communicators strive to include the recipient in their fellowship with God and with one another in the church. Therefore, "Communicators who seek to present a message recommending a relationship must model the relationship they recommend if their message is to be effective."[27]

Contextual communication presupposes that there is adequate knowledge of the recipient by the communicator.[28] In the communication process, the role of the recipient is as crucial as that of the

23 Donald K. Smith, *Creating Understanding: A Handbook for Christian Communication Across Cultural Landscapes* (Grand Rapids, MI: Zondervan Publishing House, 1992), 21.

24 Smith, *Creating Understanding*, 25

25 Smith, *Creating Understanding*, 27–29

26 Charles H. Kraft, *Communication Theory for Christian Witness* (Maryknoll, NY: Orbis Books,1991), 17.

27 Kraft, *Communication Theory*, 18.

28 I concede that this may not be true when we communicate with strangers, but the presupposition here is that mission work is with a group that we

communicator. "Recipients are active, even when they seem to be just sitting there. They are not simply passive recipients of whatever is sent their way. They interact in a transactional process in which the results are negotiated on the spot rather than predetermined."[29] That is, effective communication must be recipient-oriented.

When the communicator encodes their message and it reaches the recipient through the channel selected by the communicator, the recipient decodes the message. This is a selective filtering process, which comprises the following four stages: exposure, attention, comprehension, and retention.[30] It is the recipient who gives meaning to the message, based on their understanding of it and its relevance to their situation. Then, in responding to the message, the roles are reversed. The recipient is now the communicator, who must deal with questions such as, "Who is my recipient? What are their needs?" Thus communicators are not just senders of messages. Effective communicators are also good listeners.[31]

Contextual communication requires that the recipient is receptive to the communicator.[32] The message is not only to be spoken and heard but also seen. This means that body language plays a part in effective communication, especially in face-to-face situations. This is in line with the Burmese saying *pauk-ko-khin-hma-taya-myin*, meaning that a relationship is built between recipient and communicator, and trust is an important ingredient in the success of a relationship.

The selection of channels for the communication of a message is also crucial to the reception of that message. In other words, to communicate a message well, the communicator must understand the culture of the recipient. The communicator should choose the communication channels according to the recipient's knowledge and experiences.[33] Also,

---

have an adequate amount of knowledge of. It also signifies the importance of knowing our audience.

29 Kraft, *Communication Theory*, 67.

30 D. Broadbent, *Perception and Communication* (London: Pergamon Press, 1958).

31 Viggo Sogaard, *Media in Church*, 99.

32 Carley H. Dodd, *Dynamics of Intercultural Communication* (Dubuque: William C. Brown Publisher, 1982), 10–11; Kraft, *Communication Theory*, 150, 156–159.

33 Smith, *Creating Understanding*, 19.

the communicator should be cognizant of para-messages (secondary signal systems) that are conveyed together with the message because the unconscious use of para-messages may equally distort the message for the recipient. For example, communicating the gospel through literacy-based media in non-literate societies may give the wrong impression to people that Christianity is a religion only for those who are literate.

Contextual communication involves all three dimensions. According to Hiebert, "Taken together, cognitive, affective, and evaluative assumptions provide people with a way of looking at the world that makes sense out of it, that gives them a feeling of being at home, and that reassures them that they are right. This worldview serves as the foundation on which they construct their explicit belief and value systems, and the social institutions within which they live their daily lives."[34]

On the cognitive level, gospel communication has to do with knowledge and truth, but passing on knowledge is not enough. It must touch the affective dimensions through joy, comfort, and the like. A feeling of affection and loyalty is important. Communicating the gospel also has to do with values and allegiances. It is at the evaluative level that members of a culture judge, value, and determine right and wrong.

Culture is the vehicle of communication. That is why God entered into the Hebraic and Grecian cultures to communicate his message of love. The incarnation of Jesus is the classic example of entering into the recipient's culture for effective communication. Imposition from outside and using alien cultural symbols and channels of communication can never be effective.

Contextual communication is not just a singular event; it is a process with several events. Seen from the perspective of the communicator, it is "a consecutive, interrelated number of communication processes, some of short-term duration, others involving years, which are going on at the same time."[35] Seen from the perspective of the recipient, communication takes place through the various stages of their life. The implication of this for the Christian communicator is, as Sogaard pointed out, "Our

34 Paul G. Hiebert, *Anthropological Insights for Missionaries* (Grand Rapids, MI: Baker Book House,1985), 47–48.

35 Sogaard, *Media In Church*, 30–31.

communication messages must be designed as a process that corresponds to the needs of a recipient at his or her present position or stage in life and the needs and problems faced at that time. A person's relationship with God can be seen as a spiritual journey and if we know a person's position in this journey, we can design communication events that will be relevant at this time."[36]

As mentioned above, contextual communication needs to be recipient-oriented. For the recipient to understand a message accurately, the sender and receiver must operate within the same "frame of reference."[37] Communicators, therefore, must seek common ground. Furthermore, in contextual communication, the onus is on the communicator to adjust the medium of exchange, attuning it to the latter's frame of reference. If the gospel is not communicated in a recipient-oriented way, which Kraft calls the "identification approach," the alternative may be an extraction approach—that is, one that projects the gospel as foreign to the culture and extracts those who respond to it from their culture.[38]

Contextual communication seeks to express the relevance of the gospel in a receptive manner while truthfully declaring the content of the gospel. It presupposes that a way can be found in communicating the gospel to honor its relevance and deliver to the receiving community appropriately.[39] My understanding of the biblical text follows the model developed by Kraft called "the Bible as inspired classic casebook."[40]

> The Bible, then, is seen as an inspired collection of classic cases from history . . . exemplifying certain of God's past interactions with human beings for the instruction and guidance of those who seek to follow in their footsteps. . . . This model simply speaks to the fact that the Scriptures are a collection of "classic" materials (i.e., time-tested and found to be of enduring value) that were produced

---

36 Sogaard, *Media In Church*, 31.

37 Kraft, *Communication Theory*, 23.

38 Charles H. Kraft, *Christianity in Culture: A Study in Dynamic Biblical Theologizing in Cross-Cultural Perspective* (Maryknoll, NY: Orbis Books, 1979), 147–155.

39 Taber, "Why Communication Studies," 7.

40 Kraft, *Christianity in Culture*.

> for particular people at particular times and places. When there is in the Bible historical and theological systematization, it is done with a target audience and situation in mind. Each document is a specific presentation dealing with the problems and participants in a specific context.[41]

In accordance with this way of understanding the Bible, human beings today are expected to have meaningful communication with God as biblical persons.[42] Since the gospel is infused with various cultures and epistemes (historical worldviews), we would not be faithful to the text if we simply adopted theological and church structures from the first-century congregations in Greece, nor if we imposed modern-day Western interpretations of the text onto people of another culture. I assume that faithfulness to the text means working with people to make sense of God's message, together hoping that this twofold interaction will lead to faithful allegiance to God such as that described in the Bible.[43]

In the words of Charles R. Taber, to communicate the gospel in a way that is relevant in the context involves an "effort to understand and take seriously the specific context of each human group and person on its own terms and in all its dimensions—cultural, religious, social, political, and economic—and to discern what the gospel says to people in that context."[44] Taber explains what it means to relate the gospel to specific contexts as follows:

> What usable concepts and symbols does this religion provide for the approach of the gospel, on the analogy of Paul's use of the Athenian "unknown god?" What genuine insights does it offer into the character, activity and will of God? What are its gaps, its errors, its distortions? What obstacles does it place in the way of a true understanding of the gospel? It is based on such an analysis

41 Kraft, *Christianity in Culture*, 398.

42 Kraft, *Christianity in Culture*, 207.

43 Dean S. Gilliland, *The Word among Us: Contextualizing Theology for Mission Today* (Dallas, TX: Word, 1989), 12.

44 Charles R. Taber, "Why Communication Studies in Theological Education," *Gospel in Context* 1, no. 1 (1978): 7.

> that contextualization tries to discover in the Scriptures what God is saying to these people. In other words, contextualization takes very seriously the example of Jesus in the sensitive and careful way he offered each person a gospel tailored to his or her own context.[45]

According to Kraft, contextual communication that is faithful to the text and relevant to the context equates with the dynamic-equivalence model, which Kraft developed from translation theories: "The aim of translation is to bring about equivalence between the response of the contemporary hearers/readers of the translation and that of the original hearers/readers of the communication recorded in the document being translated. This model sees the translated Word acting as a communicational stimulus toward the re-creation of an impact on today's recipients that is (roughly) equivalent to that recorded in the Word."[46]

Therefore, just as a text is translated from one language to another, so the Christian faith in word and life has to be transliterated from one culture to another to "represent the meanings of the historical events (i.e., the dynamic interaction between God and man), as if they were clothed in contemporary events."[47] Thus the objective is to recreate equivalent events in today's cultural contexts that will emulate the same commitment to God as those of biblical persons. I propose that this model of dynamic-equivalence is pertinent to both the communication of the gospel and the development of church structures, worship forms, and all other aspects of Christian life and ministry.

Conclusion

Our God is a communicating God, and his desire to communicate with human beings through establishing relationships has been obvious from the very beginning of human existence. Thus communication is fundamental to missionizing. In this chapter, I argued that communication is a two-way or interactive process. Of the many and varied ways of God's

45 Taber, "Why Communication Studies," 7.

46 Kraft, *Christianity in Culture*, 402.

47 Kraft, *Christianity in Culture*, 280.

communication, the Bible is the predominant record of his communication to human beings and their responses to his initiatives. In communicating to humans, he expresses himself in ways human beings can understand and respond to, and in communicating to his chosen people, he commissions them to follow his practice.

The supreme form of God's communication manifests in the incarnation of Jesus Christ, thereby communicating through his son, Jesus Christ (Heb 1:1–3). Christ, in turn, communicates with the apostles and commissions them to be communicators for the church (Matt 28:18–20). It is, of course, the primary task of the church to continue in this vein, representing and communicating him to "all the nations," and since this mission cannot function without communication in specific sociocultural-religious contexts, mission is communication.

Bibliography

Augsburger, D. W. *Caring Enough to Forgive: True Forgiveness*. Ventura, CA: Regal Books, 1981.

Broadbent, D. *Perception and Communication*. London: Pergamon Press, 1958.

Bosch, David. J. "Reflections on Biblical Models of Mission." In *Toward the 21st Century in Christian Mission*, edited by James M. Phillips and Robert T. Coote, Grand Rapids, MI: Eerdmans, 1993.

Gilliland, Dean. *The Word Among Us: Contextualizing Theology for Mission Today*. London: Word Publishing, 1989.

Dodd, C. H. *Dynamics of Intercultural Communication*. Dubuque: Wm C. Brown Company Publisher, 1982.

Dulles, Avery. *The Survival of Dogma*. Garden City, NY: Doubleday,1971.

Eilers, Franz-Josef. *Communicating in Community: An Introduction to Social Communication*. Indore, India: Satprakashen Sanchar Kendra, 1996.

———. "A Simplified Theology of Communication." *Indian Theological Studies* 40, no. 1 (March 2003).

———. *Communicating in Ministry and Mission: An Introduction to Pastoral Evangelizing Communication*. Bangalore: Asian Trading Corporation, 2004.

Heinrichs, Johannes. "Theory of Practical Communication: A Christian Approach." *Media Development* 27, no. 4 (1981): 3–9.

Hesselgrave, David. J. *Communicating Christ Cross-Culturally*. Grand Rapids, MI: Academic Books, 1978.

Hiebert, Paul. G. *Anthropological Insights for Missionaries*. Grand Rapids, MI: Baker Book House, 1985.

Jorgensen, K. "Models of Communication in the New Testament." *Missiology: An International Review* 4, no. 4 (October 1976): 466–473.

Kaiser, Walter. C. *Mission in the Old Testament: Israel as a Light of the Nations*. Secunderabad, India: OM Books, 2006.

Kraft, Charles. H. *Perspective.* Maryknoll, NY: Orbis Books, 1979.

———. *Christianity in Culture: A Study in Dynamic Biblical Theologizing in Cross-Cultural Perspective.* Maryknoll, NY: Orbis Books, 1979.

———. "Contextualizing Communication." In *The Word Among Us: Contextualizing Theology for Mission Today,* edited by Dean Gilliand, London: Word Publishing, 1989.

———. Communication *Theory for Christian Witness*. Maryknoll, NY: Orbis Books, 1991.

———. *Communicating Jesus' Way*. Pasadena, CA: William Carey Library, 1999.

———. *Culture, Communication and Christianity: A Selection of Writings by Charles H. Kraft.* Pasadena, CA: William Carey Library, 2001.

Legrand, Lucien. "Communication and the Bible." *Indian Theological Studies* 40, no. 1 (2003): 9–10.

Manuel, Albert. D. *Communication and the Church.* New Delhi: ISPCK, 1994.

Nida, Eugene. A. *Message and Mission.* Pasadena, CA: William Carey Library, 1972.

Nyunt, Peter Thein. *Missions amidst Pagodas: Contextual Communication of the Gospel in a Burmese Buddhist Context*. Carlise, UK: Langham Monograph, 2014.

Palakeel, Joseph. "God's Word in Human Words: Interfaces between the Bible and Communications." In *The Bible and the Technologies of the Word, edited by* Joseph Palakeel, Bangalore: Asian Trading Corporation, 2007.

Shaw, R. Daniel. and Charles van Engen. *Communicating God's Word in a Complex World: God's Truth or Hocus Pocus*? New York: Rowman and Littlefield Publishers, 2003.

Smith, A. G. "Communication and Continuity through Oral Transmission." In *Communicating Christ Through Story and Song: Orality in Buddhist Context*, edited by Paul H. De Neui, Pasadena, CA: William Carey Library, 2008.

Smith, D. K. *Creating Understanding: A Handbook for Christian Communication Across Cultural Landscapes*. Grand Rapids, MI: Zondervan Publishing House, 1992.

Snyder, H. A. *Liberating the Church: The Ecology of Church and Kingdom*. Westmont, IL: InterVarsity Press, 1983.

Sogaard, Viggo. *Media in Church and Mission: Communicating the Gospel*. Pasadena, CA: William Carey Library, 1993.

Sundersingh, Julian. *Audio-Based Translation: Communicating Biblical Scripture to Nan-Literate.* Bangalore: SAIACS Press, 2001.

Taber, C. R. "Why Communication Studies in Theological Education." *Gospel in Context* 1, no. 1 (1978):12–15.

———. "Contextualization: Indigenization and/or transformation." In *The Gospel and Islam: A 1978 Compendium,* edited by Don M. McCurry, Monrovia, CA: MARC, 1978.

Van Engen, Charles E. *Mission on the Way: Issues in Mission Theology.* Ada, MI: Baker Academic, 1996.

4

READING THE BIBLE WITH ASIAN EYES

by Esther Park

Introduction

The term "Asianization" became prevalent in mission literature in the twentieth century, driven by *minjung* theology (Korean context),[1] Indian Christian theology (Robin Boyd), and, more recently, contextual ecotheology.[2]

I have lived and observed Christianity in Asia (Korea and the Philippines) for more than half my life, and I have spent almost that amount of time in the US. With this, I acquired a multicultural and egalitarian perspective, which I endeavor to bring to this chapter to critically examine and interpret Scripture according to the authors' (biblical) intent and to capture and reveal distinct emphases within contemporary Asian realities. Kirk stated the difficulty of interpreting the Bible from an Asian perspective: "Conceptually, it is difficult to separate belief in the Gospel from the values and institutions of Western society in which the Gospel has been subtly shaped. It is also difficult to relate the Gospel to societies molded for so long by vastly different belief systems. How does one commend a faith which has intersected with local cultures only in recent times and is

---

1 Minjung theology is a postcolonial liberation theology for the masses. Its roots are not in the evangelical tradition. My intention is not to engage with this new trend; I reject some of its thinking that is based on a universal interpretation. I use, primarily, the evangelical point of view in my chapter, which holds that the truth of God's revelation as given in Scripture is authoritative and yet transcultural.

2 Ecotheology is an emerging theology relating faith to nature in the context of interreligious dialogue.

generally seen as an intruder? The difficulties are associated both with a lack of identification and with transplantation."[3]

Regardless, I believe the Holy Spirit works in us (the interpreters) as much as in the original writers, even though differences in contexts and cultures are unavoidable. As Kaiser observed, "the interpreter must bridge the gulf of explaining the cultural elements that are present in the text of Scripture, acknowledge one's own cultural baggage as an interpreter, and then transcend both to communicate the original message of Scripture into the culture of the contemporary audience."[4]

In this chapter, I commence by outlining the background material for this study, namely, the scope of Asian contexts and my hermeneutical and methodological frameworks. I then discuss three broad themes that can be seen and appropriated through Asian perspectives: salvation, sin (and sanctification), and equality.

Background

In this section I cover the scope of the contexts of Asia and hermeneutical considerations.

The Scope of Asian Contexts

There is geographical and cultural complexity in describing Asia. Interestingly, Scarborough claimed that "even among Asian countries, there is a clear distinction between Confucian and non-Confucian societies."[5] He distinguished "doing culture" from "being culture":

> The primary difference is that the Confucian culture is a doing culture, whereas the non-Confucian is a being culture. The former places more importance on tasks relative to maintaining

3 Andrew J. Kirk, *What Is Mission: Theological Explorations* (Minneapolis, MN. Fortress Press, 2000), 946.

4 Walter C. Kaiser Jr. and Moises Silva, *Introduction to Biblical Hermeneutics: The Search for Meaning* (Grand Rapids, MI: Zondervan, 2007), 223.

5 Scarborough (1994) places Thailand, Indonesia, Malaysia, and the Philippines in the category of "being" culture.

> relationships; has a strong internal locus of control and sees nature as at least somewhat controllable; seeks to bring about change actively to conform to some idealized, abstract, improved state; prefers to think analytically, use objective information, and assign status on merit and achievement; tends to view time as linear and a valuable resource to be conserved; and takes a more compartmentalized, less holistic view of life relationships or family and keeps them separate.[6]

Eastern Asian countries, like China, Korea, and Japan, fit into the doing culture category, while some Southeast Asian countries uphold the being culture worldview.[7] Scarborough continued with a description of the uniqueness of these two worldviews:

> Being cultures tend to be more relaxed, more holistic in their worldviews, more relationship-oriented (relationships are part of work), and more accustomed to yielding power; view time as a continually recurring cycle; feel less able to control their fate; and want work, which at best can be enjoyed and at worst can be tolerated, as a necessary evil. Being people define themselves by their collective affiliations. They "work to live," whereas their "doing" counterparts "live to work." "Doing people" see "being" people as lazy, unproductive, and irresponsible. "Being" people see "doing" people as cold, compulsive, and unable to enjoy life.[8]

The distinction between Confucian and non-Confucian nations is only one way to perceive Asia's complexity and unity. Asia has different types of governments, from democratic systems to dictatorships. Also, there are different religious backgrounds, ranging from Hinduism to animism. Because of the vastness of Asia, my treatment of reading the Bible from an Asian perspective will be broad and limited to my own experiences.

---

6 Jack Scarborough, *The Origins of Cultural Differences and Their Impact on Management* (Westport, CT: Quorum, 1998), 74.

7 Scarborough, *The Origins.*

8 Scarborough, *The Origins.*

Hermeneutical Considerations and Methodology

Thiselton defined hermeneutics this way: "Hermeneutics explores how we read, understand, and handle texts, especially those written in another time or a context of life different from our own. Biblical hermeneutics investigates more specifically how we read, understand, apply, and respond to biblical texts."[9]

However, missional hermeneutics requires a deeper awareness of the mission of God and his people in both past and present contexts. We can reinterpret such narratives within our own contexts to participate in God's mission.[10] Nevertheless, Kim rightly stated the starting point of hermeneutics: "If we start with understanding human contexts . . . [we] are susceptible to exegesis—reading into the text what is not there, based on our specific cultural lens. Therefore, a more appropriate perspective, beginning with God's Word, enables us to keep our preaching grounded in the truth of Scripture. Only then do we apply it to a specific context."[11]

Kim advocated three approaches—assumption, conflict, and questions—for employing Scripture in any context.[12] First, the preacher/missionary needs to consider the *assumptions* listeners may have as they read or hear a passage. Second, to interpret Scripture in the listeners' context, the preacher needs to address the *conflicts* that the listeners have with the text. Third, the preacher needs to explore the *questions* this passage raises for the listeners. I take Van Engen and Kim's concerns and approaches seriously when I examine scriptural passages in Asian contexts. Methodologically, I use both understanding of the author's intention and its application (of this understanding) in an Asian context.

Arguably, practicing theology in a particular context is more challenging in the twenty-first century because Asian faith communities are experiencing a new consciousness of the contextualization of their own

9 Anthony Thiselton, *Hermeneutics: An Introduction* (Grand Rapids, MI: Eerdmans, 2009), 1.

10 Charles E. van Engen, *God's Missionary People* (Grand Rapids, MI: Baker Book House, 1991).

11 Heup A. Kim, *A Theology of Dao* (Maryknoll: Orbis Books, 2017), 71.

12 Kim, *Theology of Dao*, 83.

theologies.[13] Van Engen emphasized the need for a glocal (fusion of global and local) balance because "neither monolithic nor atomized uniformity is a satisfactory approach to theology in a globalizing world."[14]

In the following sections, I intend to explore three main biblical themes: salvation, sin (and sanctification), and equality. These basic themes can be approached variously by Asian cultures; therefore, missionaries need to be aware of how these themes are perceived to make mission work more relevant and effective.

Salvation through Asian Eyes

Christian missiologists have identified three responses to the biblical concept of sin in human cultures: shame, guilt, and fear. These three responses represent three types of cultures with their own worldviews: shame-honor cultures, guilt-innocence cultures, and fear-power cultures.[15] Hence, in the following subsection, I explore how shame-honor culture can construct a relevant and specific reading of the Bible.

Shame to Honor[16]

Shame-honor is not merely a cultural theme; it is also a fundamental explanation of God's salvation image: the removal of shame and the

13 Van Engen, *God's Missionary People*.

14 Van Engen, *God's Missionary People*, 57; Van Engen (2006, 172) reminds us that regardless of the enormous differences in characteristics of localities, from different worldview assumptions and cultural practices, we must stick to the concept of the *ekklesia* (the church, the new called-out assembly) (Ephesians 4:4–6): one Father, one Spirit, one baptism, and one body of Christ. At the same time, the Gospel of John 1:14, "the Word became flesh and made his dwelling among us," the concept of the incarnation, gives us an idea of appropriate contextualization as translatability (Van Engen, 2017).

15 David J. Hesselgrave, Counseling Cross-Culturally: An Introduction to Theory and Practice for Christians (Eugene, OR: Wipf and Stock Publishers, 2002); Eugene A. Nida, *Customs and Cultures: Anthropology for Christian missions* (New York: Harper, 1954).

16 Anthropologists have argued that certain cultures' behavior are determined by honor and shame (collectively called "honor cultures").

Table 4.1. Theological perspectives through culture (adapted from Jayson George's 3D Gospel, page 54).

	Shame–honor	**Guilt**	**Fear**
God (attribute)	Father, patron (superior, faithful)	Lawgiver, judge (sinless, just)	Ruler, deliverer
Sin violates—	God's face and glory	God's laws and justice	God's power and authority
Sin is—	Dishonor and disloyalty	Transgression and law-breaking	Insubordination and idolatry
Sinners are—	Rejected	Condemned	Cursed
Consequences of sin	Disgrace and impurity	Judgment and punishment	Domination and bondage
Emotion of sin	Unworthiness	Regret	Anxiety
Jesus' death	Removes our shame and restores God's face/honor	Bears the punishment for our moral transgression	Defeats spirits and power
Forgiveness	Reconciles relationships	Pardon wrongs	Removes strongholds

restoration of honor. The Bible says much regarding shame–honor.[17] Both Wu and Muller appealed to Genesis 3 to substantiate the viability of the three major ethical worldviews, also explained by Georges in his 3D Gospel: guilt, shame, and fear (see table 4.1).[18]

17 Jayson Georges and Mark. D. Baker, *Ministering in Honor-Shame Cultures: Biblical Foundations and Practical Essentials* (Downers Grove, IL: IVP Academic, 2017).

18 Jackson Wu, "How Christ Saves God's Face . . . and Ours: A Soteriology of Honor and Shame," *Missiology: An International Review* 44, no. 4 (2016): 375–387; Roland Muller, *Honor and Shame: Unlocking the Door* (Birmingham, UK: Xlibris Corp, 2000), 18; Jayson Georges, *The 3D Gospel: Ministry in Guilt, Shame, and Fear Cultures* (Kindle edition: Timē Press, 2014), 32.

The Asian societies I have worked with (in South Korea and the Philippines) belong to the shame–honor (hereafter, SH) category. SH holds a place in the Bible alongside teaching about guilt and righteousness. For this research, I only investigate the SH cultural orientation (comparison with guilt or fear is omitted).

The comparison above shows that SH culture focuses on relational languages, whereas GI culture expresses action verbs. In many Western and individualistic societies, violating the laws of the nation renders the perpetrator guilty until restitution is made and the perpetrator is restored to a state of innocence.[19] Based on the above chart, I explain a more approachable way to deal with sin issues and salvation through Jesus in certain Asian cultures, thereby helping to save face (explanation to follow).

Shame=losing face and identity: Shame is linked to revelation (of one's misdeeds) and rejection before peers or those in charge. Georges and Baker provided biblical examples of how shame causes someone to lose face, taking away their identity and value.[20] The concept of face is key in unlocking the importance of the themes of shame and honor. According to Georges and Baker, "In the New Testament, we see that many recipients of Jesus' grace bore some ascribed shame, for example, Gentiles, Samaritans, the bleeding woman, blind, deaf, lame, lepers, and demon possessed. Their shame stemmed from congenital social realities beyond their control."[21]

In the Old Testament, Naomi becomes socially marginalized because of the death of her husband and sons. Then, through Boaz, God exalts Naomi and Ruth (a Gentile widow) and recovers their joint honor. Throughout the Bible, God provides a new inheritance and an ascribed identity through Christ. Many people living in SH cultures believe their

19 Jayson Georges and Mark. D. Baker, *Ministering in Honor-Shame Cultures: Biblical Foundations and Practical Essentials* (Downers Grove, IL: IVP Academic, 2017).

20 Georges and Baker, *Ministering in Honor-Shame*, 51.

21 Georges and Baker comment that although not all whom Jesus freed from shame were in this category, the prostitutes and tax collectors "achieved shame," resulting from their sinful behavior.

identity depends mainly on the shame ascribed and inherited, such as those living under the caste system.

Wu provided a graphic and thought-provoking explanation to Chinese people about the act of sin, which is tantamount to a son or daughter spitting in their father's face.[22] When people do not recognize God, they themselves become shameful, and "God gave them over to shameful lusts" (Rom 1:26). If Christ did not die for our sins to forgive us, God would not be considered righteous (Rom 3:25–26). Therefore, God would be seen as lacking in honor; God would be shamed. Therefore, according to Wu, Jesus's atonement is the act of "saving" Father God's "face."[23]

Dumitrescu compared two different realms of the sin issue: "This creates a problem for Western missionaries because, from their perspective, the gospel requires people first to admit their status as sinners. Admitting sin is a crucial point in the [Western] conversion process."[24] Some foreign missionaries sometimes express their frustration because the locals do not admit they are sinners; they only admit to wrongdoing when they are caught, which is considered shameful. Without an understanding of sin in the cultural context, the gospel of the cross and the final judgment are meaningless.

In some Asian cultures, it is not easy to explain the concept of sin using a Western construct. However, the Bible shows that shame is the consequence of sin. For example, in the fall narrative in Genesis, Adam and Eve hid from God because they were ashamed of being naked (Gen 3:10). Asians generally refuse to admit their failures and mistakes publicly because they will lose face. Public discussions of weaknesses can lead to the view that Christianity is a shameful and foreign religion. Priest noted that consequences follow when sin is not understood adequately: "An inability to speak plausibly about sin undercuts our ability to speak persuasively of God and of what human relationship with God entails."[25]

22 Wu, "How Christ Saves," 377–379.

23 Wu, "How Christ Saves."

24 Christian Dumitrescu, "Discipleship in Asian Honor Cultures," in *Honor, Shame, and the Gospel: Reframing our Message and Ministry, ed.* Christopher Flanders and Werner Mischke (Pasadena: William Carey Library, 2020), 318.

25 Robert J. Priest, "Experience-Near Theologizing in Diverse Human Contexts," in *Globalizing Theology: Brief and Practice in an Era of World Christianity*, ed. Craig Ott and Harold A. Netland (Grand Rapids, MI: Baker Academic, 2006), 180.

In many collectivist societies in Asia, if a deed done by someone brings shame to the person or group, that action is considered wrong. The value system suggests that if telling the truth brings shame, then telling the truth is wrong. The community decides on what is honorable or shameful. Our challenge is to make truth a shared value in the community and lying a dishonorable matter, but confrontation must be exercised with delicacy (1 Tim 5:1).

The Bible acknowledges different ways of cultural expression of shame and honor. However, Georges and Baker pointed out that Romans 14 unequivocally affirms that only God's word establishes the standard of true shamefulness and honorableness: "For we will all stand before God's judgement seat . . . anyone who serves Christ in this way is pleasing to God" (Rom 14:10, 18).[26]

People in SH cultures must come to acknowledge the weakness of social shame (as seen in my examples to follow), even though initially acknowledging it may be excruciating. Social shame is prevalent in South Korea, especially among male officers in government or in a company who kill themselves on the job, either because they cannot bear the shame or prove their innocence.[27] In Acts 16, the Philippian jailer sought to kill himself to cover his shameful failure on the job. He acted to preserve the honor of his people by sacrificing his own life. Fortunately, through Paul's persuasion, the Philippian jailer overcame the weight of God's honor and the possible social shame.

As Mbuvi explained, "By clearly directing people to the correct dimension of honor and shame as the vertical relationship with God, rather than the horizontal relationship with another, we can affirm that God is the true 'significant other' who ascribes honor to us even when we do not deserve it."[28]

---

26 Georges and Baker, *Ministering in Honor,* 284.

27 South Korea has the highest suicide rate in the Organisation for Economic Co-operation and Development (OECD), with around thirteen thousand people taking their own lives in 2021. https://www.statista.com/topics/8622/suicide-in-south-korea/#topicOverview

28 Andrew M. Mbuvi, "African Theology from the Perspective of Honor and Shame," in *The Urban Face of Mission: Ministering the Gospel in a Diverse and Changing World,* ed. Harvie Conn, Manuel Ortiz, and Susan S Baker (Phillipsburg, NJ: P and P Publishing, 2002), 295.

Defilement to Cleansing

So how should Jesus's good news be presented to people mired in shame and seeking honor? Jae-suk Lee has the answer because he read Jesus's feet-washing narrative as a mission of offering freedom and forgiveness of sin (John 8:32–34; 20;23).[29] According to Lee, the central salvation theme of the Bible seen through Asian lenses is the removal of shame and the restoration of honor. We can read the following three selected Bible passages as illustrations of this interpretation.

Consecrating community, Jesus's foot washing in John 13: Jesus's foot washing in John's narrative represents how his followers are consecrated from the world. In other words, this ritualistic foot washing acknowledges that the world is defiled and that the followers of Christ need to purify the community. Anthropologist Pitt-Rivers explained that parts of the human body symbolically demonstrate honor and shame in many ways: "The right hand purveys honor with gestures like touching, waving, and shaking; the head embodies a person's honor, so it is kissed and crowned; the face is a metonym for honor; feet are the lowest and dirtiest part of the body and thus symbolize disgrace; private parts signify the shame of vulnerability and desecration; and one's blood transfers honor and is often the price in transactions of honor."[30]

These symbolic images—washing the dirtiest part of our feet (cleansing of our transgression) and Jesus's crucifixion (transferring honor) right after this ritual—spell out the ultimate ministry of Christ for us. Jesus's ministry clearly shows the actions of foot washing and, ultimately, being humiliated on the cross to be the humblest. In verse 14, Jesus commands his faith community, "You also should wash one another's feet," thereby continuously consecrating themselves to remain in him and bear fruit (John 15:2–3).

Defilement and cleansing[31]: Defilement and cleansing are easier to understand in Asian cultures because of religious washing, which has

---

29 Jae-Suk Lee, *Mission as Integrated Witness: A Missional Reading of the Foot-washing Narrative (John 13:1–38)* (Eugene, OR: WIPF and Stock, 2021).

30 Julian Pitt-Rivers, "Honor," in *International Encyclopedia of the Social Sciences*, ed. David L. Sills. (New York: Macmillan,1968), 505.

31 This is an illustration that the gifts and sacrifices being offered are not able to cleanse the conscience of the believer. These are only a matter of food and drink until the era of the new order (Heb 9:9–10).

similarities to Hebrew practices.[32] In the Old Testament, the practice of the blood of animals and the ashes of a heifer being placed on those who are unclean sanctifies them, so they are outwardly clean. According to Hebrews 9:9–10, "this is an illustration for the present time" until the time of the new order, paving the way for the cleansing of "the conscience of the worshipper" (Heb 9:9:9). What is the new order? Muller illustrated that the ultimate portrayal of God bearing our shame is discovered in Christ: "[Christ] . . . was stripped of His clothing when He was hung on the cross. Roman prisoners were often hung naked on a cross, exposed for the scoffers to see and ridicule. Consequently, even in this, Christ bore not only our sin on the cross, but also our shame. Once and for all, Christ died on the cross, bearing our shame so that we might be freed from shame as well as guilt."[33]

Therefore, those who follow Christ to the cross of shame will never be put to shame: "Anyone who believes in him will never be put to shame" (Rom 10:11).

Understanding evangelism in the Asian context: Acts 16: 22–34, the jailor's conversion story provides a suitable example of a collective cultural orientation. Inviting someone into a community and relationship building are crucial acts for evangelism in all cultures, but they are even more critical in SH cultures. Georges and Baker pointed out that Paul and Silas accepting meal invitations from nonbelievers was one way of honoring people.[34] They also accentuated the importance of creating a bond with a group or whole family because "a shared table preaches God's honor as loud as a sermon in a collectivistic society."[35] Table fellowship was also a significant way Jesus honored people.

Another case we can observe in these passages is a group conversion. In collectivist cultures, individual conversion to Christianity may bring shame to one's immediate family and neighbors. Georges articulated that

32 The ancient Chinese used water for ritual cleansing practices. In Japan, a basin—*tsukubai*—is available at Buddhist temples for ablutions. In the Philippines, animal blood is spilled in the *Padugo* ritual to ward off evil spirits. Koreans use a bronze water sprinkler, *kundika*, to purify the ground in Buddhist ceremonies.

33 Roland Muller, *The Messenger, The Message and The Community: Three Critical Issues for the Cross-Cultural Church Planter* (Independent Scholars Press, 2016), 223.

34 Georges and Baker, *Ministering in Honor*, 224.

35 Georges and Baker, *Ministering in Honor*.

many nonbelievers reject Christianity for social and cultural reasons, not for theological reasons.[36] Another missiologist, Timothy Tennent, noted that family conversion is more plausible in SH cultures because family conversion prevents the scandal of one member disgracing the rest of the family for espousing a "foreign" religion.[37] Thus the Western approach to evangelism using formulaic tools, such as Evangelism Explosion (EE) and the four spiritual laws, often misses the mark because it targets a personal or individual confession of faith in Christ, which is a problem for members of a collectivist society.

From my observation of street evangelism, foreign evangelists tend to approach strangers and present a confrontive rhetoric, which unwittingly attacks people's identities and honor. Of course, the locals will answer "yes" to accepting Jesus Christ (as a mark of politeness and hospitable understanding); however, in a collectivist society, people view conversion as shifting loyalty (and identity) to a foreign group, so they must experience salvation *as a group*. Therefore, Georges and Baker proposed that participation in the body of Christ is the initial step in the evangelism process of community (to belong), discipleship (to behave), and evangelism (to believe).[38]

Sin and Sanctification through Asian Eyes

Ascribed Honor=God's Children

Those who become believers follow Christ to the cross of shame. They inherit honor as children of God. God removes our old status as unclean and hopeless orphans and gives us the status of worthy and honorable children (John 1:12). In the New Testament, 1 Peter provides believers with a new honor code to guide their way of conduct, and 1 Peter chapters 2–5 outlines how Christians live out that divine honor in everyday life for God's

36 Georges and Baker, *Ministering in Honor,* 69.

37 Timothy Tennent, *Theology in the Context of World Christianity: How the Global Church Is Influencing the Way We Think About and Discuss Theology* (Grand Rapids, MI: Zondervan, 2007), 97–99.

38 Georges and Baker, *Ministering in Honor,* 244.

honor: "To this you were called, because Christ suffered for you, leaving you an example, that you should follow in his steps" (1 Pet 2: 21). Peter's key to discipleship in SH contexts is profoundly theological and deeply rooted in Jesus's shame-removing and honor-restoring life.

Similarly, Eng explained that the epistle of James also uses the dynamic of honor and shame to motivate his hearers: "Listen, my dear brothers and sisters . . . you have *dishonored* the poor . . . Are they not the ones who are blaspheming the *noble name of him* to whom you belong?"[39] Also, James enables us to see the priority of relationships within the collectivist concern for the group's reputation.

If a believer's honor code does not resonate with God's, then substantial parts of a believer's life "will be determined by the default values of cultures."[40] The Bible's appeals to honor, therefore, guide Christians' moral decisions in several ways. Christians should glorify God, purify themselves, and love others.[41] These three principles provide a biblical rubric for ethical discernment in SH contexts. Understanding the honor code is central to Christian discipleship in many ways; simply knowing God's honor code for life will not suffice.

Dealing with Sin

Next, I present four practical aspects of Asian realities that we must consider.

Lying/cheating issue in the Asian context: Lying belongs to our old identity. However, lying is a colossal issue among people, including Christians. For Westerners, lying is inherently wrong; however, in some cultures, a lie may not be considered faulty if one's group interests are at stake. Lying—including white lies—is acceptable in some cultures and therefore not regarded as a criminal or moral violation.

Cheating during examinations in Bible colleges has been an ongoing issue in certain Asian countries. Missionaries are sometimes frustrated by

39 Daniel K. Eng, "The Letter of James," in *An Asian Introduction to the New Testament,* ed. Johnson Thomaskutty. (Minneapolis, MN: Fortress Press, 2022), 672.

40 Daniel K. Eng, "The Letter of James", 672.

41 Georges and Baker, *Ministering in Honor.*

the way the locals view sin—not as a violation *per se* but as wrong only when found out. So, if they are caught, it is shameful. My American colleague, a missionary professor, expressed to me his frustration regarding cheating in his classroom. Sadly, his anxiety became so unbearable that it was one of the contributing factors to his departure from the mission field.

However, admitting sin is a crucial point in the conversion process. Without understanding transgression, the cross and final judgment are meaningless. In fact, in some cultural settings, it is not easy to explain the biblical concept of sin meaningfully. Priest argued that consequences follow when the sin concept is not understood adequately.[42] He continued that being a believer involves a call to repentance and specific self-understandings undergirded and informed by a particular understanding of God. The Bible harshly judges this moral failure. Throughout the Bible, many passages mention that lying causes consequences. "Thou shall not lie" is one of the ten commandments, but even Western Christians struggle with this.[43]

Sometimes harmless lies are used without hesitation or guilt because these actions create a flattering or pacifying situation. Fernando provides a specific illustration of how this habitual behavior builds up an effect on a Christian child at home: "A child cries when she sees her father leave home. Her Christian mother soothes her by saying that he is going to a shop and will come back soon. He was leaving on a two-week trip. Some years later, when someone comes to the door, and the daughter informs the mother about it, she [the mother] tells her, 'Tell him I'm not at home.' This is the mother who introduced her daughter to Christianity. Over time, the daughter comes to adopt the view that lying is acceptable for Christians."[44]

Money issue: My observation of cheating in Asia needs airing. It is an area that has brought many scandals to the contemporary church.

---

42 Priest, "Experience-Near Theologizing in Diverse Human Contexts," 180.

43 "Do not steal. Do not lie. Do not deceive one another" (Leviticus 19:11); "The LORD detests lying lips, but he delights in people who are trustworthy" (Prov12:22); "Do not lie to each other, since you have taken off your old self with its practices" (Col 3:9).

44 Ajith Fernando, "Confronting Lying Biblically in Honour-and Shame-Oriented Cultures," *Evangelical Review of Theology* 46, no. 1 (2022):171–179.

Some Christians alter the facts during funding applications or reporting fund usage. In some societies, inflating and deflating prices is almost an everyday practice. As mentioned previously, in a culture where lying is common, leaders who tell the truth may stand out as a challenge or even as a display of disloyalty to the group.

I witnessed some elders give testimonies to challenge congregations regarding paying property taxes without inflating the value, and I heard many testimonies about how the church elders had been tempted to negotiate with tax assessors to lower the value of their properties.[45] They testified how to fight against corruption and keep integrity as a truly Christian lifestyle.

Miranda-Feliciano drew attention to "a trilogy of maneuvers deeply ingrained in the Filipino psyche: *lusot*, *lakad*, and *lagay*."[46] She defined them as follows:

- *Lusot* means "to escape from something by wriggling into a hole or through a slit."
- *Lakad* means "to walk and is a euphemism for attempting to smooth out difficulties through a network of connections."
- *Lagay* means "money to smooth over a situation, such as money set aside for illegal gambling or a bribe."

Suggested strategies for combating lying: Fernando suggested strategies for the lying issue.[47] First, "make revulsion for lying a shared value; second, let Christians know that the Bible teaches that God abhors lying." This would cause a person shame when they lie. Shame is a motivator for doing right in collectivist cultures.

---

45 I lived there from 2001–2016. You can see no fixers signs all over the city hall windows. The government is also trying to eliminate this societal vice, while many Christians are still struggling with the honesty issue when dealing with money in the Philippines context.

46 Evelyn Miranda-Feliciano, *Filipino Values and Our Christian Faith* (Manila: OMF Literature, 1990), 2 –5.

47 Fernando, *Confronting Lying*, 179.

Saving face issue:[48] From this Asian perspective of integrity and honesty, maintaining honor and avoiding shame justify a lie when an untrue statement is necessary to save face. A typical Asian concern is social harmony and maintaining good relationships with the members of one's family. For example, in Filipino society, there is the sensitivity that a person's feelings should not be hurt. Lapiz introduced two Tagalog terms: *pakitang-tao* (for appearance's sake) and *pakikiramdam* (being sensitive).[49] According to Lapiz, *pakitang-tao* is superficial cordiality to conceal whatever unpleasantness may exist between parties. Therefore, this superficial cordiality of never saying "no" may cause misunderstanding. *Pakikiramdam* is also concerned with the feelings of others; it is a request to feel or to be sensitive. Therefore, it is a shared feeling, a kind of emotional *a priori*.

Sometimes foreign Christians put locals in a problematic situation because the foreigners have no idea how to identify cordiality and sincerity while they are doing an evangelistic campaign.[50] Kim testified to a case when a Korean mission team visited a local university in Chiang Mai, Thailand.[51] The team members were very excited when some students received Christ with a short acceptance prayer. Later, the local Christians conducted a follow-up with the students who had raised their hands during the meeting and found that the students had no idea of what accepting the gospel meant. Their actions were simply out of cultural courtesy to foreigners.

Equality through Asian Eyes

Partnership between Missionaries and Nationals

Throughout the history of the church and missions, equality issues in missionary-national relationships have been problematic. Primarily, the

48 "All you need to say is simply 'Yes' or 'No'; anything beyond this comes from the evil one" (Mat 5:37. NIV).

49 Ed Lapiz, *Pagpapahiyang: Redeeming Culture and Indigenizing Christianity* (Manila: Kaloob, 2010), 24.

50 Daniel Kim, "Contextualization and Evangelism," in *Ministry Across Cultures: Sharing the Christian Faith in Asia*, ed. Warren R. Beattie (Oxford: Regnum Books International, 2016), 81.

51 Kim, "Contextualization and Evangelism."

implementation of partnerships between missionaries and nationals has focused on the issue of power and hegemony.[52]

In the 1970s, tensions surfaced, and local Christians called for a "missionary moratorium."[53] The distressing voices had shocked the missionary active nations, and mission organizations started reevaluating and recapturing the heart of missionary activity within the church's mission theology, *missio Dei*. Marsh explained *missio Dei* theology in partnership as follows: "*Missio Dei* theology sought to reconstruct mission as an activity of the Trinity . . . the activity of mission was, therefore, no longer to be understood as a movement of the Church from Europe and the West to the rest of the world, but as the action of all churches participating in God's one mission as equal partners: 'partnership in mission.'"[54]

Paul's injunction in Philippians 2:3, "in humility," is a challenging way of reciprocal relations in mission. Inequality in partnership issues has been recognized yet not fully practiced, and equality is a work in progress rather than a realized perception. A plea from the evangelical national director of the Philippines Council of Evangelical Churches intimates that the issue is far from resolved: "Be intentional in your partnership with Filipino Church leaders and workers, regarding them as co-workers and not subjects in the ministry; treat Filipino workers as equal partners by allowing them to share in leadership and decision making functions in your ministry."[55] The biblical examples of Jesus's dialogues with the Samaritan woman at the well (John 4) and Nicodemus (John 3) illustrate a model of love and respect.

Gender Participation

To understand Scripture, we must be aware of the historical and cultural background at the time it was written. We must consider several specifics in the New Testament epistles, such as a church's condition and the sociocultural background. For example, rather than focusing on the fact that

---

52 Esther Park, "The Theology of Partnership: Equality Issues in the Ministry," *Asian Mission Advance* 44, (July 2014), 27–30.

53 One example was the voice from the Philippines, missionary Emerito Nacpil.

54 Colin Marsh, "Partnership in Mission: To Send or To Share?" *International Review of Mission* 92 (2003): 370–381.

55 This regrettable criticism by bishop Efraim Tendero shook the Korean Missionary gathering in 2012.

only one verse in the Bible directly prohibits women from teaching in the church, some Asian churches are drawn to the many biblical examples and instances of women involved in the ministry of teaching. Hamilton proposed that Priscilla's teaching ministry was well regarded.[56] He quoted the early church father John Chrysostom's writing, in which Chrysostom provides the reason why the order of the names is "Greet Priscilla and Aquila" (Rom 16:3; 2 Tim 4:19) and not the other way around: "He [Paul] seems to me to acknowledge a greater godliness for her than her husband. What I said is not guesswork because it is possible to learn this from the book of Acts. (Pricilla) took Apollos, an eloquent man and powerful in the Scriptures, but knowing only the baptism of John; and she instructed him in the way of the Lord and made him a teacher brought to completion." [57]

God's calling of Abraham and Sarah also confirms complementary leadership among his people. From Genesis to the New Testament era, the pairing of men and women shows the sense of equal calling in their own narratives regardless of cultural-societal environments. For example, as much as Abraham was chosen to become a father of nations, Sarah was too, according to Genesis 17:15–16, "a mother of nations." Also, the godly old man and woman in Luke 2, Simeon and Anna, who were anticipating the coming, are paired and given equal status.

When the missionaries in China in the 1860s encouraged women to read the Bible, this brought new opportunities for these Chinese women as well as for successive generations. Women missionaries and evangelists, simply known as "Bible Women," accounted for the growth of Christianity in China in the late 1800s and early 1900s.[58]

---

56 David Hamilton, "Bringing the Gospel to Sin City, AD 50," in *Why Not Women? A Fresh Look at Scripture on Women in Missions, Ministry, and Leadership*, ed. Loren Cunningham and David Hamilton. (Seattle: Youth with A Mission, 2000), 145; This switching of the list of the name has significance in Acts, where "Barnaba and Paul" becomes "Paul and Barnabas." Barnabas's name appears ahead of Paul until Paul becomes the dominant speaker from Acts 13:9 onwards: (Acts 13:43, 46,50; 15:22, 35, 36).

57 Priscilla is the wife and Aquila is her husband. This couple had a prolific ministry in the early church as associates of the apostle Paul; Hamilton, "Bringing the Gospel."

58 Alexander Chow, "The Remarkable Story of China's 'Bible Women.'" *Christianity Today,* accessed May 2, 2023, https://www.christianitytoday.com/history/2018/march/christian-china-bible-women.html

My experiences while working with a Presbyterian sectarian seminary in the Philippines, where strong foreign missionary influences are dominant, revealed the inability of foreign missionaries to understand both biblical and cultural contexts.[59] Culturally speaking, Filipino society is bilateral and relatively egalitarian. The egalitarianism present in the Filipino family was rooted in pre-colonial times; however, according to Friesen, foreign invasions changed the order: "The economic customs contributed to the autonomous stature of women within society; pre-colonial Philippines was also marked by relative sexual egalitarianism. Spanish law, however, stressed male superiority and emphasized that women belonged at home. The Roman Catholic Church taught passivity and piety as the proper traits for women. Furthermore, the American colonial experience reinforced economic control by men. Much of the pre-Hispanic culture is deeply overlaid by colonial culture."[60]

The women's leadership issue is a hot potato among missionaries and within Presbyterian circles in the Philippines. According to some female students, the unequal treatment toward female MDiv students, such as not providing them with the same preaching opportunities, is a sore point.[61] Notwithstanding this setback, I take comfort in the fact that both missionaries and locals are learning and practicing one of my favorite verses in the Bible: "Instead, speaking the truth in love, we will grow to become in every respect the mature body of Him who is the head, that is, Christ" (Eph 4:15).

Conclusion

In this book chapter, with its necessarily restricted length, I was unable to cover Asian perspectives of the Bible in depth. However, I discussed three critical areas where Asian perspectives help clarify the Bible in Asia: conversion, sin, and equality. Overall, my discussion focused on the

---

59 This seminary was founded by Presbyterians from Korea in partnership with others, like the Presbyterian Church in America.

60 Dorothy Friesen, *Critical Choices* (Grand Rapids, MI. Eerdmans, 1988), 3.

61 MDiv. is a Master of Divinity degree where preaching or homiletics is taught. My argument is that if the Presbyterian denomination had such strong views on women teaching in the churches, they should not offer the MDiv. degree to females.

theological motif of the eradication of shame and the restoration of honor in SH societies. After the fall, humans experienced shame and guilt until Jesus Christ came and bore our sin and shame, thus enabling us to enter God's family.

I also provided instances of how 1 Peter provided a new code of behavior as a checkpoint in the Asian context, drawing on the SH dynamics. Furthermore, 1 Peter also urged Christians to practice the new Christian code in a collective context, which is relevant in Asia.

My chapter is intended to stimulate readers to think more carefully about the Christian faith in their own settings. Moreover, I wish to encourage readers to pursue rigorous analyses of Asian cultures and, with appropriate lenses in place, to read Scripture with cultural intelligence.

Bibliography

Chow, Alexander. "The Remarkable Story of China's 'Bible Women.'" *Christianity Today.* Accessed May 2, 2023. https://www.christianitytoday.com/history/2018/march/christian-china-bible-women.html.

Chung, M. "Rice Is Heaven. Revisiting and Transforming Lost Korean Values in the Era of Climate Change." In *Making Peace with the Earth: Action and Advocacy for Climate Justice*, edited by Grace Ji-Sun Kim, 165–80. Geneva: WCC Publications, 2016.

Dumitrescu, Christian. "Discipleship in Asian Honor Cultures." In *Honor, Shame, and the Gospel: Reframing Our Message and Ministry*, edited by Christopher Flanders and Werner Mishcke. Pasadena, CA: William Carey Library, 2020.

Eng, Daniel K. "The Letter of James." In *An Asian Introduction to the New Testament*, edited by Johnson Thomaskutty. Minneapolis, MN: Fortress Press, 2022

Fernando, Ajith. "Confronting Lying Biblically in Honour- and Shame-Oriented Cultures." *Evangelical Review of Theology* 46, no. 1 (2022):171–179.

Friesen, Dorothy. *Critical Choices*. Grand Rapids, MI: Eerdmans, 1988.

Georges, Jayson. *The 3D Gospel: Ministry in Guilt, Shame, and Fear Cultures*. Timē Press. Kindle Edition.

Georges, Jayson, and Mark. D. Baker. 2016. *Ministering in Honor-Shame Cultures: Biblical Foundations and Practical Essentials*. Downers Grove, IL: IVP Academic, 2017.

Hamilton, David. "Bringing the Gospel to Sin City, AD 50." In *Why Not Women? A Fresh Look at Scripture on Women in Missions, Ministry, and Leadership*, edited by Loren Cunningham and David Hamilton. Seattle: Youth with A Mission, 2000.

Hesselgrave, David J. *Counseling Cross-Culturally: An Introduction to Theory and Practice for Christians*. Eugene, OR: Wipf and Stock Publishers, 2002.

Hong, In Sik. "God of Life, Lead Us to Justice and Peace: Reflection from an Asian and Korean Church Perspective." *International Review of Mission* 102, no.1(2013): 56–68.

Howell, Brian M, and Jenell W. Paris. *Introducing Cultural Anthropology*. Grand Rapids, MI: Baker Academic, 2011.

Hwang, Jae-Buhm. "A New Confession of Faith with an Eco-Theology and a Father-Centred Trinitarianism: A Critical Study of the 21st Century Confession of Faith of the Presbyterian Church of Korea." *International Review of Mission* 96 (2007):128–141. https://doi.org/10.1111/j.1758-6631.2007.tb00597.x.

Kaiser Jr., Walter C, and Moises Silva. *Introduction to Biblical Hermeneutics: The Search for Meaning*. Grand Rapids, MI: Zondervan, 2007.

Kirk, J Andrew. *What Is Mission: Theological Explorations*. Minneapolis, MN: Fortress Press, 2000.

Kwan, Simon M. *Postcolonial Resistance and Asian Theology. Routledge Studies in Asian Religion and Philosophy*. Abingdon: Routledge, 2014.

Kim, Daniel. "Contextualization and Evangelism." In *Ministry Across Cultures: Sharing the Christian Faith in Asia*, edited by Warren R. Beattie (Oxford: Regnum Books International, 2016), 81.

Kim, Heup Y. *A Theology of Dao*. Maryknoll: Orbis Books, 2017.

Kim, K. "A Conception of an Ecological Theology of Spirit and Ch'i." In *Asian Contextual Theology for the Third Millennium: Theology of Minjung in Fourth-Eye Formation*, edited by Paul S. Chung, Veli-Matti Kärkkäinen and Kyoung-Jae Kim. Translated by Paul S. Chung. Cambridge: James Clarke, 2010.

Koshy, Asish T. "The Letters to Timothy" in *An Asian Introduction to the New Testament* Minneapolis, MN: Fortress Press, 2022.

Lai, P. "Inter-Religious Dialogue on Ecology: A View from China." *Religions* 4: 82–97, 2014.

Lee, Jae-Suk. *Mission as Integrated Witness: A Missional Reading of the Foot-washing Narrative* (John 13:1-38). Eugene, OR: WIPF and Stock, 2021.

Lapiz, Ed. *Pagpapahiyang: Remeeming Culture and Indigenizing Christianity*. Manila: Kaloob, 2010.

Malina, Bruce J. "Honor and Shame: Pivotal Values of the First-Century Mediterranean World." In *The New Testament World: Insights from Cultural Anthropology*. 3d ed. Louisville, Westminster. John Knox, 27–57, 2001.

Marsh, Colin. "Partnership in Mission: To Send or To Share?" *International Review of Mission*. 92 (366): 370–381. https://doi.org/10.1111/j.1758-6631.2003.tb00411.x, 2003.

Mbuvi, Andrew M. "African Theology from the Perspective of Honor and Shame." In *The Urban Face of Mission: Ministering the Gospel in a Diverse and Changing*

World, edited by Harvie Conn, Manuel Ortiz and Susan S Baker. Phillipsburg, NJ: P and R Publishing, 2002.

Miranda-Feliciano, Evelyn. *Filipino Values and Our Christian Faith*. Manila: OMF Literature, 1990.

Muller, Roland. *The Messenger, The Message and the Community: Three Critical Issues for the Cross-Cultural Church Planter*, 4th ed. ebook: Independent Scholars Press, 2016.

Muller, Roland. *Honor and Shame: Unlocking the Door*. Birmingham, UK: Xlibris, 2000.

Nacpil, Emerito. "Mission but not Missionaries." *International Review of Mission* 60 (July 1971):356–362.

Nida, Eugene A. *Customs and Cultures: Anthropology for Christian missions*. New York: Harper, 1954.

Oh, J. S. "Salim, Ever-Recycling Energy. A Korean Postcolonial Eco-Feminist Theology of Life." In *Making Peace with the Earth: Action and Advocacy for Climate Justice*, edited by Grace Ji-Sun Kim. Geneva: WCC Publications, 2016.

Padgett, Alan. "Wealthy Women at Ephesus: 1 Timothy 2:8–15 in Social Context." *Interpretation* 4, no. 1 (1987): 19–31. https://doi.org/10.1177/002096438704100103.

Park, Esther. "The Theology of Partnership: Equality Issues in the Ministry." *Asian Mission Advance* 44 (July 2014): 27–30.

Pe-Pua, R. and E. Protacio-Marcelino. "Sikolohiyang Pilipino (Filipino Psychology): A legacy of Virgilio G. Enriquez." *Asian Journal of Social Psychology* 3 no. 1 (2003): 49–71.

Pitt-Rivers, Julian. "Honor." In *International Encyclopedia of the Social Sciences*, edited by David L. Sills. New York: Macmillan, 1968.

Priest, Robert J. "Experience-Near Theologizing in Diverse Human Contexts." In *Globalizing Theology: Brief and Practice in an Era of World Christianity*, edited by Craig Ott and Harold A. Netland. Grand Rapids, MI: Baker Academic, 2006.

Quarterman, Clayton. "The Application of Presbyterian Polity and Transfer of Leadership in Cross-cultural Situations: A Study in Presbyterian Missiology." PhD. diss., University of Wales, Lampeter, 2005.

Ross, Cathy. "The Theology of Partnership." *International Bulletin of Missionary Research* 34, no. 3 (2010):145–148.

Scarborough, Jack. *The Origins of Cultural Differences and Their Impact on Management*. Westport, CT: Quorum, 1998.

Sohn, B. "Korean Church Politics and the Problem." In *Reform of Korean Church*, edited by Young Yoon Lee. Seoul: Jeoung-Eum, 1982.

Tennent, Timothy. *Theology in the Context of World Christianity: How the Global Church Is Influencing the Way We Think About and Discuss Theology*. Grand Rapids, MI: Zondervan, 2007.

Thiselton, Anthony. *Hermeneutics: An Introduction*. Grand Rapids, MI: Eerdmans, 2009.

Van Engen, Charles E. *God's Missionary People*. Grand Rapids, MI: Baker Book House, 1991.

———. "The Glocal Church." In *Globalizing Theology: Brief and Practice in an Era of World Christianity*, edited by Craig Ott and Harold A. Netland. Grand Rapids, MI: Baker Academic, 2006.

Van Engen. *Transforming Mission Theology*. Pasadena: William Carry Library, 2017.

Wu, Jackson. 2015. *One Gospel for All Nations: A Practical Approach to Biblical Contextualization*. Pasadena, CA: William Carry University, 2013.

Wu, Jackson. "How Christ Saves God's face . . . and Ours: A Soteriology of Honor and Shame." *Missiology: An International Review* 44, no. 4 (2016): 375–387.

SECTION TWO

MISSION AND CHURCH

5

FROM PAGODAS TO THE SAVIOR—OUTREACH IN MYANMAR

by Peter Thein Nyunt

Introduction

Myanmar has been a devoutly Buddhist country for centuries. It is often referred to as "the land of pagodas" because Buddhists have erected pagodas on every hill and mountain near towns and villages.[1] According to a well-known Buddhist monk, Ashin Thittala, culture in Asian countries is religiously oriented.[2] For example, in Myanmar, the social solidarity inherent in its integrative religious overlay is strong, and the culture itself is deeply rooted in Theravada Buddhism, the conservative branch of the Buddhist faith.[3] Consequently, the Myanmar Buddhist philosophy permeates the concepts and worldview of the people and saturates their culture, language, and education with Buddhistic views. S. Ngun Ling described the pervasive nature of religion this way: "The Burman [Myanmar] culture is deeply embedded in the Theravada form of Buddhist tradition. Theravada Buddhism is the only foundation of the creativity, philosophical

1 "Bagan: The Land of a Thousand Pagodas," *The Centre For Indic Studies*, accessed April 30, 2022, https://cisindus.org/2020/05/10/bagan-the-land-of-a-thousand-pagodas/

2 Ashin Thittila, *Essential Themes of Buddhist Lectures: Given by Ashin Thittila* (Yangon: Department Religious Affairs, 2000), 213.

3 The other two schools of Buddhism are Mahayana (also known as the "great vehicle"), and Vajrayana (also known as "diamond"). Theravada is also known as the "way of the elders."

thinking, and way of life of the overall Burman people. Theravada Buddhist Abhidharma philosophy expresses their worldview, their conception of the meaning of human existence, human destiny, and the idea of the Ultimate or God. Religion and culture are, for them, just two sides of a coin."[4]

This interconnection of religion and culture in the identity of Myanmar people is often considered by Christian missionaries as an impediment to the penetration of the gospel. Thus Adoniram Judson, the first American missionary to Myanmar, exclaimed, "It was easier to extract a tooth from the tiger's mouth than to convert a Myanmar Buddhist to Christian faith."[5] Today, the population of Myanmar is estimated at 56 million, and Christianity stands at 6.2 percent.[6]

Christians are mainly from non-Myanmar ethnic groups, such as the Karen and Chin, and only 0.1 percent of Christians are *Bhama* people, the largest Myanmar ethnic group.[7] Protestant Christianity has been present in Myanmar for over two hundred years, but the Christian message is largely alien to Myanmar Buddhists, especially to the Bhama people. Anecdotal evidence from my colleagues and me (who have been in ministry for several decades) suggests that Christian communication in Myanmar has entailed hundreds of missionaries, thousands of dollars, and countless translations of texts, with few results among the Myanmar Buddhists. Among Myanmar Buddhists, Christianity is still regarded as a foreign potted plant rather than a faith that has taken root in Myanmar soil.

The problems confronting Christian communication of the gospel to the Bhama Buddhists (hereafter Myanmar Buddhists) are many. One problem that stands out is that the message Christians in Myanmar communicate

4 S. Ngun Ling, "Communicating Christ Cross-Culturally: A Dialogical Approach to Mission and Theology in 21st Century Myanmar," *MIT Festschrift Committee: Our Theology Journey* 40, no. 1 (2006): 33–51.

5 Paul Clasper, "Burma the Church amid the Pagoda," in *Christ and Crisis in Southeast Asia,* ed. G.H. Anderson (New York: Friendship Press, 1968); Judson, a pioneer missionary to Myanmar, served in Myanmar from 1813 until his death in 1850.

6 World Population Review, "Myanmar Population 2023 (Live)," accessed May 1, 2023, https://worldpopulationreview.com/countries/myanmar-population

7 M.M. Nyunt, "Myanmar Reactions to Christianity," *MIT Journal of Theology* 9, no. 1 (January 2008):104–122.

does not resonate with the spiritual quest of the Myanmar Buddhists. Christian missionaries need to be aware that Myanmar Buddhism has moved away from traditional Buddhism to incorporate the belief system of spiritism—a belief in all known spiritual beings.[8] Within traditional Buddhism, Myanmar Buddhists are taught that each person's liberation from the cycle of rebirth depends on their own efforts. However, self-induced liberation is difficult to achieve and out of fear of failure, people seek help from spirit beings and the practices of folk Buddhism.

In this chapter, I discuss how my colleagues and I engage and communicate with Myanmar Buddhists who make regular pilgrimages to the Shwedagon pagoda in Yangon.[9] Our main message to these Myanmar Buddhists is based on two presuppositions. First, because these Myanmar Buddhists are fearful, they turn to a pantheon (i.e., collection) of spirits to quell their fear. Second, Myanmar Buddhists can find true liberation in Jesus Christ. Before I embark on my recommendation for contextualizing the message to Myanmar Buddhists, I provide an overview of Myanmar spiritual realities, then of the Myanmar spiritual quest.

The Myanmar Spiritual Context

The typical identity of Myanmar Buddhists in the city of Yangon, where the famous Shwedagon pagoda is located, is "to be Myanmar is to be Buddhist," and they devote themselves to Buddhism.[10] But in daily life, their Buddhist religious practices are distinct from the mainstream teaching of Buddhism. In traditional Buddhism, believers must rely entirely on their

8 K.M. Nyunt, *Myanmar Traditional Monthly Festivals* (Yangon: Innwa Book Store, 2005), 111; En, S. P. K. *Nat Worship: A Paradigm for Doing Contextual Theology in Myanmar* (Yangon: Judson Research Center for the Myanmar Institute of Theology 2012), 56- 57.

9 Located in Yangon, Myanmar, the 2,500-year-old pagoda is in a 114-acre site on Singuttara Hill. The pagoda is the focus of religious and community activities in Yangon. For more information see: https://shwedagonpagoda.com/

10 Some information in this chapter is from my conversations with people living in Myanmar during the period 2010-2015.

own efforts, not on any external god, savior, or even the Buddha.[11] The Buddha's instruction to his followers was that everyone was their own savior, and each one must save themself through their own effort, without failure. Whoever fails in their self-effort is doomed to an existence in samsara, wandering aimlessly in a cyclic manner (samsara is the cycle of death and rebirth that human beings are subject to, depending on their deeds or misdeeds). However, even if Buddhism were to be simplified, the frailty of humanity would render the faith difficult to follow. That is why many Myanmar Buddhists turn to believing in seemingly visible, powerful beings. In Myanmar, this alternative form of religion is known as "*nat* worship" or "folk faith," and it is being practiced alongside Buddhism.

Owing to the amalgamation of animistic practices within the authentic teachings of the Buddha, idols of the Buddha and other deities flourish, and adherents worship various gods represented in the idols. The idols, as well as gods and guardians of the people and places, are kept in temples, in one's home, and in places adjacent to the home. People venerate their idols and worship them. In many instances, this folk faith is practiced in conjunction with Buddhism. Thus Buddhism in Myanmar is like "a thin veneer of philosophy laid over the main structure of animistic belief," which is practiced daily, whereas worship at the pagoda occurs only once a week.[12] As Simon Pau Enn rightly said, "Many Nat images are found on the premises of famous pagodas like Shwedagon, Sule, and Shwemawdaw, with inscriptions on the images that are worshipped by the adherents side-by-side with the images of the Buddha."[13]

The Spiritual Quest of Myanmar Buddhists

As indicated above, Myanmar Buddhists' spiritual realities dictate that they depend on self-reliance in seeking the betterment of life after death. Theravada Buddhism demands that "faith is taken without a sense of fear, or a

11 Nyunt, *Missions amidst Pagodas: Contextual Communication of the Gospel in the Myanmar Buddhist Context*, 2014.

12 R.C. Temple, *Thirty-Seven Nats: A Phase of Spirit-Worship Prevailing in Burma* (London: W. Griggs, 1906), 1.

13 En, *Nat Worship: A Paradigm*, 60.

hope for a reward, or status."[14] However, many Myanmar Buddhists do not uphold these ideals. Fear, for instance, is one of the primary motivations for their alternative forms of worship. Thus the Myanmar spiritual quest is broader than what is stipulated by Buddhism; it is a belief in all spiritual beings in the most inclusive way. Myanmar folk Buddhists seek more than welfare in daily life issues. Due to their problematic socioeconomic situation, meeting their immediate needs in daily life seems more important than life after death. They need a lord/god who can solve the problems they are facing in their daily lives. This practice of animism has become part of their indigenous religion—*mi-yo-pa-la* or *yo-ya*.[15] As Moe. M. Nyunt stated, "Animistic ideas and a belief in the existence of the supernatural power has influenced every phase, every story, every festival, every artistic performance, and the everyday life of the Myanmar until now. Every newly constructed building is necessarily preceded by paying homage to Nats with an offertory tray. Every dramatic troupe opens each performance with a nat-dance. Most Myanmar consult with Nats or fortune tellers before they start their business."[16]

As noted earlier, fear is prevalent in Myanmar spirituality. Thus the Myanmar spiritual quest is replete with daily and personal difficulties, and the citizens seek to harness a power that helps solve these problems.[17] Therefore, their actual quest is poles apart from their spiritual faith.

I now describe current popular Myanmar superstitious beliefs and practices, including the process of consulting with astrologers (*badin-saya*) and performing magical rituals (*yadayar*) at Shwedagon pagoda.

The term *badin* in Myanmar stands for astrology. For the Myanmar, astrology means "not only the methods of tracing the courses of the planets and their influence on morals, but also the ritual by which the planets are

---

14 Department For The Promotion And Propagation Of The Sasana, *How to Live as a Good Buddhist Vol. 1*, trans. U Han Htay, and U Chit Tin (Yangon: The Ministry Of Religious Affairs, 2002), 17.

15 S. Myint, *Nat-Paung-Sone* (Yangon: San Taw Win, n.d.), 22.

16 Moe M. Nyunt, *A Pneumatological Response to the Myanmar Nat-Worship* (Yangon: Myanmar Institute, 2010).

17 Melford E. Spiro, *Myanmar Supernaturalism* (Philadelphia: A Publication of the Institute for The Study of Human Issues, 1978), 94.

appeased and made to withdraw their baneful influence."[18] The one who predicts the fortunes of people through *badin* is called a *badin-saya* (astrologer). Accordingly, they advise people to solve their problems through *yadayar*, a kind of art that applies to the present life or the Myanmar form of voodoo.[19] It is prescribed by the *badin-saya* to prevent misfortune and bring good luck. Although the practice of *yadayar* cannot be found in the Buddha's teaching, most Myanmar, including country leaders and even some monks and nuns, apply it. All popular spiritual beliefs and practices that are directly or indirectly linked with Myanmar folk religion (*nat* worship) remain strong in Myanmar.

As stated above, common spiritual practices are linked with citizens' daily and personal difficulties; therefore, Myanmar Buddhists yearn for powerful beings and powers to protect them from danger and bring blessings to them. Assuming that spiritual quests cannot be attained by their own efforts, they need someone to give direction to their intra-mundane (everyday) and supra-mundane (spiritual) lives and repel their fear.

A Contextual Approach to the Myanmar Buddhists

In this section, I adapt Paul's approaches in the New Testament for communicating Christ to and reaching Myanmar Buddhists. I use the book of Acts because it depicts some of the early Christian approaches to reach non-Christians with the good news of Jesus Christ. Some of the activities mentioned are steeped in first-century Jewish and Greco-Roman cultures; however, I believe that Paul's approaches offer a guiding light to evangelize Myanmar Buddhists.

Paul's approach in Acts 17:22–34 is especially appropriate. He engaged well with people from a foreign culture, showing that he grasped both Greek society and humanity's needs. Moreover, he conveyed the message of Jesus Christ to idolaters. During Paul's time, according to reasonable

18 Maung Htin Aung 1962. *Folk Elements in Myanmar Buddhism* (London: Oxford University Press,1962), 1.

19 Christina Fink, *Living Silence: Burma under Military Rule* (Bangkok: White House, 2001), 227.

estimates, there were thirty thousand idols in Athens when the population of the city was less than ten thousand.[20] As a servant of Jesus Christ, Paul was emotionally perturbed; however, he did not express his anger toward the idols or those who venerated and worshipped them. On the contrary, he sought and found "the common interests, needs and problems and religious ideas" of Athenians to convey the message of Jesus Christ.[21] He also acknowledged and used Athenian concepts wherever they aligned with Scripture.

Christological Message: Jesus Christ as the Liberator

I contend that Christian teachers and missionaries in Myanmar can communicate the gospel effectively with the twofold approach of remaining faithful to the intent of Scripture while being relevant to the audience.[22] As Daniel Niles asserted, we are called to make the gospel understandable to the audience.[23] The primary purpose of this section is to close the gap successfully between communicators and the Myanmar Buddhist audience through the Christological message.

To begin, communicators must draw out the sine qua non (essentials) of their message. According to John T. Seamands, the effective communication of the gospel varies depending on who is giving it to whom, where, and how.[24] For example, when attempting to apply the gospel to the Bhama Buddhist group,[25] communicators must remember that this application

---

20 Andrew D. Clarke and Bruce W. Winter, *One God, One Lord in a World of Religious Pluralism* (Cambridge: Tyndale House, 1991), 138; William J. Larkin, *Acts* (Westmont, IL: InterVarsity Press, 1995), 251.

21 John T. Seamands, *Tell It Well: Communicating the Gospel Across Cultures* (Chennai, India: Mission Educational Books, 2000), 81–85.

22 This entire section has been modified from my book, *Missions amidst Pagodas Contextual Communication of the Gospel in the Myanmar Buddhist Context.*

23 Daniel Thambyrajah Niles, *Who is this Jesus?* (London, Lutterworth Press, 1968), 30.

24 Seamands, *Tell It Well*, 11.

25 The Bhama are the least evangelized people group in Myanmar. Most of the Christians come from tribal ethnic groups such as the Chin, the Karen, and the Kachin.

entails only changing the form of the presentation."[26] The main component of the biblical message is universal and cannot be changed, regardless of culture.

What do Myanmar Buddhists want to hear from the communicator when the gospel is shared with them? Before answering this question, I summarize the Buddhist teachings:

> First, Buddhists live under the spiritual law of samsara.
>
> Second, there are four noble truths:
>
> - *dukkha*: the reality that life is unsatisfactory and filled with suffering
> - *samudaya*: the knowledge that suffering is caused by craving
> - *niroda*: the teaching that to end suffering, craving must be extinguished
> - *magga*: the teaching that to end craving, Buddhists must follow the path of the Buddha (*magga* simply means path)

The way to *nibbana* (the highest spiritual state, where greed, hatred, and desire are extinguished) is to follow the teachings of Buddha, including the four noble truths, in order to eliminate craving and suffering.[27] In figure 5.1, this fourfold teaching and how life in Buddhism is controlled by the samsaric existence are illustrated.

Therefore, in answer to the question I posed earlier, *nibbana* and liberation from samsaric existence is what Buddhists long for.

My summary of Buddhist teaching indicates that the Buddha's program for *nibbana* is very demanding, and for followers who fall by the wayside, bad *kamma* is equated with sin—sin that is real and serious. This resonates with biblical teaching because the Bible views sin as humankind's wrong actions when people disobey or dishonor God (Rom 1:21). Humanity sinned by obeying Satan (Gen 2:1–7) and worshipped the things of God's creation instead of worshipping God (Rom 1:21–25). The sin that

26 Seamands, *Tell It Well.*

27 *Nibbana* (in Pali) refers to the same concept as Nirvana (in Sanskrit).

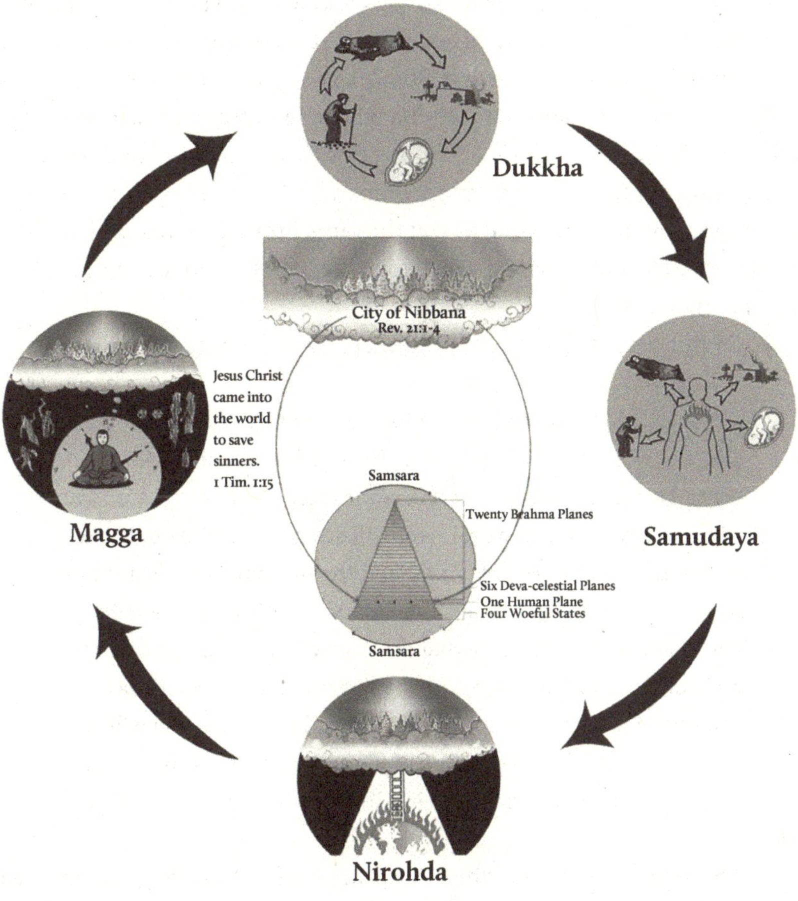

Figure 5.1. Jesus the liberator.

humankind committed could not be washed away by any human means, and it incurred the wrath of God and death.

This is the reason why everyone needs salvation from sin (Acts 4:12:1; Tim 2:5). Clearly explaining sin and virtue, the Buddha said that virtue cannot be subtracted from sin no matter how much good is done.[28] Therefore, whoever takes refuge on one's virtue to save oneself from sin is depending on the wrong thing, and this is against the Buddha's teaching.

28 K. Sri Dhammananda, *What Buddhists Believe* (Kuala Lumpur, Malaysia: Buddhist Missionary Society, 2002), 35.

It is impossible to be freed from sin by good works. The Buddha spoke to Ananda, one of his first five disciples, about a coming buddha known as Arit Metteyya: "I am not the first Buddha to come on earth, nor shall I be the last. In due time, another Buddha will arise in this world, a Holy One, a Supremely Enlightened One, endowed with wisdom, in conduct auspicious, knowing the universe, an incomparable leader of men, a master of devas and men. He will reveal to you the same Eternal Truths, which I have taught you. He will proclaim a religious life, wholly perfect and pure, as I now proclaim."[29]

Of this future savior, Inta Chanthavongsouk wrote:

> You must give alms and search for another God that will come to save the world and will help you afterward. His name is Arit Mettayya. He was before me but will come after me. In the Savior who will come to save the world, you will see puncture wounds like a wheel in the palms of his hands, and the bottom of his feet. In his side there is the mark of a stab wound, and his forehead is full of scars. This God will be the big ark that will lead you to cross the cycle of birth and death to Nirvana. Do not prefer the old way. You will not be saved. You must get rid of the old way, and you will have a new spirit which looks like the firefly and comes from above to live in your heart and continues to live in this world and in eternity.[30]

The teachings of Buddhist scripture and the writings of the two authors, Dhammananda and Chanthavongsouk, confirm that the Buddha's teachings were clear and that salvation is not from the Buddha but from the one who will come after him. This Buddhist teaching, according to Christian missiologists, serves as a clear redemptive analogy: the missiological concept that various aspects of the truth of the gospel are contained in other cultures and religions.[31] The Bible is clear that sinners cannot help themselves to get rid of sin (Rom 3:9–21).

29 Dhammananda, *What Buddhists Believe*, 60.

30 Inta Chanthavongsouk, *Buddha's Prophecy of Messiah* (La Mirada, California: The Lao Conference of Churches, 1999), 25–26.

31 Missiologists like Don Richardson have asserted that aspects of the Christian gospel are contained in a minuscule manner in all human cultures. These

The Bible also teaches that Jesus as Messiah or savior came into the world some two thousand years ago to show great mercy for sinners (Rom 5:8). Those who take refuge in him will not perish but will live in this world and in eternity (John 3:16; 5:24; 1 John 4:7). In the Old Testament, Noah built an ark that saved his family and all species of animals from the great flood. Jesus is the big ark whose compassion is great and wide for all, including Myanmar Buddhists; thus, those who enter the Jesus ark will have access to the city of Nibbana (Rev 21:1–4) when the compassionate savior comes.

Addressing the Issues

In the remainder of this chapter, I continue to expand on what Myanmar Buddhists need to hear from Christian communicators so that Myanmar Buddhists can see and respond to Jesus Christ as the liberator and the compassionate savior. Jesus is the Godman who came to earth from heaven (1 Cor 15:47). To present Jesus Christ as a liberator at this level, Christians in Myanmar must engage in dialogue with Buddhists and try to articulate how Jesus would end the cycle of rebirths (samsara) by carrying vicariously in his body all suffering (*dukkha*).

The diagram in figure 5.1 shows that Buddhists pursue liberation through self-effort, but distractions are inevitable at the *magga* stage (the teaching of the path to the end of suffering). Any distraction, such as partaking in spiritistic practices, means the person would be bound to samsara (thirty-one planes of existence: four woeful states, one human plane, six planes of deva, and twenty planes of Brahma, as in figure 5.1).

All religious beliefs have some concept of salvation from sin. According to traditional Buddhism in Myanmar, salvation or liberation is based on the law of *kamma*, as stated earlier. It is ethical retribution through morality (*sila*), concentration (*samadhi*), and wisdom (*panna*). There is no teaching on grace or forgiveness in the Buddhist understanding of liberation. The teaching is that merits or demerits are collected in one's life, depending on the good or evil deeds that one performs, and it is what is left in the balance that determines one's kammic afterlife.

---

could be paralleled in the culture's fables, teachings, values, etc. The role of the Christian missionary is to find the redemptive analogies contained in the culture.

Myanmar Buddhists believe that accumulating merits can be done for oneself, for others, and even for the dead through charitable acts. Christian communicators can use this merit-transference principle as a connection to the experience of the gospel and the death of Christ on the cross: "Savior who will come . . . you will see puncture wounds like a wheel in the palms of his hands . . . full of scars."[32] In this prophecy by the Buddha, the Lord Jesus Christ is presented as "one who accumulated infinite merits by virtue of his sinless life, good deeds, and meritorious death."[33] Although the death of Jesus on the cross symbolized this merit, what is the result for humanity? According to the Buddhist merit-transference (*pattidana*) teaching, living beings can pass on merit to the dead based on good deeds. If human beings full of sin are capable of transferring merit, how much more can the Lord Jesus Christ transfer his merit to others? Hence important insights into the loving savior, Jesus Christ, may be shared in a cyclical manner, beginning with his incarnation, coming from outside samsara (1 Tim 1:15) to overcoming the law of *kamma* by his sinless life, death, and resurrection.

As pointed out above, Myanmar folk Buddhists are constantly fearful and threatened by the *nat,* who haunt every object and every place. Therefore, there is no hope in life even when trying to appease the *nat* images in the Shwedagon pagoda. When Christ is accepted as the liberator, fear and despair will subside at the personal level, and life will be filled with hope. What Vincent J. Donovan stated as the purpose of his missionary work with the Masai people in Africa is true of the situation in Myanmar:

> I believe this is what lies at the heart of the urgency and necessity of missionary and evangelization. This is what I and others like me, are trying to do out there. Not to bring salvation and goodness and holiness and race and God, which were there before we got there. But to bring these people the only thing they did not have before we came: a hope imbedded in the meaning of the life and death and resurrection of Christ. It is a cleansing and humbling thought to see your whole life and work reduced to being simply

32 Chanthavongsouk, *Buddha's Prophecy*, 25–26.

33 Nyunt, Missions amidst Pagodas, 107.

> a channel of hope, and yourself merely a herald of hope, for those who do not have it.[34]

When folk Buddhists accept Christ as their liberator, they will study their culture from the perspective of the gospel and transform those cultural practices that dehumanize people. Thus cultural evils are challenged and transformed by the gospel.

Missiological Reflections

God is within people's reach. If they sincerely search for him, they will find him, even at the Shwedagon pagoda. God has created human beings with the capacity to search for him. Through general revelation via the created world and human conscience, God has left enough evidence about Himself for people to search for him (Acts 14:15–17).

I have observed pilgrims at the Shwedagon pagoda in Yangon offering flowers, candles, fruits, or vegetables to obtain good fortune. Others chant and pay homage to the pagoda or meditate. It reminds me of how Paul approached the Athenians. When he made a formal address to them, he did not scold them as "you foolish idolaters." If Paul were a Myanmar evangelical preacher, he would start by commending Buddhist religiosity, even though he did not sanction idolatry. In this manner, Paul respectfully recognized religious endeavors as a cultural compliment to his distinguished audience.[35] Indeed, such a positive attitude and broadmindedness are vital when encountering Buddhists with the message of Christ in the hope that the Myanmar folk Buddhists will take the chance to hear the gospel in their specific context.

Conclusion

Many Christians in Myanmar have introduced the gospel of Jesus Christ to the Myanmar Buddhists in a manner influenced by their traditional

---

34 Vincent J. Donovan, *Christianity Rediscovered* (London: SCMP Press, 2014), 193.

35 Thittila, *Essential Themes of Buddhist Lectures*, 213.

Western theology. The approach I introduced in this chapter is contextual and practical.

Due to the political and economic crisis in Myanmar, prayer for the Myanmar Buddhists is like a daily hope for freedom from poverty, hardship, and illness. Missionaries and Christian churches introduce hope for the life hereafter, but the Buddhists' hopes and prayers are very practical and aimed at this life. The premises of the Shwedagon pagoda in Yangon are surrounded by *nat* images to which Myanmar folk Buddhists pay homage. Their belief in a spirit world has several levels and a variety of supernatural powers and spirit beings. In this chapter, I argued that folk Buddhists' belief in their existence is a point of contact, whereupon Jesus Christ can be introduced as the liberator. I propose this because of my strong belief that true freedom can be found only in him.

Such missionizing requires contextualizing the gospel message within the people's religio-cultural context. The following is a three-part summary of how Paul used effective communication principles to share the gospel with the Athenian idolaters in Acts 17, linked with our approach for contextualizing our communication with Myanmar Buddhists:

First, Paul began with an affirmation of the religiosity of Athenians (v. 22). We acknowledge the religiosity of the Buddhists and their quest for spiritual success and point out how their religiosity can enable them to find the Savior, Jesus.

Second, Paul bridged the gospel by introducing familiar concepts (v. 23). We use the concept of samsara and of Christ coming from outside samsara to help us.

Third, Paul enlarged their vision (vv. 24, 25). We point out the work and ministry of Christ within the Buddhist framework and enlarge their vision to regard Christ as the one who can bring them into the heavenly city (Rev 21: 9–11).

If the Word became flesh and dwelt among us (John 1:14) and Jesus's name is Immanuel (God with us), then the gospel can be incarnated into Myanmar Buddhist culture through contextualization to enable Buddhist pilgrims to meet Jesus Christ—even at the Shwedagon pagoda.

Bibliography

Aung, Maung Htin. *Folk Elements in Myanmar Buddhism*. Oxford: Oxford University Press, 1962.

Clarke, Andrew. D, and Bruce W. Winter. *One God, One Lord in a World of Religious Pluralism*. Cambridge: Tyndale House, 1991.

Chanthavongsouk, Inta. *Buddha's Prophecy of Messiah*. La Mirada, California: The Lao Conference of Churches, 1999.

Clasper, Paul. "Burma the Church amid the Pagoda." In *Christ and Crisis in Southeast Asia*, edited by G.H. Anderson. New York: Friendship Press, 1986.

Dhammananda, K. Sri. *What Buddhists Believe*. Kuala Lumpur, Malaysia: Buddhist Missionary Society, 2002.

Donovan, Vincent J. *Christianity Rediscovered*. London: SCMP Press, 2014.

En, S. P. K. *Nat Worship: A Paradigm for Doing Contextual Theology in Myanmar*. Yangon: Judson Research Center for the Myanmar Institute of Theology, 2012.

Fink, Christina. *Living Silence: Burma under Military Rule*. Bangkok: White House, 2001.

Htay, H. and C. Tin. *How to Live as a Good Buddhist Vol.1*. Yangon: Department of the Promotion and Propagation of the Sasana, 2002.

Larkin, William. J. *Acts*. Westmont, IL: InterVarsity Press, 1995.

Ling, S. N. "Communicating Christ Cross-Culturally: A Dialogical Approach to Mission and Theology in 21st Century Myanmar." *MIT Festschrift Committee: Our Theology Journey* 40, no.1 (2006): 33–51.

Myint, S. n.d. *Nat-Paung-Sone*. Yangon: San Taw Win.

Niles, Daniel Thambyrajah. *Who Is This Jesus?* London: Lutterworth Press, 1968.

Nyunt, K. M. *Myanmar Traditional Monthly Festivals*. Yangon: Innwa Book Store, 2005.

Nyunt, M. M. "Myanmar Reactions to Christianity." *MIT Journal of Theology* 9 (January 2008):104–122.

Nyunt, M.M. *A Pneumatological Response to the Myanmar Nat-Worship*. Yangon: Myanmar Institute of Theology, 2010.

Nyunt, Peter Thein. *Missions amidst Pagodas: Contextual Communication of the Gospel in the Myanmar Buddhist Context*. Carlisle, UK: Langham Monographs, 2014.

Sayadaw, W. *The Essence of Buddha Dhamma*. Onalaska, Washington: Pariyatti, 1997.

Seamands, John. T. *Tell It Well: Communicating the Gospel Across Cultures*. Chennai, India: Mission Educational Books, 2000.

Spiro, Melford E. *Myanmar Supernaturalism*. Philadelphia: A Publication of the Institute for the Study of Human Issues, 1978.

Temple, Richard. C. *Thirty-Seven Nats: A Phase of Spirit-Worship Prevailing in Burma*. London: W. Griggs, Chromo-Lithographar to the King, 1906.

The Centre For Indic Studies. "Bagan: The Land of a Thousand Pagodas." Accessed April 30, 2022. https://cisindus.org/2020/05/10/bagan-the-land-of-a-thousand-pagodas/

Thittila, A. *Essential Themes of Buddhist Lectures: Given by Ashin Thittila*. Yangon: Myanmar: Department of Religious Affairs, 2000.

World Population Review. "Myanmar Population 2023 (Live)." Accessed May 1, 2023, https://worldpopulationreview.com/countries/myanmar-population

6

RETHINKING THE CHURCH IN THE MYANMAR BUDDHIST CONTEXT

by Peter Thein Nyunt

Introduction

The Union of Myanmar has been deeply influenced by Theravada Buddhism and its associated traditions, according to Lubeight, Thittila, and Soe.[1] Buddhism has saturated the nation's social life, ideas, manners, aspirations, and identity. However, there is a way and a place for Christianity.

From 1813 onward, Western Protestant missionaries came, one group after another, to Myanmar, but they struggled to comprehend the religious-cultural interconnectedness of Myanmar society.[2] The missionaries' Christology, developed in Western countries, did not equip them well to understand the audience's culture, nor to communicate their Christian message. The consequence of Christians' defective Christology

---

1 Guy Lubeigt, "Myanmar: A Country Modeled by Buddhist Traditions," in *Traditions of Knowledge in Southeast Asia: Part 2,* ed. Myanmar Historical Committee (Yangon: University Press, 2004), 244; Ashin Thittila, *Essential Themes of Buddhist Lectures* (Yangon: Department of Religious Affairs, 2000), 213; Tin Soe, "An Economic Interpretation of Some Myanmar Traditional Concepts in the Context of Globalization," in *Traditions of Knowledge in Southeast Asia: Part 3,* ed. Myanmar Historical Committee (Yangon: University Press, 2005), 118–119.

2 Maung Wa Shwe, *Burma Baptist Chronicles* (Rangoon: Burma Baptist Convention, 1963), 128–129.

produced a defective and alien ecclesiology (doctrine of the church). That is why Ling stated critically that "this Western orientation of church life came to Myanmar Christians not only through their missionaries' teachings but also through their colonial rulers, administrators, and civil educators."[3] As a result, the early churches in Myanmar were only replicas and potted plants of Western churches.

In this chapter, I argue that churches in Myanmar need to be indigenous churches in a Buddhist context. To support my argument, I present a brief case study about the development of an indigenous church in a Rakhine Buddhist context in Myanmar. Hopefully, the missiological insights from this chapter will ignite Myanmar Christians to rethink the structure of Myanmar ecclesiology, and perhaps the insights, rooted in the Myanmar context, will resonate to some extent with other Buddhist countries in Southeast Asia and beyond. Regardless, I believe they can be helpful for Christians generally to rethink what the true church should be.

Signs of the True Church

In chapter 3 of this book, I discussed contextual communication of the gospel in the Myanmar Buddhist context. Unstated but implied in that chapter was that the goal of such communication of the gospel is not just conversion; it is also to incorporate converts into local congregations and, in some circumstances, to establish new congregations. Therefore, in this chapter, I discuss the distinguishing signs of contextual congregations aligned with the church of Jesus Christ.

Ever since the inception of the church worldwide, the nature of the church,[4] its essence, attributes, and distinguishing features have been debated.[5] Inherent in most definitions of the church are the tension between the church as seen by God (invisible to us) and the church as seen

---

3 Samuel Ngun Ling, *Communicating Christ in Myanmar: Issues, Interactions and Perspectives* (Yangon, Myanmar: ATEM, 2005), 15.

4 Charles E. van Engen, *The Growth of the True Church: An Analysis of the Ecclesiology of Church Growth Theory* (Amsterdam, The Netherlands: Rodopi, 1981), 81–82.

5 Howard A. Snyder, *Liberating the Church: The Ecology of Church and Kingdom* (Westmont, IL: InterVarsity Press, 1983), 151–168.

by human beings (visible), or the "form-essence" dichotomy.[6] One way of dealing with this dichotomy is to state that the church is at the same time visible and hidden. The visible elements are the preaching of the word and the administration of the sacraments, whereas the faith aspect remains invisible. Since the church is at the same time visible and hidden, and since the church is always in the process of becoming what, essentially, it already is, we must look for "open concepts"—that is, signs or pointers to the reality of the church that are explicit.[7] In other words, it is useful, as far as possible, to identify palpable (plainly seeable) characteristics.

In one of the key passages in which Jesus talks about the future church, he concludes, "Where two or three come together in my name, there am I with them" (Matt 18:15–20). What qualifies a gathering of people to be the church is the presence of Jesus Christ in their midst. The church, therefore, happens when and where Christ, according to the Bible, has promised his presence.[8] Following this understanding,[9] I propose that the true church may be identified by the six signs listed below, which I have adapted from my doctoral dissertation.[10]

Church as the Relationship of People in the Name of Jesus Christ

As stated above, Jesus promised to be present when people gather in his name (Matt 18:20); therefore, to be recognized as a church, at least two or three people must come together in the name of Jesus Christ. This fellowship with Jesus, based on his authority, is a continuation of his fellowship with disciples during his earthly ministry. The church may be viewed as a sacred place, but its sacredness is not constituted by the office of a bishop or a pastor. It is a people place in which there is fellowship (*koinonia*) with Christ (1 John 1:3); thus, it is made sacred by the presence

6 Van Engen, *The Growth of the True*, 49.

7 Van Engen, *The Growth of the True.*

8 David C.K. Watson, *I Believe in the Church* (Grand Rapids, MI: Eerdmans, 1982), 336.

9 Jurgen Moltmann. *The Church in the Power of the Spirit: A Contribution to Messianic Ecclesiology* (New York: Harper and Row, 1993), 121–123.

10 Peter Thein Nyunt, "Toward a Paradigm of Christian Communication for the Bhama Buddhists in Yangon City" (PhD diss., SAIACS, 2010), 50–54.

of Christ in its midst. Just as the gospel has been described as a relationship mediated by relationships, the church in its basic form can be described as relationship-oriented.[11] Myanmar people are group-oriented or community-oriented people. A meeting between two or three of them is called *lu-su-lu-way* (i.e., a relationship—for any purpose).

Church as a Preaching Point of the Word of Jesus Christ

The presence of Jesus is primarily communicated through his word to those gathered in his name. Jesus is the word of God, which through incarnation "became flesh and made His dwelling among us" (John 1:14). A church is where the word of God is preached, for there Jesus is present with his grace. Certainly, many other components are integral to the church, but the one essential component is the communication of the gospel of Jesus Christ as revealed in the written word of God, the Scripture.[12] All the other necessary elements of the church are linked with the word. The word, the gospel of Jesus Christ, contains four classical marks of the church, which are named in the ecumenical creeds: one, holy, catholic, and apostolic.[13] But the church has only one sacrament, the gospel of Jesus, which is also communicated to us through baptism and Holy Communion.

Church as the Place That Offers Baptism and Holy Communion

Jesus is present through his spirit at the baptism in his name. As promised by John the Baptist, Jesus baptizes with the Holy Spirit and thereby incorporates the baptized person into his body, the church (1 Cor 12:13; Titus 3:5). Baptism, therefore, is a special characteristic that is uniquely associated with the church. It is through faith and baptism, administered by the church, that man is saved (Mark 15:16), and baptism is the entrance.[14]

The very words of Jesus at the institution of the holy communion (Luke 22:19–20; 1 Cor 11:23–26) indicate his presence in the church through

11 Gene A. Getz, *Sharpening the Focus of the Church* (Wheaton, IL: Victor, 1988), 94–108.

12 Watson, *I Believe in the Church*, 335.

13 Snyder, *Liberating the Church*, 96–111.

14 Snyder, *Liberating the Church.*

bread and wine, shared among the believers gathered for the Lord's supper. As baptism is the sacrament of entrance into the body of Christ, holy communion is the sacrament of continued fellowship with Jesus Christ and with the other members of the body of Christ. As a sacrament of fellowship, holy communion points to the next characteristic of the true church, unity. Just as all the church members partake of the same bread, so they all belong to the same body of Jesus Christ.

Church as the Demonstration of Love among Members

Unity, which is a characteristic of the true church, is neither necessarily organizational nor characterized by agreement in the local church on all issues. Rather, unity is communal, characterized by members genuinely loving one another. "A new command I give you: Love one another. As I have loved you, so you must love one another. By this all men will know that you are my disciples, if you love one another" (John 13:34–35). The presence of Jesus in the church may be recognized by the members of the church and those outside the church by the love that Christians have for one another.

Church as the Place of Prayer

The church was born in an atmosphere of prayer. The Holy Spirit was poured out on the followers of Jesus gathered in the upper room for prayer (Acts 2). Throughout the Acts of the Apostles and the epistles, a close connection exists between prayer and the Spirit's powerful presence in the church (e.g., Acts 4:31). Jesus Christ spoke to the church (and individuals) in their prayers and in response to their prayers. The prayers of the church are a continuation of the Lord's prayer, with which Jesus invited his disciples to join him in praying to God his heavenly Father, calling him "our Father" (Matt 6:5–15).

Church as an Agent to Continue God's Mission

Fellowship, guided by the word, brought into life, renewed by the sacraments, united in love, and breathing through prayer, is sent into the world by Jesus so that it might spread "the fragrance of the knowledge of him" (2 Cor 2:14). It is "the distinctive people of God called by him through his mission and set aside for his mission."[15] To the church intent on continuing Jesus's mission and *diaconia* (Greek for "the call to serve the poor") in the world, Jesus promises his eternal presence: "And surely I am with you always, to the very end of the age" (Matt 28:20). For people who are hungry, thirsty, naked, sick, and imprisoned, Jesus promises he will meet them in his church as they engage in *diaconia* (Matt 25: 31-46). As such, the church is people sent into the world to represent the reign of God in Jesus Christ and to invite people to enter the kingdom of God. The church is called to share his words (*kerygma* or proclamation), perform deeds of love (*diaconia* or deeds of kindness), and lead a life of love (*koinonia* or fellowship of love).[16]

All six of the following signs of the true church are demonstrated in the life and ministry of the apostolic church, as described in Acts 2: fellowship (v. 42), the word (v. 42), the sacraments (vv. 41–42), unity in love (v. 44), prayers (v. 42), and mission (v. 45 and 47).

Characteristics of Contextual Congregations

The above-listed signs constitute a true church. If one or more of these signs is absent, the essence of the church is in doubt. This signifies that it is likely to be an impaired church on the way to dying or to becoming something other than a church. Notably, the local congregation in an indigenous church always exists in a contextual nature—that is, its connection with the context ensures its relevance and longevity. The following six characteristics of contextual congregations are also adapted from my doctoral dissertation.[17]

A contextual local congregation, or contextual church, is one that reflects the biblical signs of the true church in such a way that is correctly understood by the people in the local context. The characteristics of a contextual or indigenous church may be said to belong to the well-being of

15 Gailyn van Rheenen, *Missions: Biblical Foundations and Contemporary Strategies* (Grand Rapids, MI: Zondervan, 1996), 31.

16 Franz-Josef Eilers, *Communicating in Ministry and Mission: An Introduction to Pastoral and Evangelizing Communication* (Bangalore, India: Asian Trading Corporation, 2004), 11.

17 Nyunt, "Toward a Paradigm of Christian," 55–59.

the church in a local context. However, if one or more of these contextual characteristics is absent, the congregation may still be considered a true church, but one that does not fit very well with the local context.[18]

To develop a contextual or indigenous church, it is necessary to put in place forms and structures that help a local congregation be relevant to the context (i.e., forms and structures that fit the culture of the people of that society) and that, at the same time, are faithful to the biblical text (i.e., forms and structures that fulfill the God-given functions of the church).

However, the contextual congregation may also be viewed from the perspective of the convert. Before conversion, a convert feels at home in their community and culture. A useful criterion of contextualization in congregations is that the convert, without forsaking their own culture, feels at home in the local congregation.

The dynamic-equivalence-transculturation approach to a local congregation proposed by Kraft combines the perspectives of analyzing the church in terms of its functions and the convert's perception of the church.[19] Whereas a formal correspondence church is usually modeled after a foreign church, with all its forms and structures, a "dynamic-equivalence church is an original production in a contemporary culture, not a badly fitted import."[20] The goal here is not to produce a one-to-one correspondence to any church, not even a New Testament church, but to produce a functional equivalence with the true church, as described in the New Testament:

> A dynamic-equivalence church produces an impact on the people of the society of which it is a part, equivalent to that which the scripturally described peoples of God produced upon the original hearers. In that equivalence the church will need leadership, organization, education, worship, building, behavioral standards, and means of expressing Christian love and concern to the people

18 Van Engen, *The Growth of the True Church,* 81–82.

19 Charles H. Kraft, *Christianity in Culture: A Study in Dynamic Biblical Theologizing in Cross-Cultural Perspective.* (Maryknoll, NY: Orbis Books, 1978).

20 Kraft, *Christianity in Culture,* 318.

> of its own culture who have not yet responded to Christ. But a dynamically equivalent church will employ culturally appropriate forms in meeting these needs—familiar, meaningful forms that it will possess, adapt, and fill with Christian meanings.[21]

Thus a contextual congregation is an ongoing process. Therefore, the following characteristics should be seen as indicators of the contextualization process. These characteristics may be used as checkpoints for the presence of contextual aspects in local congregations by church makers seeking that model for their congregations.

First, a contextual church should encourage and help its members to remain within their own culture and community, so the church is not regarded as a foreign object. Instead of diverting members from their culture and community, the contextual church seeks a contextual conversion wherein there is a fellowship of followers of Jesus who continue to live in fellowship with their non-Christian relatives and neighbors.[22] But in striving for context, the church should never override its unique Christian identity. Being faithful to biblical principles must be balanced with being relevant to and addressing the needs of the community.

The adage by Marshall McLuhan that "the medium is the message" is very relevant for the church.[23] The local congregation, being God's primary medium for the communication of the good news, should become the good news of renewal in the community and not be understood as bad news and in any way diminishing the local community and its culture.

Second, a contextual/indigenous church should endeavor to use the language of the converts in services and other activities. Language is crucial to context because much of a society's culture is stored in and transmitted through its language. Only when the word of God is communicated in the mother tongue of the members and only when the members communicate

21 Kraft, *Christianity in Culture.*

22 Donald A. McGavran, *The Bridges of God: A Study of Missions* (New York: Friendship Press, 1955), 9–10.

23 Marshall McLuhan, *Understanding Media: The Extensions of Man* (New York: McGraw-Hill, 1964), 23.

with one another and with God through their own language can a congregation or indigenous church be contextual.

Third, to communicate the relevant biblical message effectively, the leaders in a contextual congregation should use rituals, symbols, and worship forms that address the needs of the members. For literate and nonliterate people alike, rituals are important for the life of the congregation. According to Hiebert, "Rituals, like sacred symbols, are languages for speaking of spiritual things."[24] Hiebert asserted that rituals are especially important for teaching new Christians the meaning of the gospel and for proclaiming the gospel to non-Christians who gather to see what the Christians are doing.[25]

Fourth, a contextual congregation ensures that education for its members strengthens their faith and belonging to the local congregation and the universal church without alienating them from their original community and its values. A contextual approach to formal and informal education in the local congregation involves teaching knowledge and skills that are relevant to the members' actual Christian life in the congregation and their social service and mission in their community. The content and form of education, however, may alienate the members from their own people if the teaching is not conducted within their context and is not relevant to the values of their culture.[26]

Fifth, a contextual congregation should seek to employ indigenous organizational structures and leadership forms. Only when the patterns and styles used to govern the life of the fellowship are in harmony with those of the local culture may we speak of contextual organization and leadership for the local congregation.[27]

Sixth, the theology and ethics of the contextual church should be developed by the members of the local congregation as they reflect on their

24 Paul G. Hiebert, *Anthropological Reflections on Missiological issues* (Grand Rapids: Baker Books, 1994), 167.

25 Paul G. Hiebert, "Conversion and Worldview Transformation." *International Journal of Frontier Missions* 14, no. 2 (April-June 1997): 84–86.

26 Hiebert, "Conversion and Worldview."

27 William A. Smalley, "Cultural Implications of an Indigenous Church," in *Perspectives on the World Christian Movement: A Reader*, ed. Ralph D. Winter and Steve C. Hawthorne, (Pasadena: William Carey Library, 1992), 152–154.

life within Scripture. Instead of adopting theology developed elsewhere, a contextual church seeks its own understanding of the Christian faith.[28]

A Model for Developing Myanmar Ecclesiology

Our understanding of God's church will be much impoverished if we fail to consider the essence of the Greek word *ekklesia*, used by Jesus for church (Matt 16:13–20;18:15–20). In Jesus's time, *ekklesia* was the name for political assemblies that regularly convened for the purpose of making social and political decisions. In the secular *ekklesia*, every citizen had "the right to speak and to propose matters for discussion."[29] Considering all this, why did Jesus choose *ekklesia* as the word to describe his people and their religious gatherings? Perhaps Jesus wanted his people, the church, to function with the purposes and practices of a political institution. If so, believers would suggest matters for discussion, decide things together, make joint decisions, and experience the process of consensus. This form of government may work tolerably well in a house church, but it would be virtually impossible to operate that way in a larger church setting.[30]

In contrast to the implication contained in Christ's use of *ekklesia*, the life of the church in Myanmar is institutional and Western-oriented in structure. One of the undeniable reasons for this is that Western missionaries in Myanmar were unprepared to study the religio-cultural aspects of the people. Being the products of their age, they had no theology of culture. Furthermore, they were sent and commissioned to abolish the existing religious culture of the people. In the West, Christianity was strongly amalgamated with the economic life of society, so when the missionaries came to Myanmar, they were not ready to discern the inseparable fusion of culture and religion.

---

28 David Lim, "Radical Contextualization of Communicating the Gospel to the Buddhists," in *Sharing Jesus In the Buddhist World,* ed. David S. Lim and Steve Spaudling (Pasadena, CA: William Carey Library, 2004), 123–126.

29 Steve Atkerson, *House Church: Simple, Strategy, Scriptural* (Atlanta, GA: New Testament Reformation Fellowship, 2008), 73.

30 Atkerson, *House Church,* 74.

"The Ecclesia of Jesus Christ is to let God's power and purpose flow through her to transform and redeem his creation. For many, that requires looking at 'church' in a new way."[31] Six true signs and four characteristics of the true church have been considered above. When these considerations are brought into the Myanmar Buddhist context, the house fellowship model is significantly appropriate. The fellowship's small size and informal structure contribute to the low profile of such a congregation. In such a profile, Myanmar converts and Buddhist seekers can meet for worship, and it will probably make such a congregation less offensive to the Myanmar community. Attending such a house fellowship once a week can hardly lead to persecution and exclusion from the community. However, if persecution breaks out or members find themselves in a serious emergency, such a fellowship may not be enough to support, assist, and protect its members. Therefore, a Myanmar house fellowship may need to join a network of Myanmar fellowships that will take responsibility for each other's needs. Furthermore, although a Myanmar house fellowship is an independent local congregation, it needs to be in fellowship with the surrounding non-Myanmar churches and depend on their help and assistance.

A Myanmar house fellowship seems to be very relevant to the situation of present Myanmar converts. According to my survey, no authentic Myanmar Buddhist-background church exists in the whole country so far. Most of the Myanmar Buddhist converts are scattered across the country. This means that there are very few Myanmar converts in each location to form a Myanmar congregation built on a traditional model. A house fellowship, however, can consist of as few as two or three Myanmar converts gathering in the name of Jesus Christ, who has promised his presence among them. In many cases, assistance from a Myanmar or non-Myanmar mature Christian might be needed for developing this fellowship. Until one of the Myanmar members of the fellowship can take the role of spiritual leadership, the group will be led by this mature Christian. The house fellowship can meet at times and places that are convenient for the members and worship in ways that are meaningful to the Myanmar people.

---

31 Bambang Budijanto, Scott Todd, and Mark Yeadon, *Relentless Hope: The Unstoppable Movement of Disciple Making Communities* (London, Ontario: Compassion International, 2010), 31.

The need for Myanmar converts in the small house fellowship to experience Christian fellowship and celebration in larger settings may be met through participation in occasional gatherings led by leaders and by bringing neighboring Myanmar house fellowships together for joint meetings. This fellowship must also have access to baptism and holy communion. These rites may either be conducted by the leader or a visiting pastor, according to the tradition of the denomination.

If the leadership of the churches understands the rationale behind the Myanmar house fellowships, they should be able to accept Myanmar house fellowships and incorporate them into their mission strategy without changing any of their basic ecclesiastical principles. The Myanmar house fellowship is a flexible model of local congregation. If the pressure from the Myanmar Buddhist community grows very intense, new members of the house fellowship may remain secret believers for some time, or the whole house fellowship may go underground until the persecution subsides. Nevertheless, if the house fellowship grows or experiences a local people movement, it may transform itself into a more institutionalized congregation with a church building (a Myanmar church).

A Case Study: The Rakhine Buddhist Context

I am a Rakhine[32] by ethnicity, and before conversion, I was a Buddhist monk. I have over twenty-five years of Christian ministerial experience among Buddhist communities in Myanmar. In this case study, I describe how we developed indigenous churches within the Rakhine Buddhist communities. Rakhine is one of the ethnic groups in Myanmar, and the Rakhine mostly live in the Rakhine State. Rakhine society is clothed in the cultural garb of Buddhism and family orientation. Even though Christian

32 The Rakhine (also known as Arakanese) is one of the people groups in Myanmar. The Rakhine is also the name of a state in Northwestern Myanmar where three million Rakhine people live. The people are predominantly Buddhist, while the Rohingya, another people group in the state, are mostly Muslim. In 2020, the Rakhine State conflicted with the Myanmar army and some one hundred thousand Rakhines were displaced. See https://www.unicef.org/myanmar/rakhine-state

missions have been in Myanmar for two centuries, there were fewer than twenty Rakhine Buddhist converts in 2003, according to the oral report of the Rakhine Baptist Convention.

Rakhine Missions Band for Christ (RMBC) is a group of Buddhist-background believers with the vision to communicate the gospel to the Rakhine people to achieve their contextual conversion. The plan for RMBC is to build (i.e., plant) contextual congregations (indigenous churches) so that in time converts will be equipped to become mission-minded followers of Jesus Christ in fulfilling the Bible's Great Commission in Myanmar.

From vision and passion to action, RMBC has developed an indigenous strategy that underscores the idea that the communication of the gospel is not a single event but a series of communicational events in a spiritual journey. The conversion process is depicted as having three dimensions: awareness, conversion, and incorporation into the church.

In the dimension of awareness, the first question we raise to Rakhine Buddhists is, What does it mean for you to be an authentic Buddhist? Over many conversations, this gentle inquiry leads to gospel communication with our Buddhist friends. RMBC helps them to see that Jesus can be their liberator from *samsara* (the endless cycle of death and rebirth). Thus acquainting them with the truth of Jesus sets them free from their bondage. During this stage, RMBC communicates the foundational message of the gospel through illustrations from 550 stories in Buddhism that God is the savior from the cycle of samsara through God's mighty act of reconciliation in Jesus Christ. These stories are from the Jataka tales, a collection based on the life of the Buddha.[33]

The objective of this second stage, the dimension of conversion, is to facilitate conversion within their sociocultural context. Because communication is not an event but a process, conversion takes an indeterminate period, from weeks to months or even a year. When potential converts are convinced they need Jesus, RMBC suggests they enter a relationship with Jesus. However, instead of separating Buddhist converts from their community, RMBC encourages them to remain within their cultural community, retaining their Buddhist identity while being faithful to

33 E.B. Cowell, *The Jataka, or Stories of the Buddha's Former Births*, trans. Robert Chalmers, vol. 1, (Cambridge: Cambridge University Press, 1895).

Christ. Through this contextual process, the converts' realization of the gospel has the potential to move rapidly from individuals to families to the community and transforms them from the inside.

For the dimension of incorporation into the body of Christ, discipleship takes place in a small group. As converts need to grow in their new faith, RMBC equips them through the word of God to meet their needs and serve by introducing new people to the Christian faith. In this phase, Buddhist converts are trained through informal teaching rather than formal training.

The reader may be interested to know that Rakhine Buddhist society, through the ministries of RMBC, currently has churches in ten of the seventeen townships in Rakhine State. This translates into more than one thousand Buddhist converts who are following Jesus Christ in their sociocultural context without losing their Rakhine identity.

Conclusion

It is indeed encouraging that church and mission leaders and mission partners are now committed toward mission with Buddhists all over the country. Until recently, churches and mission organizations followed traditional Western mission principles and approaches. Consequently, the estimated Buddhist convert membership of Christian churches in Myanmar still forms a tiny minority.

Surprisingly, unawareness of the missiological mistakes of the past and, more critically, a general lack of interest among churches in the sociocultural and religious history of the Myanmar people still linger. If the mission work for Myanmar Buddhists is to be effective, church and mission leaders, mission partners, and volunteers must reexamine the scriptural concept of ecclesia, which, arguably, is the primary agent God chooses in fulfilling his Great Commission. Only with a full understanding of Myanmar ecclesiology can the church be relevantly reconstructed.

The global pandemic has impacted politics, education, economy, friendships, and religions. In the Christian ecclesiological context, this unprecedented global pandemic has brought the cancellation of worship services, closure of Sunday schools, and cancellation of pilgrimages, observances, and festivals. Many churches showed resilience by offering worship through live stream, demonstrating that if we take a serious look at the scriptural concept of ecclesia and remember what Jesus told Peter—that he would build his church with those who confess him as Christ the savior and that the gates of Hades would not overcome it (Matt 16:18)—then we will behold Myanmar Buddhist converts worshipping him in their own language and expressing their new faith in their own cultural forms not just as a single event on Sunday but every day, seven days a week. And, in the name of Jesus Christ, these converts will be saying about Jesus Christ, *Sadu, Sadu,* and *Sadu*.[34]

Bibliography

Atkerson, Steve. *House Church: Simple, Strategy, Scriptural*. Atlanta, GA: New Testament Reformation Fellowship, 2008.

Budijanto, Bambang, Todd, Scott and Yeadon, Mark. *Relentless Hope: The Unstoppable Movement of Disciple-Making Communities*. Ontario, Canada: Compassion International, 2010.

Eilers, Franz-Josef. *Communicating in Ministry and Mission: An Introduction to Pastoral and Evangelizing Communication*. Bangalore, India: Asian Trading Corporation, 2004.

Gezt, Gene A. *Sharpening the Focus of the Church*. Wheaton, IL: Victor, 1988.

Hiebert, Paul G. *Anthropological Reflections on Missiological Issues*. Grand Rapids, MI: Baker Books, 1988.

———. "Conversion and Worldview Transformation." *International Journal of Frontier Missions* 14 no. 2 (April-June 1997), 84–86.

Jenson, Ron, and Jim Stevens. *Dynamics of Church Growth*. Grand Rapids, MI: Baker Books, 1981.

Kraft, Charles H. *Christianity in Culture: A Study in Dynamic Biblical Theologizing in Cross-Cultural Perspective*. Maryknoll, NY: Orbis Books, 1978.

Lim, David. "Radical Contextualization of Communicating the Gospel to the Buddhists." In *Sharing Jesus in the Buddhist World*, edited by David S. Lim and Steve Spaudling. Pasadena, CA: William Carey Library, 2004.

Lubeigt, Guy. "Myanmar: A Country Modeled by Buddhist Traditions." In *Traditions of Knowledge in Southeast Asia: Part 2*, edited by Myanmar Historical Committee, Yangon: University Press, 2004.

34 "Sadu" is the Pali translation of "Lord;" the Buddhist canon or *Tipitaka* is written in Pali, an Indo-Aryan, liturgical language.

McGavran, Donald A. *The Bridges of God: A Study in the Strategy of Missions*. New York: Friendship Press, 1955.

McLuhan, Marshall. *Understanding Media: The Extensions of Man*. New York: McGraw-Hill, 1964.

Moltmann, Jurgen. *The Church in the Power of the Spirit: A Contribution to Messianic Ecclesiology*. New York: Harper and Row, 1993.

Ngun Ling, Samuel. *Communicating Christ in Myanmar: Issues, Interactions and Perspectives*. Yangon, Myanmar: ATEM, 2005.

Nyunt, Peter Thein. "Toward a Paradigm of Christian Communication for the Bhama Buddhists in Yangon City." PhD diss., SAIACS, 2010.

Shwe, Maung Wa, *Burma Baptist Chronicles*. Rangoon: Burma Baptist Convention, 1963.

Smalley, William A. "Cultural Implications of an Indigenous Church." In *Perspectives on the World Christian Movement: A Reader*, edited by Ralph D. Winter and Steve C. Hawthorne. Pasadena, CA: William Carey Library, 1992.

Snyder, Howard A. *Liberating the Church: The Ecology of Church and Kingdom*. Westmont, IL: InterVarsity Press, 1983.

———. *The Problem of Wine Skins: Church Structure in a Technological Age*. Westmont, IL: InterVarsity Press, 1975.

Soe, Tin. "An Economic Interpretation of Some Myanmar Traditional Concepts in the Context of Globalization." In *Traditions of Knowledge in Southeast Asia: Part 3*, edited by Myanmar Historical Committee. Yangon: University of Yangon Press, 2005.

Thittila, Ashin. *Essential Themes of Buddhist Lectures*. Yangon: Department of Religious Affairs, 2000.

Tillich, Paul. *Theology of Culture*. Oxford: Oxford University Press, 1959.

Van Engen, Charles E. *The Growth of the True Church: An Analysis of the Ecclesiology of Church Growth Theory*. Amsterdam, The Netherlands: Rodopi, 1981.

Van Rheenen, Gailyn. *Missions: Biblical Foundations and Contemporary Strategies*. Grand Rapids, MI: Zondervan, 1996.

Watson, David C.K. *I Believe in the Church*. Grand Rapids, MI: Eerdmans, 1982.

7

COMMUNICATING CHRIST IN NEPAL—PROSPECTS AND CHALLENGES

by Indra B. Rakhal

Introduction

The current multilingual and multiethnic demographic of Nepal can be traced to the early migration of people from Tibet and northern India, the Indo-Aryans.[1] Many Tibetans came in the late 1950s, but people from northern India came even earlier.[2] Today, Nepali (Deva Naagrik) is the official language; however, 123 local dialects are spoken among 125 caste and ethnic groups.[3] While the human population is only thirty million, there are thirty-three million gods and goddesses.[4] Hindu temples and shrines and Buddhists pagodas and stupas feature prominently in the nation's cultural and tourist heritage. More than 81 percent of Nepal's population is Hindu, along with 9 percent Buddhist, 4.4 percent Muslim, 3 percent Kirat (indigenous religion), and 1.4 percent Christian.[5]

---

1 Hom Nath Gartaula and Anke Niehof, "Migration to and from the Nepal Terai: Shifting Movements and Motives," *The South Asianist* 2 no. 2 (June 2023): 29–51.

2 Gartaula and Niehof, "Migration."

3 International Work Group for Indigenous Affairs, "Indigenous People in Nepal," *IWGIA,* accessed April 20, 2023, https://www.iwgia.org/en/nepal.html

4 Pandit Dasa, "The 33 Million Gods of Hinduism," *Huffpost*. August 6, 2012, https://www.huffpost.com/entry/the-33-million-demigods-o_b_1737207

5 Central Intelligence Agency, "Nepal: Religions," *The World Factbook*, accessed April 25. 2023, https://www.cia.gov/the-world-factbook/field/religions/

Prior to the eighteenth century, Nepal consisted of a collection of petty kingdoms: "There were 22 kingdoms in Karnali, 24 in Gandaki, 13 in the Kathmandu Valley, and two consortia, Rai and Limbu, in the east, making a total of 54 petty kingdoms."[6] Each kingdom was governed by a caste-based hierarchy and had its own cultural dynamics. In 1743, King Prithivi Narayan Shah of Gorkha unified the petty kingdoms under his vision of a greater, united Nepal.

An important reality in terms of Christian missionizing is that Nepal had been a sovereign country since its inception, so the Nepalese people were spared the trauma of colonial oppression experienced by many Asian nations. Most of the ethnic indigenous people live in small, segregated communities. They are interdependent for socio-religious duties and have shared values based on their economic well-being. They have a deep sense of communal solidarity. For example, when observing the annual ritual of respecting ancestors, the community comes together (as at weddings) to help, give gifts, and the like.

The earliest record of Christianity entering Nepal was February 1707, when Roman Catholic fathers were granted permission to stay and propagate the faith by the Malla king, who ruled the Kathmandu Valley area.[7] The king, Prithivi Narayan Shah, issued the fathers with a decree titled "Decree of Freedom of Conscience," apparently because a friendship had developed between the king and Father Angelo.[8] The latter had treated and cured the king's brother from injuries incurred in the Battle of Kirtipur.

However, this friendship did not last. The Catholic leaders were later suspected of forging links with the British EIC, whereupon the king became

6 Rajendra K. Rongong, *Early Churches in Nepal*, (Kathmandu, Nepal: Ekta Book Distributors, 2012), 22.

7 There are records indicating that a Portuguese Jesuit priest, Father Juan Cabral, entered Nepal in 1628; however, these records lack substantiation. See: *Apostolic Vicariate of Nepal:* https://www.ucanews.com/directory/dioceses/nepal-nepal/378

8 According to Rajandra Kumar Rongong, twenty-nine Capuchin priests (Roman Catholics) lived within the Kathmandu alley from 1715–1769. Newar King Jaya Ranjit Malla and two other Newar kings gave them permission to stay and work.

aggressively hostile to the Catholic missionaries and banished them from the country. The local Christian converts were given a stark choice: either give up their newfound Christian religion (and revert to Hinduism) or leave the country. Fifty-four local Christians left the country, and Nepal remained closed to the gospel for almost two hundred years.[9]

The second phase of gospel entry into Nepal involved Nepali Christians who had been converted in Darjeeling and Kalimpong, India in the 1890s. The Nepali leader of these converts, *Padari* (Pastor) Ganga Prasad Pradhan, was born into a Christian family in Darjeeling. Under Ganga Prasad's initiative, the Gorkha Mission was established in 1892 with the help of David Mikhia.[10] Ganga Prasad translated the Bible into the Nepali language and produced Christian literature.[11]

This was perhaps the first example of how Nepali Christians witnessed to fellow Nepalis and formed house churches, first in Nautunna (India, near the Nepal border), then in Nepal. As the house church movement grew, two notable Nepali converts, Tir Bahadur Dewan and Jagat Bahadur, provided leadership to the churches. Later, through the initiative of successive Nepali converts, the Nepal Border Fellowship was established in 1973.[12]

In this chapter, I present and discuss a four-part communication and missional framework that I have developed for witnessing to the Nepali people. As a prelude to the framework, I share the Nepali perceptions of Christians, then proceed to discuss how contextualization can be applied to the Nepali situation.

I use empirical information collected from textual sources but primarily draw on observations from my three-decade-long service in

---

9 Rongong, *Early Churches,* 22, 26.

10 Rongong, *Early Churches,* 44.
David Mikhia's parents were working with the Church of Scotland missionaries in Darjeeling (in the State of West Bengal, India on the border of Nepal). They set up a dispensary in Raxaul at the Nepal Border where David Mikhia worked and witnessed to Nepalese at the border.

11 Jonathan Lindell, *Nepal, and The Gospel of God* (Kathmandu: The United Mission to Nepal and Pilgrims Book House, 1977), 75–78.

12 Lindell, *Nepal and The Gospel of God.*

Nepal as a mission director and community worker, participating in weekly church services and discussions with attendees and coworkers both from within and without my organization.[13]

Nepali Views about Christianity

Three dominant views of Christianity are present in Nepal today.

First, even though Nepal was not colonized by Western powers, many Nepalis regard Christianity as a colonial religion.[14] According to Nepali scholars and leaders, Christian-based workers in social work, education, and health are determined to enter poor and outcast communities to colonize and proselytize.[15] Balasundaram argued that the missionary and colonization hegemonies in India are two sides of the same coin. This view was supported in 2012 by Rongong, who used the historical record of the fifty-four Nepali Christian converts expelled by King Prithivi Narayan Shah as his argument.[16] Until now, this has been the most prevalent view in the minds of the Nepalese. An extension of this view is the xenophobic sentiment that Christianity is a foreign religion, as reflected in Ram Bahadur Gurung's strong statement, "I am Nepali Hindu, not *Belayeti*," meaning British Christian.[17]

The second position on Christianity emanates from the Hindu religious ideology of caste, which is deeply rooted in the Hindu community.[18] Christianity is a religion for the untouchable caste, not for the high caste Hindus and Brahmins; therefore, Hindu Brahmins should not have socio-religious relations with these "out-caste" people.[19]

13 Since 1991, I have served in the indigenous mission Asia Evangelistic Fellowship in Nepal.

14 Franklyn J. Balasundaram, *Contemporary Asian Christian Theology* (Bangalore, India: ISPCK, 1995), 26–27.

15 Balasundaram, *Contemporary Asian Christian Theology.*

16 Balasundaram, *Contemporary Asian Christian Theology.*

17 Much of the information in this chapter is from my own field notes taken in Nepal during 2005–2008.

18 Mahadev Desai, *My Experiments with Truths, An Autobiography* (Mumbai: Jaico Publishing House 2008), 39.

19 Brahmins are the highest caste in Hindu society. This word must be differentiated from Brahman—the creator god in the Hindu trinity.

Third, Christianity is considered an unclean religion. Hindus say that Christianity is *gaikhane dharma* (the religion of beef eaters). Hindus worship cows and regard them as manifestations of the goddess Laxmi Devi. The cow is a sacred animal, and its urine is used in various purification rites and rituals in Hinduism. It is also a symbol of prosperity and wealth and is worshipped during the Deepawali festival.[20] These religio-cultural beliefs should be clearly understood by those undertaking gospel ministry in Nepal.

Challenges of Contextualization

Contextualization is an applied methodology for sharing the gospel in diverse sociocultural settings. Its core purpose is to communicate the gospel with clarity and effectiveness in cultural contexts. Contextualization in the field of evangelism does not presuppose a definitive interpretation. The interpretation of the Bible is filtered through cultural lenses, so it is dynamic. Kraft argued that God is the originator of culture; therefore, he does not deny the essence of culture.[21]

Having asserted the need for contextualization, I now touch on two potential dangers if contextualization in the Nepali context is not handled with cultural wisdom and biblical understanding.

Syncretism

"Syncretism" is defined by social scientists as an amalgamation of elements from two or more religious traditions, ideologies, or value systems.[22] Although the meaning of syncretism appears to be neutral, the term takes on a negative connotation among missiologists and theologians as something bordering on heresy or "sub-Christian."[23]

---

20 This festival is also known as Diwali.

21 Charles H. Kraft, *Christianity in Culture* (New York: Orbis Books Maryknoll, 1980).

22 Gailyn Van Rheenen, "Modern and Postmodern Syncretism in Theology and Missions," in *The Holy Spirit and Mission Dynamics*, ed. C. Douglas McConnell (Pasadena, CA: William. Carey Library, 1997), 164–207.

23 Mark Mullins, "Syncretistic Movements," in *Dictionary of Asian Christianity*, ed. Scott W. Sunquist (Grand Rapids, MI: Eerdmans, 2001), 809–810.

A careful application of contextualization is needed when sharing the gospel among multireligious and multicultural communities. Devotees of Hinduism worship *tetishkoti devata*, which refers to thirty-three million gods and goddesses. It would be a wrong perception if an evangelist unwittingly presented Jesus Christ as one of many in the pantheon of Hindu gods. The paramountcy of Jesus, as recorded in the Bible, must be clarified, and it will likely take time for Hindus to see and realize the all-embracive work of Christ before they can accept Jesus's pre-eminence as Lord.

Also, just as Christians have holy communion, Hindus have a similar practice in which the Hindu priest uses a sacred bread called *manobhog* (a rice pudding) and *panchamreet* (a sweetened drink made of sugar and milk). I regard this Hindu practice positively because it can serve as a useful point of contact to explain the Christian sacrament as well as the gospel. However, the pastor must clarify what the emblems stand for in the Christian faith to avoid syncretistic interpretation, focusing on the death of Christ who, in love, died as a sacrifice to deliver us and rose again (1 Cor 11:20–30).

Many Hindus have misconceptions about the God described in the Bible as a trinity. Hindus worship their own triune gods named Bramaha, Bishnu, and Mahesor,[24] and a clear explanation is needed to show the differences because of the Christian belief in God as one being with three personae, whereas the Hindu trinity consists of three separate beings.

Some Hindus who practice animism (the belief in spirits being incarnate in nature) offer animals as sacrifices to seek relief from the powers of evil spirits. To these people, pastors can teach about the sacrifice of Jesus Christ; however, the pastors must demonstrate that Christ died for the sin of the world and that sacrifices of all kinds are no longer necessary (Heb 10: 5–7). Without clarity in teaching, the sacrifice of animals may continue, even among Hindus who have become Christians, thus creating a practice called Christopaganism.[25]

---

24 Also known as Brahman, Vishnu, and Shiva.

25 William Madsen, *Christo-Paganism: A Study of Mexican Religious Syncretism* (New Orleans: Tulane University, 1957).

Secularism-Cum-Liberalism

The Nepali Christian community has recently engaged with discourse on secularism with a view to promoting an individual's right to espouse their own religion. This discussion is due in part to increasing pressure created by the non-Christian community (Orthodox Hindu) and the Hindu religion-based political party. The downside of this is that some in the Christian community, while advocating secularism (the government's view), have unwittingly yielded to nominal Christian living (i.e., compromising the faith and not practicing the Christian tenets).[26] Other Christians have espoused prosperity theology (i.e., the teaching that when you become a Christian, you will be wealthy), finding it a good alternative, since this teaching is not too demanding for being a true Christian.

It is important that converted believers of Christ have a "born again" experience (John 3: 3), thereby breaking free from the chains of bondage of their past immoral practices.[27] By "immoral," I refer to practices of the Mugu and Sherpa people, in which a form of polygamous culture exists (i.e., a woman can have more than one husband). Also, in the Magar culture, the dowry system during marriages has caused severe psychological and social unrest, including suicides and criminal activities.[28]

The goal of our ministry is to ensure that once people come to Christ, they are discipled in the Bible and are free from such practices after conversion. Newness of living that is righteous in word and deed is the desired outcome (Col 3:1–13). Biblical (moral and ethical) values must be the guiding principles. A converted believer must encounter Christ daily and live under the Bible's instruction.

While the gospel is a powerful vehicle for holistic transformation and conversion, the Christian life is "a redemptive journey."[29] The apostle Paul wrote, "Do not conform to the pattern of the world but be transformed by the renewing of your mind" (Rom 12:2).

---

26 Mangal M. Maharjan, *New Testament-Based Church* (Kathmandu: Patan Koinonia Church, 2011), 68

27 Maharjan, *New Testament-Based Church.*

28 Field notes, 2019.

29 Edmond Chan, *Mentoring Paradigms: Reflection on Mentoring, Leadership and Discipleship* (Singapore: Covenant Evangelical Free Church, 2008), 112.

Sharing the Gospel: A Four-Part Framework

I now share a framework that I have in my communication to people in Nepal.

Understanding the People

To reach a community for Christ, an emic cultural experience (i.e., one with a native point of view) is necessary so that the internalization of socio-religious-cultural values and norms can take place. Every cultural group has its way of functioning. When a pastor or Christian intends to share the gospel, the first step is to enter the cultural community tentatively and not assume that they have the right to teach their way of life, but to take the posture of a humble student of anthropology exploring the sociocultural values and norms of the group.

The strategy of evangelism must be based in accordance with the listening group's geographical and sociocultural specificity. I shun the idea of Christians likening mission to a tourist's adventure. The would-be missionary should be prepared to embrace the incarnational principle physically, psychologically, and emotionally.[30] This necessitates a genuine commitment to living among the people in the field for an extended time.

The apostle Paul followed this strategy in his three missionary journeys in Asia Minor (Acts 13–15; 18–21). Over the past five years, as I sought to reach out to various groups in the West Nepal region (especially among the Magar people), my team members and I spent approximately one and a half years understanding the Magar community.

The preliminary step I undertook was to gather vital information about the community. Face-to-face survey was one of the methods I used to explore the community and understand its degree of homogeneity or heterogeneity, relationships, literacy rates, income resources, religion, and languages and dialects spoken. In addition, I sought an understanding of cultural taboos, types of families (nuclear or extended), levels of

30 To serve in an incarnational way is to follow in the footsteps of Jesus, who left the glory of heaven to come into the world and enter its culture and constraints. This requires patience and foregoing one's ego.

friendliness, and power relations. Such information was crucial to formulating an effective strategy.

Understanding values, customs, and beliefs: The most sensitive issue in Nepali society, based on a sacred and profane principle of Hinduism, is the caste system.[31] In Hinduism, people are divided into four main social classes (or *varna*): Brahmin, Kshatriya, Vaishya, and Sudra. The Brahmin caste is seen as the high caste, and Brahmins rule the others in all aspects of society. Sudra is the lowest caste and subject to all kinds of discrimination. In my experience, lower caste people accept Jesus more readily than higher caste people because the lower castes are discriminated against and isolated; therefore, they see Christianity as a way of being considered equal in God's eyes.

An important consideration in our ministry is that, while Nepalis generally live peaceably as a common unit, Brahmins are not comfortable with other ethnic people groups, whom they disparagingly refer to as *matwali* (alcohol drinkers) or meat eaters (most Brahmins are vegetarians) and therefore think of as impure. This culture of exclusion normally means that in mission work, a non-Brahmin preacher, teacher, or priest would not be accepted. Thankfully, many Brahmins have come to know Jesus Christ through prominent Brahmin evangelists, pastors, and church planters in the Nepali community. Some examples of Brahmin Christian leaders are Reverend Resham Raj Paudel, Reverend Dr. Simon Pandy, and Dr. Bal Krishna Sharma.

Fortunately, the other communities in these regions generally live in peaceful social relationships despite their intercultural diversity in dialects, customs, and values. However, another regional sentiment affects our evangelism efforts, especially as we try to establish church communities. Geographically, Nepal is divided into five regions: west, mid-west, far west, east, and central. While the people in these heterogeneous communities are attracted to messengers of the gospel from their own region, the church that we establish in any region should not cater to just one ethnic entity, and it should be accessible to all people in the region. This runs

31 This social stratification system is borrowed from the classical Hindu system from India. The caste system was outlawed in Nepal in 1963, although it is still practiced in many parts of Nepal, especially in remote villages.

counter to the generally accepted mission model known as the "homogeneous unit principle," where people of the church are encouraged to be of the same ethnic nationality.[32] I appreciate that the homogeneous unit principle can be useful, but in the Nepali context, the church, when established and recognized, must be considered part of the whole community.[33]

Being the Right Messenger

A Christlike missionary who is full of love, truth, and respect for people will be welcomed in Nepal (John 1:17; Col 4:6; 1 Pet 2:17). From my field visits, I found that speaking the local dialect, sometimes referred to as the mother tongue, helps to create an instant bond and ensure a sense of positivity. I experienced this bond when I accompanied Pastor Bir Bahadur Ale (an evangelist and church planter instrumental in influencing many Magars for Jesus) to his Magar community. Even though Ale was not highly educated or politically influential, he had an extraordinary ability to make friends and win the people's respect. When I asked Ale, "How do you share the gospel and influence so many Magars to Christ?", his simple response was, "I have been working with my own people, and I speak in their mother dialect with its typical tone, known as Magar dialect. When I share, everyone is attentive; and when the opportunity comes to present the gospel, they accept the Lord Jesus Christ gladly (some with initial reservation). Those who do not accept also say to me '*Feri Rahani Hai*' [come again]."

Similarly, a friend of mine, Pastor Laxmi Lal Magharjan, who is part of the Newari community, is one of the most successful pastors among the Newaris. Hundreds of Newari people have come to Christ Jesus in churches established in the Newari community. I observed and learned

32 Donald McGavran, *Understanding Church Growth* (Grand Rapids, MI: Eerdmans, 1990).McGavran argued that missionaries should use the homogeneous unit principle to present the gospel to people. McGavran's understanding of a homogeneous unit is "a group of people that have ethnic, linguistic, social, educational, or vocational similarities." In terms of a church congregation, ethnic, social, and educational commonalities are important. People feel more comfortable when they are part of a group and they don't have to cross racial, linguistic or class barriers.

33 This is to avoid conflict and ensure social cohesion.

from his ministry that he uses his mother tongue and the Newari Bible while preaching and nurturing his congregation.

The use of native languages in the mission field is clearly an effective tool. It conveys sentimental cultural tones, not merely vernacular words. When teachers and preachers apply native vernacular dialects, they create a friendly environment and turn hostility into harmony. A similar situation of Paul's preaching is recorded in the Bible: "When they heard him [Paul] speak to them in Aramaic, they became very quiet" (Acts 2:14–28).

The titles "pastor," "evangelist," and "missionary" can carry negative connotations because they convey overtones of colonial missionary history, as even in uncolonized Nepal, there are residual sentiments of negativity from the early history with the Catholic fathers.[34] This reminded me of a conversation I had with a schoolteacher in Rampur Village, Sindhuli District who did not know I was a Christian missionary. He said, "I also do not like Hindu rituals, particularly death rituals; if I become a Christian, what are the benefits?"[35] After I tried to explain the gospel of salvation through believing in Christ Jesus, he then probed, "What is your profession?" I was momentarily unable to answer because I knew the implications of my answer. Thankfully, because I am also employed in the educational profession, I could honestly give him an acceptable answer to his question. This incident encouraged my coworkers and me to consider training bi-vocational missionaries who can be more acceptable to the Nepali community.

Using Relevant Messages

In the Bible, the Sadducees were offended by the concept of the resurrection of the dead, yet Peter used this concept sensitively, drawing on the Old Testament prophecy of David in the proclamation of the gospel (Acts 2:22–35). The truth of the message never changes, but we can change the examples, illustrations, sentences, and phrases or add historical or other contexts to ensure listener receptivity and diffuse any offense. It is all about linguistic dynamics. The reciprocity of communication takes place within

---

34 Mangal M. Maharjan, *Comparative Study of Hinduism and Christianity*, (Kathmandu: Ekta Books Distributors, 2010), 70.

35 Field notes, 2007.

cultural symbolic meanings. Specifically, Nepali Hindus take offense when preachers use terms and phrases such as "church" and "God is love." Therefore, in place of "church," we say *mandali* (a place to gather after we are free from bondage) or "house of prayer." Instead of "God is love" (more on this below), we use the term "creator God," and we use "mercy" or "kindness" in place of "love" because the Hindu concept of love is an abstract term, and sometimes love is categorized as an illusion or *maya*.

The concept of God: As mentioned earlier, Hindus believe in polytheism (a multiplicity of gods) and espouse pantheism (the belief that gods dwell in everything and live in every material and natural object and in human beings). The Bible clearly spells out the monotheistic nature of God and that he is omnipresent (Ps 139:7–10). God the Almighty can be everywhere at the same time, but God is not in everything. "The God who made the world and everything in it, is the Lord of heaven and earth, does not live in temples made by human hands" (Acts 17:24). Therefore, while sharing the gospel, as pointed out above, it is better to replace "God" with "creator of the universe" or "God the father." I have also found that "savior" and "redeemer" in relation to Jesus Christ (who is the almighty deliverer of all evil forces) are very effective.

The miracles from the ministry of the Lord Jesus Christ and the teaching passages from Jesus in John 8:32 ("the truth shall set you free") and Matthew 11:28 ("I will give you rest") are powerful in sharing the gospel. It is not meaningful to just preach about God's divine attributes; the promise of liberation from Jesus backed up by the miracles of deliverance makes a difference to Nepali ears.

The concept of sin: In Hinduism, the concept of sin is absent. Sin is just an error, and even though it may involve bad deeds, such as abandoning the forefathers' customs, cheating, speaking evil, and murder, the ultimate sin is ignorance of one's own godhood or *brahman*.

The concept of salvation: Salvation, *moksha*, is a Hindu form of freedom or liberation from the bondage of the cycle of birth and rebirth. It is also called reincarnation from death and rebirth (and from a lower-caste to a higher-caste family). There are three ways of obtaining salvation: *karma margh*, by performing good works based on the doctrine of deeds; *bhakti margh*, by devotion and repeating chants to the name of Ram, Shiva, and other deities; and *gyana margh*, which comes through attaining self-realization.

In sharing the gospel, my coworkers and I emphasize freedom, liberation, and redemption, which are relevant words for Hindus. The sacrifice of Jesus Christ for the salvation of humankind is eye-opening for most Hindus. The image of Jesus Christ's crucifixion on the cross is highly revered by Hindus because it brings out deep feelings. Many Nepali Hindu people have accepted the Lord Jesus Christ after watching the famous "Jesus films." Most Nepalis in villages are oral and visual learners, so they are attracted to Jesus's crucifixion. I have observed Hindu villagers breaking out in loud, emotional outbursts while watching a Jesus film. As a result, many have come to know Christ personally.

Using the Appropriate Approach: Word and Deed

Side-by-side with sharing the word, applying practical assistance to meet the felt needs of people plays a bridging role in reaching the Hindu and Buddhist communities in Nepal. The felt needs approach was used by the Lord Jesus Christ while he was telling people about entering the kingdom of God. He turned water into wine at Cana in Galilee (John 2:9), rectifying the scarcity of wine at the wedding. He fed five thousand hungry people, healed those who were ill, and delivered the oppressed (Matt 14:4). Later, he linked these felt needs to explain the kingdom of God: "I am the bread of life; whoever comes to me will never go hungry, and whoever believes will never be thirsty" (John 6:35, 47). Thus meeting the felt needs in the mission field prepares the way to gain the community's trust and respect.

In the Nepali context, there is a great need to extend support to orphans as well as poor and destitute children. Other programs that can be offered are literacy programs, humanitarian works, support during natural calamities, and livelihood projects. During the major earthquake in 2015, when my coworkers and I visited an affected area, bringing food and medicine, one of the villagers was so moved that he asked us, "Why did you come all the way . . . even my relatives close by did not come?"[36]

Conclusion

Drawing from my three decades of mission experience, in this chapter, I presented my four-part communication and missional framework for

36 Field notes, 2015.

witnessing to the Nepali people. This framework consists of understanding people, being the right messenger, using relevant messages, and using the approach of word and deed.

Christian mission must be, in the words of Jesus, "powerful in word and deed" (Luke 24:19). I believe God has a great plan to transform the lives of the people and develop the nation of Nepal. We, as followers of Jesus, must follow his purpose, share his words, and live out his life in this nation.

Bibliography

Balasundaram, Franklyn J. *Contemporary Asian Christian Theology*. Bangalore, India: ISPCK, 1995.

Chan, Edmond. *Mentoring Paradigms: Reflection on Mentoring, Leadership and Discipleship*. Singapore: Covenant Evangelical Free Church, 2008.

Dasa, Pandit. "The 33 Million Gods of Hinduism." *Huffpost*. August 6, 2012. https://www.huffpost.com/entry/the-33-million-demigods-o_b_1737207

Desai, Mahadev. *My Experiments with Truths, An Autobiography.* Mumbai: Jaico Publishing House, 2008.

Gartaula, Hom Nath and Anke Niehof. "Migration to and from the Nepal Terai: Shifting Movements and Motives." *The South Asianist* 2, no. 2 (June 2023): 29–51.

IWGIA. "Indigenous People in Nepal," Accessed April 20, 2023. https://www.iwgia.org/en/nepal.html

Kraft, Charles. H. *Christianity in Culture.* Maryknoll, New York: Orbis Books, 1980.

Lindell, Jonathan. *Nepal and The Gospel of God.* Kathmandu: The United Mission to Nepal and Pilgrim's Book House, 1997.

Madsen, William. *Christo-Paganism: A Study of Mexican Religious Syncretism*. New Orleans: Tulane University, 1957.

McGavran, Donald A. *Understanding Church Growth*. Grand Rapids, MI: Eerdmans, 1990.

Maharjan, Mangal Man. *New Testament-based Church*. Kathmandu: Patan Koinonia Church, 2011.

———. *Comparative Study of Hinduism and Christianity*, Kathmandu: Ekta Books Distributors, 2010.

Mullins, Mark R. "Syncretistic Movements." In *Dictionary of Asian Christianity*, edited by Scott W. Sunquist. Grand Rapids, MI: Eerdmans, 2001.

Rakhal, Indra B. "Motivating Factors on Conversion of Religion into Christianity (A Case Study of Christians in Saibu Bhaisepati VBC, Ward:3, 4 Lalitpur District)." MPhil diss., Tribhuvan University, 2012.

———. *The Biblical Foundation of God's Great Commission.* Kathmandu: Asia Educational Foundation Nepal, 2022.

Rongong, Rajendra K. *Early Churches in Nepal.* Kathmandu: Ekta Book Distributors, 2012.

The World Factbook. "Nepal: Religions." Accessed April 25. 2023, https://www.cia.gov/the-world-factbook/field/religions/.

UCA News. "Apostolic Vicariate of Nepal." Accessed April 30, 2023. https://www.ucanews.com/directory/dioceses/nepal-nepal/378.

Van Rheenen, Gailyn. "Modern and Postmodern Syncretism in Theology and Missions." In *The Holy Spirit and Mission Dynamics*, edited by C. Douglas McConnell. Pasadena, CA: William Carey University Libraries, 1997.

8

CREATING CHRIST COMMUNITIES IN THE HINDU-INDIAN CONTEXT

by Anil Yesudas

Introduction

My purpose in this chapter is to demonstrate how biblical contextualization is used in sharing Christ with Hindu-Indian communities both in India and in the US. After two decades of ministry to Hindu-Indians, I have learned to use the *satsang* (fellowship of the truth in Sanskrit) as a platform for communicating Christ to Hindu-Indians.[1]

Before explaining the *satsang* approach, I provide some background material on Christian contextualization and how it underpins my approach and practice in communicating with Hindu-Indians.

Christian Contextualization

God has chosen to communicate to human beings through the sixty-six books of the Bible and the process of canonization (how the books in the Bible were determined as authentic and authoritative). When we interact with the Bible, we are interacting with God's word, and reciprocal communication between man and God ensues. The Bible is set in history. God has entered, acted, and communicated in historical time and space.

---

1 *Satsang* is made up of two words from Sanskrit—*sat* (truth) and *sang* (to be associated with). It is a devotional platform where spiritual activities take place.

Biblical contextualization (how the Bible is interpreted and applied in a particular cultural context) may initially begin with an individual, but it will subsequently develop only within practicing communities: "The hermeneutical task is not a private or purely individual one, it must be undertaken within the community of believers. Therefore, contextualization must take place within the Church before it can be faithfully interpreted to the world."[2]

Nicholls also cautions those who tend to rush into contextualization and, in their zeal, ignore the generally accepted evangelical hermeneutical principles. Hermeneutics is interpreting and understanding what others have said and written, and, as a field of study, it originated in interpreting the Bible. God has spoken in the past, and he continues to communicate in the present through his revealed word. The writer of the epistle of Hebrews states how God has always been reaching out to humankind. In the past, God communicated through his messengers multiple times in multiple manners. His final communication is through the person and work of his eternal son, the anointed Lord Shri[3] Jesus, who himself is God incarnate. In the person of Lord Jesus, the medium and the message merge into one another.

Contextualization as practiced by conservative faith communities, such as my own evangelical tradition, is best done, as Bruce Nicholls insists, "within the Church." I believe the best framework to communicate faith is in the context of corporate devotion. Worshipping in the contextual framework of a particular people group helps in the communication of his unchanging message to those who live within a set of cultural values. Thus contextualization must be practiced *within a community of believers* over time for it to communicate the biblical message. We cannot perform contextualization as a superficial momentary drama to entice people. It must become the consistent primary lifestyle of the individual *bhakta* (devotion) and the *bhakta-mandali* (circle of devotees).

2 Bruce Nicholls, "A Living Theology for Asian Churches: Some Reflections on the Contextualization-Syncretism Debate," in *The Bible and Theology in an Asian Context, ed.* Bong Rin Ro and Ruth Eshenaur (Taichung, Taiwan: Asia Theological Association, 1984), 134.

3 *Shri* is a generic title of respect.

Worship can be offered by an individual, family, or community. Many kinds of worship are accepted by God. However, not all kinds of worship are acceptable. The worship of Abel was accepted, but Cain's was rejected. For acceptable worship, the object of worship should be none other than the true creator God, and the worshipper must be sincere.

A local church typically begins with the divine calling of a particular individual who is engaged in worship. When that individual hears the call of God, they begin to form a small core group. The initial core group may be the family and others who have heard the divine call, and they come together for worship. Over time, a small body of believers is formed as a local church/ecclesia that offers rhythmic corporate worship to the triune God. A local church can offer worship in spirit and truth to the true triune God in a particular cultural context as the Lord leads. Lord Shri Jesus said, "I will build my church" (Matt 16:18). All local churches globally are part of the one universal church that the Lord Shri Jesus is building.

A contextualized group can meet both as a *mandir* (temple, gathering of regenerated believers) or a *satsang* (fellowship with the truth; that is God or a fellowship of truth-seekers). Several other contextualized labels exist for such groups. Normally, *mandir* refers to the local church that comes together as a corporate group and practices the ordinance of *jal sanskar* (baptism) and *maha-prasad* (breaking of bread/communion service); however, *satsang* can be a devotion that does not include *maha-prasad*.

A local church can practice its faith in any given cultural context. All cultural contexts, if they are in sync with the Bible, are valid and acceptable forms of worship. In the context of India and the Indian diaspora, practicing biblical faith in the Hindu-Indian cultural context will deepen our faith and make us better communicators. In this chapter, I use the term *satsang* in a generic manner.

Satsang and Its Content

The Hindu-Indian context has a tradition of offering worship in sixteen formalities. The Hindus treat God as their guest, and all the formalities they observe in welcoming a guest are used for God. The Sanskrit term for these sixteen formalities of worship is *sodashopchar puja*.

What follows is my proposed *sodashopchar puja* format for a trinitarian, Christocentric *satsang*. Despite possible variations, this format for biblical devotion has been developed since 2003 and is contained in a few liturgical booklets.[4]

For *satsang*, participants take off their shoes and, if possible, sit on the floor, squatting. All the chants contained in this format of *sodasopchar puja* are in Sanskrit. The translations in English and vernacular Indian language are also provided in a liturgy booklet so that participants can understand the meaning of the chants. After every chant, parallel translations are read out for the devotees. This format of devotion works particularly well in small groups numbering fifteen to twenty, allowing active participation for all the attending devotees. The sixteen formalities of worship are as follows:

- *trieak parmeshwar vandan* (praise to the triune God)
- *dhuup* (incense)
- *deepak* (lamp)
- *muul mantra* (root/theme verses)
- *prarthana* (prayer)
- bhajan (song)
- *naam jap* (names of the triune God)
- *pavitra atma abhinandan* (acknowledgment of the Holy Spirit)
- *pravachan* (ministry of the word)
- *dhayan manan* (meditation)
- *punaragaman shloka* (second coming verses)
- *yachana* (supplication)

4 For example: Anil Yesudas, *Christ Context Satsang* (Indore, India: Destiny Communications, 2016).

- *aarti nirankari* (a particular song toward the end of the devotion)
- *kshama yachana* (prayer for forgiveness)
- *aashirvadam* (benediction)
- *prasaad* (grace/sacred food)

Trieak parmeshwar vandan is a Sanskrit chant of praise to the eternal Father, eternal Son Lord Shri Jesus, and eternal Holy Spirit. This is an important early chant for the object of our worship. *Dhuup* is for the lighting of incense, and it contains chants in Sanskrit stating that God's name will be great among the nations where the sun rises to where it sets, and in every place, incense and pure offerings will be brought to God (Mal 1:11). The lighting of the lamp is *deepak*, accompanied by a chant about Lord Shri Jesus being the light of the world.

Each *satsang* format has a basic chant, *muul mantra*, and a theme for devotion. An example of a *muul mantra* is a Christocentric chant from the book of Colossians about the supremacy of Lord Shri Jesus (Col 1:15–20). A prayer of worship, *prarthana*, is offered, acknowledging God as creator, savior, and sustainer and that he is worthy of worship, as revealed in the Bible. Songs, *bhajan*, are sung in vernacular Indian language with melodies and musical instruments. It is preferable to have *bhajans* that are trinitarian and point to Lord Jesus as savior and other important scriptural truths. *Naam jap* is the chanting of the names of God and selected names of Jesus from the Bible. During *naam jap*, each name begins with the word *shalom* (peace) and ends with the word *namaha* (I worship you). With much reverence, we acknowledge the presence of the Holy Spirit, *pavitra atma abhinandan*. The Father, who has sent us the person of the Holy Spirit in the name of Jesus, will teach us all things and will remind us of the revealed things in the Bible (John 14:26). The core of contextualized devotion is *pravachan*, in which the life of Lord Shri Jesus is presented in a story format. The main text typically comes from the four Gospels, and when required, the Old Testament and the epistles are quoted. However, as the Spirit leads, a presentation from any other portion of Scripture can be made during *pravachan*.

The twenty-to-forty-minute message from Scripture is followed by a brief time of silent meditation, *dhayan manan*. This is a subtle, personal, silent altar-call for all participants to communicate with the triune God as a response to the message that was just delivered. *Punaragaman shloka*, the second coming chant, reminds us that Lord Shri Jesus will supernaturally come again, and we will live in a new, recreated divine realm. The chant is usually concluded by blowing the *shankh* (a religious horn, a conch shell) as a symbol of the last trumpet. *Yachana* is another formality in which, through a prayer of supplication, all needs, material and spiritual, are presented to the triune God. All requests are made in the name of Lord Shri Jesus with the attitude that he is sovereign and that his wishes will be done. *Trieak Parmeshwar aarti nirankari* is a trinitarian, Christocentric, cross-centric, and salvation-centric *bhajan* (song).

In the Hindu mind, the word *aarti* connotes the wave-offering of lamps to deities. The word *nirankari* points to God, who cannot be contained or limited to a shape or idol. This word *nirankari* is a reminder that the living God cannot be represented through a nonliving object. Asking for forgiveness of sins is *kshama yachana*, an acknowledgment and reminder that we are sinners by birth and by deeds and that our souls are steeped in sin. When we come and surrender to Shri Lord Jesus, all our sins are washed away. A trinitarian benediction, *ashirvadam*, is spoken toward the end (2 Cor 13:14). The final formality is *prasad*, which literally means "grace." *Prasad* is a small snack at the very end of the devotion while we chant about Lord Shri Jesus as the bread of life (John 6:36).

The Hindu mind wants to worship with all five senses: sight, sound, touch, smell, and taste. *Prasad* involves the sense of taste, but one should not confuse and equate *prasad* to the breaking of bread/communion, which is a separate ordinance using regular chapatti (Indian bread) and juice, found in any Indian home.

Thus those who are followers of the triune God have a format with sixteen formalities of worship (*sodashopchar puja*). In classical Hindu fashion, God is treated as a guest, but from a biblical point of view, God is the host and the devotees are the guests. We sit around God's table. This is the predominant biblical idea during contextualized *sodashop-char puja*.

Satsang and Time

A regular rhythmic *satsang* is typically no longer than one hour. However, on certain special occasions, an arrangement can be made to extend *satsang* for more than one hour.

The *satsang* can be held on a daily or weekly basis. A monthly routine of *satsang* would not be of much value because the continuity of thought would be lost, and when the participants skip attending, the gap is much too long. In the case when a brand new *satsang* group is starting, a monthly routine is acceptable, but it should be upgraded to a weekly routine as soon as possible, and, further, the group should aim for a daily *satsang*.

A Hindu temple is open all day, every day. Devotees of the triune God cannot afford to imagine themselves as contextualized into the Hindu-Indian context if they attend a *satsang* only occasionally. Hopefully, in the future, there will be places that are open all day, every day, where the triune God can be worshipped multiple times a day. While academic studies about *satsang* and conversations about *satsang* are valuable, the most important act is doing *satsang*.

The best scenario for a daily *satsang* is for it to happen at the same place and at the same time. When the time and location are fixed, it is easy for community members to walk in, and daily *satsang* in the evenings helps all age groups find an appropriate time to attend.

Satsang Size and Space

It is useful to remember anthropologist Margaret Mead's quote, "Never doubt that a small group . . . can change the world."[5] Lord Jesus had a selected group of twelve people. While occasional large gatherings have benefits, a small grouping is preferable for regular, routine *satsang*. Smallness enhances close relationships, reduces overhead costs, develops community, and multiplies *satsang* leaders. Small groups make it easier to practice the breaking of bread/communion on a weekly basis.[6] Moreover, a

5 NYC Radio, "Margaret Mead," NYC Radio, accessed March 25, 2023, https://www.wnyc.org/people/margaret-mead/

6 The term "the breaking of bread" refers to a communion service used in certain Protestant churches.

small group can comfortably sit in a circle. When the mother and brothers of Lord Jesus came to see him, the small group sat in concentric circles (Mark 3:32).

Satsang Posture

In the Bible, we see several postures for devotion. There is no obligation to favor or prescribe one correct posture. However, certain postures can be awkward to the Hindu mind and should be avoided. A cursory look in the Bible indicates many postures for communing with God: Enoch took long walks while meditating (Gen 5:24). Hezekiah faced the wall and prayed (Isa 38:18). Moses removed his shoes (Exod 3:1–6) and, at another time, raised his hands in prayer (Exod 17). People bowed down in worship (Exod 4:31). Eli sat on a chair, waiting and praying (1 Sam 4:13). The leper came to Lord Jesus and knelt before him (Mark 1:40). Abraham fell prostrate before the Lord (Gen 17:3). David mentioned lying down and meditating (Ps 63:6) and urged stillness (Ps 46:10). A psalmist mentioned dancing (Ps 149:3). Lord Jesus looked up while praying (John 11:41). The tax collector stood and prayed in the synagogue, and he kept his head and eyes down (Luke 18:9–14).

Indian spirituality favors sitting on the floor cross-legged while engaged in spiritual activity. Those who practice their faith in the Hindu-Indian cultural context may comply with traditional Indian posture for spiritual activities. Sitting on the floor suggests humility, like sitting at the feet of the Lord.

If participants are elderly or disabled and cannot sit on the floor, chairs must be provided for them. However, by and large, *satsang* should be done while sitting on the floor. In the Hindu-Indian subconscious mind, political speeches should be made while standing, whereas religious leaders usually prefer to sit and speak. When the devotees of Jesus stand and speak, it gives an aura of politicism to the Hindu-Indian mind. The devotees of Jesus are already under suspicion and falsely accused of having a vague divisive political agenda; therefore, standing and speaking only enhances prejudice.

When Peter met Lord Jesus, before the great catch of fish, Jesus taught the people while sitting in his boat (Luke 5:3). Lord Jesus gave the sermon on the mount while sitting (Matt 5:1). When Lord Jesus came back to Nazareth, he went to the synagogue, read the portion from Isaiah, and sat down to speak (Luke 4:20). When the crowd brought the woman caught in adultery and tried to stone her, they came to Jesus and found him sitting and teaching (John 8:2). Lord Jesus told the parables of the kingdom while sitting in a boat (Matt 13:2). The discourse during the last supper occurred when Lord Jesus was sitting at the table (Matt 26:20). Most probably, there were times Lord Jesus stood to speak, but when it is documented multiple times that Lord Jesus was sitting while speaking, it encourages us to readily sit for *satsang*.

Satsang Vocabulary

In this chapter, I deliberately use Western Christian vocabulary; however, during *satsang*, one must use a vocabulary familiar to the participants wanting the message of Jesus. The Indian Christian and Western Christian vocabulary must be consciously shed in the context of *satsang*, and Hindu-Indian spiritual vocabulary must be embraced. It is often observed among Indian Christians that when a person is speaking in any Indian language, especially when preaching the word of God, the punchlines are uttered in English as if speaking in English elevates them or makes them look more literate. Western vocabulary is not necessary in *satsang*; rather, it is a hurdle and creates the false notion that biblical faith can by equated with Western culture.

Many good Indian spiritual vocabularies are better suited to the Hindu-Indian cultural context. There is no dearth of words in the Sanskrit-based languages.[7] It takes much time and effort to change vocabulary; however, it is necessary to do so. In biblical narrative storytelling, one can appropriately provide boundaries and meanings to contextualized terminologies because they are being used for *pravachan* (religious discourse), but when contextualized vocabulary is used, it must be explained through the Bible.

7 Words like *mandir, puja, sadhana, bhajan, kirtan, shastrartha, guru, satguru, Abhishikth Prabhu Shri Yesu ji, Ved-pustakam, Bhagwan, Paramatma, param-prasad,* and *moksha*, to cite a few examples, can be explored.

Jesus said, "I am the Alpha and Omega" (Rev 1:8). Lord Jesus is the personified eternal word. Lord Jesus owns all the alphabets: alpha, omega, and everything in between. The words we speak are permutations and combinations of alphabets. Lord Jesus is the lord of language. The Hindu culture is large-hearted, and Hindu devotees of Lord Jesus have the spiritual right to use any vocabulary for the purpose of clear and meaningful expression.

It is understandable that for some diasporas, English may be the most suitable language for *pravachan*. However, whenever possible, all the key words should be in a contextualized vocabulary, and *pravachan* must be translated into the vernacular. Of course, the chanting and songs must also be in an Indian language.

Satsang Structure

The egalitarian structure of a small group is desirable and workable for most purposes. However, each *satsang* should have a leader or guru (teacher) figure with the final say, whose main task is to keep everything within the Hindu-Indian cultural and biblical frames of reference.

The *pravachan* should be given by various able people taking turns to speak at different *satsangs*. It is not good practice for one guru figure to give *pravachan* all the time. Notwithstanding, *pravachan* must only be led by those who are deeply rooted devotees of Jesus. A person with a new or nominal interest in the Bible may interpret Scripture with unbiblical presuppositions, creating more confusion than clarity. Guarding the *vyasgaddi* (i.e., the seat from which *pravachan* is given) is essential.

Nevertheless, it is not appropriate to restrict *satsang* leadership to people of ethnic Indian origin; that ideology is a form of racism. Any person, irrespective of their ethnic origin or financial standing, who has decided to incarnate and contextualize the Hindu-Indian cultural framework, is eligible to be a *satsang* leader.

At the global level, all the devotees of the triune God, irrespective of their locations, languages, cultures, and ethnicities, are one in Lord Jesus. Therefore, a loose, dotted-line, horizontal relationship with global or local ecclesiastical counterparts can and should be maintained, providing the ecclesiastical counterparts do not attempt to dictate terms to *satsang* groups. A *satsang* should be open for all who want to participate sincerely and respectfully.

Satsang Setup

Initially, many *satsang* groups may not have a physical space of their own. It is perfectly acceptable to meet in a home, shop, or small rented hall if the legal restrictions are met. Under exceptional circumstances, a well-established Hindu group may be willing to share its space.[8]

While the *satsang* should last for approximately one hour, selected *satsang* leaders should arrive at least an hour earlier to set up the space. Also, they should stay for an hour to wrap up the *satsang* space. The space should be ready before the devotees come in. Setup and wrap-up can be delegated to a devotee and are part and parcel of devotion itself.

During fellowship time, only vegetarian food must be offered. Non-vegetarian food must not be used or discussed within the *satsang* space. Regarding the daily *satsang*, there is no need for an elaborate meal. A monthly meal may be more feasible and desirable.

Satsang Training

Many Indian Christians currently follow a format of worship that is Western in cultural context, and they have become used to it. It is easy for them to join any group, any time, and with short notice, pick up a guitar, organ, piano, or drums, and begin to worship in a completely Western format. This ease encourages Christian leaders to confine themselves to the established Western format. When it seems easy for new members to fit in with the format, the leaders are further encouraged because they do not need to bother with training for newcomers.

8 The author, Anil Yesudas, between 2003 and 2008, conducted rhythmic weekly *satsang* in Kalamazoo Hindu Temple, Kalamazoo, Missouri and for two-and-a-half years at Vivekanand Monastery, Ganges, Missouri in the US and is grateful for the positive relationships and large-heartedness of Hindu friends at those temples.

However, I contend that for the format of *satsang*, training is necessary. Learning the *satsang* format is easy enough—at a superficial level—but it takes humility, time, and energy to learn *satsang* thoroughly. It is the task of the *satsang* leader, the guru figure, to teach newcomers to worship the triune God in the Hindu-Indian cultural context.

The good news of Lord Jesus is not a set of formulas that can be dispensed via marketing or propaganda-style communication. The biblical message is not a commercial product to be sold for profit. The gospel is the work of the anointed Lord Jesus and is expressed through worship of the triune God. In this process of worship, the historical living Lord Jesus, as revealed in the Bible, is introduced. Instead of consciously or unconsciously employing marketing methodology, people must be trained to translate the designs of their lives to live as regenerated and transformed individuals and as a community of practicing believers in the Hindu-Indian cultural context.

Satsang Safeguards

Making standalone, short doctrinal statements to people, such as "Jesus died for your sins," would not necessarily communicate that Lord Jesus is the true and only savior. During *satsang*, the life and work of Lord Jesus are narrated multiple times in small doses to a small group of people. Anything and everything about the life of Jesus is unique, and the uniqueness is built over time in the context of storytelling.

I propose that it is better to avoid question-and-answer (Q&A) sessions after *satsang*. The Q&A format may satisfy the curiosity of Christian leaders looking for material for their newsletters, but in my experience, these sessions often lead to unfriendly debates. Furthermore, certain people who may be described as fanatical may be keen to disrupt these sessions. Over time, *satsang* usually answers all the silent questions in the minds of the participants. Patience is a virtue. If need be, Q&A can be easily handled at a personal level outside *satsang* time.

Something else to be avoided is personal testimonies that amount to "I was a Hindu, now I am a Christian," especially during *satsang*. None of the Hindus are attracted by that sort of presentation; they only get irritated. If anyone were to give the testimony "I was a Christian, now I am a Hindu," would the Christian audience dance with joy? The reactions of the Hindus are no different. Bible stories are far better and infinitely more important than elaborate personal stories. During *satsang*, the time for *pravachan* is precious and should be dedicated entirely to Scripture. There is no personal story more important than the story of God working in history, as revealed in the Bible. Personal stories should be set aside for personal conversations at a much later time. After devotees have exhausted all the Bible stories (which is nigh impossible), then they can think of releasing their "I was a Hindu, now I am a Christian" testimonies.

Yes, there is a place for very short, anecdotal life incidents during *pravachan* in conjunction with a particular biblical story being presented. However, an elaborate personal life story at the expense of Scripture presentation time should be completely avoided. *Satsang* is a worship format to genuinely express following Lord Jesus in the Hindu-Indian cultural context. One can remain Hindu culturally and be a genuine follower of Lord Jesus; extreme transformation from Hindu to Christian is not necessary.

During casual conversations in *satsang* fellowship time, there should not be any discussion of strategies of communication, stories of success, or stories of persecution. Avoid discussing the progress of others toward Lord Jesus. Educate your Christian guests not to ask questions like "Are you a Hindu?" or "Are you a Christian?". These only cause divisions and hurdles. Also, avoid newsletters that portray others as projects. We who are from the East need to depend on God, not the West.

Conclusion

Without changing the original meaning and intent, I would like to rephrase (italics mine) the statement made by Nicholls that I shared at the beginning of this chapter: "The hermeneutical task *may begin as a private or purely individual attempt*; however, *it must soon* be undertaken within the community of believers. Therefore, contextualization must take place within the Church before it can be faithfully interpreted to the world."[9]

9 Bruce Nicholls, "A Living Theology for Asian Churches."

The divine revelation contained in the Bible is the only way we can know God. What begins as an individual understanding soon can be practiced and validated by the community of *bhaktas* (devotees). We respond to God's communication through individual and corporate worship. When we begin to know God, we will not be able to contain that information within ourselves and will need to share the truth about the activities of God and his immense love for humankind, who are created in his image. God is "not wanting anyone to perish, but everyone to come to repentance" (2 Pet 3:9).

Followers of Lord Jesus look toward a paradigm beyond the traditional church to express their biblical faith in a format that is culturally familiar. Lord Shri Jesus said, "Go into all the world and preach the gospel to all creation" (Mark 16:15).

If the gospel is communicated by an individual to another individual, it is likely that the individual will come to Christ. If the gospel is communicated by a family to another family, it is likely that the family will come to Christ. If the gospel is practiced contextually by a community that communicates with another community, it is likely that the new community will come to Christ, sparking further Christ-ward movements.

Lord Jesus is best understood and communicated in the context of worship. It is perfectly possible to worship the triune God in a manner that is culturally Hindu-Indian and theologically biblical. We strive to become a community serious about biblical truths and a clear communicator of the unchanging message of Lord Shri Jesus.

In his essay titled "A Living Theology for Asian Churches: Some Reflections on the Contextualization-Syncretism Debate," Bruce J. Nicholls wrote, "The translation of the gospel into other cultural forms so that it assimilates and absorbs elements that are not contrary to the gospel itself is not syncretism."[10] In other words, one can contextualize in a manner that conserves biblical truths that have collectively been unearthed in the past two thousand years of theologizing.

The idea of contextualization is not new, but it seems that in history, contextualization efforts have died with various leaders who pioneered these movements. However, plenty of wisdom has come out of their

10 Nicholls, "A Living Theology."

lifestyle that can now be built upon. As Roger Hedlund wrote, "One of the most interesting contextual experiments in mission history took place in the early seventeenth century in India . . . Roberto de Nobili (1577–1656) . . . stands as a model of adaptation . . . De Nobili is castigated by modern critics for methods designed to appeal exclusively to the Brahmins and other 'twice-born' castes. It should be noted however that most converts were from the lower castes who were not excluded by his ingenious approach."[11]

We are living in times when many spiritual leaders favor a contextual approach; therefore, one can look forward to the day when this will become the norm in India and among Indian diasporas. "To him who sits on the throne and to the Lamb be praised and honor and glory and power, for ever and ever!" (Rev 5:13).

The Hindu-Indian culture is very conducive to practicing biblical faith in the triune God. In this chapter, I have proposed *satsang* as a methodology for creating Christ-centered, conservative, contextual, communicating communities.

Bibliography

Hedlund, Roger E. *Christianity Made in India—From Apostle Thomas to Mother Teresa.* Minneapolis, MN: Fortress Press, 2017.

Nicholls, Bruce J. "A Living Theology for Asian Churches: Some Reflections on the Contextualization—Syncretism Debate." In *The Bible and Theology in Asian Contexts: An Evangelical Perspective on Asian Theology*, edited by Bong Rin Ro and Ruth Eshenaur, 119–138. Taichung, Taiwan: Asia Theological Association, 1984.

NYC Radio. "Margaret Mead." Accessed March 25, 2023. https://www.wnyc.org/people/margaret-mead/

11 Hedlund R.E., 2017, 220–221.

9

CHRISTIAN OUTREACH TO MUSLIMS IN THE EAST AND WEST—OBSTACLES

by M. T. Amjad

Introduction

The church has had little success with Muslim evangelism and outreach worldwide. Missionaries who worked among Muslims in the past expected the gospel to penetrate the Muslim world, but it rarely happened in their lifetime. Stacey noted, "Apart from a movement into the church in Spain in the thirteenth century and large movements in Indonesia, there has been no large take-up to the Christian message in the Muslim world."[1]

In 1900, the Muslim population was only 200 million, compared with 558 million Christians.[2] According to the prediction of the Pew Research Center in 2015, Christianity will continue to be a dominant religion in the world within the next few decades; however, Islam will grow faster than any other major religion. By 2050, Christians will constitute around 31.4 percent of the world's population, with Muslims at 29.7 percent.[3] If this

---

1 Vivienne Stacey, "Toward a Current Strategy: Discerning God's Hand in Islam Today?" *Missiology* 4, no. 3 (July 1976): 363–372, https://doi.org/10.1177/009182967600400310

2 "Christianity in View: Statistics and Forecasts for World Religions: 1800–2025," *Gordon-Cornwell Theological Seminary*, accessed April 12, 2022, http://christianityinview.com/religion-statistics.html

3 "The Future of World Religions: Population Growth Projections, 2010–2050," *Pew Research Center*, accessed April 2, 2015, https://www.pewresearch.org/religion/2015/04/02/religious-projections-2010-2050/

trend continues, the Muslim population will exceed that of Christians by 2070, when Muslims will be 34.9 percent and Christians 33.8 percent.[4]

At present, there is a sizable population of Muslims in Southeast Asia, the Middle East, Europe, North and South America, Australia, and other parts of the world. Incidentally, with a high birth rate of 3.1 children per woman, Muslims have higher fertility levels than the world average.[5]

In recent times, several demographic and sociological studies have been conducted on the fifty million Muslims in Europe with the purpose of assessing their propensity to "fit in" with their local multicultural communities.[6] Other research, with missiological intent, has been performed by Christian organizations in the UK, Europe, and Southeast Asia, focusing on the conversion of and the dynamics of assimilating Muslims into local churches and the Christian community.[7] However, these studies have yielded little substantial evidence for what induces successful conversions from Islam to the Christian faith. This issue has baffled the church in both the Eastern and Western worlds for decades.

This chapter is concerned with the factors that hinder Muslims from accepting the Christian message and faith. I have spent thirty years conducting informal ethnographic studies of Muslim seekers and Muslim believers (hereafter Muslim background believer, MBB, and Muslim background believers, MBBs) from the regions and countries mentioned above.[8] I have found numerous hindering factors that have played a part

---

4 Pew Research Center, "Muslims," *Pew Research Center*, accessed April 12, 2022, https://www.pewresearch.org/religion/2015/04/02/religious-projections-2010-2050/

5 Pew Research Center, "Muslims."

6 Pew Research Center, "Religion in Europe," Find Easy, accessed June 18, 2021, https://www.findeasy.in/europe-population-by-religion/

7 Marc Coleman, "The Muslim Spiritual Progress Scale: Aiding Muslims in Coming to Christ," *Digital Commons @Andrews University*. https://digitalcommons.andrews.edu/do/search/?q=aiding%20muslims%20coming%20to%20christ&start=0&context=6860132&facet=

8 By "informal ethnography," I mean meeting Muslim seekers in an informal way and compiling my findings for my own ministry. The results of these compilations were neither peer-reviewed nor published.

in snubbing the evangelistic methods and efforts—factors that need to be overcome if outreach and church planting for Muslims are to be fruitful.

In this chapter, I use the knowledge I have gained from the MBBs who were discipled during my ministry to Muslims in Southeast Asia and the UK from 1992 onward. This amounts to over 500 MBBs with whom I have interacted through relationships, fellowship, and hospitality. These Muslim converts represent thirty nationalities from Eastern and Western countries but all from a Muslim background. My colleagues and I reached out, discipled, and provided fellowship and family to them. Sadly, most of the converts lost their families because of their conversion to the Christian faith.

The purpose of my research was to gain an understanding of why Christian approaches, outreaches, and evangelistic efforts toward Muslims have mostly failed. Hopefully, by sharing my understanding of the hindering factors in this chapter and the enabling factors in the next, readers will be better equipped for their missionary work in the future. I commence with some background information, followed by definitions and methods for contacting Muslims. Then in the main body, I identify the hindering factors. The identities of the MBBs I interviewed and interacted with are coded and credited in the footnotes.

Background Information

To begin, I propose that the results of our outreach and evangelistic efforts with Muslims should not be attributed entirely to the approaches and strategies of evangelism. The latter is undoubtedly important, but we must not forget the power of the Holy Spirit and his influence on whether Muslims come to Christ. God uses us as a vessel to accomplish his purposes, employing our skills and gifts. Therefore, although the methods, strategies, skills, and understanding of the process of evangelism, discipleship, and fellowship of MBBs are vitally important, if God is not part of the process and we have no enduring relationship with Muslims, we will not get far in discipling them.

Most evangelistic programs for communicating the gospel to Muslims overlook the importance of missionaries' relationships and interactions with the receivers. Muslims do not read the Qur'an the way Christians read the Bible. They usually spend more time and effort on their reading and receive considerable reinforcement from teaching and information by imams at mosques. Therefore, information-based evangelistic strategies do not go deep enough to take root with Muslim receivers. We need to have a deeper relationship and share the gospel in the context of love and relationship to transform Muslims' lives from the inside out.

We have many inspirational messages in Scripture. The Bible says, "Clearly you are an epistle of Christ" (2 Cor 3:3) and "We are therefore Christ's ambassadors" (2 Cor 5:20).

Our lives must reflect Christ. Muslims may not read the Bible, but they read you and me. We are the ones who are going to lead Muslims to Christ and the biblical message in the context of relationships and love.

I believe that church planting to bring about the fellowship of believers' groups for converts is the best strategy to reach out to Muslims and show them the love of Christ. That Muslim converts lose their Muslim family, relatives, and community is common knowledge that has been handed down to us.[9] Therefore, Christian fellowship and the church must become the family for young believers from Islam.

This approach and method were evaluated and applied by the apostles in the book of Acts 2. It worked for them in the first century, and it has the potential to work for us in the twenty-first century. Indeed, it has provided family, relationships, and fellowship for younger and older converts in the Eastern and Western world. Next, I discuss the factors hindering Muslim conversion to the Christian faith.

Most of the MBBs in our ministry in the UK were born to parents living in the UK who originated from such regions and countries mentioned above in this chapter. We also have 100 to 120 MBBs from Southeast Asia, the Middle East, and African backgrounds. All the information quoted here was collected through open-ended conversations with them. They shared information with me voluntarily, either one-on-one or in a group, during times of fellowship. It took years to develop these relationships in which we could talk from the depths of our hearts.

The Muslim population living in Western countries enjoys privileges that are not available to them in the Eastern world. Modern Britain is a

9 Coleman, "The Muslim Spiritual Progress Scale."

multiracial, multicultural, and multireligious country. Freedom of speech and religious freedom are guarded by legislation. It is a basic human right to practice or not practice religion. Despite such privileges, Muslim converts in the UK and other parts of Europe face challenges similar to Muslim converts in the Eastern world: They wish to preserve their religious, social, and cultural beliefs and customs.

Definitions

I now define the following terms which will be used in this and the following chapter.

Da'wah: an invitation to all that is good and a communication of the Islamic message to Muslims as well as non-Muslims.[10]

Shi'as: followers of Ali, first cousin of Mohammed and husband of his daughter Fatima Musk.[11]

Sunnis: followers who accept the sunnah and the historical succession of the caliphs. Sunnis form most of the worldwide Muslim community.[12]

Sunnah: the sayings and teachings of the prophet Muhammad.

Sharia law: Muslim religious law based on the Qur'an.[13]

Shirk: derogatory term for Muslims who associate with other gods..[14]

Halal: food that is pure and lawful. According to Islamic law, the animal must be slaughtered by a sharp knife penetrating the inner part of its neck while the name of God is being invoked.[15]

Haram: impure and unlawful. If God's name is not spoken with intent at the time of slaughtering the meat, it is regarded as *haram*.[16]

---

10 R.A. Wu, *The Call to Islam: A Contemporary Perspective* (Singapore: Muslim Converts' Association 1990), 63.

11 B.A. Musk, *Touching the Soul of Islam* (MARC: Crowborough, UK. 1997), 223.

12 Musk, "Touching the Soul," 224.

13 Anne Cooper, *Ishmael My Brother: A Christian Introduction to Islam* (MARC: Crowborough, UK. 1997), 314

14 Cooper, *Ishmael My Brother.*

15 Muhammad M. Ahsan, *Islam: Faith and Practice* (United Kingdom: Islamic Foundation 1977), 35.

16 Ahsan, *Islam: Faith and Practice.*

Din: in Islamic terminology, *din* refers to the way of life Muslims must adopt to comply with divine law. It encompasses beliefs, character, and deeds.[17]

Wudu: Rizvi wrote that *wudu* is an act of Islamic ritual washing and cleansing of the human body.[18] It is derived from the Qur'anic teachings: "O you who believe! When you stand up for ritual prayer, wash your face and your hands up to the elbows, and wipe a part of your head and your feet up to the ankles" (Sura 5:6).[19]

Methods for Contacting Muslims

I have used the following methods to contact Muslims.

Bookstall/Book Table

At our bookstall on the high street in our town, during market day, we distribute Bibles, Christian literature, worship CDs, and DVDs of the Jesus movie. This is one of the evangelist tools or methods we use to reach out to Muslims. The main purpose of the bookstall is to develop relationships with Muslims who are interested in friendship and gospel discussions, either at the book table or in follow-up meetings one-on-one.

Most of our lasting contacts with Muslims are made through the book table ministry—follow-up gospel discussions conducted individually or within a group. Most of our ministry activities include food, relationships, and fellowship over meals.

Amn-O-Aman: Peace and Faith Community امن-و-ایمان

Amn-O-Aman (AOA) is a community of people from Muslim and Christian beliefs who meet to build bridges and establish a strong community in our town. The group meets to discuss social, cultural, spiritual, and political

17 John Esposito, *The Oxford Dictionary of Islam* (Oxford: Oxford University Press, 2014).

18 Sayyid Muhmmad Rizvi, "The Ritual and Spiritual Purity," Ahlul Bayt Digital Islamic Library Project 1995–2023. https://www.al-islam.org/ritual-and-spiritual-purity-sayyid-muhammad-rizvi/ii-wudu

19 Rizvi, "The Ritual."

issues. We talk and ask questions, and we try to deal with misunderstandings among Muslims and Christians to discover the truth through the holy scriptures. Mutual respect for religious beliefs, practices, and culture and listening to each other are central to our discussions, gatherings, and events. The group tries to find diverse ways to understand each other better. We want to develop long-term friendships and interpersonal relationships among Muslims and Christians to build AOA (i.e., community).

Door-to-Door Visitation and Outreach

We also visit Muslim families by going door-to-door. Friendship is developed, and invitations are given to discuss spiritual and cultural issues and questions.

Factors That Hinder Conversion

Now I identify the factors that hinder the conversion of Muslims to Christianity, derived from the responses of MBBs during the twenty-five years I worked in the UK and five years in Southeast Asia. The identified factors fall into four categories: theological or spiritual, social, cultural, and political.

Theological/Spiritual Factors

Most of the MBBs expressed that Islamic theology differs from Christian theology. Muslims find it difficult to reconcile Muslim and Christian theologies. The following three areas are the most difficult to understand for Muslims: the Trinity, the authenticity of the Bible, and the crucifixion and resurrection of Jesus Christ.

Understanding of the Trinity: About three-quarters of MBBs indicated that the enigma of the Trinity is one of the hindering factors for Muslims to come to Christ. One MBB mentioned, "The complexity of the Trinity hinders conversion. Trinity is a *shirk*. The Qur'an forbids it."[20] Whenever Christians refer to the triune God, Muslims think it means three gods. This is unacceptable to Muslims. They believe there is only one God; thus, if Christians believe in three gods, this is a *shirk*.

---

20 CMMMS2.

Many Muslims think that the Trinity refers to God the father, Mary the mother, and Jesus as the biological son of God and Mary. As such, even if they accept that Christians do not believe in three gods, they still reject it. This is a *shirk* because they think Christians believe Mary and Jesus to be equal partners with God, and they wonder, "How can anyone be equal to God when there is only one God?"

The Qur'an also warns and forbids anyone to mention the Trinity. The Qur'an states, "Do not say Trinity, for Allah is one God" (Sura 4:171). Another MBB mentioned that "Jesus is not the Son of God, according to Qur'an."[21] Yet another MBB expressed a similar opinion, "Muslims cannot accept Jesus as the son of God because it is not mentioned in the Qur'an; this makes it difficult to reconcile the two [the Bible and Qur'an]."[22]

Authenticity of the Bible: About half of the MBs indicated that the corruption of the Bible is one of the hindering factors for conversion. Two MBBs mentioned that, according to the Qur'an, the Bible is corrupt.[23] Another MBB said, "The Bible with many versions is evidence that it has been corrupted." The Qur'an also mentions that the Bible is corrupted (Sura 3:78). Hence for Muslims "It is difficult to refute this claim in the Qur'an and to accept the Bible."[24]

Muslims consider the Qur'an to be the only word of God. All other scriptures are regarded as written by humans and are therefore corrupted. This claim is written in Sura 2:79. Since there are different Bible versions and translations, Muslims question the validity and authenticity of the Bible as being the word of God.

Sura 4:82 states, "If it [Qur'an] had been from other than Allah they would have found therein much incongruity." This implies that there should be no incongruity found in the Qur'an and there should not be any clash in the Bible if it is from God. However, when Muslims find variations of narration in the synoptic Gospels, they regard these variations as incongruities. This causes them to reject the Bible as the authentic word of God.

21 CMMFS10

22 CMMFS1.

23 CIMMS12 and CMMFS1.

24 CIMMS11.

Crucifixion and resurrection of Jesus Christ: About three-quarters of the MBBs identified the crucifixion and resurrection of Jesus Christ as one of the factors that hinder conversion among Muslims. One MBB mentioned, "Muslims cannot accept that Jesus was crucified on the cross for man's sins; men must be responsible for their own sins. This teaching is not according to the Qur'an's teaching, which makes it difficult for Muslims to believe."[25] Another stated, "The crucifixion of Jesus Christ is not mentioned in the Qur'an."[26]

The Qur'an says, "But they killed him not, nor crucified him, but it was made to appear to them so, and those who differ therein are full of doubts with no knowledge, but they follow only conjecture, for of surety they killed him not" (Sura 4:157). It is difficult for Muslims to oppose their holy book. Muslims reject the crucifixion of Jesus Christ; therefore, they cannot accept that through the death and resurrection of Jesus Christ, the sins of humanity can be forgiven. One MBB said, "I was confused about the truth of the resurrection of Jesus, which is a core teaching of Salvation in the Bible. It is not mentioned in the Qur'an that Jesus really died on the Cross."[27]

According to the Qur'an, Jesus was not crucified. He was taken to heaven on his way to be crucified. Muslims believe that God substituted someone to be crucified in Jesus's place. However, according to the Bible, Jesus was crucified, and he was also resurrected so that God could forgive the sins of humanity. This confuses Muslims and puts them in a dilemma as to which is the truth and whether they should commit their lives to Jesus.

Social Factors

Several MBBs referred to social factors, such as fear of Islamic *ummah*, fear of persecution from the Muslim community, fear of ostracism, the attitude of Christians, and disunity in the church, all of which hinder Muslims in their decision to convert to Christianity.

25 CMMFS1.
26 CMMMS15.
27 CMMFS16.

Fear of ummah: About a quarter of the MBBs singled out the Islamic *ummah* as a major deterrent to conversion. Muslims believe in the brotherhood of Muslims around the world, which unites them in the *ummah*. This principle runs against the sovereignty of states, the central pillar of the secular international system. Latif said, "[They] live in nations but their true loyalty is to the global Islamic domain."[28] This sense of brotherhood knits Muslims together as a family unit.[29] It is a prevalent sentiment, especially among younger Muslims, and young people say things like, "I am British because that is my nationality, but Islam is who I am." This is a common self-identification among Muslims in both Eastern and Western countries.

The *ummah* is a strong bond in the Muslim community. To be separated from it means dire consequences, such as ostracism and persecution, including a possible death penalty. This is one of the reasons Muslims are so fearful of leaving their community and converting to the Christian faith, even if they are convinced by the gospel.

Fear of persecution from the Muslim community: Almost all the MBBs acknowledged fear of persecution from family and community as a factor that affected their conversion. Persecution ranges from alienation, ostracism, and disownment to threats of being beaten or even killed. One MB admitted, "When my conversion was discovered, my mother wanted to kill me. I miraculously escaped death when my mother could not find a knife in her own kitchen."[30] To sum up, Muslims are fearful of converting because they are afraid of being disowned by their family.

According to the *Daily Mail* newspaper, a British couple of Pakistani background was convicted of suffocating their teenage daughter, Shafilea, in a so-called honor killing for bringing shame on the family by becoming Westernized (Christian).[31] In another such incident, Abdullah Yones

28 A. Latif, "The Global Islamic Community: What Ummah Means to Believers, Muslims in Multi-religious Singapore Taking Practical Approach," *The Straits Times*, March 14, 1998, 66.

29 CMMMS2, CMMMS6, and COMMS7.

30 COMFS5.

31 Stephanie Linning, "The Tragic Schoolgirl Victim on UK's First 'Honour Killing'," *Daily Mail*, February 18, 2021, https://www.dailymail.co.uk/femail/article-9270103/

stabbed his sixteen-year-old daughter Heshu to death at their home in Acton Town, West London, on October 12, 2002. Yones killed his daughter because she was becoming Westernized (Christian).[32]

Scotland Yard and the Metropolitan Police have reported a huge rise in recorded incidents motivated by "honor," and the British press reported that there were more than eleven thousand cases of honor crimes in the UK from 2010 to 2014.[33]

Another MB said, "Muslim friends and relatives influence your parents to go against you. They also persecute your parents and family if they cannot do anything to you."[34] This makes Muslims fearful of converting to the Christian faith because other members of their families will be affected by their decision as well.

Fear of ostracism: About three-quarters of the MBBs highlighted the fear of ostracism as another strong social factor that hinders conversion. It is a horrible thought to be shunned by a supportive community, blood relatives, and other Muslims. It is even harder for women living in an Eastern country where there is no social security provided by the state. This fear is very common in Western countries as well, where 70 percent of converts are women.[35] One MB mentioned, "Fear of being cut off from family members and loved ones causes loneliness."[36] Another hindering factor is the possibility of being condemned and treated as an outcast or a "weirdo." Two other MBBs also indicated that "fear of ostracism hindered conversions."[37]

Attitude of Christians: About a quarter of the MBBs mentioned that the attitude of Christians and Christian leaders is one of the hindering

32 Stephanie Linning, "The Tragic Schoolgirl Victim on UK's First 'Honour Killing.'"

33 Divya Talwar and Athar Ahmad, "'Honour crimes':11,000 UK cases recorded in five years," *BBC News*, July 9, 2015, https://www.bbc.com/news/uk-33424644

34 CMMFP1.

35 FSSPX.News, "Investigation Into the Persecution of Christian Converts From Islam in Europe," *News: Information and Analysis on the Life of the Church*, July 20, 2022, https://fsspx.news/en/news-events/news/investigation-persecution-christian-converts-islam-europe-2-75143

36 CMMFS4.

37 CMMMS13 and CMMMS14.

factors for conversion. Several MBs said they were disgusted by the attitude of Christians leaders who regarded them with suspicion or indifference. One MBB said, "I was treated with suspicion by the leaders. They made me feel as if I was there to seek financial help or to function as a spy to seek information. They interviewed me and asked very personal questions before admitting me into membership. I struggled a lot and underwent persecution to leave the Muslim community. I faced such a condescending attitude and a poor reception by the Christian leaders. I was very discouraged and disappointed. I wondered if I should stay on or would it be better for me to return to the warm Muslim community."[38]

Another MBB narrated, "After my conversion, I faced many problems. I approached my pastor and cried out to him for help. I was shocked by his outburst, 'Why did you convert? Did you not know you must undergo such problems?' He left me in the lurch without any offer of help or comfort."[39] And another MBB said, "Initially my pastor was rather warm and enthusiastic; however, when I got into trouble, his attitude changed. I was questioned by the church authorities regarding my conversion, and he simply denied any affiliation with me!"[40]

Muslims typically come from warm, friendly, and supportive communities. Therefore, when they convert to Christianity, they expect the same from the Christian community. However, they are often extremely disappointed to find that it is not so, and they receive negative treatment from Christians leaders. This hinders their growth and increases their yearning to be back with the Muslim community. Many of them leave the church. Thus, in some instances, the attitude of Christians hinders conversion.

Politics and disunity in the church: One MBB stated, "Conflict among Christians and church politics gives Muslims the impression that the church is disunited, thus hindering conversion."[41] Several others made a similar claim.

Other Muslims noticed that the leaders of various Christian denominations often teach and hold different views of Christianity, and some

38 COMMS7.
39 CMMFS9.
40 CMMFS4.
41 CMMMS6.

leaders even condemn others' denominations. Muslims regard the different denominations as evidence that the church is disunited.

When Christian leaders fight each other for prominent positions, especially in the Eastern world, such politics may be all too familiar to Muslims. Nevertheless, this kind of conflict makes Christianity unattractive to them and thus hinders their conversion.

Cultural Factors

About half of the MBBs responded that cultural factors hinder conversion. The commonly identified cultural factors were bigotry, food, the handling of the holy book, the character of church leaders, and swaying away from biblical teachings.

Bigotry: About a quarter of MBBs mentioned Christian bigotry as a cultural factor that hinders conversion. For example, one MBB, who was baptized in her local Western congregation just outside London, said, "I was wearing *Shalwar Kameez* (Pakistani women's clothing) during my baptism. At the end of my baptism, the pastor asked me, 'When are you going to stop wearing these funny clothes?' I answered him, 'I have not become an English woman, but I have become a follower of Christ. So, I can wear these cultural clothes and still, I can follow Jesus. I do not have to be a Westerner to follow Jesus.'"[42]

Another MBB asserted, "Christians are giving the impression that they are better people."[43] Yet another MBB expressed the same opinion, "Muslims feel that Christians are bigots when they communicate verbally and nonverbally that their religion and community are better than Islam; Christ didn't call us into a religion but into a relationship to follow him."[44]

Some Muslims perceive Christianity as a white man's religion and Christians as followers of Western religion and culture. Most Christians come from non-Muslim backgrounds, so Muslims perceive church culture as dominated by Western culture. They conclude that simply adding a few local (Muslim) cultural elements to the practice does not attract local

42 PCMSZL.

43 CMMMS6.

44 COMMS7.

Muslims toward the Christian faith. Muslims also resent the possibility of having to give up their own language and culture if they become Christians.

Giving up language is a highly provocative thought for Muslims because they regard Arabic as Allah's language, and many regard their cultural heritage as superior to any other culture, especially Western culture. It is unthinkable for Muslims to reject their own culture and embrace a hybrid of Western and local cultural elements because both are foreign to them. One MBB said, "If we cannot change our mother, we cannot change our Muslim faith and culture."[45]

Food: Food is another factor that hinders conversion. Muslims observe strict dietary rules about haram and halal food. One MBB explained, "Christians consume pork and alcohol, which are considered haram according to Muslim culture and religion."[46] MBBs are afraid that if they convert to Christianity, they also must eat pork. This is a repulsive thought because they have been taught from birth that pork is a forbidden food. It is also challenging for converts to find food in Western countries unless they live in communities with sizable Muslim communities. However, one MBB admitted, "I initially felt disgusted when I ate pork, which was haram food, but now I don't have a problem with it."[47]

In the UK, Christians eat mostly non-halal food because they are Westerners or of non-Muslim backgrounds. Similarly, in Southeast Asian countries, where I worked for many years, Christians do not follow any dietary rules, but Muslims do. Most Muslim seekers and converts do not eat haram food because they have never acquired a taste for pork and alcohol. Therefore, most Muslims perceive that if they convert, they must change their diet and eat haram food, which kills their appetite for food as well as their interest in Christianity. It often becomes obvious to the MBBs, when they are invited by local churches to mingle with believers for fellowship over food, that there is no provision for halal food.

Handling of the holy book: About a quarter of the MBBs identified the way Christians carry and manage their Bibles as a factor that hindered their conversion. One MBB stated, "The way Christians manage the Bible

45 CMMMS6.

46 CMMMS15.

47 COMFS5.

is different from the way Muslims handle their Holy Book."[48] Another MBB asserted, "Muslims treat their Holy Book with much reverence. It is an appalling sight for Muslims when they observe that Christians place their Bibles on their seats, almost sitting on them. Muslims find such mishandling of the Holy Book to be very offensive and irreverent, so much so that this affects their receptivity and regard for Christianity."[49]

Muslims regard the holy scriptures as a sacred book. They are trained to follow strict rules to manage it with reverence because it is God's holy word. Before they touch or read the Qur'an, they must perform cleansing rituals (*wudu*), which may extend to having a full bath and changing into clean clothes. Then the Qur'an is removed from its protective casing and carefully placed on a special stand for reading. No marking or anything is to be placed between the pages of the Qur'an.

The way Christians handle their Bibles affects Muslims very much. When they see that the Holy Bible is treated like an ordinary book, they consider such action as an insult to God and his word. Muslims are appalled and enraged that Bibles are found lying all over the place, with all sorts of things kept between their pages. They feel that if Christians do not respect their holy book, then they have no respect for God.

Character of church leaders and swaying away from biblical teachings: An increasing number of churches, denominations, and leaders are accepting same-gender marriages in Western countries. Even conservative church members are divided over this issue, let alone Muslims and Muslim converts. Many church leaders and members feel that they should uphold biblical standards, but others advocate for the inclusion of LGBTQ Christians in all aspects of church life. However, most Muslims and Muslim converts are offended by such advocacy. The Western church and culture consider such a position as an accommodation for equal rights, but Muslim seekers and converts consider it as departing from biblical and conservative values. Therefore, it has become one of the hindering factors for Muslims to follow the Christian faith and go to a church that believes in and practices such diversions from conservative values.

48 CMMMS15.

49 CIMMS12.

Political Factors

According to the European Court of Human Rights guarantees in Article 9:

> The right to freedom of thought, conscience, and religion: this right includes freedom to change his religion or belief and freedom, either alone or in community with others and in public or private, to manifest his religion or belief, in worship, teaching, practice and observance. The freedom to manifest one's religion or beliefs shall be subject only to such limitations as are prescribed by law and are necessary in a democratic society in the interests of public safety, for the protection of public order, health or morals, or for the protection of the rights and freedoms of others.[50]

Thus, legally, freedom of speech and freedom of religion are guaranteed in the UK, but in some instances, political pressure is put on Christians to conform to secular values. For example, teachers in some Christian schools must choose between their job or their faith. Therefore, Muslim converts expect to receive the same treatment as Western Christians. There are many examples of Christians in schools and even in public service who must deal with fear and intimidation in the workplace.

In 2006, a British Airways check-in clerk, Nadia Eweida, was fired by her manager for refusing to remove her cross necklace.[51] British Airways allowed Muslims to wear hijabs, Sikhs to wear turbans and bracelets, and Jews to wear skullcaps, but the manager forbade Eweida, an Egyptian-background Christian employee, from wearing her necklace. Such pressure to conform to secular values has become a deterrent even to Christians in the workplace.

The British Broadcasting Corporation (BBC) reported on October 30, 2018, that Rimsha Masih was the first non-Muslim to be acquitted in a blasphemy case in 2012 in Pakistan. It was discovered that she had been

50 ECHR, "Guide on Article 9 of the European Convention on Human Rights," European Court of Human Rights, 31 August 31, 2022, https://www.echr.coe.int/documents/guide_art_9_eng.pdf

51 BBC News, "British Airways Christian Employee Nadia Eweida Wins Case," *BBC News*, January 15, 2013https://www.bbc.com/news/uk-21025332

framed by a local Muslim cleric.[52] Previously, in a well-known 2010 case, Asia Bibi was accused by Muslim women of having blasphemed.[53] Masood noted that in the period 1987–2017, the Pakistan Centre for Social Justice recorded approximately 1,500 charges of blasphemy, and at least seventy-five people involved in accusations of blasphemy were killed.[54]

Conclusion

In this chapter, I reported responses from multiple Muslim seekers and MBBs who disclosed many hindering factors for their conversion. The factors fell into four major themes: theological, social, cultural, and political factors.

The commonly identified theological factors were grouped according to Muslim perceptions of the Trinity, the authenticity of the Bible, and the crucifixion and resurrection of Jesus Christ. The factors of social concern were fear of the Islamic *ummah*, fear of persecution from the Muslim community, fear of ostracism, the attitude of Christians, and disunity in the church. The cultural factors that hindered conversion were concerned with bigotry, food, and the handling of the holy book. The political factors were mostly related to human rights issues that directly affect the freedoms of practicing Christians in the UK, including Muslim converts.

In the next chapter, I turn the table and discuss the factors that contribute to the conversion of Muslims to the Christian faith.

Bibliography

Ahsan, Muhammad M. *Islam: Faith and Practice*. United Kingdom: Islamic Foundation, 1977.

BBC Ethic Guide. "Honour Crime." *BBC News*, 2014. Accessed December 24, 2022. http://www.bbc.co.uk/ethics/honourcrimes/crimesofhonour_1.shtml.

52 BBC News, "Why Are Pakistan's Christians Targeted?", *BBC News*, October 30, 2018, https://www.bbc.co.uk/news/world-asia-35910331

53 BBC News, "Why are Pakistan's Christians."

54 Salman Masood, "Hindu Veterinarian Is Latest to Face Blasphemy Charges in Pakistan," *The New York Times*, May 30, 2019, https://www.nytimes.com/2019/05/30/world/asia/pakistan-blasphemy-law.html

BBC News. "Why Are Pakistan's Christians Targeted?" *BBC News*, October 30, 2018, https://www.bbc.co.uk/news/world-asia-35910331.

———. "British Airways Christian Employee Nadia Eweida Wins Case." *BBC News*, January 15, 2013, https://www.bbc.com/news/uk-21025332.

Coleman, Marc. *"The Muslim Spiritual Progress Scale: Aiding Muslims in Coming to Christ."* Digital Commons @Andrews University. 2012. https://digitalcommons.andrews.edu/do/search/?q=aiding%20muslims%20coming%20to%20christ&start=0&context=6860132&facet=

Cooper, Anne. *Ishmael My Brother: A Christian Introduction to Islam*. Crowborough, UK: MARC, 1997.

Esposito, John. *The Oxford Dictionary of Islam*. Oxford: Oxford University Press, 2014.

European Court of Human Rights, Guide on Article 9 of the European Convention on Human Rights, *European Court of Human Rights*, August 31, 2022, https://www.echr.coe.int/documents/guide_art_9_eng.pdf

Find Easy, "Religion in Europe." Find Easy, June 18, 2021. https://www.findeasy.in/europe-population-by-religion/

Gordon-Cornwell Theological Seminary. "Christianity in View: Statistics and Forecasts for World Religions: 1800–2025," *Gordon-Cornwell Theological Seminary*, Accessed April 12, 2022, http://christianityinview.com/religion-statistics.html.

Latif, A. "The Global Islamic Community: What Ummah Means to Believers, Muslims in Multi-religious Singapore Taking Practical Approach." *The Straits Times*, March 14, 1998.

Linning, Stephanie. "The Tragic Schoolgirl Victim of UK's First 'Honour Killing.'" *Daily Mail*, February 18, 2021, https://www.dailymail.co.uk/femail/article-9270103/.

Masood, Salman. "Hindu Veterinarian Is Latest to Face Blasphemy Charges in Pakistan." *The New York Times*, May 30, 2019.

Musk, B. A. *Touching the Soul of Islam*. Crowborough, UK: MARC, 1997.

News Information and Analysis. "Investigation Into the Persecution of Christian Converts from Islam in Europe (1)." *News Information and Analysis*, July 20, 2022. https://fsspx.news/en/news-events/news/investigation-persecution-christian-converts-islam-europe-1-75128.

Pew Research Center. "The Future of World Religions: Population Growth Projections, 2010–2050." *Pew Research Center*, April 2, 2015. https://www.pewresearch.org/religion/2015/04/02/religious-projections-2010-2050/.

———. "Muslims." *Pew Research Center*, April 2, 2015. https://www.pewresearch.org/religion/2015/04/02/muslims/.

Rizvi, Sayyid Muhmmad. *The Ritual and Spiritual Purity*. Ahlul Bayt Digital Islamic Library Project 1995–2023. https://www.al-islam.org/ritual-and-spiritual-purity-sayyid-muhammad-rizvi/ii-wudu.

Stacey, Vivienne. "Toward a Current Strategy: Discerning God's Hand in Islam Today." *Missiology* 4, no. 3 (July 1976): 363–372. https://doi.org/10.1177/009182967600400310.

Talwar, Divya and Athar Ahmad. "'Honour Crimes': 11,000 UK Cases Recorded in Five Years." *BBC News*, July 9, 2015. https://www.bbc.com/news/uk-33424644.

UPI. "Reports of 'Honor' Crimes Rise in London." UPI, December 9, 2009. https://www.upi.com/Top_News/World-News/2009/12/07/Reports-of-honor-crimes- rise-in-London/37251260206655/?ur3=1

Wu, R. A. *The Call to Islam: A Contemporary Perspective*. Singapore: Muslim Converts' Association, 1990.

10

CHRISTIAN OUTREACH TO MUSLIMS IN THE EAST AND WEST—OPPORTUNITIES

by M. T. Amjad

Introduction

In the previous chapter, I discussed the obstacles to Muslim evangelization and named four hindering factors: theological or spiritual, social, cultural, and political. In this chapter, I reverse the focus to identify and discuss factors that help Muslims convert from Islam to Christianity. I also share my experiences of Christians showing love to Muslims and the importance of an indigenous church specific to Muslim believers. I commence with the five categories of helping factors and follow with two sections, radical love, and the church as a family, which provide perspectives on the difficult conversion process for Muslims. Finally, I argue that the insider movement is not an effective contextualization method.

As in my earlier chapter, I draw on my informal ethnographic study of Muslim seekers and MBBs from Southeast Asia and the UK since 1992.

What Helps Muslims Come to Faith in Jesus?

Many factors contribute to conversion from Islam to Christianity. I have sorted the responses I received from MBBs into five major themes: extraordinary events, relationships with individual Christians, the role of the church, personal struggles, and Christian literature and outreach.

Extraordinary Events

Many of the Muslim seekers and converts reported extraordinary events, such as visions, dreams, and miracles, that contributed to their conversion. Muslims can relate to extraordinary events because they believe in miracles. When Muslims experience miracles in their own lives and hear testimonies that Jesus performed miracles, they feel a life-changing affinity. The Qur'an states that Jesus performed miracles. An MBB[1], mentioned, "I saw a vision of Jesus Christ standing in front of me, assuring me of his presence that led to my decision to follow Christ."

While I was talking to a Muslim seeker[2] in the summer of May–June 2000, I discovered that he had been searching for the truth about Jesus for over a year. He said his desire was to see Jesus in person. I encouraged him to pray and ask Jesus to show himself to him. I said to the seeker, "If you believe that Jesus is still alive according to the Qur'an, he should be able to respond to your prayer and requests." After a few days, he told me that he had a dream in which he was standing in the front row (*saff*) of his mosque for evening prayers. A man in a white robe appeared in the mihrab (the arch where the imam or sheikh stands to lead prayers), facing toward the congregation, which was unusual because Muslim worshippers usually see the imam's back. He saw that his face was shining, and the whole room was lit up with bright white light from his presence. The person in the white robe said, "Come and follow me." At that point, the whole congregation fell on their faces and bowed down to him and worshipped him. The mysterious man called my informant by name three times, and the congregation bowed down to him as he called out again, "Come and follow me." In this way, the seeker realized that Jesus is alive, as he gave a clear call to follow him. Another MBB said that he personally experienced a miracle: "When my mother discovered that I was attending church secretly (I had lied that I was working overtime), she became very angry. She dragged me into the kitchen and looked for a knife to kill me and then herself. But somehow, she could not find a single knife or sharp

1 CMMFP4.

2 ASCFA.

object in her own kitchen! This was very unusual, and, in this way, God showed us his grace and mercy. He spared our lives miraculously."[3]

Hence, when these Muslims encountered visions and miracles in their own lives, the impact was much greater. Visions and miracles are powerful means of drawing Muslims to believe in Jesus.

Relationship with Individual Christian Believers

A quarter of the Muslim seekers and converts claimed that the good impressions they received from their Christian colleagues and other Christians contributed to their conversion. One convert proclaimed, "A Christian office colleague who eventually became my spouse was the one who influenced my conversion to Christianity."[4] Another convert acknowledged, "A layperson with a golden heart . . . greatly influenced my decision to follow Christ."[5] Still another convert declared, "My mother married my father, who was a Muslim, and she had to convert to Islam because she was formerly a Christian. She told us about Jesus and miracles in the Bible through storytelling. As a result, both my sisters and I became Christians."[6]

Thus Muslims can see Christ in the character and lifestyles of Christian believers. Acts of kindness and compassion from Christian workers and believers, such as teachers, nurses, and doctors, help them to see the transforming love of Christ.

The Role of the Local Church

Almost all the MBBs I interacted with revealed that the church had no influence on their conversion. They only went to church after they converted, and they often faced challenges in fitting into church culture.

However, once in the confines of the church, several MBBs were impressed by "the way Christians love each other like family members."[7] About half of the MBBs stated that they like the way Christians fellowship with each other, and about half said they liked the friendliness and

3 COMFS5.

4 CMMFS1.

5 CMMMS6.

6 CMMMS14.

7 CMMFS8.

openness of a Christian group. One of the MBBs claimed, "After my conversion . . . the church played its spiritual role by providing a friendly atmosphere with preaching of the Word."[8]

Personal Struggles

All the MBBs said that personal struggles played a part in their conversion. Their struggles varied, but all MBBs had arrived at a stage when they were looking for a personal relationship with God. One MBB, said, "I always wanted to have a personal relationship with God. I tried to be a good Muslim, but in my heart, I could not reach to the upper level or be assured that God would accept me. Eventually, I found that Christianity showed me the answer to my struggles, causing me to accept Jesus as my Savior."[9]

Another MBB claimed, "The teachings of Islam, conflicts among the Muslims, and vagueness of the Qur'an were factors that caused me to be dissatisfied with Islam. As I struggled with this dissatisfaction, I found revelation in the Bible that was not vague and satisfied me spiritually."[10] Another MBB attributed his conversion to "inconsistencies between the teachings and practices of Islam, which caused me to seek for the Truth. I found my answers from the Bible and converted to Christianity."[11]

As indicated above, many of the MBBs had struggled with the Islamic concept of sin and forgiveness, which led them to search for it in other religions, hence the pathway to Christianity, which assured them that their sins could be forgiven. One MBB confided, "I was not satisfied with what Islam can offer because Islam did not provide assurance that my sins can be forgiven. I was not sure if I would attain God's standard and get to heaven. I was always afraid of the consequences in my future life—will I go to heaven or hell? I began to search for the answers, and the Bible showed me that I can reach the goal and have my sins forgiven in Jesus Christ."[12]

However, a quarter of the MBBs also struggled with the concept of how the sacrifice of Jesus made it possible for God to accept sinners. One MBB said, "I struggled a lot to understand the issue of how a holy God can

8 CMMFS8.

9 CMMFS1.

10 CMMMS6.

11 CIMMS11.

12 COMFS3.

accept a sinner because of the sacrifice of Jesus for sinners. But I understood this when I read the Bible."[13]

Half of the MBs had struggled with the meaning of life and felt there was no purpose in their lives. Some common remarks from the MBBs were "missing something in life, no satisfaction," "spiritual hunger," and "emptiness in life."[14] One MBB expressed, "During my turbulent time, I felt God's helping hand and, through prayer and communication with God, I found strength and comfort and felt God's touch in my heart."[15]

In my twenty-five years of ministry in the UK and beyond, I witnessed many personal struggles that take someone either closer or further away from God. Surprisingly, many Muslims sought Jesus when they were in prison, and eventually these seekers were baptized by the prison chaplaincy teams and volunteer pastors who came to help them in the prisons. This was also common among hospitalized patients struggling with chronic diseases. They were introduced to Jesus by someone and prayed to Jesus for healing and miracles, and some were eventually healed by the miraculous power of Jesus Christ.

One MBB recounted that he had an accident in Pakistan and was told that his damaged eye from the accident would not heal.[16] Someone challenged him to pray and ask Jesus for healing. He did pray to Jesus, and he was healed. He gave his life to Jesus because of this miracle.

Christian Literature and Evangelistic Outreach

Many of the MBBs claimed that the Bible was both the most powerful literature they had read and the factor that led them to their conversion. One of them pointed out that reading the Holy Bible (New Testament) in his own language was particularly helpful.[17] Another MB said she was converted while studying the Bible as a compulsory religious knowledge subject for O level in a mission school.[18] A few MBBs stated that, in addition to the Bible, their conversion was assisted by other evangelistic materials and outreach.

13 CMMFS10.

14 CMMFS9, CMMMS13, and CMMMS14 respectively.

15 CMMFS8.

16 AMPMBB.

17 CMMMS6.

18 CMMMS2.

These evangelistic materials were "navigators' materials" and "a correspondence course" (the MBB could not remember the name of the course).[19] The evangelistic outreach comprised "Billy Graham's crusade"[20] and visual presentations of Christian organizations, such as "*Hiding Place* film", "Every Home Crusade in 1978, United in Christ Fellowship 1979."[21] "The Christian Seamen's Fellowship" also contributed to conversions, and the book *Table Ministries* in 2014 and 2019 were also acknowledged.[22]

To sum up, the five contributory themes above encapsulate the responses from the MBBs to the question, "What contributed to your conversion to Christianity?" It was interesting to find that the local church did *not* play a significant role in their conversion, but it did help them in their subsequent spiritual growth through the teaching and preaching of God's word. Sadly, some converts dropped out of Christianity when confronted by negative social, cultural, spiritual, and political circumstances.

As noted above, many of the MBBs had personal struggles in their lives that were mitigated by answers from the Bible, inducing them to follow the Christian faith. Also mentioned was the phenomenon of conversion by many men and women who were imprisoned, which is more common among prisoners in Western countries than in the Eastern world. Incidentally, the common issues identified by prisoners were emptiness, dissatisfaction, and meaninglessness in life, concern about sin, and the need for forgiveness of sins, which led to a yearning for a personal relationship with Jesus.

Reaching Out to Muslims with Radical Love

A study of the life and ministry of Jesus shows that his strategies were simple but radical. Mostly, he ministered to Jewish individuals, groups, and the community at large. He worked within his own culture and the people who spoke his language. He presented the message that "the kingdom of God is at hand" (Mark 1:15). He used Jewish theological knowledge, interpretation of Jewish law, and cultural understanding to communicate his

19 CMMFS4 and CMMFS1.

20 CMMFS1 and CMMMS6.

21 CMMMS6.

22 CMMFS8, BNMB, and PNMB, respectively.

message and show his radical love—for example, in Acts 4:13: "Now when they [Jews] saw the boldness of Peter and John, they perceived that they were uneducated, common men, they were astonished, and they recognized that they had been with Jesus."

I have observed that Jews are like Muslims in many ways, especially in their culture and religious laws. Jesus connected with Jews at marketplaces, workplaces, homes, and different events (such as at the wedding at Cana), at the temple, during his travels, at the well, and in many other ways. His methods of connecting with people were simple, but they were incredibly profound.

Jesus's methods of connecting were not important in terms of who he met and how he met them, but the delivery of his message in the context of relationships and love penetrated people's hearts and transformed their lives from the inside out. They became his followers because of his message and radical love.

I propose that reaching out to Muslims should be like the ways Jesus approached Jews and shared the good news of the kingdom of God during his ministry. In our ministry, we contact Muslims through a bookstall at the marketplace, visiting the mosque, Muslim and Christian discussions, door-to-door visits, teaching (free of charge), legal and family counseling, and hospitality. We seek Muslim seekers like Nicodemus: "Now there was a Pharisee, a man named Nicodemus who was a member of the Jewish ruling council. He came to Jesus at night and said, 'Rabbi, we know that you are a teacher who has come from God. For no one could perform the signs you are doing if God were not with him'" (John 3:1).

We find many Nicodemuses in the Muslim community through relationships and the love of Christ shown to them. As with Jesus, our methods of making contact are not significant; they are just a starting point toward the process of friendship and relationship to share the love of Christ. Jesus called his disciples and discipled them in the context of relationships and love, so we are also reaching out to Muslims with love and relationships. We cannot do what Jesus did; however, we might be able to follow the example of his disciples. For example, Paul said, "I will not venture to speak of anything except what Christ has accomplished through me in leading the Gentiles to obey God by what I have said and done by the power of signs and wonders, through the power of the spirit of God. So, from Jerusalem all the way around to Illyricum, I have fully proclaimed the gospel of Christ. It has always been my ambition to preach the gospel where Christ was not known, so that I would not be building on someone else's foundation" (Rom 15:18–20).

The Church as a Family

In the book of Acts chapter 2, the followers of Jesus became a family of believers in Jesus Christ. However, this transition has become more complicated in multicultural and multireligious societies, especially in Western countries. Churches in most societies and communities have modified their practices to comply with multicultural policies. Nevertheless, the MBBs found it hard to assimilate into Western-style churches because they longed for Eastern culture and values.

To solve these cultural and value problems, many church planters have tried to contextualize the church and fellowship for believers. However, many church planters or reformers have struggled to find the right balance and have ended up with churches that are either over-contextualized or under-contextualized. Over-contextualization has resulted in syncretism, an attempt to combine opposing belief systems. By contrast, under-contextualization has produced Western-style churches into which MBBs are unable to fit and eventually reject. Therefore, the attrition rate is extremely high among MBBs, and many Muslim seekers never realize their chance to explore the Christian faith. They disappear or drop out (see figure 10.1).

As indicated earlier in this chapter, many Muslim seekers and MBBs are unable to adjust to Western churches because they are unable to solve the dilemma of wanting to follow Jesus Christ while facing the prospect of losing their families, relatives, and Muslim communities (see figure 10.2). Many times, converts are left with the choice of no fellowship with other Muslim families and friends or being secret believers. If they do step forward and enter a church or fellowship, they are often misunderstood because they do not fit into the normal mold of their fellow churchgoers.

In such a predicament, MBBs are very sensitive about sharing personal information because they never know how the information

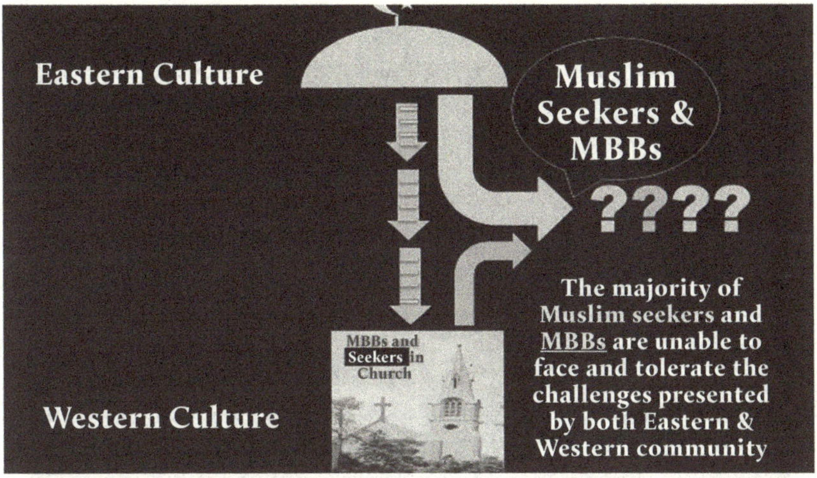

Figure 10.1. Attrition rate (Source: Amjad 2023).

will be handled by both their Muslim communities and Christians at the church. On one side are possible grounds for their persecution, and on the other side are church people who regard MBBs' secrecy as an unwillingness to share. And if church leaders and fellow believers withdraw their support for Muslim seekers and MBBs, the latter are left stranded.

Let us consider a linear graph (figure 10.3) showing the relationship between Muslims on the y-axis and Christians on the x-axis. They are both human beings at the starting points (0) of their relationships. If Christians (x) start developing relationships with Muslims (y) by showing radical love as Jesus loved us, they will grow together in relationships, and all the variables on the x-axis and y-axis will have a positive correlation. Understanding each other and going deeper in a relationship and love result in a straight line as a resultant mean line in the middle of the graph for a balanced relationship (and contextualization). But if the resultant lines are not directly proportional to x and y, they will be under the resultant mean line, representing under-contextualization (see figure 10.4).

Contrastingly, if the resultant lines fall above the resultant mean line, it will indicate over-contextualization. This may be because missionaries have encouraged MBBs to stay close to their Eastern

Figure 10.2. Differences between Muslims in the East and West (Source: Amjad 2023).

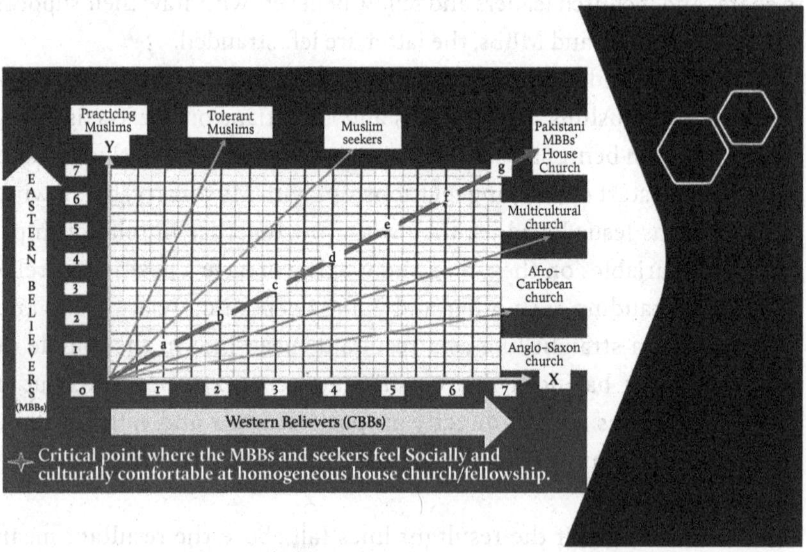

Figure 10.3. Variables along the x-axis and y-axis (Source: Amjad 2023).

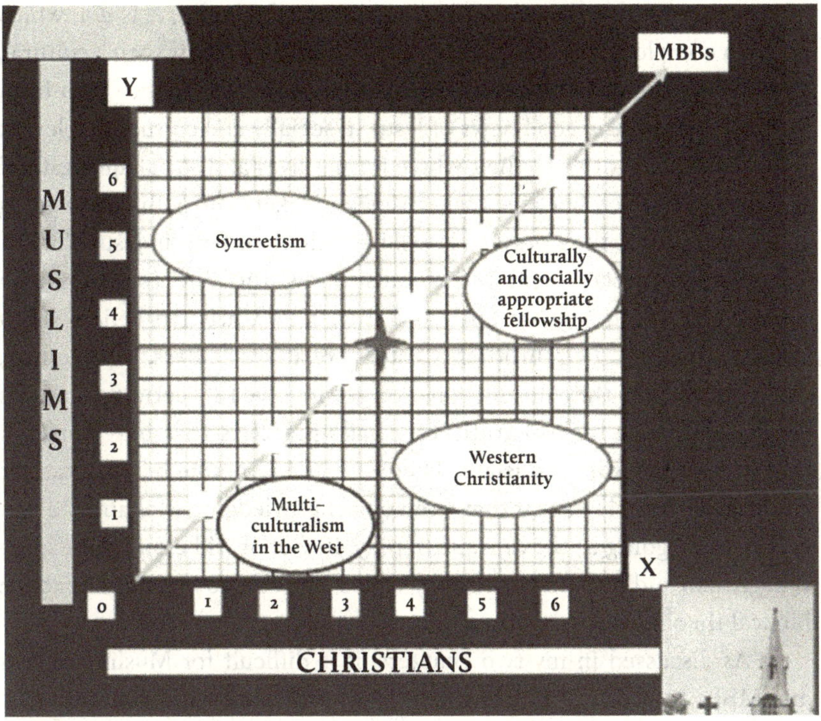

Figure 10.4. Over- and under-contextualization (Source: Amjad 2023).

cultures where they feel comfortable, but there is a danger that the new church plants are moving too close to the y-axis and syncretism. To achieve balance, the MBBs' identities should not be of either Eastern or Western believers, but of transformed believers who are changed by radical love and relationships, and they can understand the sensitivities of both cultures and willingly believe and practice a sound biblical theology.

Many Western missionaries working among Muslims, including in the UK, favor keeping MBBs and Muslim seekers within Muslim culture, families, and communities. They even advocate calling Mohammed a prophet and attending a local mosque while they are praying in the name of Jesus. I call this approach and strategy an over-contextualized syncretistic missionary approach to Muslims.

We need to realize that Islam is not just a religion; it is *din*, which means a complete way of life for Muslims. It includes their social, cultural, spiritual, and political lives. It is true that to break through into their lives, we must present the good news of Jesus in socially and culturally relevant ways that are sensitive to their whole former lives and social and cultural practices. However, I believe that if Muslim seekers and MBBs keep going to the mosque for their prayers, it will not help their faith in Jesus Christ.

Muslim seekers and MBBs must draw the line to distinguish between their old Muslim faith and their new Christian beliefs. They need to respect their brothers, sisters, relatives, elders, community, and *ummah*, but they do not have to get involved in certain practices that compromise biblical truth, especially practices that have spiritual significance according to Islam. Therefore, it will not be helpful in their spiritual walk with Jesus if they keep on acknowledging Mohammad as a prophet and going to the mosque to pray. In fact, it will cloud their spiritual growth and faith in Jesus. They will not be able to learn and practice biblical theology.

As discussed in my two chapters, it is difficult for Muslim seekers and MBBs to break away from their Muslim relatives and communities, especially when living in Muslim-dominant countries, but the truth can be liberating. Jesus said, "Then you will know the truth, and the truth will set you free" (John 8:32). For MBBs to keep on calling Mohammad the prophet and going to the mosque to pray is too large a compromise.

It may be useful to reflect on the churches that existed in what is now Pakistan before the partition of India and Pakistan in 1947. These churches were planted by Western missionaries with minimal consideration of Muslim contextualization. Eventually, they turned into Eastern churches with Western culture and theology, even though the worshippers were all Pakistanis. The new believers spoke their local languages and lived mainly in their own cultures, but they followed the Western way of religion and had to change some aspects of their lives. Many MBBs even changed their first names to follow the Christian faith. However, these prior changes make it complicated and more difficult in contemporary times for church leaders and believers to attract Muslims to their local churches.

The Insider Movement

I am in favor of balanced social and cultural approaches to Islam without compromising biblical theology and the truth found in Jesus Christ. And, as stated above, I am mindful of over- and under-contextualized approaches being used. I contend that an example of an under-contextualized approach is the "insider movement."[23] Advocates of this approach (hereafter "insiders") propose that Muslims believe in one God who is called Allah and that this is synonymous with the Christian God, which is justified because Muhammed preached the same Judeo-Christian message. But when we compare Muhammed's message with the biblical truth, we find it is entirely different. Therefore, I regard the insider movement as a variant of Western approaches wherein missionaries have tried to reach out to Muslims for decades and centuries with very little to show for it.

As mentioned above, the fundamental problem of Western churches is that they have not been able to compensate MBBs for their loss of family and community. Based on my everyday observations and research in Southeast Asia and Europe, I have found that many MBBs have not been able to sustain their conversion. They go back to Islam because of the social and cultural issues they face in Western-oriented churches.

I assume that insiders, realizing that Westernized churches have not adequately accommodated MBBs, offer MBBs a hybrid religion that keeps them in a socially and culturally relevant Muslim community where they will feel at home. Farrokh made a similar observation about the insider movement's proponents: "Muslims can come to faith in the Lord Jesus Christ, retain their Muslim identity, and remain in good standing with their respective Muslim communities."[24] Pullella and Eljechtimi noted that even Pope Francis told the tiny Catholic community in the predominantly Muslim country of Morocco that

23 Fred Farrokh, "Indigenous Perspectives on Muslim Identity, and Insider Movements," *Global Missiology*, 2, no. 12 (January 2015), http://ojs.globalmissiology.org/index.php/english/article/view/1757/3897

24 Farrokh, *Indigenous Perspectives on Muslim Identity.*

"their mission was not to convert their neighbors but to live in brotherhood with other faiths."[25]

I acknowledge that the insiders' approach might be helpful in reducing the historical problem of converts being killed or ostracized, but it creates a bigger problem. Apparently, the insiders have not analyzed the impact of their movement on the integrity of biblical theology and clashes between the biblical, Qur'anic, and hadith explanations of the key issues of Muslim and Christian beliefs.

It is fair enough to try contextualized approaches to reach out to Muslims, but we must not forget that outreach methods and strategies themselves do not persuade Muslims. It is God's prerogative to convert their hearts to realize the need for the saving grace of God and salvation. Keeping MBBs in their former communities and expecting them to disciple others in their communities may be compared with the actions of "insiders" like Paul and Peter. Paul and Peter were clear about their convictions and the message; however, they were eventually killed because of their openness and opposition to the gospel message.

Even if insiders answer the objections above and propose solutions, the insider movement may not provide the right motivation and approach in terms of deep theological issues. Moreover, it would be an abdication for Western missionaries to place so much responsibility on the shoulders of freshly converted Muslim seekers or MBBs.

The reality is that committed MBBs need to sever ties with their families and communities, but to do so is very risky, and they may even be killed according to the sharia law in their native Muslim countries. Alarmingly, such killings are becoming more prevalent even in the UK. The other worst-case scenario is that if MBBs survive their conversion in the UK and return to such places as Pakistan, they will either be forced to revert to Islam or be victims of honor killing.

We do not know the exact number of honor killings each year in the UK. The police estimated that twelve honor killings took place in the UK in 2002. According to the police database, there were twenty-nine cases of

25 Philip Pullella and Ahmed Eljechtimi, "Conversion Is Not Your Mission, Pope Tells Catholics in Morocco," *Yahoo Finance*, March 31, 2019, https://uk.finance.yahoo.com/news/1-conversion-not-mission-pope-150040407.html

killings or attempted killings from 2010 to 2014 (eleven attempted killings and eighteen actual killings).[26]

In my experience, very few MBBs want to be insiders, as they know well the consequences of being deceptive and working under the noses of their Muslim communities. It is Western missionaries who are guiding MBBs to take this approach. I have known hundreds of MBBs during my twenty-five years of ministry in Europe and Southeast Asia. The MBBs will not stay in their former communities, and they will not even visit the towns where they were born or grew up, let alone work as insiders.

Staying within the Muslim community in disguise would be considered a deceitful act toward their Muslim friends, relatives, communities, and Islamic *ummah*, which will not be tolerated by Muslims. When it becomes known that Muslim seekers and MBBs are pretending to be Muslims but believe in opposing teachings to the Qur'an and hadith, they will be dealt with harshly.

We can find a similar example in the book of Acts 2:46, with reference to the disciples of Jesus. It says, "Every day they continued to meet in the temple courts. They broke bread in their homes and ate together with glad and sincere hearts." They hid their beliefs from the temple authorities for some time, but when it became general knowledge that the disciples were following Jesus Christ and that they claimed him as savior and the son of God, they were no longer welcome to meet at the temple courts. We see in Acts 4:1–4 that "the priests and the captain of the temple guard and the Sadducees came up to Peter and John while they were speaking to the people. They were disturbed because the apostles were teaching the people, proclaiming in Jesus the resurrection of the dead. They seized Peter and John and, because it was evening, they put them in jail until the next day. But many who heard the message believed it; so, the number of men who believed grew to about five thousand."

This approach and the message that Peter and John were proclaiming were contrary to Jewish beliefs and theology and were not acceptable to the Jewish leaders and many citizens. Similarly, the insiders' approach

26 Emily Dyer, "'*Honour' killings in the UK*," *The Henry Jackson Society*, January 2015, https://henryjacksonsociety.org/wp-content/uploads/2015/01/Honour-Killings-in-the-UK.pdf

contravenes Muslim beliefs and theology and brings persecution to MBBs. I accept that Western missionaries and insider movement proponents cannot abandon Muslim countries in such challenging times. However, it would be unfair to expect MBBs and seekers to promote the insider movement in Muslim-majority countries. Since many MBBs are already being killed for Jesus in the Muslim world, Western insiders should not add fuel to the fire. We need to trust God, and we must not force or push controversial approaches that carry the risk of dire outcomes.

Conclusion

In this chapter, I focused on the factors conducive to the conversion of MBBs, with an emphasis on what happened under my watch in the UK. However, the reality is that even in Muslim minority countries, Muslim conversion is problematic and often dangerous. Therefore, Christians who want to reach out to their Muslim communities must use sensitive approaches, strategies, vocabulary, and codes of conduct. I have found it helpful to contact Muslims in appropriate and safe places; build relationships with respect, friendship, and radical love; and try very hard to avoid compromising biblical truth and theology.

Bibliography

Dyer, Emily. "*'Honour' Killings in the UK*, London." *The Henry Jackson Society*, January 2015. https://henryjacksonsociety.org/wp-content/uploads/2015/01/Honour-Killings-in-the-UK.pdf.

Farrokh, Fred. 2015. "Indigenous Perspectives on Muslim Identity and Insider Movements." *Global Missiology*. 2, no.12, (January 2015). http://ojs.globalmissiology.org/index.php/english/article/view/1757/3897.

Pullella, Philip and Ahmed Eljechtimi. "Conversion Is Not Your Mission, Pope Tells Catholics in Morocco." *Yahoo Finance*, March 31, 2109. https://uk.finance.yahoo.com/news/1-conversion-not-mission-pope-150040407.html.

11

ASIAN MUSLIMS—CHRISTIANS' "NEIGHBORS" IN SOUTHEAST ASIA

by Markus Ching

Introduction

In a real sense, the Asianization of Christianity brings the discussion back to where it began. Christianity did not originate west of the Caucasus mountains, nor was Jesus Christ a Caucasian. He was a Jew from the Middle East and the western region of Asia. To investigate the Asianization of Christianity and its mission, one must retrace the teaching of the gospel to its roots in the divine economy and mention of God's divine mission, as recorded in Genesis 3:15, to the establishment of the table of nations in Genesis 10–11 and their "power plays" around the Tower of Babel, and, significantly, to the eventual calling of Abram (later Abraham) in Genesis 12 to bless the nations. Likewise, the following core questions pertinent to the topic must be framed in the primary source document: the Bible, which faithfully records the story of God's redemptive plan through his people, including the Asian peoples.

In this chapter, "neighbor communities" refer to the largest non-Christian religious communities in Southeast Asia. In most countries, these neighbors are Muslims. According to Pew Research, "Muslims living in the Asia-Pacific region, which includes 61 countries and territories, constitute 62% of all Muslims worldwide." The six Asian countries with the largest Muslim populations are Indonesia (229 million), Pakistan (200 million), India (195 million), Bangladesh (153 million), Iran (82.5 million), and Türkiye (formerly Turkey; 74.4 million). Together, these six countries are home to 85 percent of Asia's Muslim population and more than 50 percent of the global Muslim population.[1] Therefore, it is appropriate to say that Muslims are the most significant other to Christian communities in Asia.

There other religions in Asia, such as Buddhism, Taoism, Sikhism, Confucianism, and spiritual animism, but the one that presents the biggest challenge to the Christian evangelism instituted by Christ is Islam. Since Muslims are in close geographical proximity to Christians across Asia and Southeast Asia, and because I advocate friendly, respectful engagement between Muslims and Christians, the term "neighbors" seems appropriate. In this chapter, I focus on neighbor communities in Indonesia and Malaysia, and I deem the following questions pertinent for gospel ministry to and with this large unreached group:

- How do Christians reach Asian Muslims for Christ?
- What unique communication principles should we use?
- How do we present the Bible in the Muslim frame of reference?
- How do we start worship centers?
- What type of liturgy resonates with their culture? Are they oral learners?

I now address each question in turn.

How Do We Reach Asian Muslims for the Lord?

Unfortunately, the twenty-first century has been marred by sociopolitical, interreligious, and interracial dissonance and conflicts between the followers of Christianity and Islam, especially in radicalized

1 Pew Research Center, "Asia Pacific Overview," *Pew Research Center*, accessed February 8, 2022, https://www.pewresearch.org/religion/2009/10/07/mapping-the-global-muslim-population9/

Muslim-majority areas of Southeast Asia. Even a cursory reading of current and past reports underscores this reality.[2] This situation evokes the need for better education in Islamic religion and culture for Christians who desire to intelligently reach out and engage with Muslims for Christ.

Robert C. Douglas, who spent many years serving in the Muslim world, stated that traditional Christians need to be equipped and empowered to respond to their Muslim friends and seekers with sound understanding. This edict, presumably, was intended for *all* concerned Christian laity, not just professional missionaries, to help them avoid the common misunderstandings and confusion Muslims and Christians typically display toward each other.[3]

I believe that first and foremost, Christians need to establish the foundational principle that God has a plan of salvation for all humankind—no single race, religion, or nation is excluded. I presume that the following key learning points are relevant for concerned Asian Christians. First, Jesus Christ's death on the cross was for any who would come to him to receive his gift of salvation that was purchased by his precious shed blood. Christopher Wright noted that the God of the Christian Bible is himself a missional God from the very beginning, as evidenced in Genesis 1, 3, 10, and 12.[4] Just after the account of the fall of Adam and Eve and the confrontation of God with the serpent, the author of Genesis recorded God's curse on the serpent, which was the perpetrator, while at the same time providing a veiled promise of divine redemption in Genesis 3:1415: "The Lord God said to the serpent,

2 Malaysiakini, "Family of alleged 'enforcement disappearance' victim takes plight to Jokowi," *Malaysiakini*, accessed March 30, 2023, https://m.malaysiakini.com/news/469948Also, Malachi E. Vethamani, "The Malaysian Albatross of May 13, 1969 Racial Riots," *Sun Yat-sen Journal of Humanities* 49, no. 2 (2020):19–41.

3 Robert C. Douglas, "Research and Training," *Muslims and Christians on the Emmaus Road,"* ed. J. Dudley Woodberry (Pasadena: Zwemer Institute of Muslim Studies, 1989), 350–435.

4 Christopher J.H. Wright, *The Mission of God's People: A Biblical Theology of the Church's Mission* (Grand Rapids, MI: Zondervan 2010), 28–29.

'Because you have done this . . . I will put enmity between you and the woman, and between your offspring and her offspring; he shall bruise your head, and you shall bruise his heel.'" Embedded in these words is humankind's only hope, as God declared in Genesis 3:15: the seed of the woman, who is coming as the deliverer, the savior, the Messiah. God had begun the work of redeeming and saving humankind from the effects of the fall, even from the Garden itself, with the prophetic announcement of the gospel of hope.

Second, it is the Holy Spirit's prerogative that converts the heart of the hearer and effects the work of salvation in their life, not Christian efforts alone. In John 3:3–8, Jesus explained his distinct truth of spiritual rebirth by the work of the Holy Spirit to Nicodemus, the Hebrew rabbi and private seeker of truth:

> Jesus answered him, 'Truly, truly I say to you, unless one is born again, he cannot see the kingdom of God.' Nicodemus said to him, 'How can a man be born when he is old? Can he enter a second time into his mother's womb and be born?' Jesus answered, 'Truly, truly I say to you, unless one is born of water and the Spirit, he cannot enter the kingdom of God. That which is born of the flesh is flesh, and that which is born of the Spirit is spirit. Do not marvel that said to you, "You must be born again." The wind blows where it wishes, and you hear its sound, but you now know where it comes from or where it goes. So, it is with everyone who is born of the Spirit.'

It is also the Spirit that seals the hearts of all believers that they truly belong to God, and the Spirit bears witness in their hearts to the guarantee of what they will ultimately own and become in Christ (2 Cor 1:21, 22). The same spirit of Christ gave the mandate to his believers to proclaim the gospel to all creation (Mark 16:15–16) and equips all who would be witnesses for the task. It is the same Holy Spirit who moves the hearts of Asian Muslims, not just Christians' stalwart human efforts to convert them. By relying on the guidance of the Holy Spirit, we may avoid human disappointment and avert Muslims' accusations and charges about "Christians proselytizing Muslims," which are common in many Asian societies with Muslim majorities.[5]

Third, God used his Christian believers to bring the message of salvation to all seekers. The Lord Jesus gave us a very clear and unmistakable cultural mandate in Matthew 28:19 to make disciples of all nations and baptize them in the name of the Holy Trinity. The Lord Jesus Christ also invites Asian Christians to join him in fulfilling his Great Commission in the world to proclaim the good news of his kingdom and to invite others to join him as reconciled children. I contend that this is the invitation of a lifetime from him and should carry the highest priority for Asians. Jesus calls us to enlist in his service and to be his ambassadors for his kingdom and his good news as he sends us out to do the following:[6]

- proclamation: to explain to Muslim seekers and believers the good news that sins can be forgiven, the kingdom of God is now open to them through Jesus's death on the cross, and a vicarious reconciliation with God is a reality
- compassion: to care about their physical, emotional, mental, and relational needs
- justice: to take a stand against unjust persecution, the suppression of fundamental human rights, and every form of exploitation and cruel tyranny, which includes freedom of religious choice, conscience, and thought
- restoration: to introduce disciples to Jesus Christ by teaching believers how to live by making a difference upon entering the kingdom of God

Thus the gospel of Jesus Christ is not merely a system of beliefs and doctrines for Christians to study intellectually and discuss. It proposes a

5 For example, in the Malaysian Constitution's Article 11, where there is such an explicit prohibition.

6 Richard Stearns, *Unfinished: Believing Is Only the Beginning* (Nashville: Thomas Nelson, 2013), 89.

way of living that we are called to adopt and demonstrate daily. It is indeed through Christ's regenerated believers that God works his plan to bring salvation to all seekers and the unbelieving. And these believers need an understanding and discernment of the worldview and mindsets of seekers. This, in turn, aids the communication of any witness who seeks to make the gospel relevant to anyone with little understanding of, much less appreciation for, the historic message of the gospel of Christ.

Therefore, to reach out to neighbor Muslims, Christians need to have a greater understanding of Christianity-Islam interfaith communication, including Islamic worldviews and confusion about the gospel.[7] It calls for a need to distinguish Biblical-based tenets of faith from common Islamic misunderstandings, which was a key finding of Catholic researcher J. M. Gaudeul, who documented and studied scores of conversion events and testimonies of ex-Muslims who converted to Christ in modern history.[8]

Fourth, it is important that Christians proceed with openness and willingness to overcome fears and prejudices of reaching out to Muslims. The simplest way to begin is for Asian Christians to support and participate in group prayer meetings that involve like-minded Christians. Apart from that, Christians can engage churches in church-wide prayer meetings for Muslim seekers, pre-believers, and converted Muslims for their protection and spiritual nurture to aid in building their faith and confidence.

Finally, Christians can go one step further by empathically addressing the felt needs of Muslim inquirers and relating to their doubts, fears, family insecurities, and spiritual struggles. Prayer and genuine friendship build the foundation to reach Muslim seekers, and both require commitment, time, sacrifice, and effort because there will be obstacles along the way where either party may be tempted to give up. Practitioners need to see beyond the barriers of fear and prejudice by allowing the Lord to open their eyes to Muslims' need for a savior who also died for their sins.[9] The Lord

---

7 George Cheng, "Equipping Asian Christians to Communicate the Gospel with Muslim Seekers" (Doctoral diss., Faith Evangelical Lutheran Seminary, Tacoma, 2021).

8 Jean-Marie Gaudeul, *Called from Islam to Christ: Why Muslims Become Christians* (Arroyo Grande: Monarch Books, 1999), 33–123.

9 In the Qur'an chapter 4 verse 157, the crucifixion of Jesus Christ is expressly denied and rejected. So, Muslims reject the need to consider Christ's vicarious death and crucifixion as the means of their salvation. Thus there is

Jesus Christ loves them as much as he loves Christians; therefore, sharing the good news of salvation with neighbor Muslims is equally urgent.

Considering the foregoing evangelical points of the sociocultural gospel mandate and the Great Commission regarding neighbors, I now share feedback from Muslims in the context of Christian-Muslim engagement and interaction that I have experienced over the last few years.

What Unique Communication Principles Should We Use?

Positively and perhaps surprisingly, I have received considerable feedback from Muslims in Asia, especially Southeast Asia. This feedback has emanated from the growth in Internet and social media interactions between Christians and Muslims, typically in open-ended, meaningful dialogue between people genuinely interested in spiritual and interfaith engagement. This feedback from Muslims underscores the confusion, lack of knowledge, and need for the right information that Muslims and Christians display toward each other's doctrines. Below are samples of chats between Malay Christians and Muslims in English or translated from the Malay language into English during the period 2000–2002.

An email from a Malay Muslim from Malaysia studying abroad:

> Monday, August 6, 2001, 07:22:25 BST
> From: "Robbie Wayne" waynern01xxx@yahoo.co.uk
>
> Hi, I am a Malay-Muslim, 20 years old. I have been reading your webpage and [am] interested to know more. Can you suggest if there is anyone I can get in touch with?
>
> Wednesday, August 8, 2001
> From: The AI Team[10]
>
> Hello Wayne, thank you for writing in and expressing interest in the contents of *www.answering-islam.org*. We are happy that you have a growing interest in it. May we know

the pertinent need to clarify the purpose and event of Jesus's crucifixion to Muslims.

10 "AI" stands for the "Answering-Islam" website.

a little more about you and what stirred your interest in Christianity, please?

Friday, 10 August 2001
From "Robbie Wayne" <waynerno1xxx@yahoo.co.uk>

Thank you for the e-mail. As you might guess, Wayne is not my real name since I am a Malay by ethnicity. Now, I live near Leicester (UK). I am a Malaysian and from K.L. (Kuala Lumpur).

I have been exposed to Christianity even since I was in Malaysia, through a good friend of mine who converted to Christianity from Buddhism. She has been talking to me about Christ, as you probably know that isn't allowed in Malaysia. Although I wasn't very interested, I did visit her church once in PJ, but was so afraid that I totally avoided [it] since then.

Then I found your website and have been reading about it again. To be honest I don't know where to start since this is all new to me. I do feel scared and [it] would be nice if I could speak to someone similar about it.

Will write again, bye, Wayne.

An email from "Harry," a Malay Muslim studying at a local Malaysian university, translated from the Malay original:

June 10, 2001

Dear A.I. Team,

My name is Harry, [and] I am a Malay Muslim studying engineering at a local university. I would like to [ask] if you could kindly send me a Bible to read. I would prefer it if you could send me one in the Malay language so I can understand it better in my mother tongue?

This is my postal address:[11] Yyyyyy, Zzzzzz, Malaysia.

11 Upon receiving Harry's request for a Malay Bible, we mailed a Bible to him at the above address, upon which he duly acknowledged receipt of it.

June 27, 2001

Dear Sir,

Praise be to God! I just returned from the College Post Office this morning, June 25 at 1.30PM. I truly hope that you would be willing to help teach me [to] understand the Bible. There are many things in it that I find new and unfamiliar to understand, reading as a Muslim. Thank you.

June 28, 2001

Dear Harry,

We are so pleased that the packet containing the Malay language Bible has arrived safely at the College Post office at your university.

I hope that you will start reading it daily, if possible, and gain a clearer picture of what the Bible really teaches. I am also happy to explain to you further [about] what it says. Please do not hesitate to contact me [at] any time should you require any further clarifications.

Best regards,
Michael

June 20, 2001

Dear Michael,

Thank you very much, and thanks be to God, finally, the Malay language Bible that I was longing for has arrived and [is] in my possession. I am very happy indeed, thank you! From the moment I received this Bible ("Al-Kitab") I started reading it right away. I could not put it down as I wanted to know the stories and teachings that followed each chapter and book in it. There are some parts I found hard to follow or understand, [and] I will ask you about them when I encounter them, okay? What I want to do first is to finish reading the whole book first. Currently, it took me just three days to finish reading the book of Genesis. I must have read it three times. Now, I am in [the] middle of the book of Exodus. Michael, is it possible for us to meet up one day, in KL? This coming July is my mid-semester break, and I can travel back to my hometown in Selangor, and we could meet up to discuss further if that is okay with you? Could we visit some churches at that time, as well? As I have never entered a church building before.

January 7, 2000
From: Jason K. jackson333@usa.net

Dear Sir,

I have been reading your website "Answering-Islam" in the Malay and Indonesian languages. And I believe that the Torah, Psalms, and the Gospel of the Holy Bible are true and resemble the books of Islam. I also discovered this before coming across this website. That is because there is not a single verse in the Qur'an that says that the Scriptures of the Christian[s] and the Jews are wrong or false.

I desire to read the Torah, Psalms and Gospel, and [I] wish that more Muslims would read them. But I think that many Muslims won't read them because the Christians publish them as the "Old Testament" and "New Testament" and they use Roman names. The Muslims of Southeast Asia are used to Islamic and Qur'anic concepts through the Arabic language.

What I am suggesting to you is that you publish the Scriptures in Malay and Indonesian using Arabic terms. Like "Isa al-Masih" for Jesus Christ, Matta for Matthew, Mariyam for Mary, Baitul Muqaddis for Jerusalem and so on.

I believe that the Muslims from Indonesia, Malaysia, Singapore, Brunei, and Thailand will surely be happy to

> receive the Gospel, Torah and Psalms in their respective languages using the Arabized names and terms.
>
> I truly enjoyed reading the Biblical texts and wish for my fellow Muslims to also read them because in the Qur'an there are many references to those scriptures and many stories of the prophets in them. It would be a great loss if the Muslims do not read these scriptures. I hope you and your team can look into my suggestion and request above.
>
> May God bless your works and thank you.
>
> Dear Jason K,
>
> Your advice and encouragement are well-taken. We thank you for it. It is really important to have the Christian scriptures in the heart language of the Muslim readers, [and] we fully agree with you. I pray and hope that one day you will also be able to embrace the message of the Gospel of Christ.

Note: "Jason K" kept studying the Bible and other Christian literature. He engaged in various doctrinal inquiries and relevant discussions with local Christians to his satisfaction, and then he left Islam to become a Christian with his family. Jason keeps his Christian faith to this day.

How Do We Present the Bible in the Muslim Frame of Reference?

I propose three ways to engage with the Muslim frame of reference.

By Having a Good Understanding of Muslim People

The Malay and Indonesian Muslims, who make up the majority population of non-Christians in Southeast Asia, seem to be so near and yet so far from the gospel's core concepts and message. Christians and Muslims need to be prepared to discuss and openly engage and freely interact with our differences in worldviews, tenets, and dogma in the context of ethnographic and religious-anthropological mindsets. The aim is to primarily promote sincere freedom of thought and better mutual understanding in our modern plural societies.

Christians and Muslims share some concepts; however, many obstacles and contrasting ideologies also exist—prejudiced ideas that make Muslims and Christians antagonistic toward each other. Understanding the Muslim mindset and worldview will help Christians avoid unhelpful heated arguments and vice versa. Christians need to understand and appreciate the wholistic and collectivist nature of Muslim ideology, such as believing that there is no division between secular and sacred in life.

Malaysian Muslim scholar Rashid Moten affirmed that "Islam is a belief system that encompasses all political, cultural, economic, and spiritual aspects of life for the individual. The Muslim is mandated not only to propagate their faith but also to act upon it, promote it, and enforce it, this emphasizes power, authority, and political action,"[12] and so presented pragmatic challenges for Christians to address contextually.

The most significant areas that divide Christianity and Islam are what both positions claim exclusive rights to. They are:

- the identity and divine nature of Jesus Christ
- the mission, crucifixion, and roles of Jesus Christ
- the Holy Trinity
- the authenticity and validity of the Holy Bible
- the claim that the prophet Muhammad is prophesied in the Bible[13]

A deeper study of the respective doctrines would afford Christians and Muslims today a thorough understanding that would facilitate constructive interfaith activities and interaction anywhere. For this to

12 Abdul Rashid Moten, *Political Science: An Islamic Perspective* (London: Macmillan Press, 1996).

13 Norman L Geisler, *Answering Islam: The Crescent in the Light of the Cross* (Ada, MI: Baker Publishing, 2002). This resource for interfaith dialogue clarifies these points in greater, helpful details.

happen, training workshops would need to be conducted to enlighten both parties on how best to bridge the gap or divide between them.

By Adopting Interfaith Communication of Biblical Concepts

Closing the gap of socioreligious differences between Christians and Muslims in our society requires special and extraordinary efforts on the part of each to promote genuine sociocultural affinity and mutual religious understanding. It would be necessary to first seek come common ground for Christians and Muslims and, from there, to begin to build meaningful bridges for dialogue between them. These dialogues have the potential to:

- overcome the deep chasm of misrepresentations that exists
- provide an effective way to convey the authentic position of the gospel to Asian Muslims precisely, clearly, and respectfully and to minimize the confusion and polemics that exist on both sides[14]

Such interfaith and interreligious interactions go both ways, as Christians also misunderstand many things about the Muslim mindset and worldview through erroneous and flawed notions that Islamic theology and the Qur'an misread onto Christian ideas, such as the identity and nature of Jesus Christ, the crucifixion and redemptive role of Jesus Christ, the Holy Trinity, the authenticity and validity of the Holy Bible, and Muhammad's prophecy.

By Enhancing Relational Learning in Various Social Media Contexts

Such dialogue can improve situations and communication between followers of different religions, enabling personal, relational, and structural change. The dialogue involves transformative learning and is amenable to a variety of learning domains, both inside and outside the classroom. Thus there is a tremendous need for relational learning to include enhanced

14 Andreas Maurer, *Ask Your Muslim Friend: An Introduction to Islam and a Christian's Guide for Interaction with Muslims* (Maitland, FL: Xulon Press, 2008).

communication skills among communicators. This applies even in our approach to communicating the gospel message to neighbor seekers. Pertinent training programs and new curricula are necessary for the interfaith learning needs of targeted audiences.

In recent years, the accessibility of social media, high-speed bandwidths, and online training has become the preferred way for many, including Muslims. They have resorted to new means and methods to access the information they need, circumventing the restrictions placed upon them. Social media platforms such as Facebook, YouTube, Twitter, Instagram, TikTok, chat blogs, and video logs have become increasingly popular, especially with the younger generation.[15] Their users collectively number in the hundreds of millions across global regions. For example, in December 2018, the number of Facebook users in Malaysia surpassed the twenty-two million mark.[16] Facebook has its critics, but it enables Internet users to connect in the online world for personal, social, political, and business uses, and this powerful platform provides Christians with a means to fully avail of and share the message of the gospel, as it is now borderless and unrestricted.

It is now passé for seekers to travel across the globe to attend evangelistic meetings. These can be beamed right into our homes on a television monitor, cell phone, or tablet. Social media transcends the boundaries of state-sponsored and enforced restrictions and prohibitions, particularly for Malaysian Muslims who seek to learn more about Christianity or other non-Muslim religions, hitherto restricted from doing so.[17] New technologies have resulted in increasing access, engagement, and interactivity with deeper and more detailed Christian knowledge and information by

15 "Connectivity: The New Human Evolution," accessed January 26, 2021, https://theedgemalaysia.com/article/connectivity-new-human-evolution

16 Statistica, "Number of Facebook Users in Malaysia 2018–2027," Statista, accessed January 26, 2021. https://www.statista.com/statistics/490484/number-of-malaysia-facebook-users/

17 Such as the restrictions imposed upon Malay Muslims caused by constitutional prohibitions preventing them from being taught any non-Islamic religious knowledge, enshrined in Article 11 (4) of the Malaysian Federal Constitution. See footnote 5 above and footnotes 18 and 19, below.

Muslims. Indeed, the internet and social media have effectively become the new media for communicating the gospel of Jesus Christ to this generation. They provide us with a viable means to communicate the message of the gospel to millions more Malay Muslims in the privacy of their homes, the library, the office, schools and campuses, coffee shops, airports. When gospel web content was developed using the heart languages and with cultural sensitivity for neighbor seeker communities, I saw a dramatic increase in interfaith and multicultural interactions.

Malay Muslims who seek to investigate the gospel go on the internet to consult Christian websites, web blogs, and social media to obtain information. They can also freely engage in Christian-Muslim interfaith conversations. App designers, webmasters, and content producers can develop content and media in accordance with the intellectual, emotional, and spiritual aspirations of Muslim users. Indeed, the Internet and online technology have facilitated widespread access to Christian knowledge and deeper interfaith engagement between Christians and Muslims in Muslim-majority states, such as Indonesia and Malaysia.

How Do We Start Worship Centers for Muslim Converts to Christ?

Bearing in mind the vulnerability[18] of Malay Muslim seekers[19] who decide to accept the offer of salvation vouchsafed through the atoning blood of Jesus Christ, safety and security factors will be issues to consider, whether for a mainstream church building or a public worship center.

As in the days of the early church, when Christians met in homes to break bread and worship the Lord, the at-home location may be the best way to go for Christians from a Muslim background. This would

18 Article 11 (Clause 4), *Federal Constitution of Malaysia with Index*. Kuala Lumpur: MDC Publishers Printers, 1998. This clause forbids the teaching, educating, or spreading of any religious ideologies among Malaysian Muslims *except* Islam.

19 Article 160 (Clause 2), *Federal Constitution of Malaysia, defines a Malay as "a person who professes Islam, habitually speaks the Malay language and conforms to Malay customs (culture)."*

reduce the likelihood of unnecessary attention from curious outsiders and maximize the safety of the small group. Apparently, underground house churches also helped Christians in China to grow and flourish despite several attempts to close them.[20]

The recent COVID-19 pandemic has opened another avenue for believers from a Muslim background to join other Christians: the aforementioned online live streaming of worship services. This affords Muslim-background believers the opportunity to worship in the privacy of their homes while being part of a larger congregation. Online worshippers can also attend virtual Bible studies to ground them in their growing faith, and many churches today offer such courses to anyone interested.

Online technology also enables church leaders to reach out to those willing to reveal their identities, either for direct contact with them or to facilitate fellowship between like-minded believers on a regular basis. Nothing is impossible with God as the day of our Lord Jesus's return draws near, and he is opening doors of opportunities for many to enter his kingdom (Matt 24: 14). Nothing can stop a thirsty soul from drinking from the water of life that Christ offers and in the community of newfound fellow believers.

What Type of Liturgy Resonates with Asian Muslim Culture/Are They Oral Learners?

Muslim neighbors are both oral and literate learners. I have found that Indonesian-Malay (or other local) languages provide the optimal means for spiritual conversations and Scripture comprehension. This was confirmed by the feedback received from Malay readers and seekers who contacted me, as well as from ex-Muslim converts who are now Christian disciples. It is well-known that Muslims place a premium on reciting and chanting the Qur'an in Arabic. We have uploaded the gospel and biblical texts online in Arabic (e.g., the psalms and Gospels) and Malay to aid them in

20 Lauren B. Homer, "Registration of Chinese Protestant House Churches Under China's 2005 Regulation on Religious Affairs: Resolving the Implementation Impasse," *Journal of Church and State* 52, no.1 (2010): 50–73.

reciting and understanding the texts' meanings.[21] Neighbor converts have generally been pleased with the indigenized translations and used them in their house churches, fellowship groups, and Bible studies. Likewise, we have composed indigenized worship songs, sermons, and Bible studies for adults, youths, and children in the languages of the Muslim converts.

Even music styles, songs, and lyrics have been adapted to the local believers' flavor and style—for example, *dangdut*, *keronchong*, *pantun*, and *zikir* genres and styles. Samples of such indigenous spiritual ethnomusicology can be found in the footnote.[22] These comprise worship hymns, songs, and choruses used during Sunday worship, holy communion, and fellowship. Recitals of the Psalms are in Arabic, Malay, and Indonesian; devotionals from the Psalms are in Bahasa; and the full Scripture (Old Testament and New Testament) and digital resources to further investigate the Bible are in the local dialects and Bahasa.

The new creeds that Muslim converts confess are essentially scriptural truths from the biblical texts, which are appropriate in light of their Islamic background that elevates to a practical veneration of a holy book in their practices.[23] Examples of the biblical texts confessed or recited are the Lord's Prayer (Matt 6:9–13), the Logos confession (John 1:1–4, 14), and the shepherd psalm (Ps 23). The sacrament of holy baptism is also practiced with these new believers, in line with Matthew 28:19–20.

---

21 The reader may look at these websites for more information: https://www.answering-islam.net/fileadmin/bahasa/mp3/Zabur/zabur23.mp3; https://www.answering-islam.net/fileadmin/bahasa/mp3/Zabur/zabur1.mp3; https://www.answering-islam.net/fileadmin/bahasa/mp3/Zabur/zabur103.mp3

22 The reader may look at these websites for more information: https://www.answering-islam.net/bahasa/nada-kemuliaan.html; https://www.answering-islam.net/fileadmin/bahasa/mp3/Pujian_Segala_Bangsa/02_Track_2.mp3; https://www.answering-islam.net/fileadmin/bahasa/mp3 /Kasih Yang Menyelamatkan/Kalimatullah.mp3; https://www.answering-islam.net/Bahasa/Santapan/zabur23.html; www.SABDA.org, www.komuniti-digital.com

23 For example, it is mandatory for a Muslim to perform ritual ablutions before touching and reciting an Arabic Qur'an as demanded in Qur'an chapter 56:77, 79.

Conclusion

In this chapter, I addressed the question, "How can Christians and Muslims be good neighbors in Southeast Asia?" In keeping with this metaphor, I sought to identify common ground between neighbors and respectful ways to converse and interact with each other. As responsible and loving evangelists, it is our hope that our neighborliness will lead to a heartfelt embrace of the historic and biblical Christ though our words and deeds.

Thus I argued that neighbor communities and societies in Asia are not beyond the reach of the gospel of Christ. There is indeed a growing trend in Asia today of many such neighbor Muslims turning to embrace Christ as their Lord and savior. Missiologist David Garrison said there is a "wind in the house of Islam" today, with multiple movements of Muslim peoples around the world who are, in greater numbers and momentum, finding and exercising their religious freedom and freedoms of choice and expression in unprecedented ways.[24] These movements, coupled with strong indigenized expressions of local ecclesiae (churches) of such disciples across Asia, augur well for church planting among neighbors worldwide.

Bibliography

Cheng, George. "Equipping Asian Christians to Communicate the Gospel with Muslim Seekers." DSL diss., Faith Evangelical Lutheran Seminary, 2021.

Douglas, Robert. C. "Research and Training." In *Muslims and Christians on the Emmaus Road,* edited by J. Dudley Woodberry. Pasadena: Zwemer Institute of Muslim Studies, 1989.

Federal Constitution of Malaysia. (Article 11, Clause 4). Kuala Lumpur: MDC Publishers, 1998.

Garrison, David. *A Wind in the House of Islam: How God is Drawing Muslims Around the World to Faith in Jesus Christ.* Colorado, USA: WIGTake Resources, 2014.

Gaudeul, Jean-Marie. *Called from Islam to Christ: Why Muslims Become Christians.* Oxford: Monarch Books, 1999.

Geisler, Norman L. *Answering Islam: The Crescent in the Light of the Cross.* Ada, MI: Baker Publishing, 2002.

24 David Garrison, *A Wind in the House of Islam: How God Is Drawing Muslims Around the World to Faith in Jesus Christ* (USA: WIGTake Resources, 2014).

Homer, Lauren B. "Registration of Chinese Protestant House Churches Under China's 2005 Regulation on Religious Affairs: Resolving the Implementation Impasse." *Journal of Church and State,* Volume 52, no.1 (2010): 50–73.

Malaysiakini website. "Family of Alleged 'Enforcement Disappearance' Victim Takes Plight to Jokowi." Accessed March 30, 2023, https://m.malaysiakini.com/news/469948.

Maurer, Andreas. *Ask Your Muslim Friend: An Introduction to Islam and a Christian's Guide for Interaction with Muslims.* Maitland, FL: Xulon Press, 2008.

Moten, Abdul Rashid. *Political Science: An Islamic Perspective.* London: Macmillan Press, 1996.

Ng, Stephen and Hwa Beng Lee. *Where is Pastor Raymond Koh? Selangor.* Malaysia: Semai Maju, 2019.

Pew Research Center. "Asia Pacific Overview." Accessed February 8, 2022, https://www.pewresearch.org/religion/2009/10/07/mapping-the-global-muslim-population9/

Statista website. "Number of Facebook users in Malaysia 2018–2027." Accessed January 3, 2023, https://www.statista.com/statistics/490484/number-of-malaysia-facebook-users/,

Stearns, Richard. *Unfinished: Believing Is Only the Beginning.* Nashville, Thomas Nelson, 2013.

The Edge. "Connectivity: The New Human Evolution." Accessed January 26, 2021, https://theedgemalaysia.com/article/connectivity-new-human-evolution.

Vethamani, Malachi E., "The Malaysian Albatross of May 13, 1969, Racial Riots," *Sun Yat-sen Journal of Humanities.* 49: (2); 19–41.

Wright, Christopher J.H. *The Mission of God's People: A Biblical Theology of The Church's Mission.* Grand Rapids, MI: Zondervan, 2010.

Online Website Resources

https://www.pewresearch.org/religion/2009/10/07/mapping-the-global-muslim-population9/

https://www.answering-islam.net/fileadmin/bahasa/mp3/Zabur/zabur23.mp3,

https://www.answering-islam.net/Bahasa/Santapan/zabur23.html,

https://www.answering-islam.net/bahasa/nada-kemuliaan.html

https://www.komuniti-digital.com, https://www.SABDA.org,

https://www.statista.com/statistics/490484/number-of-malaysia-facebook-users/

12

CHURCHES IN SUMBA, INDONESIA—CONTESTATION AND CONVICTION

by Daniel Trihandarkha

Introduction

On the topic of planting churches in Indonesia, Java Island comes readily to mind because Java played a significant role in the history of the whole archipelago. Java was the site of the battle for sovereign control of Indonesia, determined by mammoth leadership and religio-cultural struggles in Indonesia. This began with the Majapahit Hindu-Buddhist empire, the Islamic sultanate, followed by Dutch Christian colonialism. Java's prominence is further explained by it being the epicenter of the nation's population, technology, and cultural centers, and it being the location of the nation's capital, Jakarta. The focus of my chapter is Sumba, an island 800 kilometers east of Java.

Most people regard Indonesia as the largest Muslim nation in the world. However, some historical and chronological context is needed. In the span of four centuries, starting soon after the beginning of the tenth century, three catalytic events occurred in Indonesia, all of which significantly impacted Christianity's cultural and political situation.

The first event was when the Majapahit Kingdom,[1] the Indianized Hindu domain in Indonesia based in Eastern Java, was at its pinnacle

1 Nazeer Ahmed, "Islam in Indonesia," in *History of Islam: An encyclopedia of Islamic History*, (web version 2001), https://historyofislam.com/contents/the-post-mongol-period/islam-in-indonesia/According to Ahmed (2001),

under the rule of King Hayam Wuruk and Gadjah Mada, the king's viceroy in East Java.[2] Quite suddenly, in the late fifteenth century, the golden era of the Hindu empire ended because of the second event: the coming of the Islamic sultanate of Demak. Finally, the most significant catalytic event was the arrival of the Dutch colonials in 1595, who were oppressive destroyers of most of the Islamic kingdoms in Java.[3]

Hence, in a relatively rapid and devastating manner, Indonesia was subjected to invasion and colonialization from three national bodies with world religions: Hinduism, Islam, and Christianity. Each religion brought its own worldview into Indonesia, with long-lasting impacts. In terms of sentiments, the Hindus feel that the Muslims were their oppressors, and the Muslims think the Christians were their oppressors. Hence, Christians who are intent on planting churches in the twenty-first century must be aware of history and the residual perceptions that linger among those who are being ministered to.[4]

Just as the Greeks ushered in the Hellenistic period, which incorporated the worship of deities from their conquered regions, the rise and fall of the Hindu, Islamic, and Christian kingdoms shaped the religious and political culture of Indonesia. For example, Hinduism from the Indian subcontinent formed the Balinese Hindu belief system, along with co-opted local variants distinct from the traditional Hindu religion

---

this empire had a "Hindu ruling class over a Buddhist-Hindu-animist matrix. The first infusion of Indian elements into the Archipelago occurred during the reign of Ashoka (269–232 BCE.). Ashoka was the first to consolidate his power over much of the Indian subcontinent. His early reign was characterized by a relentless war to expand his dominions. However, after the Battle of Kalinga (circa 250 BCE), he was so moved by the slaughter and destruction of the war, that he embraced Buddhism. Ashoka's edicts of non-violence, reflecting the teachings of Buddha, were carved into stone, and were sent to Sri Lanka, Burma, Afghanistan, and the Indonesian Islands."

2 George Cœdès, *Asia Tenggara Masa Hindu-Budha* (Jakarta: Kepustakaan Populer Gramedia, 2010).

3 J.M. Roberts, *History of The World* (Oxford: Oxford University Press, 1993).

4 Victoria C. Scott and Susan M. Wolfe, *Community Psychology: Foundations for Practice* (Thousand Oaks: SAGE Publications, 2015).

practiced in India, although both emphasized the worship of Brahma, Vishnu, and Shiva.[5]

The transnational cultural-religious fusion between Indonesia and India is not unique. From a Hegelian philosophical perspective, Christianity is a synthesis of Judaism and the early apostolic church.[6] Christianity was birthed in the Greco-Roman world, and it used the prevalent *koine* Greek as the language for the Christian Scriptures. Some scholars believe that the apostle Paul, when formulating the concept of Christian marriage and celibacy, was reacting against contemporary Greek culture's low regard for purity in temple worship and family life.[7] Paul's references to "ritual-cleanliness"[8] and purity in worship were borrowed from Judaism and the Old Testament depiction that those who served in the Tabernacle must be Levites, *and* they must undergo various purification rituals.

The scholar Deming argued that Paul, while teaching the dangers of sexual promiscuity, did not focus on taboo asceticism; instead, Paul focused on undivided devotion to Christ.[9] This was congruent with the concept of cleanliness and uncleanliness in Judaism. It was not mere morality and physical and visual purity, but the devotion of the heart to the one true God of Israel, referred to as Yahweh or YHWH.[10] This holistic notion of purity would subsequently affect Christianity and the morality of

---

5 Some scholars are hesitant to equate the Balinese belief system with India's Hinduism.

6 George E. Ladd, *A Theology of the New Testament* (Chicago: Eerdmans, 1993).

7 Sara Keating, "'Sacred Prostitution': An Ancient Tradition Based on Respect for the Woman," *The Irish Times*, February 20, 2017 2021, https://www.irishtimes.com/culture/stage/sacred-prostitution-an-ancient-tradition-based-on-respect-for-the-woman-1.2975529#:~:text=%5BSacred%20prostitution%5D%20involved%20women%20having,seen%20as%20a%20powerful%20person.

8 Will Deming, *Paul on Marriage and Celibacy: The Hellenistic Background of 1 Corinthians 7* (Grand Rapids, MI: Eerdmans, 2004).

9 Deming, *Paul on Marriage and Celibacy*, 15.

10 Yahweh, the name for the God of the Hebrew people, represents the biblical pronunciation of "YHWH." The name YHWH is based on the sequence of Hebrew consonants *Yod, Heh, Waw*, and *Heh*, called the tetragrammaton.

its people.[11] Arguably, this discourse on purity first appeared in the Pentateuch (the first five books of the Hebrew Bible) to teach the Israelites to live as a people with a firm biblical standard, unlike the nations around Israel who worshipped idols and multiple deities: "Out of all nations you will be . . . a kingdom of priests and a holy nation" (Exod 19:5–6).

However, the evolution of Christianity was not determined primarily by the cultural and social predilections of various communities. Evangelical Christians believe Christianity is based on the conviction that God "breathed" his words in the Bible; therefore, the Bible is the preeminent guide to a distinct way of life for Christians (2 Tim 3:16), and since belief in the Bible is based on it, faith is the starting point for evangelical Christians.[12]

Having sketched the historical and cultural contexts of Indonesia in relation to Christianity in Greco-Roman society some two thousand years ago, I now devote the rest of this chapter to describing, in narrative fashion, two "civil war" cases of how churches were birthed on the island of Sumba (south of Java Island).

I write these two cases in my capacity as one of the leaders overseeing the local leadership of these churches. I have selected the two cases with the intent of showing the distinct context and peculiar challenge of building churches in the villages of Sumba. I use primary source materials collected through in-depth interviews over a period from 2008 to 2022.

The common element of these two cases is that both churches were engaged in a conflict—not with non-Christians, but with Christians—hence

11 Tremper Longman and Raymond B. Dillard, *An Introduction to the Old Testament* (Grand Rapids, MI: Zondervan, 1993).

12 The classic debates about the source of the story of Noah's flood being from the *Gilgamesh* epoch included seculars and skeptics attacking the Scripture for adopting the Sumerian epoch. However, there is no clear substantiation of this alleged adoption. Some hostile evidence-based scientists, who deny the faith, are eager to refute God's revelatory divine truth. It is only with faith that we will see and know God. God made science and rightly understood that science testifies to God and the veracity of his word. As the Scriptures declare, "And without faith it is impossible to please God, for the one who draws near to Him must believe that He exists and rewards those who seek Him" (Hebrews 11:6 NIV).

my depiction of the conflicts as civil wars. The case studies also foreshadow two important lessons that will be raised later: the need for strong Christian discipleship when converts come from other worldviews and the primacy of purity and holiness in Christian living once conversion takes place.

Central Sumba: A Christian "Civil War"

Before I share my first case, I include a brief background to Sumba.

Historical Background of Sumba

Sumba, at one time a vassal state of the Hindu Majapahit empire, is one of the few islands in Southeast Asia with a tradition of head-hunting.[13] Although some local people deem this tradition a thing of the past, others prefer to keep it alive, either as a legacy or a boost for tourism.

Two head-hunting tribes, Loli and Waweya, are mortal enemies living in the eastern part of the island and using Kamberan as their sole language. Residents in the eastern part of the island routinely share head-hunting stories to add to the distinctive flavor of their culture when selling their handwoven fabrics.[14]

Meanwhile, in the western part of the island, with more than ten languages in use, the Waweya, the most powerful clan in Sumba, regard head-hunting as a noble legacy and extol their prowess to defend their community and sustain their established cultural tradition.[15]

In 1998, the Waweya and Loli[16] were involved in the battle of Bloody Thursday, in which four thousand people were involved in horrific violence.

---

13 The Dayaks in Kalimantan and the island of Borneo, as well as the Nagas in Northeast India, also practiced head-hunting. Head-hunting is a practice of animistic people which involves the hunting and killing of victims followed by collecting the severed heads of victims for use in rituals to appease the gods.

14 Janet Hoskin, *Head Hunting and Social Imagination in South East Asia* (Stanford: Stanford University Press, 1996).

15 Hoskin, *Head Hunting*.

16 My use of "rival" does not mean that Loli is the mortal enemy of *Waweya*, but there have been some clashes between these two clans that share the

This melee resulted in more than a hundred casualties.[17] The conflict was triggered by the allegation that a Loli official won an election through fraudulent means. The Waweyan tribe reacted to this, and a battle ensued. Understanding Waweyan history will help the reader to understand the problems that occurred when building a church in Waweyan territory. It is relevant to also mention the significant influence of Merapu, the dominant local animistic religion. Today, many professing and baptized church members still practice their old animistic ways while attending church. "Christians persist in following both Christian tradition as well as Merapu rituals, including worship of their deceased ancestor's spirit,"[18] which is clearly unbiblical.

Cornelius and Wilhelmina

I introduce an admirable Waweyan couple, Cornelius and Wilhelmina, a husband-and-wife team[19] who have faithfully served as indigenous Christian missionaries for twenty-five years. Their names are Western because Wilhelmina, the wife, has Dutch ancestry from the early twentieth century. She proudly told me about her grandma named Ambu Bolu, whose beauty attracted a Dutch man to marry her. Before knowing Christ, Cornelius and Wilhelmina were a very devout Merapu (animistic) couple.

Cornelius is one of the few people in the community who received the education made available by the Dutch Reformed Church in the late 1940s.[20] The Dutch Reformed Church missionaries came to Sumba after violence among the local nobles was pacified in 1912. These missionaries established many schools throughout the island and gave selected locals an

---

same language and have a similar culture. An incident in 1991, for example, involved a land dispute between the two clans, which resulted in a significant number of casualties. In my twelve years of interacting with the locals, there have been occasions when the Waweyan stereotyped Loli as criminals and opportunistic liars.

17 Jacqueline A. C. Vel, "Tribal Battle in a Remote Island: Crisis and Violence in Sumba (Eastern Indonesia)," Indonesia Cornell University 72, no. 72 (2001): 141, https://doi.org/10.2307/3351484

18 Vel, "Tribal Battle in a Remote Island."

19 Sometimes referred to as *Sumbanese*.

20 Vel, "Tribal Battle in a Remote Island."

opportunity to get an education.[21] Although Cornelius is very smart and respected in the community, he was also known, prior to his conversion, as a fierce warrior with anger issues.

John Pote is Cornelius's brother-in-law. A new convert, John preached the gospel to Cornelius and Wilhelmina in 1993. Cornelius was furious and accused John of apostasy. This reaction destroyed the family harmony, and chaos ensued. However, John, formerly a fierce warrior who practiced animism, maintained his composure and, in future encounters, continued to talk to Cornelius about Jesus Christ and the gift of salvation that he brings. Yet Cornelius remained hostile to these entreaties.

Wilhelmina, who loved her brother John Pote dearly, secretly accepted Christ. She prayed every night for her husband in the hut. Once, when returning from the farm, Cornelius saw his wife praying in a Christian way, in a posture of kneeling. Cornelius was outraged, took a stick, and beat his wife and children. But Wilhelmina persevered in her newfound faith. Cornelius, in his anger, shouted at his wife, "If your God is real, he should come and show himself to us!" Then he left the house in a bitter rage.

In December 1993, while Cornelius was tending a herd of water buffalo in the field, he was suddenly struck by lightning, rendered temporarily unconscious, and suffered severe burns. For a few days, Cornelius

21 Chronologically, there have been various debates on who initiated the first evangelism in Sumba. The Dutch mission started in 1886, but the Jesuits were also in Sumba. One of the Jesuits opened a mission in Laura, West Sumba. See Janet Hoskins, *The Play of Time: Kodi Perspectives on Calendars, History, and Exchange* (Berkeley: University of California Press, 1993).In 1907, D. K. Wielenga, a Protestant missionary who had been working in East Sumba for three years, traveled to West Sumba and decided to use the abandoned buildings at Pakamandara for his own evangelical activities. He opened a Protestant school, bringing Christian Indonesians from other islands (Roti, Savu, and Ambon) as teachers to educate the sons of local rulers and noblemen. Consistent with Dutch colonial policy at the time, the school was established to train future administrators, and admission was contingent on a hereditary claim to rank. Soon the Dutch Reformed Church built other elementary schools in neighboring districts. By 1913 there were seventy Protestant village schools and four secondary schools, as well as a theological seminary near the original mission station in Karuni, where promising students could continue their studies.

Wilhelmina and Cornelius at Taman Mas Village in 2014 (Source: Trihandarkha).

was bedridden and extremely frustrated. Wilhelmina cared for Cornelius and kept praying for him. Then John Pote came and prayed for Cornelius. Shortly after John's prayer, Cornelius was healed. Stunned by the prayer that set him free from paralysis, Cornelius visited his ssbrother-in-law and willingly received Christ. Cornelius asked to be baptized in a river nearby. Having tasted the kindness of God, Cornelius and Wilhelmina decided to serve Christ and moved from West to Central Sumba.

The Defiled Godforsaken Land (Lev 18:24–25)

Although Sumba is regarded as a predominantly Christian island, witchcraft and promiscuity are commonly practiced there.[22] These practices are

22 "Do not defile yourselves with any of these ways, because this is how the nations that I am about to drive out before you became defiled. Even the land was defiled, so I punished it for its sin and the land vomited out its inhabitants."

usually done in secret in the central part of the island. Many young women experience unwanted pregnancies, often because of unreported incest and rape. Many women also experience domestic violence, and marital unfaithfulness by both genders is common.

In July 1994, Cornelius and Wilhelmina, after completing short-term bible training, moved to the district of Anakalang in the third largest tribal clan area in central Sumba. They intentionally searched for an area where witchcraft, violence, and immorality were rampant. They chose Taman Mas, a location that the church's previous pastor reportedly fled from; allegedly he went insane because of strong opposition from the darkness and evil of the community.[23] Incidentally, Taman Mas means "garden of gold." Legend has it that in the middle of the jungle, there are abundant yet elusive treasures of gold, and many people have died or gone astray in their search for this gold.

Cornelius and Wilhelmina found Taman Mas to be a barren land, in contrast to its garden image, with enormous limestone sedimentation because of the frequent burning of the fields by locals in the previous hundred years. Cornelius and Wilhelmina struggled to find water, and every crop they planted was unfruitful.

The couple's first attempts to preach the gospel were equally unrewarding. The locals avoided them and spread false rumors that Cornelius and Wilhelmina had been sent by assassins[24] to steal land and livestock from the locals. These locals also professed that baptized Christians and churchgoers practiced evil every day but Sunday.[25]

Dramatically, in their first three nights in Taman Mas, the couple experienced what they termed "demonic attacks." Wilhelmina, who was seven months pregnant, reported seeing a female spirit with two sharp, long fangs.[26] Then while she was working in the field, Wilhelmina was severely attacked by other evil spirits, resulting in debilitating fevers and

23 Much of the information in this chapter is from my own field notes taken in Sumba, Indonesia during the period 2008–2016.

24 In Sumba, because of the history of tribal warfare and the present robbery of livestock, the nobles often sent assassins to kill their adversaries and sometimes decapitate them and take their heads as trophies.

25 Field notes, 2008.

26 Field notes, 2008.

insomnia that haunted her. Wilhelmina's baby boy was born prematurely and had cognitive and socioemotional problems. Day after day, for eight months, the couple felt attacked by visible demons. Their household possessions were stolen more than once, and they were even poisoned by the local shaman.

Once, in the middle of the night, Cornelius was dragged from his house by a group of people who seemed intent on lynching him. Wilhelmina watched in horror as Cornelius was dragged ruthlessly down a stony gravel road, and she was forcibly restrained from assisting him. However, when Cornelius was accused of stealing the villagers' possessions, he was filled with the "spirit of wrath of the Lord, similar to the Old Testament time when Saul was full of wrath" (1 Sam 11:6).[27] Cornelius, burning with furious anger, shouted at the mob, "If you are ready to kill me, come and do it quickly! If any of you have the legal authority to punish me, do it! Kill me now!"[28]

Cornelius could see that some of them were wavering. One by one, they left him until he was alone, surrounded only by the sound of crickets. Cornelius sat alone, sobbing and thanking God for his divine protection. Then he went home and, with his wife and son, worshipped God. Through countless ordeals and deliverances that followed these physical attacks, Cornelius became convinced that Taman Mas was a promised land where God was using the couple to bring his message of salvation and grace to people who were in bondage to darkness.

Cornelius began to dig wells, and he found abundant water that had not been found by the locals. With this discovery, the couple planted corn, banana, and various spices and herbs. By God's grace, the crops grew exceptionally well in a very short time. They claimed that the biblical words in Leviticus 26:3 had come true for them.[29] Cornelius and Wilhelmina were also blessed with another son and two daughters.

27 Field notes, 2008.

28 Field notes, 2008.

29 "If you follow my decrees and are careful to obey my commands, I will send you rain in its season, and the ground will yield its crops and the trees their fruit. Your threshing will continue until grape harvest and the grape harvest will continue until planting, and you will eat all the food you want and live in safety in your land" Lev. 26:3–5.

They started a local church a couple of years after they arrived. They taught thirty people from their local area, who were former robbers, and several other families came to faith in Christ. Their priority in the church was to teach people how to observe biblical commands and rid themselves of animistic ways, such as sorcery and witchcraft. However, Cornelius and Wilhelmina became caught in a civil war with the professing Christians, who were still immersed in animistic practices.

Having personally experienced the evil done by the hands of professing Christians in Indonesia, I challenge the traditional distinction between pastoral care for nonbelievers and for believers. Typically, in pastoral theology, for non-Christians, pastoral care is called "evangelization," and for members of the church, it is called "pastoral care." But Scripture clearly distinguishes people not by their membership in the church or religious identity but by whether they are born again (John 3:3–5). However, pastors providing pastoral care in places like Sumba cannot assume people are born again. Pastors in Sumba must include the component of evangelism for all their pastoral care, as evidenced in Cornelius and Wilhelmina's story. Now for the other civil war.

West Sumba: A Martyr in the Christian "Civil War"

As mentioned above, Cornelius was baptized by his brother-in-law, John Pote, who was named Umbu Pote before his conversion. John's story of his salvation and obedience to Christ is another remarkable testament to mission work in the life of the people on the isolated island of Sumba.

Revival

Umbu Pote was widely regarded as a ferocious warrior. He was also a *ratu*, a religious priest in the animistic Merapu belief system, and he practiced witchcraft. Umbu Pote was known to go to other peoples' properties and take possession of their belongings, including animals like water buffalo. People allowed him to do this because his notoriety induced fear in them. In the early1990s, Umbu Pote, who lived in Wonga village, organized a band of robbers and warriors and raided a rival village nearby. With both demonic-induced power and his well-honed fighting skills, he overpowered the rival villagers and stole their livestock and their harvested produce. Those who tried to stop him reportedly ended up hypnotized.

Sumba is the area where the Merapu religion was founded in the late Bronze Age, around the time of Moses.[30] Dutch colonization, which commenced in the early sixteenth century and ended in the mid-twentieth century, only encroached as far as the coastal parts and larger towns of Sumba. There were seven religious sites of "abomination" in the Southwest and West Sumba regions. They were called "abomination sites" because of their huge residual collections of decapitated human skulls and flayed human skins and because animism continued to thrive in the sites. Christianity was practiced merely as a customary religion in these places.

In 1991, all eight notorious sites were struck by lightning, which burned most of the accumulated skulls and flayed human skin. Some people argued that this incident was a mere coincidence, while others were convinced it was an act of the Christian God to show his wrath for these worship sites or *kampung adat*. The case for the latter argument was substantiated by the fact that the houses of the common people were unscathed, and only the Merapu worshipping sites were burned to ashes. The lightning phenomenon occurred again in 2022, further reducing the number of worship sites.[31]

Yearning for the True God

In late 1991, Umbu Pote was going about his normal daily activity of tending his water buffalos when he suddenly felt something unusual in his body. He explained in detail:

> I felt a tremendous electric current in my feet that went up to my chest, and debilitating pain overwhelmed my head. I fell into a trench of water. I had never felt something like that before. I was in my prime, healthy, powerful, and no one dared to challenge my decision. I hated the feeling of powerlessness, and yet my body was

30 Around 3300 BCE to 1200 BCE.

31 Petrus Piter, "Diduga Disambar Petir, Delapan Rumah Adat di Desa Waikaninyo Sumba Barat Daya Terbakar," *Pos-Kupang.com*, Accessed January 13, 2022, https://kupang.tribunnews.com/2022/01/13/diduga-disambar-petir-delapan-rumah-adat-di-desa-waikaninyo-sumba-barat-daya-terbakar

One of eight sites burned down by lightning strike in January 2022 (Image courtesy of Kupang Tribun News and used with permission).

> unable to be controlled at all. As I lay in the finger depth of water, I gazed up at the sky. There were beautiful clouds with birds flying overhead. And, as I gazed upward, writhing in pain, I wondered whether there was a true Creator?[32]

Brought back to his house by his relatives, Pote rested on a woven bamboo mattress. At first, he thought that it was only exhaustion and a little fever that provoked the episode and assumed that he would fully recover in the next day or two. He waited and waited. Yet after two months, Pote still could not move, and the fever had worsened. He was brought to the local hospital, but the doctor could not find a medical cause. His followers were dismayed by this situation. Pote was frustrated, but he did not know with whom he should be angry. At the beginning of the third month, Pote finally realized that God was working on him.

When he thought he was going to die, Pote said, "God, if you are really there, I am sorry." Pote explained that, during a restless night with a high fever, he saw a long-haired man dressed in a robe whose face shone very brightly. The man said to Pote, "I have loved you, so I died for you. Now I want you to do the same for these people that I love. I will destroy

32 Field notes, 2008.

the power of the three demons who lived inside you."[33] Pote was amazed because the man knew his secrets. Pote had made a covenant with demons to attain a high level of witchcraft. Pote realized that the three ancient demons, symbolized by the dragon, horse, and fish, had been with him almost his entire life. Pote then woke up from his dream. He thought he had been hallucinating until he asked his Christian friend and learned that the person in his dream was Jesus Christ. Pote sensed unusual freedom and knew that the three demons had left his body. He fully recovered, and his walk to carry the cross of Christ began.

Opposition

Pote started reading the Bible. He was fortunate to have access to an extremely rare Waweyan translation. Pote focused on three words, *pamalangi, ama, mori* (Col 1:3), which mean "thankful to God the father." Pote learned what it meant to be thankful, and he learned what it meant to have a merciful and loving father who sent his eternal son Jesus Christ to die for him. Pote has been filled with joy ever since.

Pote wanted to study the Bible and serve the Lord faithfully. When Pote's henchmen came to him, they realized he was a changed man. Once a ferocious man with dreadful-looking warlord features, he became an ordinary man. They were angry with him because he had stopped raiding other villages, which brought a fortune to the gang. Moreover, when Pote told them he was a Christian, they vowed to kill him.

In August 1992, the henchmen came with a mob of about a hundred people to lynch him. Pote was unmoved by this threat and just sat on the veranda of his house. The henchmen came with many people because they were afraid Pote might still have the same power in him. Pote's family urged him to take refuge in another village, but he said, "If I must die, let me die." The mob went from one house to another in the village compound, but they could not find him. Pote was sitting comfortably, but the Lord hid him from their sight.[34] Frustrated, they went home and never came back.

Pote realized that the Lord wanted him to reach out to those violent criminals. A local pastor persuaded him to be baptized. At his baptism,

33 Field notes, 2008.

34 Field notes, 2013.

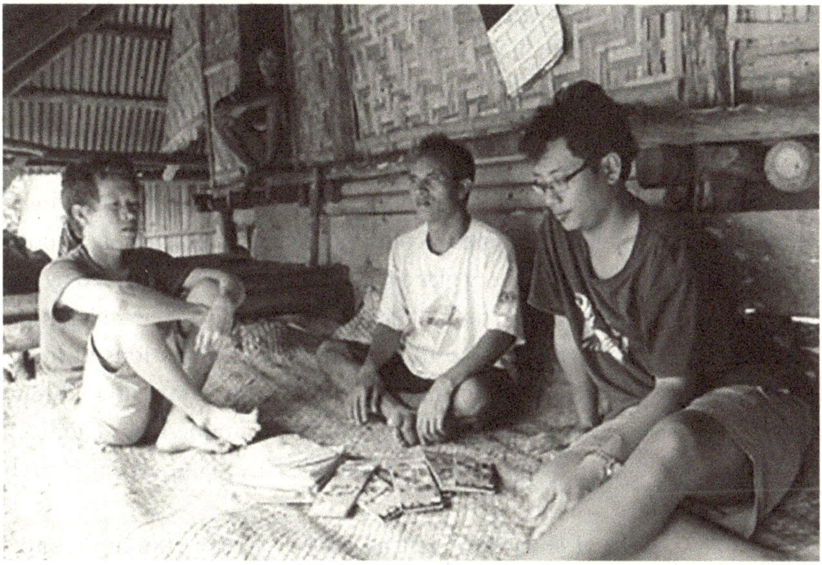

The veranda where John Pote (in white T-shirt) was "divinely" hidden (Source: Trihandarkha).

Pote was named John, and he assumed the characteristics of the apostle John, who was quiet in manner, and of John the Baptist, who fearlessly proclaimed the kingdom of God.

When Pote went to those criminals, some were afraid and fled from him, while others stayed to receive Christ. Thirty people from the gang became believers and were the first members of the fledgling church that John built with bamboo-woven walls and simple roofing.

Pote's ministry to the village children was also effective in reaching their parents. He worked tirelessly, and the church number swelled to four hundred people, mostly from violent, animistic backgrounds. This was the time when John met Cornelius and healed him by the Lord through prayer.

John Pote's long-term dream was to have a permanent church building where all his disciples and families could come together and have regular Scripture readings in a place of worship. In 2013, after saving money for more than a decade, he was able to buy land for the church site. His dream was within his grasp, and all his disciples shared the excitement. However, this coincided with the beginning of a period of prolonged, dreadful opposition from "Christian" men who did not share his convictions.

Cross

The Republic of Indonesia has a distinct policy for managing religious differences among its almost 300 million citizens. Unlike Western countries, the government of Indonesia controls the affairs of religious groups in Indonesia. For instance, every place of worship must be registered by the Ministry of Religious Affairs, and all citizens must state their religion on the national identity card. There are 332 church denominations in Indonesia, such as Evangelical, Reformed, Methodist, Lutheran, and Charismatic. However, church denominations are not immune from conflicts, power, and greed. In 2017, there were lawsuits involving eleven church denominations.[35]

By law, all local churches must be part of a legal church denomination in Indonesia, so Pote decided to join one of the denominations. He was asked to collect the names and details of all his church members, such as birth certificate numbers and national identity cards, as part of this process. It was a difficult task for him, but when the job was completed, the church denomination denied his church's membership because his coleaders refused to pay a bribe to the denomination officer to speed up the process.

Yet Pote was undeterred and continued in his calling to evangelize and disciple violent criminals in his church. Seeing the rapid growth of his disciples, which exceeded 1,000 members, major churches in the surrounds felt threatened. Several well-educated[36] pastors from other churches accused him of being an ordinary uneducated buffalo herder, a practicing warlord, and a false teacher. Consequently, some members

35 The Director of Religious Affairs in Indonesia mentioned this statistic at the graduation of KADESI, a theological seminary, in December 2017. The director argued that churches should act differently in keeping with their biblical ethics—church lawsuit cases should not be the main concern of the denominations.

36 Access to higher education in theology outside Sumba, such as in Java and Kupang, is available only to noble or influential families.

deserted Pote, but others continued to rally around him, seeing him as their spiritual father.

In 2019, a well-educated theologian cornered Pote in the market and punched him in the face. He walked home with a swollen face. His adversaries became even more furious in 2020, when they heard that he had started preparing to dig the ground for the foundation of a permanent church. Gossip, humiliation, and violence over four years did not stop him.

Some of the churchgoers who hated Pote practiced witchcraft and sent him spiritual attacks involving magic charms called *santet*. These are done by chanting, targeting specific organs of a person's body to cause physical illness. In the middle of September 2021, Pote fell sick. His lungs were swollen with fluid, and his sister Lena, who helped him with church ministry, rushed him to the hospital. After being hospitalized for two weeks, Pote was sent home with some medicine because the doctors could not find what was wrong with him. He decided to continue his ministry for another three months, but his health deteriorated, and on May 16, 2022, John Pote died. Before he passed away, some of his disciples who were former assassins were on the way to kill the fugitives in the neighboring church. Pote, in pain, ran to them and hugged them, saying, "If we pay evil with evil, how then can they tell us apart in this world?" He also quoted a few verses from Matthew 5 from memory (Matt 5:43–48).[37]

Legacy

There was great confusion after Pote's passing. The opposing churches spoke of his passing as the "demise of a sorcerer," but others, who were former animists, thieves, and assassins, mourned the passing of "their father."[38]

---

37 "You have heard that it was said, 'Love your neighbor' and 'hate your enemy.' But I say to you, love your enemy and pray for those who persecute you, so that you may be like your Father in heaven, since He causes the sun to rise on the evil and the good, and sends rain on the righteous and the unrighteous. For if you love those who love you, what reward do you have? Even the tax collectors do the same, don't they? And if you only greet your brothers, what more do you do? Even the Gentiles do the same, don't they? So then, be perfect, as your heavenly Father is perfect."

38 Field notes, 2022.

Lena continued the ministry and is currently intent on carrying out Pote's dream to build a church in their village. At first, Lena felt inadequate, but, supported by the many people impacted by Pote's ministry, she is dedicated to persevering with the legacy of her martyred brother.[39]

Conclusion

Both narratives in my chapter were framed in the context of Christians living in two worlds, attending churches on the one hand and yet practicing animistic practices.

I believe the church planting by Cornelius, Wilhelmina, John Pote, and Lena was exemplary indigenization, showing how the gospel can prevail over a violent culture with animistic beliefs. Remarkably, in these cases, the ministers were former animists and had checkered histories before coming to faith in Christ.

As described in this chapter, Christianity was conveyed to Sumba initially by Dutch missionaries, whereupon it was treated by many converts as a nominal faith rather than a transformative one. In other words, the Christianity brought by the Dutch to Sumba was a hybrid of Christianity and animism. Hence the lesson learned is that effective discipleship of new believers from animistic backgrounds requires persistent evangelization to avoid the conflict and contestation evidenced in the above two narratives.

Bibliography

Ahmed, Nazeer. "Islam in Indonesia." In *History of Islam: An Encyclopedia of Islamic History*, web version, 2001. Accessed April 21, 2023, https://historyofislam.com/contents/the-post-mongol-period/islam-in-indonesia/.

Cœdès, George. *Asia Tenggara Masa Hindu-Budha*. Jakarta: Kepustakaan Populer Gramedia, 2010.

Deming, Will. *Paul on Marriage and Celibacy: The Hellenistic Background of 1 Corinthians 7*. Grand Rapids, MI: Eerdmans, 2004.

39 Lena finally got the church to come under the *Gereja Bethel Indonesia* denomination (GBI), and the church is, at the time of writing, still waiting for the church building registration from the government.

Hoskin, Janet. *Head Hunting and Social Imagination in Southeast Asia*. Stanford, CA: Stanford University Press, 1996.

Keating, Sara. "Sacred Prostitution: An Ancient Tradition Based on Respect for the Woman." *The Irish Times,* February 20, 2017. https://www.irishtimes.com/culture/stage/sacred-prostitution-an-ancient-tradition-based-on-respect-for-the-woman-1.2975529#:~:text=%5BSacred%20prostitution%5D%20involved%20women%20having,seen%20as%20a%20powerful%20person.

Ladd, George Eldon. *A Theology of the New Testament*. Grand Rapids, MI: Eerdmans, 1993.

Longman, Tremper and Raymond B. Dillard. *An Introduction to the Old Testament.* Grand Rapids: Zondervan. 1993.

Pos-Kupang.com. "Duduga Disambar Petir, Delapan Rumah Adat di desa Waikaninyo Sumba Barat Daya Terbarkar." Accessed January 13, 2022. https://kupang.tribunnews.com/2022/01/13/diduga-disambar-petir-delapan-rumah-adat-di-desa-waikaninyo-sumba-barat-daya-terbakar.

Roberts, J.M. *History of The World*. Oxford: Oxford University Press, 1993.

Scott, Victoria C., and Susan M. Wolfe. *Community Psychology: Foundations for Practice*. New York: SAGE Publications, 2015.

Vel, Jacqueline A. C. "Tribal Battle in a Remote Island: Crisis and Violence in Sumba (Eastern Indonesia)." *Indonesia Cornell University* 72, no. 72 (2001): 141. https://doi.org/10.2307/3351484.

SECTION THREE

TRAINING AND DISCIPLESHIP

13

DISCIPLESHIP AND TRAINING IN THE THAI CONTEXT

by Pracha Thaiwatcharamas

Introduction

Christians comprise a little over 1 percent of Thailand's population of seventy million people in 2023.[1] The Thai educational system, with its emphasis on the study of history, the monarchy, and Buddhism, is different from other Southeast Asian countries. With a low number of Christians and an educational system that is steeped in Buddhism, Christian leaders ask, "How should Christian missionaries conduct discipleship programs and training?"

My father first encountered miraculous healing from the Lord Jesus when I was about nine or ten years old. Then my whole family went to the Christian Fellowship church in Udon Thani, now under the Churches of Christ denomination. I had the assurance of salvation and rededicated my life at about fifteen years of age and was baptized in 1964. After graduating from the Faculty of Communication and Arts at Chulalongkorn University in Bangkok, I joined the mission Operation Mobilization and traveled on its ship *Logos* from 1977 to 1978. During that year, I was exposed to many cultures and experienced culture shock.

Then came the time for me to choose where to obtain my theological education for a future ministry in Thailand. I looked for a theological school with similar belief systems to my country, in terms of its history and religion, which is Theravada Buddhism, but I could not find a fit.

---

1 Other agencies, such as the World Bank, give a lower figure of the percentage of Christians at 0.5 per cent.

However, with the help of a Baptist missionary in Thailand, I ended up going to a school in South Korea, the Asian Center for Theological Studies and Missions (ACTS), from 1979 to 1981. The Republic of South Korea was the fastest-growing Christian nation in the world at that time, with six churches birthed per day. At ACTS, I was exposed to theological education, Korean culture, and Korean church history. Another privilege I had was to attend special seminars conducted by three visiting professors: Dr. Donald McGavran, Dr. Peter Wagner, and Dr. Paul Hiebert, known as the "fathers of church growth," all from the Fuller Theological Seminary in the US. Through them, I realized the scope and depth of mission work. I also learned aspects of missionizing that helped me to analyze my church back home.

A huge challenge came after graduating and returning to Thailand: I was asked to present a paper at a theological consultation in Bangkok on the topic "Christ in the context of Buddhism." The challenge for me, then and now, is how to frame the gospel and ministry in the Thai context while being conscious that Asian Christians are under the umbrella of Western cultural influences in many ways. When I was appointed president of the Baptist seminary in Bangkok from 1983 to 1999, I was most troubled that our library was full of English theological books. A few of the books were translated into Thai, but not a single theological book was written by a Thai Christian. How could we train our future Christian leaders for Thailand when there was such a dearth of Thai Christian writing?

During my sabbatical year in 1990, I had the privilege to obtain my doctoral education at the Asia Baptist Graduate Theological Seminary in Baguio City, Philippines. My dissertation in 1997 was titled "A Church Growth Plan for the Thailand Baptist Churches Association." During my doctoral study, the Lord opened my eyes to learn many new things, some of which I share in this chapter.

In the remainder of the chapter, I commence with a brief historical sketch of the Thai church, then discuss Thai culture before focusing on the challenges and prospects of discipling and training Thai people in the Christian faith. The chapter is not scholarly; it is a case study in which I share my observations and experiences, first as a local church pastor at the Sajatharm Baptist Church (SBC) from 1998 onward and second as Thailand director of Asia Evangelistic Fellowship (AEF Thailand) in 2021. I hope my chapter will benefit mission practitioners, especially those serving in Thailand and other predominantly Buddhist nations in Asia.

A Brief History of the Thai Church

Roman Catholics began their mission in Siam, the former name of Thailand, in 1511. More than three centuries later, in 1828,[2] Protestant missionaries arrived.[3] However, it is evident that mission work was conducted in 1819 among the Karen tribe and prisoners of war by Ann Judson, wife of Adoniram Judson, a noted Baptist missionary in Myanmar.[4] The mission work in Thailand among immigrant minorities, such as the Karen, Chinese, and Vietnamese, was fruitful in terms of winning over the minority peoples and starting churches.[5]

The first Chinese-speaking church in Thailand was the Mitrichit Chinese Baptist Church, founded by Reverend William Dean in 1837. This is considered the first Chinese church in the Orient.[6] Many early mission agencies used Thailand as a stepping stone for mission work in China. Many missionaries hoped to return to China when communism was quashed. The American Presbyterians also began their work with immigrant minorities in 1840, but they later focused their attention on

---

2 "Christ Church Bangkok the English Church in Convent Road," Tour Bangkok Legacies, accessed March 19, 2023, https://www.tour-bangkok-legacies.com/christ-church.html

3 The Catholic Church left both a positive and negative legacy in Thailand after almost 300 years of their presence. Positively, they gave us modern education for the common people—good schools from preschool to high school in most Thai provinces. Unfortunately, they do not share our evangelical doctrines. Although they are ahead of the Protestant churches in terms of the contextualization of the gospel into Thai tradition, they seem to have gone too far and adopted a syncretistic Buddhist-Christian version of the faith.

4 Pracha Thaiwatcharamas, "A Church Growth Plan for the Thailand Baptist Churches Association" (PhD diss., Baptist Graduate Theological Seminary, 1997).

5 John Telford, *Women in the Mission Field: Glimpses of Women among the Heathen* (London: Paternoster Row, 1895).

6 Thaiwatcharamas, "A Church Growth Plan."

the Thais. It took them nineteen years to win their first Thai convert, Nai Chune, who was baptized in 1859.[7]

In the early 1970s, a movement was formed among Thai Protestant churches from three major organizations: the Church of Christ in Thailand, the Evangelical Fellowship Thailand, and the Thailand Baptist Churches' Association. They formed a united committee called the Thailand Protestant Churches Coordinating Committee (TPCCC), in which I represented the Baptist denomination for several years.

Today, the TPCCC has matured. It organized an all-Thailand Christian leadership congress in April 2023.[8] In 2028, TPCCC will celebrate the bicentennial of Thailand's Protestant church history, and in conjunction with the celebration, there is an ambitious plan called Love Thailand III, a call to double the number of Christians, existing churches, and Christian workers in Thailand.[9]

Cultural Context of Thai People

Many aspects of Thai culture are contrary to biblical teaching, and many aspects are positive to a new life in Christ.[10] I focus on some aspects that are relevant to evangelization, discipleship, and training of future workers.

Three Thai Institutions

There are three national institutions: citizenship, religion, and kingship. Every Thai is taught to be patriotic and devote themselves to these institutions. I will explain these three briefly.

---

7 Thaiwatcharamas, A Church Growth Plan."

8 It was postponed for three years during COVID-19. TPCCC has suggested that each province form a similar group or committee from the three major Christian groups where it is applicable. My Baptist group is the smallest of the three groups; nevertheless, we are committed to this goal. So far out of seventy-seven provinces, there are seventy such committees.

9 *Love Thailand III Manual* (Konkhaen City, Thailand: Northeastern Bible School, 2022).

10 One aspect of Thai culture that contrasts with biblical teaching arises from the Buddhist teaching not to trust in anything until you can prove or experience it by yourself. The other contrary Thai cultural value is the Buddhist doctrine that Creator God is a lower deity because he still has a desire to create. Desire negates the possibility of reaching Nirvana.

Citizenship: Every Thai is required to love and be loyal to the country. Thai students are taught to salute the national flag in school before they start classes in the morning and after school before they go back home. All media outlets, such as television and radio stations, broadcast the national anthem at 8 a.m. and 6 p.m. All Thais, and even non-Thais, are expected to stop and stand still upon hearing the anthem played in public places.

Religion: The Buddhist monk is considered the ideal person and citizen, fully detached from all involvement, especially the cares of this world. The monkhood is the largest Thai institution, and many people allege that there are more monks in Thailand than soldiers in the Thai army. Students can become monks during their school vacation at the age of twenty, and many Thai men sign up as short-term monks for a period to honor their deceased loved ones or living parents. Monks represent a way of life and an institution, which all Buddhist Thais share because they are the "living witnesses of Buddhism today."[11] This aspect of Thai culture, where monks sign up for national service, is regarded positively in Christian mission. In my ministry, I have encouraged young Thai Christians to dedicate their lives to serving God at a certain age (e.g., after earning their bachelor's degree). Many teens and young adults have taken up this challenge.

Although Thailand claims to espouse Theravada Buddhism, Thai people generally are syncretistic; that is, they combine their Buddhism with elements of other belief systems. For example, many Buddhists also worship spirits, ancestors, Chinese gods and goddesses, nature, and supernatural beings.

Another twist is that some conservative, almost fanatical, Buddhists advocate that Buddhism be instituted as the national religion by law. Other Thai Buddhists have gone further to propose that all Thais must be Buddhist. These extreme movements can be an impediment to Christian mission because, according to their ideology, converts to Christ would be betrayers of Thai culture and nationalism.[12] Thankfully, since King Rama V, Thai kings have enshrined religious freedom in the constitution.[13]

---

11 Thaiwatcharamas, "A Church Growth Plan."

12 Thaiwatcharamas, "A Church Growth Plan."

13 Nantachai Mejudhon, "Meekness: A New Approach to Christian Witness to the Thai People" (PhD diss., Asbury Theological Seminary, 1997).

Kingship: Although the king supports and provides for people of all faiths in Thailand,[14] he is bound by law to be a practicing Buddhist. This is yet another example of how religion, the monarchy, and identity are entwined. Unfortunately, early missionaries came to Thailand without understanding the intersection of religion and nationality. They came with the mindset of the Western colonizers, and naturally, Thai kings were threatened by the Westerners at that time. The fear of missionaries and Westerners was palpable during the colonization of Burma by the British in the 1880s and Indochina by France.[15] In this context, becoming a Christian was equated with becoming a foreigner, thereby betraying one's family, or dishonoring one's parents.[16]

Characteristics

I now discuss four Thai cultural values or ways of life that Thais consciously or unconsciously partake in.

Self-centeredness: There is a common view in Thailand that a Thai person can do anything they wish. This is the Thai version of independence or individualism, and it probably derives from the Theravada Buddhist teaching that "one can obtain the highest good by one's perseverance and action in all aspects of life."[17]

Related to this concept is the Thai attitude toward foreigners, which is to distance oneself from them. The concept of *krengklua* implies feelings of suspicion primarily arising out of fear in one's mind. Another aspect of *krengklua* is avoidance and noncommitment. It is a trait to avoid confrontation with outside powers, both human and supernatural. For example, I brought a foreign missionary to see a friend who needed some work done. The foreign missionary had the skills and the willingness to help my friend; however, sadly, my friend was not able to overcome his *krengklua*, and he

14 Other religions in Thailand include Islam, Hinduism, Sikhism, Judaism, and folk religion.

15 David K. Wyatt, *Thailand: A Short History* (New Haven: Yale University Press, 2003).

16 Thaiwatcharamas, "A Church Growth Plan."

17 Thaiwatcharamas, "A Church Growth Plan."

quietly refused help even though he needed it.[18] Arguably, *krenglua* has two manifestations: One is aloofness or disregard for authority and strangers, and the other is an inclination to worship familiar spirits of nature, such as rivers, the sky, trees, and animals.[19]

Survival: Most rural Thais subsist by deriving their daily food from their own gardens or the surrounding areas. Many still live a nonindustrial way of life without electricity, gas stoves, or modern household appliances.

Young people typically leave their villages to work in cities to add to their family income. Some go overseas for work and, sadly, must subsequently sell all their assets to pay for the high costs incurred in relocation. Many male workers who go overseas to work lose their wives because the wives leave them for other men.[20] The situation is compounded by some of the overseas male workers taking other wives in overseas locations. Children then become a responsibility and burden for aged grandparents `or close relatives.[21]

This chain of problems often challenges our discipleship-making process. Teenagers and young adults moving away from their homes for work or higher education create a brain drain or loss of manpower. Pastors in provincial churches must, therefore, train new leaders to ensure continuity in church ministry leadership. This is another challenge for ministry in rural Thailand.

Bondage: In my decades of experience as a pastor, I have seen people in physical and spiritual bondage be diverted away from healthy and productive living.

For example, unpaid debt affects Thais at all levels of society, from poor peasants to elites. The easy banking system, credit cards, and leasing grants entice people to borrow beyond their means and become trapped. I know a couple who came to Jesus Christ in one of our ministries and possessed more than twenty credit cards. Finally, these people were

18 Much of the information in this chapter is from my conversations with local believers and non believers in many locations in Thailand during the period 2001-2023.

19 Field notes, 2022.

20 Field notes, 2022.

21 Field notes, 2022.

blacklisted by the financial bureau for many years. My wife has had to redeem several people from this kind of bondage.

The gambling spirit is evident in many forms, including lottery, sports betting, cockfighting, fish fighting. Every first and sixteenth day of the month, the streets are busy because people are queuing to purchase lottery tickets. Many people lose their sense of right and wrong, borrow too much money, and turn to stealing or even robbing shops.

Another example of bondage is gender fluidity. When I first moved to Udon Thani, I was surprised to see males dressing and acting like females. I had thought this gender fluidity was restricted to Western societies or urban centers like Bangkok. However, over the last two decades, it has become widespread. In 2022, the Thai parliament voted overwhelmingly in favor of legalizing same-sex marriage despite strong objections from Thai Christians.[22] These issues are proving to be a challenge for churches in Thailand.

Learning styles: Reading levels are not high in Thailand, and the cynical joke often expressed in Thai society is that "Thais only read eight lines a year."[23] However, researchers have found that Thais aged between fifteen and twenty-four are reading more now, especially via digital media.[24]

A recent study of learning English as a foreign language found that auditory learning was most preferred by Thai adults, followed by kinesthetic learning (learning linked to physical activity), tactile learning (learning linked with touch), group learning, and visual learning.[25] These

---

22 Parliament's lower house approved bills that would allow same-sex marriages and permit civil partnerships. The legislation must pass through several more hurdles before becoming law, but this vote has signaled a step towards same-sex marriage.

23 Pongsak Sangkhapinyo, "Discourse on Reading in Thai Society," *TLA Research Journal* 12, no. 2 (2019): 2–18.

24 The Nation, "Thais Spending More Time Reading: Survey," *The Nation,* March 30, 2016, https://www.nationthailand.com/national/30282915 This 2016 survey show that Thais on average now spend sixty-six minutes per day reading, nearly double the thirty-seven minutes they were found to spend reading in 2014.

25 Attapol Khamkien, "Demystifying Thai EFL Learners' Perceptual Learning Style Preferences," *The Southeast Asian Journal of English Language Studies* 18, no.1 (2012): 61–74.

results resonate with my own experience and are inculcated in the formulation of my discipleship and training proposal below.

Training and Discipling Thais

In the main, there are four aspects of training that I will share.

Holistic Ministry

The situation in rural Thailand, where people live off the land, sometimes in nonindustrial conditions, has prompted me to reread the Bible with Thai eyes. According to the Bible, the whole world is the arena of God's dominion and mission. God plans to fulfill his will through human beings, whom he created according to his image. God has distributed a scope of responsibilities to human beings since the creation of the world (Gen 1:26, Ps 8:5–9).

The sin of disobedience separated us from God, so God sent his only begotten son to redeem us and restore people to be the people of God who ably "subdue the earth" (Gen 1:28). This act of subduing calls for a holistic ministry. Jesus demonstrated his power over all realms of life, spiritual and physical. Jesus responded to needy people in his day, ministering to the whole person (Matt 9:35–36). Furthermore, holistic ministry was the essential practice of the life of the New Testament churches. The disciples shared what they had to meet the needs of other disciples (Acts 2:43–45, 11:30; 2 Cor 8:1–4, 14).

Therefore, we should have the same mindset. The Thai church needs to be a kingdom-minded ministry that takes care of both the spiritual and physical needs of the church and community (Rom 15:2; Gal 6:9–10). I liken the pastor of a church in rural Thailand to the governor of a local district, not in status but in service, who serves under the kingship of Christ. Pastors need to see the whole situation of their flock and come up with holistic strategies.

I have seen some good models of churches with holistic ministries in Udon Thani and elsewhere in Thailand. For example, in the Srithat district, there is a church called Nariang. In the early days of this church, four lay-pastors who owned land pooled their resources and trained people, both Christians and non-Christians, to farm. The pastors used self-sustaining farming methods developed under the late King Rama IX. Now their church has become a learning center recognized by the province and approved to receive financial support from the Udon Thani government. The church uses a social media phone chat application called Line to share its farming insights widely, along with the gospel message of Jesus Christ. Although the church has no full-time pastors, its leadership and influence in this community of farmers and beyond are very strong.

Another church with this model is Thaveeporn Church in the Pakko district of Udon Thani. The pastor has been there since the church began, and he patiently serves the church people and the community with many ministries, including the Immanuel soccer ministry that I introduced to him. Furthermore, his daughter returned from her workplace in Japan with the express purpose of countering the growing brain drain problem. She has helped to build a small factory that manufactures automobile body parts, creating job opportunities for over two hundred villagers, mostly non-Christians, enabling them to stay in the home villages and thereby avoid the social and family separation mentioned earlier. This district church has about two hundred attendees each Sunday, which makes it one of the larger congregations in my province.

A new movement in Thailand was started by a Christian businessman who felt a responsibility to build food storage in every part of Thailand to help nonbelievers and believers withstand any crisis, such as drought and famine. From his own wealth, he provides a facility to each local church to store one ton of rice grain and 200 kilograms of polished and packed rice, ready to be used. He distributes freezers, food preservation ovens, water purifiers, and solar panels. Many churches in North, Central, and Northeast Thailand are participating in this scheme, enabling them to share Christ in word and deed, especially in times of crisis.

Bi-vocational Training

I am currently leading the SBC in our discipleship and ministry programs with the holistic concept in mind. We train our new Christian leaders with the Theological Education by Extension curriculum under the Siam Mission Thailand. Church members are discipled and trained to become leaders of the church without leaving their jobs and homes. They are also involved in vocational training, such as baking classes and cardiopulmonary

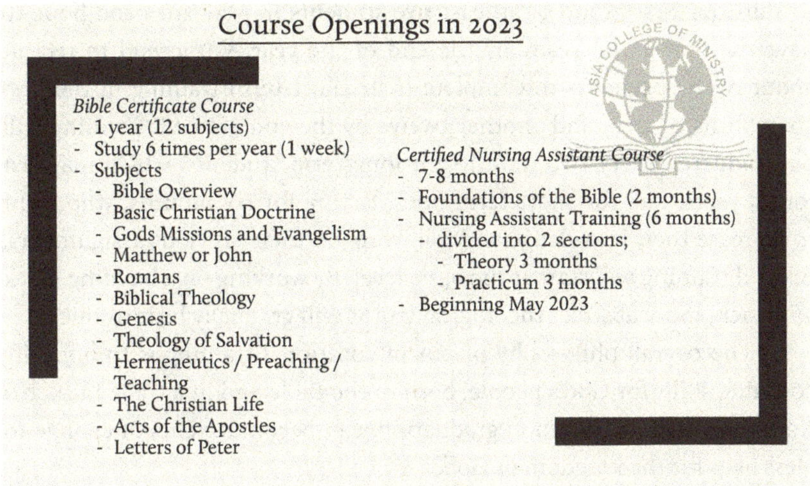

Figure 13.1. Asia College of Ministry Thailand (Source: Thaiwatcharamas 2023).

resuscitation (CPR) training to help people in emergencies. I am grateful that eight months after we introduced this CPR training, two of our church members used their newly acquired skills to rescue a young boy from drowning.

The Asia College of Ministry (ACOM)[26] I am setting up also uses the holistic approach to train future church planters and pastors. We provide biblical knowledge and vocational skills, such as nurses' aid training to minister to newborn children and senior citizens, carpentry with construction techniques, barista and bakery training, domestic work skills, and related topics. In figure 13.1, the first column indicates that the biblical courses comprise twelve subjects, and the second column shows an example of how the nursing assistant course is merged with biblical subjects. The nursing course takes six months, with a government-accredited body providing the nursing subjects, while Asia Evangelistic Fellowship Thailand and ACOM teach the biblical courses.

Through the ACOM program, we will also train people to plant new churches with the Love Thailand III goals in mind. We have planned

26 This is the training arm of Asia Evangelistic Fellowship Thailand.

to start our first group of at least five students in May 2023 and hope to have the first group ready by the end of the year. We intend to recruit about twelve students to complete their short-term training in the first six months of 2024 and another twelve by the end of 2024. Training will be conducted every two months for long-term students, which may last for 1.5 years, and for short-term ones, lasting for six months, who want to increase their knowledge and follow up on their previous assignments. Biblical training will start at the basic level. By working on a building block approach, more abstract theological truths will gradually be introduced.

The overall philosophy of our bi-vocational training is to offer life coaching skills for God's people, both in the Bible and in a trade in such a way that our trainees, upon graduation, can become agents of change to bless lives for the kingdom of God.

Culture-specific Focus

Considering the learning styles of rural people in Thailand, as mentioned above, the ACOM teaching style will be oral (speaking), backed by visual representations in small group settings. Rather than inundating students with doctrinal teaching and heavy theology, we will intentionally draw out aspects of biblical theology that speak to the current issues of Thailand, such as gambling, indebtedness, and gender identity. Traditionally, Thai citizens respectfully and thoughtfully give their best things to the Buddhist monks. We adopt this practice and teach Christians to come to church to give, not receive (Acts 20:35).

The Bible overview subject is a good starting point, wherein we systematically compare the Christian worldview with the Thai Buddhist worldview so that our students can appreciate what it means to be a Thai Christian in contemporary Thailand. In the subjects Basic Christian Doctrine and Acts of the Apostles, we include the Christian approach to signs and wonders because many Thai people have become Christians through healing and miracles.[27]

Just as Thai citizens are taught from day one to be loyal to the king, Christians discover the king of kings, Jesus Christ, through studying the

27 My anecdotal evidence suggests three out of ten of the conversions are due to healing, signs, and wonders or deliverance from evil spirits.

Bible and become subject to his wishes. To serve the king is an honorable thing in one's family, so we take advantage of this and teach people to render their service wholeheartedly and diligently to Jesus, meaning we love Jesus so much that we are willing to die for him.

Evangelism

Why do I mention evangelism in this discussion on discipleship and training? In Western Christian models of ministry, discipleship usually comes after evangelism. In Thailand, I have found it better to offer discipleship as the first step in Christian ministry because Thais take a long time to grapple with the worldview of Christianity. Therefore, after only one session of discipleship following the teachings of Christ, we teach evangelism.[28]

In the New Testament, Jesus asks his disciples to follow him at least thirteen times, but only after many years and after his death and resurrection do the disciples gain a full understanding of Christ. However, the practice of discipleship preceding evangelism does not stop my church members at SBC in their evangelism activities. We focus our resources on bringing people to Christ whenever possible. We divide our existing disciples into four groups, call them *ban pra porn* (house of blessing), and locate them in different parts of Udon Thani. Some members open their homes to host weekly meetings at convenient times. During the 2011 Christmas evangelistic events, a few people accepted Christ, and some joined our group activities.

Thai society is collectivistic rather than individualistic; therefore, the family should be the starting place for evangelism. In the past, missionaries, church planters, and pastors have mistakenly focused on individuals instead of the family, which has proven harmful and even dangerous. For example, it has caused new converts to be persecuted and many to leave the church. When my father was converted, he was the only convert in the family, and he experienced persecution from various family members, including my grandmother. Thankfully, my father practiced a holistic concept. He bought and developed land with various projects to help and support both his family and the people in the neighborhood. This positively

28 And after a Thai comes to Christ, the discipleship process continues.

changed many minds and hearts, including those of his family members, who had initially ostracized him.

With family conversion in mind, I started a soccer ministry at SBC. Through this, our church has had many blessings, including that of a Christian teenager who led his family to Jesus three months after his parents and two sisters watched him play for his team.

I also started marriage encounter seminars in 2007. At SBC, we organized weekend seminars with couples, which continued fruitfully until the worldwide COVID-19 pandemic hit us. The encounter weekends lasted for forty-eight hours. Christians invited their friends, relatives, and others, regardless of their faith, to attend these seminars. The felt needs of many Thai couples were met through systematic teaching on biblical marriage and family life, and a bonus was that many Thai families came to know Jesus Christ. Those who came to Christ were discipled and built up to become part of church leadership teams. After each weekend seminar, we conducted another ten follow-up sessions before starting a new marriage encounter seminar.

What is my church, SBC, doing now? We have purchased a twenty-five-acre plot of land where we are planning to grow rice, banana, coconut, and other fruit trees. We have dug more than ten lakes and canals for water reservoirs and plantations, and we have fisheries in place. Our goal is for our church to speak to Thai people through architecture, which resembles God's immanence and his incarnation in stooping to become a human being. Our goal is also to build a gospel theme park demonstrating the Bible from creation to the white throne judgment to share Christ tangibly in a context where learning takes place visually.

Conclusion

In this chapter, I discussed the great challenges of Christian ministry in Thailand. After more than five hundred years of Christian influence, including two hundred years of evangelical mission work, Thailand still has one of the lowest percentages of Christians in Asia.

I also shared my journey in Christian ministry to show that after decades of experience, I am still learning and putting many things into practice through trial and error.

Furthermore, I discussed at some length the various dimensions of culture, because failure to understand and appreciate cultural norms is usually the main obstacle to effective gospel work in Thailand. I then discussed the issue of discipleship and training in Thailand, concluding that discipleship must take a holistic approach, be bi-vocational, and include evangelism based on winning over whole families rather than individuals.

Even though Thailand is steeped in Buddhism and a new wave of religious nationalism is rising, Thailand's churches are quietly but confidently addressing deep-seated challenges. Our programs are enabled and enhanced by cultural awareness, indigenous pastors, local training programs, and a holistic approach to mission. Led by local leaders and funded increasingly by Thai Christians, our movement is a force for good in our nation.

Bibliography

Love Thailand III Manual. Konkhaen City, Thailand: Northeastern Bible School, 2022.

Khamkien, Attapol. "Demystifying Thai EFL Learners' Perceptual Learning Style Preferences." *The Southeast Asian Journal of English Language Studies* 18 no. 1 (2012): 61–74.

Mejudhon, Nantachai. "Meekness: A New Approach to Christian Witness to the Thai People." PhD diss., Asbury Theological Seminary, 1997.

Sangkhapinyo, Pongsak. "Discourse on Reading in Thai Society." *TLA Research Journal* 12, no. 2 (2019): 2–18.

Telford, John. *Women in the Mission Field: Glimpses of Women among the Heathen.* London: Paternoster Row, 1895.

Tour Bangkok Legacies. "Christ Church Bangkok the English Church in Convent Road." Accessed March 19, 2023, https://www.tour-bangkok-legacies.com/christ-church.html.

Thaiwatcharamas, Pracha. "A Church Growth Plan for the Thailand Baptist Churches Association." PhD diss., Baptist Graduate Theological Seminary, 1997.

The Nation. "Thais Spending More Time Reading: Survey." *The Nation,* March 30, 2016. https://www.nationthailand.com/national/30282915.

Wyatt, David K. *Thailand: A Short History.*2nd ed. New Haven: Yale University Press, 2003.

14

DISCIPLESHIP TRAINING IN CHINA—CHALLENGES AND OPPORTUNITIES

by Peter Fu

Introduction

Any attempt to analyze Christianity in contemporary China is fraught with challenges, which are revealed throughout this chapter, along with proposed opportunities for improving discipleship training. But first, I offer some background information that may be useful. There are two kinds of churches in China:Three-Self Patriotic Movement (TSPM) and the illegal or house/underground churches (hereafter "underground").[1] TSPM is the government-controlled organization for Protestantism in the People's Republic of China, commonly referred to as the Three-Self Church.[2] The underground churches operate without government control and are, therefore, considered illegal; however, these underground churches arguably honor the Bible and its teachings.

The rapid growth of Christian churches in China is evident, but due to the government's interventionist policy, official records of church attendance, number of Christians, et cetera, are not readily available. Unsurprisingly, the churches, both TSPM and underground, seem reticent about revealing these statistics.

1 Daniel H. Bays, *A New History of Christianity in China* (Chichester, West Sussex: Wiley-Blackwell, 2012).

2 Bays, *A New History*.

As indicated above, my chapter contains limited statistical data. Nevertheless, I use some textual sources and rely primarily on anecdotal interviews and records provided by Christian leaders and church members. My sources have been gathered from both TPSM and underground churches. In this chapter, the only distinction I make between these two types of churches is their structural differences.

Having been involved in ministry for ten years, I believe the priority for churches in China should be to strengthen their discipleship training. Even though it is not possible to thoroughly investigate current discipleship training in China, as intimated above, I contend that my anecdotal evidence supports this priority.[3] The question pastors frequently ask in China is, "How can we improve the quality of discipleship for a believer?"

Incidentally, based on a nationwide survey of Protestant pastors in US churches in 2019,[4] 96 percent of the pastors indicated that they considered discipleship an important factor in church life and therefore carried out discipleship training programs to strengthen their churches.[5] I presume that pastors in China would respond in a similar way to their US counterparts about the importance of discipleship training despite their struggles.

In this chapter, I outline four elements of discipleship training: the theological principle vis-à-vis our local context, the purpose of discipleship training in an atheistic nation, the training methodology, and the content used for training in China. In my view, the four elements are interrelated rather than separate components. Hopefully, this outline and ensuing discussion convey to the reader a better understanding of and useful resources for discipleship training in China.

---

3 Xu Yi Hua, (徐以骅) *How to comprehend Christianity in today's China* (如何理解中国今日的基督教) (Hong Kong: Heavenly Wind, 2014).

4 Carol Pipes, "Most Pastors Satisfied With Discipleship Efforts, But Recognize Room for Growth," Lifeway Research, Published April 11, 2019, https://research.lifeway.com/2019/04/11/new-research-most-pastors-satisfied-with-discipleship-efforts-room-for-growth/

5 Yu Han Qin, (玉汉钦) *Awakening of the Common Believers* (唤醒平信徒) (Seoul: Library Publishing International, 2009).

The Theology of Discipleship Training in China

The word "disciple" in Hebrew takes two forms: a noun and a verb. The noun *talmid* (בן) means "a son, student, apprentice, or scholar," and the verb *limmud* (לודמ) means "being taught."[6] In the original Greek Bible, the word for disciple is *mathetes* (αθητης), which means "a student or follower." Therefore, a disciple is a student or follower of a teacher in a certain subject. Through the teacher-student relationship, the teacher imparts their philosophy, teaching methods, and characteristics to the disciple.

In the Gospels, it is evident that Jesus was the ultimate teacher of his small group of followers (Mark 15:40–41). He was also the person whom the group wanted to know and imitate.[7] Therefore, Christian discipleship training is modeled on two components: knowledge (truth and doctrine) and imparting a way of life (the life of Christ). Discipleship training emanating from this definition is seen as the path of growth for a Christian follower toward maturity.[8]

There is a misperception of the concept of discipleship in China. In China, a scholar, teacher, or professor is highly revered, and only the wealthy can afford to be instructed by notable teachers. When this idea is applied to the Christian context, discipleship training may be regarded as training for the elite—that is, for the wealthy who can afford the cost of studying under a Christian scholar. Therefore, in China, believers tend to explicate, "I am only a believer in Jesus—I cannot afford to reach the 'status' of a disciple of Jesus."[9] Related to this perception is another misconception: Whereas in the West, many people go to Bible colleges without the

6 In the NIV Bible, "למד" has been translated as disciples; "בן" has been translated as company, team.

7 Lee Fang Zhou, (李方舟) *Great Commission Disciple Training-Third stage* (Hongkong: Christian Communications, 2002), 28–29.

8 Yang Mu Gu (杨牧谷), *Reconciliation Theology and Renewal of Church* (复和神学与教会更新) (Hong Kong: Seed Publisher, 1987), 68–78.

9 Field notes, 2022.

aspiration of becoming a pastor, in China, a seminary education is reserved for those who aspire to full-time pastoral ministry.[10]

Hence the elitist misconception is far-reaching, and it distracts many Chinese believers from pursuing learning about Jesus's doctrines and being helped to live under the power of the Holy Spirit. Furthermore, the elitist mentality opens the door for believers to be influenced by false teachings, which are rampant in China.[11] For example, an influential Christian woman in one of the churches disclosed that she had discontinued her private health insurance because holding an insurance policy is an act of trust in humans rather than the almighty God. Unfortunately, this woman's belief influenced followers to give up their insurance policies—to the detriment of some who were later diagnosed with cancer and experienced serious financial difficulties.

Sadly, these kinds of scenarios have been detrimental to the lives of believers and have even divided churches.[12] I have been heartbroken to witness the rise of internal strife, confusion, disputes, and church dismemberment over the last five years.[13] Clearly, the elitist mentality of Christian discipleship training is a contributory factor to the abovementioned problems.

I now present five instances of localization or theological contextualization that affect how discipleship training is practiced in China. The first four are inspired by the teachings of well-known local Christian theologians, while the last viewpoint is a recent government directive of the Chinese Communist Party (CCP).

Wu Lei Chuan

The controversial teacher Wu Lei Chuan (吴雷川) asserted that the main tenets of Christianity are already found in the teachings of Confucius

10 F.E. March (马尔舒), *Disciple Handbook* (Hong Kong: Corner Stone Publisher,1993), 3.

11 The rise of various cults and heresies has been well documented. See: "Cults and Christianity in China," https://www.chinasource.org/resource-library/chinese-church-voices/cults-and-christianity-in-china/

12 Zhao Tian En (赵天恩), *Discipleship Training in Mainland* (Taipei: China Ministries International [中国福音会], 1999).

13 Zhao Tian En (赵天恩), *Discipleship Training in Mainland,* 23–24.

(551–479 BCE), considered the father of sages and philosophers in China. Wu's construction implies that since Confucius is superior, Christianity should emphasize Confucian teachings in its approach to discipleship-making, thereby contextualizing Christianity and making it more acceptable within Chinese society.

Fan Zi Xin

The Christians represented by Fan Zi Xin (范子美) teach that both Christianity and Chinese culture exist on their own merits, and there is no way of determining whether one is better than the other. Their advice is to balance the two and allow their coexistence.

Zhao Zi Cheng

Zhao Zi Cheng (赵紫宸) criticized Chinese culture. One weakness he identified in China is that a wealthy man can have many concubines. Zhao proposed that Christianity could check and overcome this weakness by promoting the Bible's teaching on the sanctity of a monogamous relationship within the bonds of marriage. In this way, Christianity could renew and improve Chinese culture.

Reverend Wang Ming Dao

However, in the opposite camp, the group represented by Reverend Wang (王明道) asserts that the relationship between the Christian faith and Chinese culture is like the relationship between Christ and *bi lie* (彼列). *Bi lie* is a reference to Baal in the Old Testament, the king of the devils. Wang's position, therefore, is that Christians have no place in Chinese culture. However, since the 1950s, the followers of Wang have amended this view, pointing out that the Christian faith is beyond any culture.[14] Indeed, Christianity is not a culture. If Christianity were a culture, it would be for one nation only. Christians believe Christianity is transcultural and for all people. Its tenets are unchanging, although its applications may differ.[15]

14 Yang Mu Gu, *Reconciliation Theology*, 68–78.

15 Yang, *Reconciliation Theology*.

Chinese Communist Party

Hence there are differing views within the Christian camp on the relationship between Chinese culture and Christianity. To add to this already complex repertoire of views, the government has an official view articulated by the CCP. In March 2018, the committees of TPSM and the China Christian Council[16] published their inaugural five-year strategic plan to promote China's sinicized Christianity.[17] The Sinicization (or Chinaization[18]) of Christianity is a government initiative to indigenize Christianity. Arguably, it is part of a larger, pervasive ideological movement undertaken by the current CCP leadership, in which Christianity must become subservient to the overall principles of the state ideology and the CCP leadership. In practical terms, the following will be enforced by the end of the five-year plan in 2023: Relationships with foreign churches must cease, all pastors and theological professors must be trained within China, and foreign funding of local Christian works will be prohibited.[19]

How are churches responding? As I move around in churches, I hear two extreme views. At one end of the spectrum stand the compliant churches. They have agreed to serve the interests of the government and have started discussing ways and means to make Sinicization work. At the other end are the churches that reject this policy. They have dubbed the government's Sinicization initiative as a type of "beast" in reference to the antichrist in Revelation 13:1–10.[20]

---

16 The CCC was founded in 1980; it is believed to be separate entity to bring together churches for its outreach, as distinct from the direct political involvement of the TPSM. It is hard to see the CCC as an entity with any measure of independence from the government.

17 Some scholars do not like the term "sinicization" or "sinicized" because it comes from Sino, the defunct Quing dynasty of the eighteenth century. However, sinicization is becoming widely used.

18 Yang, *Reconciliation Theology.*

19 China Law Translate, "Five-Year Planning Outline for Advancing the Sinification of Christianity (2018–2022)," *China Law Translate,* published June 18, 2019, https://www.chinalawtranslate.com/en/outline-of-the-five-year-plan-for-promoting-the-sinification-of-christianity%ef%bc%882018-2022%ef%bc%89/

20 Some of the information in this chapter are taken from my field notes in various parts of China during the period 2018–2022.

To sum up, I have offered various perspectives on how discipleship training in China might proceed with respect to the fit between Christianity and Chinese culture, four from Christian scholars and one from the CCP. I have also noted the misinformed concept that discipleship training in China is confined to the elite.

It is time to introduce the view of Reverend Zhou Lian Hua (周联华牧师). He has proposed that localized theology in China must be discussed and worked through with everyday Christians rather than scholars.[21] Once this happens, Zhou contends, believers would be in a better position to accept localized theology.[22]

It is also timely to invoke the instruction of Jesus in his discourse on the Great Commission: "Go therefore and make disciples of all nations" (Matt 28:19). Note that the term "disciple" is not a reference to apostles or elites, but to every person who comes to know Christ. Therefore, discipleship training should not be bogged down by considerations of whether one is a full-time pastor or evangelist, academically inclined, or of a particular age or gender. Discipleship training "is not a course meant to give people an air of superiority, but for all who are followers of Christ . . . [so that they] become better imitators of Jesus."[23] In practical terms, discipleship training caters to those engaged in a wide range of church activities, such as worship, fellowship, visitations, small group gatherings, and Bible studies. I propose that regarding all believers as candidates for discipleship training would increase the likelihood of believers becoming strengthened in their faith and better equipped for various lay ministries.

The Purpose of Discipleship Training in the Context of Atheism

Atheism, the belief that there is no god, has been the prevalent belief system in China since 1949, when the CCP took over.[24] In such an environment,

21 China Law Translate.

22 China Law Translate.

23 Yu Han Qin, *Awakening of the Believers*,109.

24 Katharina Wenzel-Teuber, "Statistics on Religions and Churches in the People's Republic of China—Update for the Year 2016." *Religions and Christianity in Today's China* 8, no. 2 (2017): 25–53.

the starting point of discipleship training is to address God of the Bible as he is presented in the book of Genesis as the creator. After this foundation is laid and accepted, a logical next step would be the gospels, where Jesus is presented as the son of God who became fully human.

However, discipleship training is not just conducting Bible study lessons to make disciples more informed, teaching believers techniques of evangelism, or conducting revival meetings to make believers more zealous for God.[25] All these are good, but they are inadequate. Discipleship training that merely focuses on knowledge and skills for ministry will ultimately cause a conflict between faith and life. As mentioned above, churches have split over many theological issues.[26]

The ultimate purpose of discipleship training is to mold disciples so that they can be attuned to the image of God, which was marred after the fall of humankind in Genesis 3. Since the starting point of Christian doctrine is the creation of human beings by God, as distinct from atheism's presupposition, discipleship training in China must be holistic and embody the following aspects: the soul, body, emotions, will, worldview, and value system of the believer.[27] Holistic molding and renewing of discipleship training entail disciples following in the footsteps of Jesus—imitating his examples and nurturing others' lives.[28]

How, then, could we put holistic training in place? I believe the way to teach holistic discipleship is to begin in Genesis and explain the concept of creation. As created beings, we are accountable to our creator; hence, there are moral and ethical principles that God has revealed for us to obey through his word.[29]

We begin discipleship training in Christian groups in the northeast and south regions by asking group members if they believe in evolution. In my experience, some people in every group answer in the affirmative.

---

25 Wenzel-Teuber, "Statistics on Religions and Churches," 145–148.

26 Peter Au-Ou Ying Yu (欧应毓), *Educational comprehension and Christian Education* (Cheng Du: Si Chuan University Publisher, 2005), 316.

27 Yu, *Educational Comprehension*, 315.

28 Yu, *Educational Comprehension*, 317.

29 Shen Jue Shan (沈介山), *Believer's Theology* (信徒神学) (Taipei: China Evangelical Seminary Publisher, 1997), 150.

Thus, by highlighting creation and renewal in the worldview of Christian believers, we put our discipleship training in sync with the Bible. Lee (李方舟) does not take creation for granted in his popular workbook, *The Way of a Disciple* (门徒之道). He invites readers and students to fill in the blanks: "In the beginning, God created ______," and in Genesis 1:27–28, "God created ______ in his ______, in the image of God he ______, And God blessed them."[30]

Shen (沈介山) also uses Genesis 1:27 to illustrate that the creation of human beings is the great work of God and the pivot of our existence. The main purpose of life for the believer is to recognize their relationship with the creator. This is the beginning of the formulation of the biblical worldview,[31] which is vital for Chinese Christians who have been raised in the doctrine of atheism. Therefore, it is appropriate to start with Genesis in discipleship training.

The next pillar of our holistic training is character training. Since God created us, we need to live for him with a character that is acceptable to him. God provided an example by sending his son Jesus Christ into the world. Jesus was not only fully divine but also fully human, an apt model for our character development. Following Jesus will renew believers' value systems and mold them into becoming fully human. Therefore, we devise a training system imitating the life of Jesus, according to his interactions with disciples, so that believers can apply Jesus's principles in their lives and grow their Christian maturity.[32] According to the teaching of the apostle Paul, this discipleship molding is to attain "the whole measure of the fullness of Christ" (Eph 4:14–14). Wang concluded that this type of discipleship training is the closest example to biblical teaching and learning.[33] Moreover, discipleship training that moves toward this holistic objective and is biblical will help the church develop both in quantity and quality.

---

30 Lee Fang Zhou (李方舟), *Great Commission Disciple Training-Third stage* (Hongkong: Christian Communications, 2002), 22.

31 Shen Jue Shan, *Believer Theology*, 175–176.

32 Zhao Tian En, *Discipleship Training in the Mainland*, 8–9.

33 Wang Han Qin, *Awakening of the Believers*, 152.

The Training Method and the Teacher's Qualifications

Once we have outlined the objective of discipleship training, we consider the aspect of strategy. I mentioned above that church ministries, such as worship, visitation, and bible study, can also be strengthened through discipleship training. Discipleship training can be delivered through various agencies: theological seminaries, Christian organizations, and local churches. Training can be conducted in various time frames, depending on the situation, such as short-term training over a few days of intensive sessions or longer-term training over a few months.

At a mission conference in Hong Kong in 2016, the organizers suggested implementing an "adopt a people" strategy in which disciples adopt a certain group of foreigners across the world, who are nonbelievers, to pray for and with them and find ways to witness to them about Jesus Christ.[34] This was a paradigm shift in the curriculum of discipleship training in China because Chinese Christians normally interact only with their own people in evangelism and mission.[35]

I recently had contact with a theological training project operating in a church in Southwest China. This project comprises three people in discipleship training: the teacher, the trainee, and the pastor of the trainee's church. These three participate in the training for up to three years, with a view to molding and discipling new believers. This training program was designed according to an appraisal of the trainees' results as students and of the trainees' lives and ministry in the church. An obvious advantage of tailor-made training is that the teacher is willing to make needed adjustments to the curriculum instead of mechanically following a set syllabus. I believe this is what the apostle Paul meant when he described his ministry: "I did not shrink from declaring to you the whole counsel of God" (Act 20:17).

The abovementioned training method signifies another important principle I have learned: Discipleship training is not a ministry that can be achieved in a short time. It is deliberate, careful, and time-consuming, and it continues steadfastly until the believer matures in the faith. The key to

34 Zhao Tian En, *Discipleship Training in the Mainland*, 29.

35 Field notes, 2022.

this method is not the theory or the techniques but the people, especially the teacher.

It follows that we must include in our discussion the qualification of teachers for discipleship training. Sadly, one of the weaknesses in our Chinese churches is the lack of qualified teachers who can take a holistic view of discipleship training. This is due to many reasons, two of which are China's background in atheism and the fact that Christianity is marginalized because of the government's control over churches.

Currently, in our churches, teachers who are experienced and can teach are kept very busy. Furthermore, they are unable to give a long-term commitment to their discipleship training due to the other demands of church ministry. Also, due to the aforementioned government constraints, churches tend to adopt a survival mentality. Their priority is to take care of urgent issues, often neglecting the long-term strategic issues concerning discipleship training.

Naturally, students expect high-quality teaching in their discipleship training; however, students who are new and learning the faith on their own are not experienced or mature enough to discern what constitutes quality in a teacher.

I contend that living a godly life is the bedrock of quality teaching. As part of this godly life, teachers need to put a high premium on prayer, since the situation in China is tense, and the challenges are immense.[36] Based on Jesus's model of discipleship training, teachers of discipleship need to know God's word well. Teachers, as well as pastors and leaders, need to guide the disciples to apply what they learn from the Bible.[37] Hence Paul's advice, "Find faithful men who will be able to teach others" (2 Tim 2:2), must be heeded by Chinese churches today. So what can be done about the shortage of teachers?

I propose two ways to ease the shortage. The first is to make pastors responsible for discipleship training. As disciples of Christ, pastors are best placed to disciple believers, although they will probably need to enlist help with their other duties.[38] That means the pastors in local churches must

36 Ying Yu, *Educational Comprehension and Christian Education*, 318–319.

37 Wang, *Awakening of the Believers*, 170.

38 Wang, *Awakening of the Believers*, 153–155.

make discipleship their priority and refrain from delegating discipleship training ministry to coworkers. By being the first to sow the seeds of discipleship training in their churches, pastors will demonstrate the importance of this activity, and the nurtured disciples will be more inclined to undergo further training and, eventually, assume the role of discipleship training themselves.

The second is for pastors and other leaders to use the current well-developed digital platforms to deliver teaching. However, it is better to combine online teaching with face-to-face teaching and learning because discipleship training is also about lifestyle and the holistic molding process into Christlikeness. Pastors cannot achieve this objective solely through online platforms. Ultimately, a discipleship training approach that is at the center of a church's life would be a source of strength for the development of the Chinese church in both quantity and quality.

Teaching Content and Using Traditional Chinese Stories

Finally, regarding discipleship training materials, I believe we cannot depend on a particular organization or a certain type of teaching material to cover everything thoroughly. Having outlined discipleship training in Chinese churches, I now focus on how pastors might improvise and source appropriate materials for the job.

Training materials come in all shapes and sizes. Some share the gospel in a formulaic way, others are focused on doctrine, and yet others are application-oriented.[39] In terms of content, one can choose lessons from church history, systematic theology, the life of Jesus Christ, apologetics (giving biblical answers to cults and heretical groups), hermeneutics, and growth.[40] However, the chosen topic must relate to evangelical, historical doctrines of the Bible.

Furthermore, the teaching materials must fit the circumstances and needs of the local church. Pastors should avoid the temptation to select

39 Wang, *Awakening of the Believers*, 176–181.

40 For details of the categorization of the content, refer to Zhao Tian En (赵天恩) and the book *Discipleship Training in the Mainland.*

teaching materials because of a good relationship developed with a certain organization or because the pastors hope to receive financial support by using them.

In keeping with the theme of this book, we must be mindful of how the materials relate to Chinese culture. The concern is that discipleship training materials must be localized or indigenized. For example, translated materials (mostly from Western churches) may contain idioms, examples, and styles of writing that are strange or offensive to the Chinese. Moreover, plenty of Western theological writing is difficult to digest because of its academic style.[41]

Fortunately, due to globalization and collaboration with overseas Chinese Christians, opportunities to obtain good resources have improved significantly. However, sourcing discipleship training materials that are localized and suitable for believers remains a challenge. For instance, there is a dearth of teaching materials for educated people in the Chinese church.[42] This brings me to the viability of Chinese folktales, legends, and myths to teach biblical truths.

In Luke 16:1–13, Jesus told the disciples the parable of the dishonest manager. A manager was sacked by his master, but the manager, who shrewdly wanted to win friends for his future, took the initiative to reduce the debt of the master by going to his debtors. Surprisingly, the manager was later commended by the master for his shrewdness.

This passage may be difficult to explain to Chinese Christians, but Chinese history contains a story that may provide a useful analogy. *Stratagems of the Warring States*, an epic record of diplomacy when China was divided into states in 475–221 BCE, contains an anecdote with two characters: Adviser Feng Yuan (在拼音中) and Meng Chang Jun (冯言爱客孟常君), a prince of the region.[43] The prince's friends were against Feng, describing him as a parasite. Prince Meng decided to test Feng's loyalty by giving him the job of collecting all of Meng's debts. Feng agreed and then asked Meng what he wanted to be done with the money once it was collected. Prince

41 Zhao Tian En, *Discipleship Training*, 24.

42 Zhao Tian En, *Discipleship Training*, 9.

43 This work, *Zhan Guo Ce*, known in English as *Strategies (Intrigues or Stratagems) of the Warring States* was compiled by Lin Shaohua.

Meng replied that Feng should use the money to buy whatever the prince lacked. Feng agreed to this request, but instead of collecting the debts, Feng burned the debt records of the debtors and advised them that their debts were cancelled. When Feng returned, the prince asked Feng, "Why did you burn the records instead of recovering the debts?" Feng replied, "You asked me to buy something that you lacked; I thought you needed the people's love and gratitude, so I burned the records."[44] The prince was extremely angry with Feng, but because the people were celebrating Feng's actions, the prince was forced to retract his criticism and honor Feng's actions.

This Chinese story can be used to explain the parable told by Jesus. A difficult passage in the Bible can be helped by a parallel story in Chinese culture, illustrating that a prudent believer can be assured of a good life through the reciprocity of friendship.[45] Stories and fables like this can be used if they are true to biblical teachings and relevant to discipleship training. These stories can replace Western examples and Greek mythologies typically used in Western Christian texts. Thus localized teaching materials can add another dimension to discipleship training in Chinese churches.

Conclusion

In this chapter, I explored four elements of discipleship training: the theological principle, the purpose for training in an atheistic nation, the training methodology, and the content used in local churches in China.

I emphasized that discipleship training must be provided to all Christians, not just the elite or seminary students training for ministry. I also stressed the importance of conceiving discipleship training as a molding process in which disciples not only acquire knowledge but also emulate the mind of Christ as they negotiate life in a country with an atheistic background and a government that exercises control over churches. I argued that discipleship training that integrates stories and examples from the traditional culture with the gospel could be useful and enriching for Chinese churches.

---

44 My translation.

45 Sun Po Ling (孙宝玲), *Subversion: A Dazzling Light to the World* (逆道-路加福音品读) (Hong Kong: De Hui Culture, 2015), 227–229.

The future of the Chinese church is, at best, uncertain, given the current political context, but one thing is clear: The longevity and depth of the Chinese church depend on the quality of the church's discipleship training.

Bibliography

Bays, Daniel H. *A New History of Christianity in China.* Chichester, West Sussex: Wiley-Blackwell, 2012.

China Law Translate. "Five-Year Planning Outline for Advancing the Sinification of Christianity (2018–2022)." *China Law Translate,* June 18, 2019. https://www.chinalawtranslate.com/en/outline-of-the-five-year-plan-for-promoting-the-sinification-of-christianity%ef%bc%882018-2022%ef%bc%89/.

China Source Team. "Cults and Christianity in China." *China Source,* March 31, 2015. https://www.chinasource.org/resource-library/chinese-church-voices/cults-and-christianity-in-china/.

Lee, Fang Zhou (李方舟). *Great Commission Disciple Training-Third Stage.* Hong Kong: Christian Communications, 2002.

Lin, Shaohua. *Strategies (Intrigues) of the Warring States: Zhan Guo Ce*. Hong Kong: Lijiang Publishing, 2017.

March, F.F. (马尔舒). *Discipleship Training Handbook.* Hong Kong, Corner Stone Publisher, 1993.

Shen, Jue Shen (沈介山). *Believer's Theology* (信徒神学). Taipei: China Evangelical Seminary Publisher, 1997.

Sun, Po Ling (孙宝玲). *Subversion: A Dazzling Light to the World* (逆道-路加福 音品读). Hong Kong: De Hui Culture, 2015.

Yu, Han Qin (王汉钦). *Awakening of the Common Believers* (唤醒平信徒). Seoul: Library Publishing International (图书出板国际门徒训练院), 2009.

Wenzel-Teuber, Katharina. "Statistics on Religions and Churches in the People's Republic of China—Update for the Year 2016." *Religions and Christianity in Today's China* 8, no. 2 (2017): 25–53.

Xu, Yi Hua (徐以骅). *How to Comprehend Christianity in Today's China* (如何理解中国今日的督教). Hong Kong: Heavenly Wind (天风), 2014.

Yang, Mu Gu (杨牧谷). *Reconciliation Theology and Renewal of the Church* (复和神学与 会更新). Hong Kong: Seed Publisher, 1987.

Yu, Au-Ou Ying P. (欧应毓). *Educational Comprehension and Christian Education* (教育 理 解与基督教教育观). Cheng Du: Si Chuan University Publisher, 2005.

Zhao, Tian En (赵天恩). *Discipleship Training in the Mainland*. Taipei: China Ministries International (中国福音会), 1999.

15

THE FILIPINO DIASPORA IN SINGAPORE—OUTREACH AND DISCIPLESHIP

by Jingle D. Cortes

Introduction

The Philippines is the third largest exporter of migrant workers in the world.[1] Remittances from Filipino workers in more than 200 countries amount to 30 percent of the home country's gross national product.[2] Filipino workers are the country's most valuable export.[3] Under former president Benigno Aquino III (2010–2016), the number of overseas Filipino workers (OFWs) leaving the Philippines increased due to low employment and wages in their home country.[4] President Rodrigo Duterte

---

1 Maruja M.B. Asis, "The Philippines: Beyond Labour Migration Toward Development (Possibly) Return," Migration Policy Institute, accessed February 20, 2019, https://www.migrationpolicy.org/articles/philippines-beyond-labor-migration-toward-development-and-possibly-return.

2 "Overview of Philippines-Singapore Relations," accessed February 2, 2023, https://www.philippine-embassy.org.sg/about-us-2/overview-of-philippines-singapore-relations/; "A Rising Tide of Filipinos," The Star/Asia News Network, accessed February 17, 2015, https://sg.neahws.yoo.com/rising-tide-filipinos-0723003671.html.

3 Victoria P. Garchitorena, "Diaspora Philanthropy: The Philippines Experience," The Ayala Foundation, accessed February 8, 2023, https://www.cbd.int/financial/charity/philippines-diaspora.pdf.

4 "SONA2015 Number of OFWs Leaving Daily Rose from 2,500 in 2009 to 6,092 in 2015," accessed May 25, 2016, https://migranteinternational.org/sona2015-number-of-ofws-leaving-daily-rose-from-2500-in-2009-to-6092-in-2015/.

(2016–2022) affirmed the importance of exported labor.[5] Newly installed President Ferdinand Marcos, Jr. has made OFW protection a priority, addressing OFW complaints and providing predeparture seminars to prepare for life in foreign lands.[6]

Singapore is a foreign-labor-dependent country.[7] It opened its doors to Filipino domestic workers, semiskilled workers, and professionals in the 1970s.[8] In 2004, the majority of Filipinos in Singapore were domestic workers.[9] Now Singapore is a trade and investment partner of the Philippines. Data from the Philippine embassy in Singapore show that in 2021 there were over two hundred thousand Filipinos working in Singapore, approximately 60 percent of whom were professional and highly skilled workers (with dependents), and the rest were employed as household service workers.[10]

In my doctoral study, I examined the ways and extent to which five selected Singaporean evangelical churches were reaching Filipinos in Singapore. I started with a preliminary survey of fifty-eight churches ministering

---

5 "State of the Nation Address 2016," *Official Gazette*, accessed February 6, 2017, https://www.officialgazette.gov.ph/2016/07/25/rodrigo-roa-duterte-first-state-of-the-nation-address-july-25-2016/.

6 Marita Moaje, "Protection of OFWs, Utmost Priority of Marcos Admin: CFO," *Philippine News Agency*, accessed February 8, 2023, https://www.pna.gov.ph/articles/1190869.

7 "A Sustainable Population for a Dynamic Singapore: Population White Paper," National Population and Talent Division, accessed May 25, 2016, https://www.strategygroup.gov.sg/images/chart7.png.pdf.

8 Shirlena Huang and Brenda S.A. Yeoh, "Ties that Bind: State Policy and Migrant Female Domestic Helpers in Singapore," *Geoforum* 27, no. 4 (1996): 486–88.

9 Jean Nicole R. Casabuena, "Socio-Economic Impact of Increasing OFWs in Singapore: An Assessment," SCRIBD, accessed March 3, 2018, https://www.scribd.com/document/374039743/CASABUENA-Socio-Economic-Impact-of-Increasing-OFWS-in-Singapore-an-Assessment.

10 "Overview of Singapore-Philippines Relations," The Embassy of the Philippines Singapore, accessed April 19, 2023, https://www.philippine-embassy.org.sg/about-us-2/overview-of-philippines-singapore-relations/#:~:text=An%20estimated%20200%2C000%20Filipinos%20live,both%20the%20Philippi nes%20and%20Singapore.

to Filipinos and followed up by singling out and interviewing leaders in five churches that had more than two hundred Filipino attendees. My interviews focused on the churches' goals, strengths, weaknesses, growth inhibitors, and ministry opportunities. From the interview responses, I derived the commonalities of these churches ministering to the Filipino diaspora. Then, based on the two sets of data, I constructed a set of principles for reaching and discipling Filipinos in Singapore, followed by a framework for their ministry.[11] However, due to the length of this chapter, I have *not* included the principles and framework.

Nevertheless, I illustrate many of the ideas from the principles and framework in two ways: a case study of my involvement with discipleship and outreach for Filipino members of the Bethesda Bedok Tampines Church (BBTC) and a model of the common practices in the five Singaporean churches for ministering to Filipino domestic workers (FDWs).

However, I precede the case study and model with information about several aspects of my research, commencing with a definition of terms, followed by a brief sketch of the history of diaspora missions in Singapore. Then I provide accounts of and outcomes from my preliminary survey and interviews with the leaders of the five selected Singaporean churches.

Definition of Terms

Diaspora, from the Greek word διασπορά, meaning "dispersion," refers to the Jewish dispersion after Babylonian captivity. In the New Testament, these were the Christians living outside Palestine. "Diaspora" in this chapter refers to people who have voluntarily immigrated to a host country.

"Filipino diaspora in Singapore" refers to Filipinos who have moved to Singapore in pursuit of employment and a better life and are naturalized citizens, permanent residents, or OFWs who stay or work in Singapore on one of the following work permits: employment pass, S Pass, student pass, dependent pass, or long-term visit pass.[12]

---

11 Maria Carlisle Dans-Cortes, "Examining the Outreach and Discipleship Efforts of Selected Evangelical Churches to the Filipino Diaspora in Singapore," (DMin diss., Singapore Bible College, 2019).

12 Cortes, *Examining the Outreach and Discipleship.*

Evangelism and discipleship: Evangelism is the proclamation of the good news of God's salvation in Jesus Christ.[13] Discipleship is a process of training in which a Christian is transformed and committed to the mission of Christ (Mark 4:19; Matt 28:19–20).[14]

A Brief History of Missions to the Filipino Diaspora

Since Singapore commenced hiring Filipinos as household workers, Singaporean Christian employers have brought their domestic helpers to their churches—some of the helpers joined church services. Churches seized the opportunity to gather the FDWs and invited them to services, Bible studies, and church-sponsored outings.[15]

Between 1985 and 1990, a few churches started Bible study groups for Filipinos.[16] In the 1990s, several Filipino and Singaporean pastors responded to "missions at our doorsteps" (a catchphrase used in missions to diaspora people) and formed the Filipino Outreach for Christ (FOC) to organize and gather resources to reach Filipinos through national outreach.[17] The FOC became an arm of Asia Evangelistic Fellowship in 1994.

Desiring more autonomy and ministry ownership, the *Kapatiran ng mga Simbahang Pilipino sa* Singapore (KSPS, translated as Brotherhood of Filipino Churches in Singapore) was organized in 1997.[18] KSPS launched creative outreach, such as interchurch basketball and volleyball tournaments. The more established churches introduced multiple levels of training on evangelism, worship, and mission.[19]

---

13 William J. Larkins, Jr., "Evangelise, Evangelism," in *Evangelical Dictionary of Biblical Theology*, ed. Walter A. Elwell (Grand Rapids, MI: Baker, 1996), 216.

14 Jim Putman, *Real-Life Discipleship: Building Churches That Make Disciples* (Colorado Springs, CO: NavPress, 2010), 25–31.

15 Maria Carlisle D. Cortes, *The Diaspora of Filipinos in Singapore: Its Impact on Missions and Evangelism*, (paper, Asian Church History at Singapore Bible College, Singapore, 2000), 7.

16 Cortes, *The Diaspora of Filipinos in Singapore*, 7.

17 Cortes, *The Diaspora of Filipinos in Singapore*, 9–10.

18 Cortes, *The Diaspora of Filipinos in Singapore*.

19 Cortes, *The Diaspora of Filipinos in Singapore*, 11.

In 2009, KSPS metamorphosed into Net Fil, which is now a registered society operating in Singapore. Net Fil organizes training, outreach projects, and mission activities. It has supported a Filipino missionary couple in Timor Leste.[20] Additionally, it collaborated with projects of Love Singapore.[21] Other bodies concerned with Filipino migrants are the Singapore Bible College, which includes missions to migrants and diaspora people as part of its curricula.[22] The Singapore Centre for Global Missions, a catalytic organization and coordinating body enabling other organizations to fulfill the Great Commission, is now at the forefront of highlighting migrant and urban missions.

Aspects of Research on Outreach and Discipleship

In my research on the outreach and discipleship of the Filipino diaspora, I commenced with a preliminary survey of fifty-eight churches. Here are some observations from the responses.

Preliminary survey: [23]

- Most of the participating churches ministered to 11–30 Filipinos, and 9 percent had a congregational strength of 201–2000.
- Most of the Filipinos attended churches located within a ten-minute radius of the Metro Rail Transit (62 percent) or their bus stop (79 percent).

---

20 Ruth Ursua, interview by Maria Carlisle D. Cortes, June 8, 2018.

21 Love Singapore is a unity movement birthed in 1995 motivated by love, fueled by prayer, and inspired by a common vision to catalyze kingdom transformation in the Seven Gates of Cultural Influence in Singapore (Arts and Entertainment; Business, Science and Technology; Communications and Media; Divine Institution and Religion; Education and School; Family and Home; Government and Leadership). Love Singapore, accessed February 17, 2019, http://www.lovesingapore.org.sg/curiousaboutus2.html.

22 "School of Theology English," *Singapore Bible College*, accessed February 8, 2023, https://www.sbc.edu.sg/academics/school-of-theology-english/master-of-arts-in-intercultural-studies/.

23 Maria Carlisle Dans-Cortes, *Examining the Outreach and Discipleship*, 192–196.

- More work permit holders attended churches than other work pass categories. The majority of these were domestic helpers.
- The highest percentages of church attendees belonged to the age ranges of 22–35, 36–45, and 45–55 years old, in that order.
- Ministries prominent among the participating churches were worship, evangelism, cell groups, discipleship, prayer, and the pulpit ministry.
- For special events, churches tried organizing activities in keeping with the outgoing and communal nature of Filipinos.
- Discipleship occurred in discipleship classes, follow-ups, one-on-one mentoring, and training on worship and discipleship.
- The language used was mostly English, followed by Taglish (a combination of English and Tagalog) and Tagalog.
- 47 percent of the churches had Filipino leaders or pastors.
- Migrant issues included family conflicts back in the Philippines, employer–employee relationship, days off, loneliness, finances, punctuality, infidelity, and cultural adjustments.

Interviews with leaders in the five churches:[24] In the five churches, which were Christ Commission Fellowship; Cornerstone Community Church, Filipino; Hope Church Singapore, Filipino; The Living Word Fellowship; and Word International Ministries Singapore, I conducted interviews with pastors, key leaders, and selected congregants familiar with the ethos and ministry of their churches. All five churches had five hundred or more congregants. The interview questions posed to the congregants mirrored the questions posed to the pastors and key leaders. The interview respondents' collective views provided rich and varied pictures of their ministries, such as:

- Four of the five churches were from independent and charismatic denominations, established for more than ten years, and led by elders and full-time pastors.

24 Cortes, *Examining the Outreach and Discipleship Efforts*, 189–192.

- Four of the churches conducted services in English, catering mostly to professionals. One church conducted its main service and six satellite services in Tagalog or Taglish for FDWs, work permit holders, and S Pass holders.
- Three churches had 90 percent or more professionals, neglecting FDWs.
- Two churches had a 50/50 ratio of professionals to FDWs.
- The five churches had multiple ministries and services catering to various groups and needs.
- One church, Cornerstone Filipino Community Church, catered mostly to Tagalog-speaking members. It had decentralized its ministry by renting rooms in Singapore with high concentrations of Filipinos. This attracted FDWs, those unable to come to the main church, and those with irregular work schedules.

Summary of the five churches' ministry goals: [25] The primary goals of all five churches for reaching Filipino members were evangelism and discipleship. However, each church had its own training and discipleship structure. According to Filipino pastor Hazeil Minosa, the keywords for the approach taken by Cornerstone Community Church were "solidify" and "simplify": "Solidify is all about the health of the church. This involves training, equipping, and discipleship. When they are strong, they know their identity, their value system. Then they can be good leaders. Simplify is when you simplify how you run the church. What does God want us to do? Go and make disciples of all nations. If the church is doing something aside from discipling, then the church is not really doing anything. Let's simplify. . . . That's my goal."[26]

Cornerstone used Tagalog and Taglish in its pulpit messages and training materials prepared by the pastor. The congregation ministered to professionals and FDWs. Having grown up as the daughter of an FDW, Pastor Minosa was especially concerned about the plight of FDWs.

The Hope Church focused on reaching Filipinos in Singapore and the Philippines. Evangelism as a lifestyle was done through relationships

25 Cortes, *Examining the Outreach and Discipleship Efforts*, 196–199.

26 Cortes, *Examining the Outreach and Discipleship Efforts*, 137.

and care. Training followed outreach. The Hope Church leadership recognized that the transient nature of Filipino migrants requires Filipinos to be equipped before they journey elsewhere.

Pastor Butch Yu of Word International Ministries Singapore reported that they leveraged the diaspora nature of Filipinos to reach other nations and had penetrated 142 countries. Pastor Wu said Word International's primary goal was to raise spiritual leaders whose transformed lives would impact the marketplace and equip them for other nations. His church had thirteen bi-vocational pastors.

Church Growth Factors

The following growth factors emerged from the interviews:[27]

Small groups: The number one growth factor overall was small groups, which varied in character and purpose from church to church. Except for one church, which operated satellite congregations in the central area of Singapore, discipleship, fellowship, care, love, follow-up, and mentoring occurred in small groups.

Discipleship and discipleship processes: As mentioned above, each church had its own discipleship process:

- Pastor Minosa's Cornerstone church conducted training and equipping in Tagalog.
- The discipleship process of Christ Commission Fellowship began with relational evangelism, followed by gospel sharing, joining a discipleship group, and undergoing the global leadership course, the training ground for future D group leaders.
- At Hope Church Filipino, discipleship, outreach, and care were all conducted at the life group level.
- Word International had developed its own discipleship process, which was used worldwide by the various Word International churches.

27 Cortes, *Examining the Outreach and Discipleship Efforts*, 199–201.

Different ministries and services: The growth in numbers in the churches generated multiple services and ministries to disciple families, children, youth, singles, and parents.

Intentional leadership and accountability structures: Discipleship goals, woven into the structure of small groups, the discipleship process, and creative services and ministries, led to the expansion of leadership development, leadership training, and accountability. For example, Hope Church had a hierarchical structure of leadership that wove from the life group upward.

Word of God and solid teaching: The teaching was grounded in the Bible.

Outreach/evangelism: Outreach, mostly done through small groups, was strategic in the growth of all five churches. One church organized a weekly informal gathering of professionals for one year and provided a social space for them to interact. When the professionals grew exponentially, many joined the FDW small groups.

Strong leadership: Churches were led by female pastors, male pastors, bi-vocational pastors, pastoral and administrative staff, and elders. The leaders communicated the church vision regularly—essentially, the vision to make disciples.

Home, family, and love environment: Family, home, belonging, and genuine love and care are values and emotions that are expressed in action like beads strung together, and they are certainly a magnet for Filipinos. The five churches bore witness to love, acceptance, going the extra mile, remembering special occasions, and the like. Where there was loneliness, the churches provided friendship within a community. For those uprooted from their home country, the churches provided a home away from home and a family in Christ. For identity displacement, there were teachings on purpose and destiny in Christ. Those Filipinos facing the uncertainties of job loss were encouraged to plant churches and disciple their compatriots. Thus an army of economic migrants was transformed into a conquering army of purposeful migrants, thanks to the reaching and discipling of the churches in Singapore.

Location: Location matters. When FDWs with limited days off and tired professionals with heavy work schedules come together, they look for a place to gather within a reachable distance.

Encounters with the Holy Spirit or God: Most Filipinos who come to Singapore experience dysfunctionality and brokenness. Breakthrough ministries, such as the Holy Spirit Encounter or Encounter with God, offered emotional release and spiritual freedom.[28] They helped Filipinos understand their identity in Christ and enabled freedom from the baggage of the past.

Strong mission emphasis and ownership: Three of the churches had strong missional ownership. Leveraging the migration and return of Filipinos, they supported and founded new extensions and daughter churches. While one church gravitated toward leadership development, church planting, and civic projects, another church was intent on bringing the presence of God to every *barangay*.[29]

Strong follow-up: The discipleship process included a strong follow-up culture. Continuous connection with a new Christian happened until retention occurred. For instance, a life group member of one church was assigned to a new believer for follow-up. The new believer would go through the follow-up material, where many foundational truths were taught.

Church Growth Inhibitors

The number one inhibitor to church growth was the pressing requirements and consequences of work. Overtime, no days off, irregular hours, long work hours, and illegal part-time work were typical work exigencies. Government regulations on work tenure have resulted in employment turnover, eventual migration, or return to the Philippines. The length of stay for most Filipinos in Singapore, as designed by law, makes the church a revolving door for Filipinos.

Case Study of Discipleship in a Singaporean Church

In 2018, I began ministry in BBTC,[30] a disciple-making church with a small group of professionals ministering mostly to FDWs.

---

28 Cesar Castellanos, *The Ladder of Success* (Bogota, Colombia: Editorial Villit and Company, 2003), 25–50.

29 A barangay is the smallest political unit in the Philippines.

30 This ministry was started by three Singaporean ladies who had the heart to reach the FDWs in the church.

At that stage, I constructed the aforementioned proposed discipleship framework derived from my research and applied a basic structure to tie up the various elements in BBTC Filipino ministry. Our ministry was to an eclectic combination of approximately 70 percent FDWs and 30 percent professionals, dependents, permanent residents, and naturalized citizens. I adopted the core values of BBTC and its strong leadership accountability structure (see figure 15.1).

Initially, four ministries—worship, house of prayer, audiovisual, and ushering—were committed to serving weekly. To support these ministries, a kitchen ministry was developed with four teams of FDWs and professionals rostered to cook and feed the Filipinos after Sunday services. This promoted fellowship and a third-place community. Because Filipinos value birthdays, we celebrated "Everybody's Birthday" monthly. In 2019, three training sessions were conducted:

- Spiritual parent training:[31] a seminar to teach leaders to share the gospel, craft personal testimonies, and follow up with new converts. Thirty FDWs and professionals were trained.
- Andrew Initiative: a training program to teach everyone how to share the gospel in a three-day initiative by the National Council of Churches of Singapore, Evangelical Fellowship of Singapore, and Love Singapore.[32]
- Cell leaders' training and worship training; geared toward training specialized leaders for ministries.[33]

Besides the above, an intentional discipleship training and equipping ministry was introduced. Forty leaders and members attended a six-week Class 101 course called New Beginnings.[34] The following training was included:

31 This was part of aligning with the leadership structure of BBTC.

32 THIR.ST, "When Churches Unite: Got Hope?", THIR.ST, accessed February 20, 2023, https://thirst.sg/when-churches-unite-got-hope/.

33 This was adopted from the leadership structure of BBTC for alignment.

34 Jingle Dans-Cortes, *New Beginnings* (Singapore: Bethesda Bedok-Tampines Church, 2019).

- ministry giver training for FDWs and professionals to run the breakthrough ministry
- big idea homiletics training to develop a pulpit ministry team[35]
- cell supervisors' training
- The Significant Woman (TSW) facilitators' training to develop facilitators for the TSW
- Man of Impact training, the male equivalent of TSW[36]

When COVID-19 struck, BBTC Filipino modified many things. Services, meetings, and training were conducted online. This spawned the BBTC Filipino Multi-Media Ministry. Cell groups that met online for prayer and study, allowing families stationed in the Philippines and other countries to join using Messenger, Zoom, and WhatsApp as the main platforms.

Surprisingly, the pandemic strengthened BBTC Filipino because the online ministries created a bigger stage for our evangelism and discipleship programs. Other churches were sadly losing members during this time, but BBTC Filipino grew exponentially.

The mentoring of leaders and the structural framework to support the vision and mission of the congregation in 2019 strengthened BBTC Filipino, and the cell groups multiplied from seven to fourteen (nine FDW and five professional cell groups).

BBTC Filipino was determined to reach both FDWs and professionals, who were discipled under the same curriculum using the principles derived from my doctoral study, as indicated by the following features:

- Lay teachers were empowered to teach the word.
- English, Tagalog, and Taglish remained the main languages of instruction and communication.

---

35 Haddon W. Robinson, *Biblical Preaching* (Grand Rapids, MI: Baker Book House, 1980).

36 Campus Crusade for Christ (Singapore), *Man of Impact*, (Singapore: Campus Crusade for Christ, 2018).

- Food played a big part in bringing fellowship and cohesion.
- Outings on fifth Sundays continued to bring members and guests together.
- Pre-evangelistic cell groups, evangelistic cell groups, and harvest events became a part of the DNA of BBTC Filipino.
- The Seven Anointed Pillars, organic to BBTC,[37] continued to be emphasized.
- Social space was provided, allowing members to stay in church until evening.

During the BBTC Filipino anniversaries in 2021 and 2022, we received an encouraging thread of messages from attendees: "BBTC Filipino is a loving church beyond walls . . . BBTC Filipino is worship, food, love, community, Word, resilient . . . BBTC Filipino is family."

As the practitioners discipled the Filipino diaspora, intentional discipleship was the key. My research, which provided a wealth of data and helpful information as a possible framework for discipleship, was tested and somewhat modified at BBTC Filipino.[38]

Now, for a change of focus and setting, I present a model for ministry to FDWs based on my thirty-plus years of practical ministry with FDWs and data collected in my PhD study of FDWs in Singapore.

Model for Ministry to Filipino Domestic Workers

When discipling FDWs, the practitioner should first note contextual issues, such as education, culture, language, family situation, and social and economic issues. It is also useful to know such details as the FDWs' days off for physical meetings and their accessibility to communication platforms. An elaboration of these contextual matters follows.

37 Anointed Word, Anointed Worship, Anointed Body Life, Anointed Leadership, Anointed Ministries, Anointed Altar, Anointed Works of Faith.

38 Cortes, *Examining the Outreach and Discipleship Efforts.*

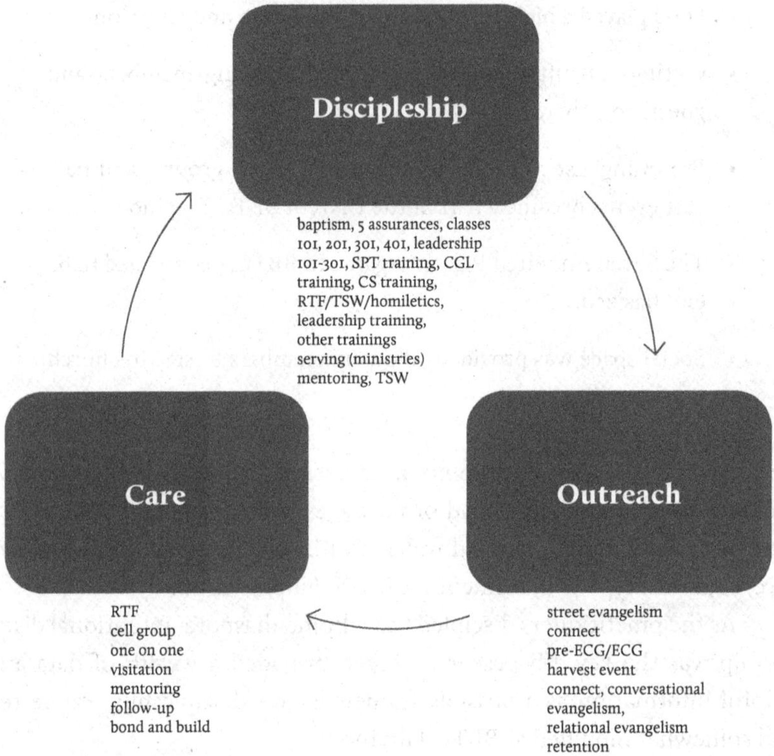

Figure 15.1. Bethesda Bedok Tampines Church Filipino discipleship process (Source: Cortes).

Legend:

Pre-ECG—pre-evangelistic cell group
ECG—evangelistic cell group
RTF—restoring the foundation
TSW—The Significant Woman
CGL—cell group leader
CS—cell supervisor
SPT—spiritual parent training

Education and Medium of Communication

Most FDWs who come to Singapore have a high school education or a few years in college or vocational school. A few are degree holders.[39]

39 *Migrant Domestic Worker Eligibility*, Ministry of Manpower, accessed 10 February 2023, https://www.mom.gov.sg/passes-and-permits/work-permit-

Since English is the lingua franca in Singapore, employers prefer Filipinos because they are generally better educated than helpers from other countries. But this does not mean all Filipinos are proficient in English; in fact, most communicate among themselves in Taglish, Tagalog, or a native dialect.[40]

In my research, most of the five churches indicated that church leaders used English, Taglish and Tagalog in their pulpit ministry.[41] The pastor of Diakonia Christian Fellowship said that their church used Taglish in the pulpit, English for discipleship materials from Western sources, and a mixture of English and Tagalog for worship songs. His congregation comprised 75 percent FDWs.[42] The same was true for Light at the Crossroads Church, which had a congregation of 40 percent FDWs.[43] Cornerstone Filipino Community Church mainly used Taglish and Tagalog.[44]

Because BBTC Filipino was composed of 60 percent FDWs, it was committed to using English, Taglish, and Tagalog. It deputized some helpers to translate teaching materials into Tagalog, Cebuano, and Ilocano.[45] BBTC Filipino also used other dialects for discipleship, training, and equipping. Every newcomer who responded to salvation was given the preferred Tagalog language Bible.

At AEFI, Jonathan Cortes conducted Cebuano Bible studies to cater to Cebuano-speaking FDWs. This program included at least three online Cebuano Bible studies with families of the FDWs and three cell groups in Tagalog.

Social Media Platforms

At the height of the pandemic, several physical restrictions were put in place by the Singaporean government, paving the way for online meetings,

---

for-foreign-domestic-worker/eligibility-and-requirements/fdw-eligibility #:~:text=Minimum%208%20years%20of%20formal,they%20are%20first %2Dtime%20helpers.

40 Philippines Ethnologue, *Languages of the World*, accessed May 26, 2018, https://www.ethnologue.com/country/PH.

41 Cortes, *Examining the Outreach and Discipleship Efforts*, 129.

42 Rey Navarro, Survey by Maria Carlisle D. Cortes, December 31, 2022.

43 Domingo Naz, Survey Light at the Crossroads Church, January 3, 2023.

44 Cortes, *Examining the Outreach and Discipleship Efforts*, 197.

45 Major dialects used by Filipinos.

Bible studies, training, and outreach. FDWs who were able to plug into weekly meetings mostly used the free apps Messenger chat, WhatsApp, and Zoom for communication.

Priority Issues

Priority issues for the practitioners called to minister to FDWs were unity, healing and emotional support, and self-transformation. Filipinos value unity because of their cultural concept of *kapwa*, loosely translated in English as "fellow being," which implies the "recognition of shared identity."[46] However, this concept was ineffective in integrating Filipinos into Singaporean churches because the FDWs felt restricted in expressing themselves when they were in church with their employers and other Singaporeans.

Integrating FDWs into a local church was difficult for the following reasons:

- It was difficult for FDWs to be themselves in the presence of employers.
- Most Filipinos were uncomfortable due to cultural and language barriers.
- Many desired to serve in the local church but were not happy about competing with locals.[47]

If a church practitioner thinks that the integration of FDWs into local churches is a necessary approach to ministry, the following example of a Filipino couple's experience with Bible study for FDWs may provide a reason to reconsider: "The Bible study was separate from the main congregation. The FDWs were mostly employed by Singaporean employers, who participated in the main service and in the Bible study meetings. The

46 Virgilio Enriquez, "Kapwa: A Core Concept in Filipino Psychology," in *Philippine Worldview*, ed. Virgilio Enriquez (Singapore: Institute of Southeast Asian Studies, 1986), 6–19.

47 Joseph Nathan Villamonte Cruz, "Evangelical Communities and Filipino Migrant Workers," (MA thesis, National University of Singapore, 2013) 67–68.

couple observed that the church was far from the egalitarian ideal because some of the FDWs *were forbidden by their employers to attend the Bible study*."[48] This experience indicated that a third space for Filipinos to freely fellowship and interact among themselves might provide greater relational connection and belonging.

Even among Filipinos, boundaries are formed. Joseph Cruz cited the former pastor of International Baptist Church (IBC), Rey Navarro, who resisted creating separate fellowship groups for Filipino professionals and FDWs but relented due to pressure from his congregation. IBC found that it had to address the different needs of young professionals who preferred to gather on Friday nights, unlike FDWs, who met only on Sundays. Clearly, there is no hard and fast rule for how churches should promote egalitarian social relations between local Christians, FDWs, and Filipino professionals.[49]

The interviews with the five churches, where a thriving community of professionals existed, showed that their focus had shifted to favoring professionals as influencers, to the exclusion of the domestic helpers.[50] A pastor of Hope Filipino Church said, "We have neglected the domestic helpers. We were focused on the professionals. That's because the helpers were available only on Sundays, and their attendance was irregular for follow-up. So we had the option to reach out more to the professionals who are freer on Saturdays and night-time."[51]

A leader at Christ Commission Fellowship stated, "The Filipinos in Singapore are basically either professionals or domestics. When you try to cater to the professional group, you tend to miss out on the helpers."[52] However, the hybrid model at BBTC Filipino of professionals and FDWs assembling for corporate worship, discipleship training, equipping, retreats, and outings showed that it is possible to integrate the two groups. At BBTC, the imaginary demarcation between the two was erased in such ministries as the house of prayer, dance ministry, audiovisual

48 Cruz, *Evangelical Communities and Filipino Migrant Workers*, 69–70.

49 Cruz, *Evangelical Communities and Filipino Migrant Workers*, 70–71.

50 Cortes, *Examining the Outreach and Discipleship Efforts*, 173.

51 Cortes, *Examining the Outreach and Discipleship Efforts*, 174.

52 Cortes, *Examining the Outreach and Discipleship Efforts*, 176.

and multimedia, and worship. Both sectors served together in unity, but there was some homogeneity. FDWs were put into cell groups led mostly by fellow FDW leaders, while most of the professionals were in separate cell groups.

The major issues for FDWs are isolation and emotional loneliness, as their worlds are mostly limited to their workplaces. This world expands when an FDW forms a romantic relationship, which may lead to sexual activities. Joseph Cruz asserted that loneliness and sexuality are related issues. However, most of the FDWs' problems concern their workplace and families in the Philippines, including sickness, finances for school enrollment, medical expenses, husbands' infidelity, or children in trouble. Sexual immorality is likely "a symptom of underlying problems, such as loneliness, a sense of helplessness, and low self-esteem arising from being an unskilled foreigner without the support network of family and friends."[53] In my doctoral survey of fifty-eight churches, I identified the following issues the churches faced.[54]

Table 15.1. Cultural and contextual issues (Source: Cortes).

Data on cultural and contextual issues	Number of cases	Percentage
Family conflicts in the Philippines	45	78%
Employer–employee relationship	44	76%
Loneliness	39	67%
Rest days and days off	38	66%
Debts and borrowing	36	62%
Financial management	33	57%
Punctuality	31	53%
Infidelity	30	52%
Cultural adjustment	28	48%
Workplace abuse	21	36%
Language communication	18	31%

53 Cruz, *Evangelical Communities and Filipino Migrant Workers*, 74.

54 Cortes, *Examining the Outreach and Discipleship Efforts*, 133–134.

The churches addressed these cultural and contextual issues in various ways.[55] Cruz suggested that the most important agenda for the church is to address and promote self-transformation among the Filipino domestic diaspora. When the issue is low self-image, FDWs need to see God's divine purpose for them as diaspora. Net Fil embraced the vision that the Filipino diaspora in Singapore and elsewhere has a divine purpose.[56] Below is an excerpt from an interview that Cruz conducted with Pastor Vargas of Marine Parade Christian Centre on March 5, 2009. Vargas stated:

> I experienced a vision . . . I was in a dark room. I couldn't see anything. . . . [T]iny candles appeared. . . . God told me that the candles were the spiritual testimony of migrant workers. The dark room was the world. I complained to God that the candles were so small, their light too faint. God told me, "The darker the room, the brighter the light." I wept for my arrogance and shortsightedness. While my heart loved migrant workers, in truth, I was not giving them the respect they deserved. I doubted their ability to be witnesses. . . . As I shared with them what God revealed to me, their perspectives changed, and so did their self-image.[57]

As part of inculcating a higher purpose for Christ, Filipino pastors are now teaching the FDWs to witness through relationships, and the pastors lead people to Christ.[58]

As cited earlier, there is a strong discipleship thrust by churches to transform beliefs and attitudes. The offshoot of discipleship is a sense of purpose. Angie Tabaquero led a discipleship group of young people, FDWs, professionals, IT workers, and businesspeople. Tabaquero was herself an FDW who came to know Christ when she was in Hong Kong. She used this training to disciple Filipinos when she moved to Singapore. The church became an environment where she gained skills, learned new perspectives,

55 Cortes, *Examining the Outreach and Discipleship Efforts*, 134.
56 Cruz, *Evangelical Communities and Filipino Migrant Workers*, 72.
57 Cruz, *Evangelical Communities and Filipino Migrant Workers*, 73.
58 Cruz, *Evangelical Communities and Filipino Migrant Workers*, 73.

and acquired knowledge. Sunday became the focal point of her week, and she discovered the higher purpose of discipling Filipinos.[59]

Pastor Minosa at Cornerstone led the way in empowering FDWs, and at BBTC Filipino, as reported in the previous section, we followed the model of training, equipping, and empowering FDWs for ministry: discipleship training and equipping facilitated growth among FDWs. FDWs were called to leadership and became actively involved in ministries, discipleship, outreach, and care within cell group settings.

Conclusion

In this chapter, I described the aspects of my doctoral research on how churches in Singapore provide ministry to the Filipino diaspora in Singapore. Hopefully, my ideas will be useful for Singaporean churches or churches in countries where Filipinos work.

I am grateful for the many churches that have recognized the importance of reaching Filipinos in cosmopolitan Singapore. The Filipinos came to Singapore to work and support their families. They also came as a gift to Singapore, progressing the nation's economy. In return, Singaporean churches have offered a gift to the Filipinos and God. Discipled Filipinos are a gift to other nations when they leave Singapore. Thus the Filipino who is well-trained and discipled by a Singaporean church is an instrument of blessing to Jesus—the migrant God who came into this world to share the light of God.

Bibliography

A Guide to Churches in Christian Organizations in Singapore, 2015–2016. Singapore: National Council of Churches, 2015.

"A Rising Tide of Filipinos." *The Star/Asia News Network*. Accessed February 17, 2015. https://sg.neahws.yoo.com/rising-tide-filipinos-072300367l.html.

"A Sustainable Population for a Dynamic Singapore: Population White Paper." *National Population and Talent Division*. Accessed May 25, 2016. https://www.strategygroup.gov.sg/images/chart7.png.pdf.

59 Cruz, *Evangelical Communities and Filipino Migrant Workers*, 75–80.

Asis, Maruja M.B. "The Philippines: Beyond Labour Migration Toward Development (Possibly) Return." *Migration Policy Institute*, Accessed February 20, 2019. https://www.migrationpolicy.org/articles/philippines-beyond-labor-migration-toward-development-and-possibly-return.

"Barangay," Philippines Statistics Authority. Accessed February 9, 2023, https://psa.gov.ph/content/barangay-1.

"Breakthrough Weekends." *Covenant Evangelical Free Church of Singapore*. Accessed November 26, 2018. http://www.cefc.org.sg/index.php/bts-faqs.

Casabuena, Jean Nicole R. "Socio-Economic Impact of Increasing OFWs in Singapore: An Assessment." *B Foreign Service/FS302, International Political Economy, SCRIBD*. Accessed March 3, 2018, https://www.scribd.com/document/374039743/CASABUENA-Socio-Economic-Impact-of-Increasing-OFWS-in-Singapore-an-Assessment.

Castellanos, Cesar. The Ladder of Success. Bogota, Colombia: Editorial Villit and Company, 2003.

Chong, Calvin. "Diaspora Missions in Singapore." *SCGM Breakfast Fellowship*. November 3, 2017.

———. "Transforming Migrant Place Conditions and Experiences as Good News." in *Servants at the Fringes: Christians Serving Foreign Workers in Singapore*. Singapore: Singapore Bible College, 2018.

Cortes, Maria Carlisle Dans. "Examining the Outreach and Discipleship Efforts of Selected Evangelical Churches to the Filipino Diaspora in Singapore." Thesis: Doctor of Ministry at Singapore Bible College, May 2019.

———. *New Beginnings*. Singapore: Bethesda Bedok-Tampines Church, 2019.

———. "The Diaspora of Filipinos in Singapore: Its Impact on Missions and Evangelism." Paper for the course Asian Church History at Singapore Bible College. Singapore, 2000.

Cruz, Joseph Nathan Villamonte. "Evangelical Communities and Filipino Migrant Workers." Master's thesis, National University of Singapore, 2013.

Devashayam, Theresa W. "Placement and/or Protection? Singapore's Labour Policies and Practices for Temporary Women Migrant Workers." *Journal of the Asian Pacific Economy* 15, no. 1 (2010).

"Diaspora," in *Universal Dictionary, Reader's Digest*. Boston: Houghton Mifflin, 1993.

Ko, Lawrence. *Ethnic Rhythms: Life in the Global City*. Singapore: Singapore Centre for Global Missions, 2015.

Feldman, Dian, Gail L. Porter, and Susan M. Heckmann. *The Significant Woman*. Singapore: Campus Crusade for Christ, 2018.

Garchitorena, Victoria. "Diaspora Philanthropy: The Philippines Experience." The Philanthropic Initiative and The Globe; Equity Initiative, Harvard University. Accessed February 8, 2023. https://www.cbd.int/financial/charity/philippines-diaspora.pdf.

Gavilan, Jodesz. "FAST FACTS: Things to Know About Philippines-Singapore Relations," *Rappler.* Accessed February 8, 2023. https://www.rappler.com/nation/things-to-know-philippines-singapore-relations/#:~:text=Singapore%20is%20home%20and%20workplace%20of%20many%20Filipinos&text=Data%20from%20DFA%20shows%20that,live%20and%20work%20in%20Singapore.

Gornik, Mark R. *To Live in Peace: Biblical Faith and the Changing Inner City.* Grand Rapids, MI: Eerdmans, 2002.

"How to Open an Account with Overseas Filipino Bank." OWWA Member. Accessed February 1, 2023. https://owwamember.com/overseas-filipino-bank/.

Huang, Shirlena, and Brenda S.A. Yeoh. "Ties that Bind: State Policy and Migrant Female Domestic Helpers in Singapore." *Geoforum* 27, no. 4 (1996): 486–88.

Enriquez, Virgillo G. "Kapwa: A Core Concept in Filipino Psychology." In *Philippine Worldview,* edited by Virgilio G. Enriquez, Singapore: Institute of Southeast Asian Studies, 1986.

Love Singapore. Accessed February 17, 2019. http://www.lovesingapore.org.sg/curiousaboutus2.html.

Man of Impact. Singapore: Campus Crusade for Christ, 2018.

Menguin, Jeff. "Malasakit: The Filipino Culture of Caring for Others." Accessed February 9, 2023, https://jefmenguin.com/malasakit/.

"Migrant Domestic Worker Eligibility." Ministry of Manpower. Accessed February 10, 2023. https://www.mom.gov.sg/passes-and-permits/work-permit-for-foreign-domestic-worker/eligibility-and-requirements/fdw-eligibility#:~:text=Minimum%208%20years%20of%20formal,they%20are%20first%2Dtime%20helpers.

Moaje, Marita. "Protection of OFWs, Utmost Priority of Marcos admin: CFO." *Philippine News Agency*. December 15, 2022. Accessed February 8, 2023, https://www.pna.gov.ph/articles/1190869.

Overview of Philippines-Singapore Relations. Accessed February 2, 2023. https://www.philippine-embassy.org.sg/about-us-2/overview-of-philippines-singapore-relations/.

Peterson, Christopher. "Happy Places, Third Places," *Psychology Today.* December 1, 2009. https://www.psychologytoday.com/us/blog/the-good-life/200912/happy-places-third-places.

"Philippines." Ethnologue: Languages of the World. Accessed May 26, 2018. https://www.ethnologue.com/country/PH.

Putman, Jim. *Real-Life Discipleship: Building Churches that Make Disciples.* Colorado Springs, CO: NavPress, 2010.

Robbe, Brett. *Connect, Grow, Serve, Go: Moving Toward a Balanced Approach to an Adult Ministry*. Nashville, TN: Lifeway Press, 2010.

Robinson, Haddon W. *Biblical Preaching.* Grand Rapids, MI: Baker Book House, 1980.

"RTF@BBTC," *Bethesda Bedok-Tampines Church*. Accessed November 26, 2019. https://www.bbtc.com.sg/rtf-bbtc/.

S.A., Brenda, and Shirlena Huang. "Home and Away: Foreign Domestic Workers and Negotiations of Diasporic Identity in Singapore." *Women's Study International Forum 3,* (Singapore: Elsevier Science, 2000), 413–29.

"School of Theology English." *Singapore Bible College*. Accessed February 8, 2023. https://www.sbc.edu.sg/academics/school-of-theology-english/master-of-arts-in-intercultural-studies/.

Singapore Centre for Global Missions. Accessed June 8, 2018. http://www.scgm.org.sg/ethnic-rhythms-life-inthe-global-city-book-launch-3-sept-2015/.

"State of the Nation Address 2016." Official Gazette, Government of the Philippines. Accessed February 6, 2017. https://www.officialgazette.gov.ph/2016/07/25/rodrigo-roa-duterte-first-state-of-the-nation-address-july-25-2016/.

"SONA2015 Number of OFWs Leaving Daily Rose from 2,500 in 2009 to 6,092 in 2015." Accessed May 25, 2016. https://migranteinternational.org/sona2015-number-of-ofws-leaving-daily-rose-from-2500-in-2009-to-6092-in-2015/.

"The WIN Discipleship Process." Accessed February 9, 2023. https://www.winsingaporechurch.com/discipleship-process. The Discipleship Process is: "Connect, Belong, Believe, Serve, Lead."

THIR.ST. "When Churches Unite: Got Hope?" Accessed February 20, 2023. https://thirst.sg/when-churches-unite-got-hope/.

"What is Messenger." Webwise. Accessed February 15, 2023. https://www.webwise.ie/parents/explained-what-is-messenger/.

"What is Zoom Video Conferencing," Zoom Support. Accessed February 15, 2023. https://support.zoom.us/hc/en-us/articles/4420426401037-What-is-Zoom-Video-Conferencing-.

"What is WhatsApp?" Webwise. Accessed February 15, 2023. https://www.webwise.ie/parents/explainer-whatsapp/.

Wong, David. "Foreign Domestic Workers in Singapore." *Asian and Pacific Migration Journal,* 5, no.1 (1996).

16

TRAINING AND DISCIPLING VILLAGE PASTORS IN THE PHILIPPINES

by Metosalem Castillo

Introduction

The Philippines is an Asian Christian nation.[1] Roman Catholicism was introduced from Spain as early as 1521 when the Philippines was "discovered" by Magellan. Protestant missionaries arrived with US forces around 1900.[2] American mission agencies came with urgency to accomplish a threefold mandate: to educate, civilize, and Christianize the Philippines. Driving these goals was a mission agreement aimed at reaching the whole nation as quickly as possible.[3] Protestant missionaries from various denominations divided the nation into segments and assigned mission bodies to serve and operate in each segment. In so doing, mission organizations believed unnecessary duplication and competition would be avoided.

However, the dominant plan for evangelizing the entire nation quickly and efficiently meant that some components of a truly Christian mission were overlooked. Evangelism, discipleship, and church establishment may

1 86 percent of the population is Roman Catholic and approximately 2 percent belong to the one hundred or so Protestant denominations according to the Asia Society: https://asiasociety.org/education/religion-philippines

2 Teodoro Agoncillo, *A Short History of the Philippines* (New York: Mentor Books, 1969).

3 Agoncillo, *A Short History of the Philippines.*

have been the core concerns, but pastoral and leadership training were slow in development, and most training institutions, such as Bible schools and institutes, were established in cities and large towns. This centralization meant that students had to leave their families and villages and travel long distances. Sadly, when they returned to their villages, many could not relate to the villages' sociocultural and economic scenarios. Consequently, many, if not most, of those trained in such Bible schools had to remain in cities and towns, leaving the rural villages devoid of the blessings of proper Bible and theological training.

Thankfully, the situation has somewhat improved in the last decade. Theological training is finding its way to key provinces, bringing the opportunity closer to many villages. However, city Bible schools and seminaries, particularly in Metro Manila, remain the beacon, so those who can afford the fees for study still try to find their way to the metropolis. But what about those who need to remain in the villages?

In this chapter, I describe and discuss the minority situation of training and discipleship that takes place in the villages of the Philippines. I begin with a brief overview of some cultural perspectives that are pertinent to the discussion, then go on to explain my methodology. Later, I will present a case study of how effective training is taking place in the provinces of the Philippines. I use the example of Asia Evangelistic Fellowship Destiny Ministry Incorporated, which is typically shortened to ADMI,[4] to draw out the salient principles of training and discipleship in Filipino villages.

Cultural Perspectives and Methodology

Before colonization by the Spanish, Filipinos worshipped a form of animism with a pantheon of gods, spirits, and mythical creatures who supposedly watched over the mountains, forests, rivers, and even houses.[5] Among the gods was the supreme being, Bathala, who created humankind

4 ADMI stands for AEF Destiny Ministry Incorporated. AEF is the initialism for Asia Evangelistic Fellowship.

5 "Religion in the Philippines," *Asia Society,* accessed March 25, 2023, https://asiasociety.org/education/religion-philippines

and the world.[6] People who exercised power over the supernatural were immediately recognized and given status and positions of prominence. Every village had shamans and holy men who performed ritual cleansing and curing.[7] People craved *anting-anting*, a kind of charm that would help overcome all human enemies.[8]

After more than four centuries of Western colonization, the Philippines still has a strong and unique cultural ethos alongside certain Western influences. The family is the basic unit of society, underpinning Filipino identity and belonging. Next to the family, the *barangay* (district or smallest unit of government) is significant in the social milieu of Filipinos. Filipino culture is based on *kapwa* (fellowship or togetherness). At the family or *barangay* level, Filipino identity is strong despite differences in social status or wealth.[9] Related to this reality is *bayanihan* (teamwork) in the context of community living.

In the villages, Filipinos come together for a cause, such as to help build someone's house or to volunteer for a community cause.[10] Linked with this concept is the idea of *hiya* (shame or embarrassment), which almost always relates to another key concept, *utang na loob* (indebtedness).[11] When someone has done you a favor, you feel obliged to return it—at some other time or in some way. So that is where *hiya* and *utang na loob* come into play.[12]

I use anecdotal evidence drawn from my more than five decades of mission experience in the Philippines. In the case study to follow, I recount lessons and principles from the ADMI's work in the Philippines. Some of

---

6 Maximo Ramos, *Creatures of Philippine Lower Mythology* (Quezon City, Philippines: University of the Philippines Press, 1971).

7 Asia Society, "Religion in the Philippines."

8 Ramos, *Creatures of Philippine Lower Mythology.*

9 Chara Scroope, "Filipino Culture: Core Concepts," *Cultural Atlas,* https://culturalatlas.sbs.com.au/filipino-culture/filipino-culture-core-concepts

10 Niels Mulder, "Filipino Culture and Social Analysis." *Philippine Studies* 42, no. 1 (1994): 80–90, http://www.jstor.org/stable/42633420.

11 Virgilio G. Enriquez, "Developing a Filipino Psychology," in *Indigenous Psychologies: Research and Experience in Cultural Context, ed.* U. Kim and J. W. Berry (Thousand Oaks, CA: SAGE Publications, 1993), 152–169.

12 Mulder, "Filipino Culture and Social Analysis," 80–90.

the lessons are drawn from memory, and others from field interviews, my lectures, and leadership discussions with my staff and ministry leaders.

The Case of Asia Evangelistic Fellowship Destiny Ministry Incorporated's Attempt to Train and Disciple

ADMI is registered with the Philippine government as a nonprofit religious organization. Its primary objective is to reach Filipinos everywhere with the gospel and train believers to undertake development projects for disadvantaged communities. In its eleven years of existence, ADMI has set its ministry focus on villagers: pastors, church leaders, and people. In 2019, the leadership set a five-year discipling and training goal for village pastors and church leaders, particularly in the northern Philippines. Due to the restrictions imposed by the national health department during the COVID-19 pandemic, the ADMI board of trustees extended the program for another five years (from 2020 to 2025) with the expanded goal of establishing additional training sites in other provinces and regions.

ADMI's workforce consists mostly of volunteer servants of the Lord, who are classified into two groups: leaders and the core ministry team (five leaders and five core ministry leaders) and the field representatives who look after the local ministries and personnel. Most field representatives are bi-vocational, combining their secular work with their ministry work. Our relationships with each other are not defined by our corporate organization but by a less complicated relational understanding, which is culturally valued among the village folk. Its core values are trust and respect. We respect and trust the villagers, and we seek their respect and trust. And these values are enacted in Christ.[13]

Villagers work in farming, fishing, and small businesses. Many healthy villagers commute to cities like Manila to work as domestic helpers and construction workers or overseas under the government-endorsed program called OFWs. Despite this scenario, village populations are on the rise. However, poverty, illness, lack of education, and other forms of

---

13 2 Cor. 5: 17; Rom. 8: 1 and Eph. 2: 10 are some of the many verses that signify a new relationship Christians have in Jesus Christ.

suffering and deprivation remain the day-to-day realities in the villages. The weak, poor, and most needy are there, which is likely why Jesus included villages in his preaching, teaching, and healing itinerary (Matt 9:35).

ADMI's training and discipling countryside mission, which is offered to pastors and church leaders, is code-named "The 4-E Plan" and comprises encouraging, equipping, empowering, and engaging.[14] Next I discuss each segment, but first, I want to acknowledge that before this plan/methodology was applied in the northern Philippines, it was field-tested for years in Mindanao (southern Philippines), known as the country's frontier.

Encouraging: To encourage is to give help, support, and confidence and to embolden. Our first approach is to come alongside the village pastors and church leaders as encouragers, just like Barnabas, whose name means "son of encouragement," did in the New Testament (Acts 11:22–24). These servants of God are often victims of discouragement and loneliness because of their isolation and substandard living conditions. In one of our training sites, a pastor poured out his heart to me the first time we met. He said his superiors had never visited him in the fourteen years of his ministry there. With tears of joy, he added, "Praise God that you and your team have come to our humble town."[15] This meeting was like a lamppost that lit the beginning of an ongoing ministry partnership among the pastors and church leaders of two isolated but vibrant towns in the countryside.

Encouraging village workers may sound trivial compared with the other aims of the plan, but so much depends on how we encourage them. At first, we tried to reinvent the wheel, but we soon settled on prioritizing establishing relationships through prayer and pastors' fellowships.

Our first task was to make contact and get acquainted with our intended audience. We refrained from the usual fashion of sending out attractive promotional leaflets and advance parties. Instead, we adopted their cultural practice of engaging with trusted informal Christian village leaders to introduce us to the pastors in the area. Our main aim was to

14 This is my own idea developed for lectures to my students at various Bible colleges and at ASOM.

15 Much of the information in this chapter is from my field notes gathered from various regions in the Philippines during the years 2009–2023.

establish relationships based on trust and confidence, which have proven to be crucial in our ministries across denominational boundaries, such as evangelical communities within Protestant churches.

Bible study took precedence over prayer. Recognizing that these were aural learners, we focused on reading, listening, and participative study of the word of God. We took time to listen to their concerns about their families, ministries, churches, and villages. To encourage the open sharing of prayer requests, we ensured that each request would be prayed for because we realized that individual recognition was of great value for these folk.

Our entire program was capped each day with a fellowship *merienda* (snack time) consisting of native coffee and pastries or a main meal, depending on the time of day. Eating together remains a vital cultural sign of friendship and goodwill. Before leaving each visit, we checked to ensure our pastors had Bibles. Some only had a New Testament, and others had worn-out copies.

Pastors' fellowship is the other key component of encouragement. Fellowship is usually one or two days in duration, with three primary objectives: to encourage, give instruction, and raise vision. The instruction relates to the Bible, Christian living, evangelism, discipleship, mission, and community and livelihood development. To assist with raising their vision in ministry, we conduct workshops on visioning, planning, and implementing.

Our main challenges in convening pastors' fellowships are issues of denominationalism and the time factor. Regarding the last challenge, many pastors in the villages engage in some form of farming or fishing to augment their meager income; therefore, even one day taken out of their daily chores means a "big loss" for them,[16] and scheduling pastors' fellowship meetings must be taken seriously to ensure good participation. The book of Ecclesiastes informs us that everything has a season (Eccl 3:1–8). We try to target fellowship days for when conditions are not conducive to working on the farm or fishing, and we take advantage of the town and village fiestas (festivals)—holidays that are perennial socioreligious events in the Philippines (more on fiestas below). Participants learn to adjust

16 Field notes, 2022.

and prioritize these special days assigned for their spiritual feeding and upliftment.

I conclude this section by identifying some exciting outcomes of this ministry. Besides encouragement, instruction, and spiritual upliftment for the participants, the pastors' fellowship meetings often revitalize their existing ministerial associations or form new ones.

Notable examples of such revitalization are:

- the ministerial associations that occurred in the municipalities of Dinalungan, Province of Aurora; San Pablo, Province of Isabela; Laoag, Province of Ilocos Norte; and Caba, Province of La Union
- the new pastors' fellowships established in Tuguegarao and Santiago in the Cagayan Valley region

Alongside Bible teaching and preaching and the usual fellowship meals and coffee breaks, we give out Bibles, books, and other material goods. Thank God for ministry partners who supply Bibles and books from time to time. Often we drive home with loads of fruits and vegetables, which are readily available in the countryside. Thus we set out to encourage others, and we return home encouraged.

Equipping: Equipping village pastors and church leaders in ADMI's 4-E Plan involves intensive teaching and training. Through teaching, the pastors grow in knowledge, and through training, they either develop new skills or improve existing ones. Bear in mind that a great number of our trainees have had insufficient schooling and training for the ministry. However, their desire and dedication to learn and obtain further training in ministry more than compensates for the lack of foundational learning. Thankfully, the ADMI team responds positively to the realities and uses a two-prong teaching-training program: leadership training seminars (LTSs) and the ADMI School of Ministry (ASOM). I now explain the mechanics and functions of each.

In LTSs, the objective is to augment the biblical and professional knowledge and training of village pastors, church leaders, and workers with intensive teaching and practical training for ministry. The program content includes the Bible, doctrine, Christian life, evangelism, discipleship, mission, church planting, pastoral care, community and health, and livelihood development. An LTS is an ongoing in-service training program designed to enhance effectiveness in the Lord's work, and we can only cover one or two courses or themes at a time. The duration of an LTS is normally two to three days. In places where lighting facilities are subnormal, training sessions are held in the morning and afternoon hours only. Where lighting is available, we use the evening for preaching and sharing testimonies.

The lecturers and speakers for LTSs come from our ADMI team and friends who share their time and talent. Moreover, team members and invited lecturers and speakers contribute toward the cost of the LTSs. We have a 3-P motto: pray, plan, and pay together. Begun by the ADMI team several years ago, this practice continues today by the grace of God.

Another big help in the operation of this program comes from our field representatives (field reps) who serve as volunteers. They are officially chosen and appointed by ADMI. As mentioned above, a key Filipino social value is *bayanihan*, and while it may be diminishing in urban centers, it is very much alive among the village folk.

ADMI's established friendships and volunteer brigades in the ministry's work are, I believe, an example of what I call "slingshot theology." Christians all recall how young David felled Goliath (1 Sam 17:41–52): a slingshot with the Lord does the job. This theology does not imply that ADMI can function without financial assistance, but when financing is not readily available, we use our God-given resources. A lack of funds may hinder God's work, but not always.

Field reps primarily serve as our contact people in the villages. Our communications affecting ministry coordination and community relationships go through them. To provide growth and ministry effectiveness among them, we conduct a weekly online Bible study (OBS), where everyone is given the opportunity to teach an OBS lesson, and the overall coordination of OBSs is in the hands of an ADMI team member. Thus we have weekly, continuing contact with the villages through our reps.

ASOM, which is the LTS's twin, is a more intensive and extensive training program in terms of both content and duration. ASOM is ADMI's response to the cry for help from village pastors and other workers to equip them for ministry—as an alternative to the traditional campus-centered Bible schools and seminaries that take students away from their families and communities for several years. Thus ASOM is a peripatetic training program intended for people in their places of residence and work. ("Peripatetic" means going or walking around.) We bring training to where our trainees live and work, just as Jesus trained his disciples wherever he went. He "went through the towns and villages, teaching in their synagogues and preaching the good news of the kingdom and healing every disease and sickness" (Matt 9:35).

ASOM's curriculum includes courses on biblical, theological, and professional studies. The first two are foundational, while the third is practical. The Bible and doctrine are the foundations of life and ministry, and their courses are for two credits each. Forty credits are required for the Diploma in Ministry Studies (Dpl. M.S.). We hold teaching-training through face-to-face classes in the places where most students live. Each session is four days. Classes are held morning and afternoon, with two coffee breaks and a lunch break. The fourth evening is for a fellowship dinner the students and teaching staff provide, using the Filipino potluck. Before or after dinner, we have a fun program: sharing testimonies and experiences during the four-day training.

Every ASOM training session offers two courses written in English with Tagalog translations.[17] To maximize learning and understanding with practical application, ASOM exposes the students to the teaching material four times:

- They are given the materials upon enrollment so that the material can be read prior to class.
- In class, the material is presented by the lecturer and discussed with the students in a participative and interactive manner.

17 Tagalog (or Filipino), according to the 1987 constitution is the main national language understood by most Filipinos. However, local languages (sometimes called dialects) such as Cebuano and Ilocano are also spoken, and it is ADMI's aim to conduct training and Bible studies in the regional languages, which are the heart languages of the people.

- The students review the study questions at the end of the material and select and answer questions for submission at the next scheduled class.
- The students select a topic from the study material, prepare and present a lesson on the topic, and report on their teaching and its outcomes.

The first ASOM training site is in the town of Dinalungan, Province of Aurora. It is a beautiful beachside facility where training is offered free of charge, thanks to funding support from friends of ADMI. We lodge there for five nights, prepare our meals, enjoy a very large swimming pool (the Pacific Ocean), and conduct classes in a nearby church. Students come from the towns of Dinalungan and Casiguran in Aurora. We conducted five ASOM training sessions in 2022 and look forward to holding another five in 2023. We began with thirteen students—all pastors and deaconesses. The first graduation is planned for the end of 2023, after which another training program will commence at another site.

ADMI's training and coaching of church planters in seminars is the third aspect of equipping. This is open to all church and mission groups in the Philippines. There are two kinds of training seminars: one-time, face-to-face meetings of three to four days and three-time seminars (four days per meeting, twelve in total). We use the textbook *Let's Plant Viable Churches* as the main resource material.[18]

Those who opt for the longer training seminar (twelve days) are usually the serious pastors who go on to the church planting ministry. We offer coaching assistance at every stage, from planning to implementation. We use the blessings of modern communication technology, except in places without an internet connection, where we conduct face-to-face meetings. We often combine such meetings with other related ministry occasions. We are aware of the cost, but the outcomes outweigh the cost.

In the past, we have coached church plant projects for mostly small and independent church groups, first in Mindanao and later in northern

18 *Let's Plant Viable Churches* (2020) is a book authored by Met Castillo and published in the Philippines.

Luzon. In the former, we assisted a new group by training and coaching five of their village workers, four of whom were successful. One of the Mindanao churches was among an indigenous people group in the town of Banga, South Cotabato Province.

In northern Luzon, we trained and coached the church planting pastors of an independent group in the Province of Ilocos Norte. The goal was to establish daughter churches in the villages. Over fifteen years, the number of churches increased from fourteen to thirty-two local congregations.

Currently, we are coaching three church planters from within ADMI and several other church and mission groups. Our church planters work in different social, economic, and cultural settings. For example, Pastor Bal works on the shores of the West Philippine Sea among village folk who fish and cultivate vegetable gardens. This place is eight to ten hours by public bus, plus another forty minutes by motor tricycle. In addition to our usual good morning messages,[19] we connect bimonthly online using Facebook Messenger.

For over a year, a congregation (i.e., a new church) in the town of Pililla, Province of Rizal, has been meeting in a tent for worship and Bible studies. Across from this location, we are coaching a sixteen-month-old church plant project led by Pastor Onil, a former student of mine in the Great Commission Training Center. He and his wife Aurora work as a team. On November 23, 2022, they held their first worship service. Onil and I regularly meet face-to-face, in addition to exchanging messaging and emails.

Finally, Pastor Arvin is reaching an indigenous people group living on the mountain ranges of Tanay, Province of Rizal. This is pure pioneering work. Arvin was trained by one of our partners, Dr. Jason Tan, who also continues to provide basic coaching and counseling.

Empowering: Most of our audiences comprise pastors and church leaders who are already functioning in their respective villages. These people are not like fresh high school graduates seeking some kind of Bible school or seminary training. High school graduates, we surmise, have a

19 These are locally written daily devotionals sent via social media to pastors in the groups we work in.

need for some type of pre-ministry preparation, and, as mentioned earlier, Bible and theological schools abound in large towns and cities. ADMI comes alongside these humble servants of almighty God to encourage, equip, and empower them for service.

The call to ministry is the prerogative of Jesus Christ, the Lord of the church (Matt 28:18). Our responsibility is to recognize and attend to the needs of those called. We come alongside and do whatever we can under the guidance of the Holy Spirit to give them a push in the right direction. In short, we enable them to pursue their God-given ministries and vision. As mentioned, the people we are currently reaching are, in many respects, tentmakers or bi-vocational pastors (Acts 18:3).[20]

Here are examples of our enabling:

- In the coastline third-class (lower socioeconomic) municipalities of Dinalungan and Casiguran in the northeast, we assisted one pastor by installing an engine on his personal fishing boat and another by repairing his old fishing boat.
- We are currently helping a pastor and his family restore their mini goat-raising project, which they lost due to a lack of proper care and feed.
- We provided start-up capital for a small-scale native food business for deaconesses, and seed money for purchasing materials for a woodwork shop belonging to a gifted village pastor.
- Most importantly, we taught these folk to be good stewards of their time and income and to guard their motives.

One pastor goes deep-sea fishing on Tuesdays, returns on Thursdays, and reserves Fridays through Sundays for pastoral responsibilities. Monday is his rest and restoration day. To sum up, they do what they are doing to gain additional income for their families and, primarily, so that they can remain in the Lord's work.

20 Acts 18: 3 informs us that the apostle Paul made tents to support himself, and hence the term "tentmaker" has become the Christian term for bi-vocational missionaries or pastors.

Perhaps it is appropriate to mention ADMI's social concern program, ADMI Care. Besides the activities mentioned, ADMI Care assists in developing livelihood projects for needy workers and fellow believers.

Engaging: This is the final component of our training and discipling ministry among village pastors and church leaders. Engaging means involving them in the Lord's service. We are unable to employ everyone we have the privilege to train, but we provide guidance and counseling for those who need it. We also endorse them to partner ministry entities, as in the Philippines, commendation through direct sponsorship is a revered sociocultural value, especially among church and mission leaders.

We train and disciple these pastors and church leaders the best we can until it is time to release them for service. Like the disciples of Jesus, who were with him, these village workers were with us, especially during the training classes and four-day, face-to-face lecture. We are convinced that we are uniquely responsible for connecting them to service in God's kingdom.

How do we engage them in ministry? We do it using a threefold approach of confirmation, communication, and consignment. I will explain each aspect with specific illustrations.

Confirmation: As stated above, most pastors and deaconesses who have undertaken training already have pastoral and/or ministry responsibilities. However, not everybody is clear about these duties. For those who are certain about their pastoral assignments, in consultation with their leaders we simply confirm and encourage them to continue in their present ministry placements. But we add a very important dimension: We assist them in implementing their ministry plan for the ensuing year, typically a plan to grow their church membership through intentional evangelism and purposeful discipleship. We introduce to them a training seminar called "Evangelism Deep and Wide" (E-Deep and E-Wide). E-Deep ensures that everyone who attends church and every family member is truly a born-again believer. E-Wide aims to take the gospel to nearby neighboring homes, communities, and *barangays* or villages. Thus the gospel moves inwardly to every person in the church and outwardly to every group of people geographically. By comparison, the trajectory of the gospel movement in Acts 1:8 is from the center outward, or centrifugal: "from Jerusalem to Judea and Samaria, and to the ends part of the earth."

Pastor Jes, one of our ASOM students, is the pastor of a growing church in Dinalungan, Aurora. He is a bi-vocational fisherman-pastor. His wife is one of the deaconesses and a trainee at ASOM. Early in 2022, they launched a project to replace their present church building to accommodate a growing congregation. Their church hosted the first E-Deep and E-Wide seminar in that province, and together with the church board, they rolled up their sleeves and applied what they learned.

Pastor Joel and his deaconess wife are conducting pioneer church planting among the tribes living in small *kubos* or huts made of light materials from the forest in a scenic mountain range across the sea from Dinalungan. Pastor Joel is also bi-vocational. He plants vegetables, bananas, coconuts, and fishes in his boat at night when the weather is favorable. Joel's wife is involved in training at ASOM, and she is doing well despite her difficult and sometimes dangerous commute by small boat between home and the training site. Pastor Joel has assigned his wife to teach Bible study and Sunday school, which was welcomed by her because it qualified as part of the fulfillment of her practical application requirement from ASOM. Incidentally, Pastor Joel has admitted publicly that his wife teaches the Bible much better than he does.

Communication: As mentioned above, we get together with those who seek ministry involvement to pray, discuss their prospects, and assist them in finding their places. Spending time with friends and acquaintances, praying, and discussing essential matters in life over a cup of coffee mean a lot to the village folk and us. However, it is not just meeting and talking; it is talking mixed with light jokes and serious purpose. I heard the following remark some time ago: "When people meet, 25 percent of the problem is solved; when people meet and talk, 50 percent of the problem is solved; when people meet, talk, and pray, 75 percent of the problem is solved. And when people meet, talk, pray, and work together, the problem disappears completely."[21]

Incidentally, some friends have coined "cafellowship" to mean our usual meeting over coffee. Inevitably, native pastries are served with the ever-present coffee, reinforcing acceptance, hospitality, and friendship. An

21 Field notes, 2022.

outsider might misjudge the occasion as a frivolous use of time. But for Filipinos and us, the meetings secure consensus and cooperation.

Allow me to share a detailed example of our engagement of village pastors and church leaders in ministry. It concerns an extremely lonely pastor who, immediately following a short Bible school course, was sent from his hometown near Metropolitan Manila to a remote town in the northeast Philippines for a pioneer mission and church planting. Unfortunately, soon after his arrival in the remote location, his promised support was discontinued due to a lack of funds from his sending church. However, he chose to remain in that small town and support himself through various small, income-generating schemes. "It was so difficult for me that I wanted to quit and return home," he remarked with teary eyes.[22] His difficulty more than doubled when he married, had children, and needed to provide for them. He started a bicycle repair business, which helped to sustain his family but not very well. Then his situation worsened because other pastors and church members criticized him as a compromiser.

Eventually, the tide turned. In the words of the pastor, his backyard bicycle repair shop was "blessed by the Lord." It became a full-fledged bicycle and parts store, and he emerged as a bi-vocational pastor in his own right.[23] We met this pastor in 2018 during a pastors' visit and prayer in his town. In a series of one-on-one meetings, we talked and prayed about his situation, generating a friendship in the ministry that extended to other pastors and church leaders in neighboring towns.

I believe that because of our intervention, the pastor became a more faithful student of the word and a more dependable supporter of providing pastoral and leadership training to village workers. For such things, we rejoice, but most importantly, he finally established a local church in his town, and he is the current pastor.

Nevertheless, in a recent meeting, he shared his heart's desire, admitting that his gift seemed to be helping rather than pastoral work. He requested prayer and further light on this issue, and as part of the ongoing process, we agreed to look for an assistant pastor; so the engaging ministry continues.

---

22 Field notes, 2022.

23 Field notes, 2022.

Consignment: Webster's New World Dictionary states that the original meaning of consign is "to mark with the sign of the cross." We use consignment to mean "assign or give over" when our trainees have no ministry assignments due to their resignation, transfer, or contract termination.[24] Consigning entails connecting them with other church groups or mission entities that might use the gifts of their training.

For instance, we consigned one ASOM trainee to assist her husband in planting a church in the town of Pililia, Province of Rizal. She is involved in teaching outreach home Bible studies and in children's ministry. Moreover, in Santiago, Province of Isabela, after training Pastor Ruelson, we consigned him to an indigenous mission group that directed his efforts in planting a church, of which he is currently the pastor. And in rural Mindanao, after training them on-site, we consigned several trainees to church planting and working with churches and mission groups in the villages. These dedicated national leaders trained by ADMI are establishing churches in the countryside.

Culture and Faith Intertwined

Previously, I mentioned the concepts of *utang na loob* and *bayanihan*. Now, I will show how fiestas and funeral wakes are used to share the word and Christian fellowship. As stated previously, the fiesta is a popular part of Philippine culture that was introduced by the Spaniards in the 1500s. Originally designed to honor the patron saint of the city or town, fiestas are a one-to-three-day celebration for towns and villages, where friends and relatives gather for lively merrymaking of all sorts.

Up until the 1970s, many believers were unsure of how to celebrate fiestas. For example, some participated in sports and community activities but shied away from the religious aspect. Through proper teaching and instruction, most have learned to harness the occasion for gospel proclamation and Christian witness. They invite friends and other guests to dinner in their homes and use the opportunity to share the good news through Bible study and witnessing. Many churches have opened their doors to conducting services honoring the Lord Jesus. Women's groups

24 ADMI field notes, 2019.

are going out with the word of God and distributing gospel literature to the public. Youth groups, likewise, are doing their part among fellow young people. Thus, coincidentally, Christian activities during fiestas have become a strong component in the growth of churches and the expansion of Christian witness.

However, not all fiestas are religious by nature. In the villages, the harvest festival ranks very highly in value and significance to farmers. It is primarily a thanksgiving festival, but some of our village brothers and sisters have harnessed the cultural aspect for the Lord's glory.

Another sociocultural practice in the Philippines, the funeral wake, is a pre-burial event usually held in the evenings. It is not only a time to watch over the dead body of a loved one; it is a community event at which the deceased's friends and relatives mingle to greet each other and offer condolences to the surviving family members. During the wake, village Christians and workers may offer to conduct nightly meetings to show solidarity with the bereaved. These services consist of reading appropriate portions of Scripture, spiritual songs designed to comfort, and a short gospel message. Although this kind of service has become an essential part of village wakes, it rarely happens in cities.

Conclusion

In this chapter, I explained how, in the past, rural Philippines was typically deprived of proper training for Christian leaders for church ministry. Using ADMI as a case study, I endeavored to show with practical examples how this situation has been turned around through our training and discipleship of Christians in line with the unique culture underpinning Filipino village life.

Participative and relational learning is our style, with a curriculum that addresses the issues facing village folk, such as superstition and lingering Roman Catholic traditions. ADMI tailor-makes its training programs, but they all include ongoing fellowship and Bible study meetings. Instruction to farmers, fisherfolk, tradesmen, and others is provided through collective sharing and learning—all for the purpose of supporting and establishing pastoral and other Christian leaders for the church in the rural Philippines.

Bibliography

Agoncillo, Teodoro. *A Short History of the Philippines*. New York: Mentor Books, 1969.

Asia Society, "Religion in the Philippines." Accessed March 25, 2023. https://asiasociety.org/education/religion-philippines.

Enriquez, Virgilio G. "Developing a Filipino Psychology." In *Indigenous Psychologies: Research and Experience in Cultural Context*, edited by U. Kim and J. W. Berry, 152–169. Thousand Oaks, CA: SAGE Publications, 1993.

Miller, J. 2023. "Religion in the Philippines." *Asia Society.* https://asiasociety.org/education/religion-philippines#:~:text=The%20Philippines%20proudly%20boasts%20to,well%20over%20100%20Protestant%20denominations.

Mulder, Niels. "Filipino Culture and Social Analysis." *Philippine Studies* 42, no. 1 (1994): 80–90. http://www.jstor.org/stable/42633420.

Ramos, Maximo. D. *Creatures of Philippine Lower Mythology*. Quezon City: University of the Philippines Press, 1971.

Scroope, Chara. "Filipino Culture: Core Concepts." *Cultural Atlas,* 2017. https://culturalatlas.sbs.com.au/filipino-culture/filipino-culture-core-concepts#filipino-culture-core-concepts.

17

DISCIPLING THE DAYAK PEOPLE IN KALIMANTAN, INDONESIA

by Muner Daliman

Introduction

Kalimantan, Indonesia, occupies 73 percent of the island of Borneo. The remainder of the island comprises the nations of Malaysia—Sarawak and Sabah (26 percent)—and Brunei (1 percent). The total population of Kalimantan is seventeen million, of whom three million are Dayaks.[1]

The equator crosses through Kalimantan, which is a blessing because the land is rich in biodiversity. However, the downside is that various endemic tropical diseases, such as dengue fever and malaria, also thrive. Therefore, living in Kalimantan was not easy for the first Protestant missionary who entered Kalimantan in 1829, nor for the two missionaries from the Rhenish Missionary Society who arrived in 1834.[2] Apart from climatic difficulties, missionaries had to struggle with high mortality rates and a lack of transportation facilities. They also struggled to reach souls steeped in animism, magic, and sorcery as they endeavored to bring Dayaks to Christ.

In this chapter, I focus on how the Protestant church in Kalimantan can effectively disciple Dayaks, the indigenous people, who have turned

1 "Jumlah Penduduk Menurut Provinsi di Indonesia (RJ), 2020–2022," *Badan Pusat Statistik*, accessed March 30, 2023, https://sulut.bps.go.id/indicator/12/958/1/jumlah-penduduk-menurut-provinsi-di-indonesia.html

2 See footnotes 22, 31, and 32.

Figure 17.1. Map of Kalimantan on Borneo Island (used with permission).

to Jesus Christ.[3] But first, I provide an overview of the historical, social, and religious contexts of the Dayaks in Kalimantan. I use textual sources and draw heavily from my own experience as a Dayak convert, together with primary sources gathered from interviews conducted in 2018 in Balai Berkuak, Kalimantan, during an Asia College of Ministry (ACOM) training course on missiology.

3 I was born into a Catholic Dayak tribe, but my family still practiced the culture of animism. From 1982–1985 I worshipped in a Protestant church and began to believe in the Lord Jesus Christ. In 1985, after finishing high school, I continued my studies at the School of Theology, and in 1987 I finally broke free from the shackles of animism and became a full-time minister of the gospel.

Dayaks in Kalimantan

The term "Dayak" refers to the non-Muslim, indigenous people who live in Kalimantan. Conflicting theories exist about the origin of this word. Some scholars claim that Dayak is derived from *daya* in the Kenyah (indigenous Austronesian) language, which means upstream or inland,[4] whereas King[5] contended that Dayak came from the word *aja*, a Malay word meaning "native," which itself originated from a Javanese word meaning "inappropriate behavior."[6]

Currently, Kalimantan is inhabited by several tribes who live side-by-side with the Dayak tribe.[7] The flow of migration has had a major influence on the culture of the Dayak tribe, which explains why some Dayaks have chosen to live inland to maintain their cultural identity. The Dayak tribe can be divided into six clans: Bidayuh, Iban, Apokayan, Murut, Ot Danum-Ngaju, and Punan.[8]

The West Kalimantan region shares a land border with the state of Sarawak, Malaysia. This geographical position has given West Kalimantan residents easy road access to and from Malaysia and Brunei Darussalam. But in the rest of Kalimantan, the roads and related infrastructure are poor.[9]

---

4 Joshi Laxman, Kusuma Wijaya, Martyua Sirait, and Elok Mulyoutami, "Indigenous Systems and Ecological Knowledge among Dayak People in Kutai Barat, East Kalimantan—a Preliminary Report," *ICRAF Southeast Asia Working Paper* 3, (2004): 1–25.

5 Victor T. King, *Essays on Borneo Societies* (Oxford: Oxford University Press, 1978).

6 Yekti Maunati, *Dayak Identity* (Jakarta: PT LKiS Pelangi Aksara, 2003), 28–45.

7 Dayak Kanayatn is one of the many subgroups of the Dayak tribe who inhabit the island of Borneo. Apart from the Dayak tribe, there are also other tribes that live side by side with the Dayaks tribe, there are other people groups such as Malay, Chinese, Batak, and Javanese. In general, the Javanese people are more prone to migrate, partly due to the government's transmigration policy.

8 Masri Singarimbun, "Beberapa aspek kehidupan masyarakat Dayak," *Humaniora* 3, no. 2 (January 1991):139–151.

9 The government announced in 2022 that Nusantara in East Kalimantan is the proposed new capital of Indonesia, replacing Jakarta, which is in the island of Java.

History

"Dayak" is a word that lexically connotes both an ethnic group in Kalimantan and the language used by the Dayak tribe.[10] "Dayak," or *Dajak* in Dutch, refers to the non-Muslim indigenous people on the island of Borneo, most of whom live near the banks of the large rivers.[11] The Dayaks, the original "Borneo wild people," were head-hunters who lived under the *ngayau* tradition (*ngayau* can be interpreted as head-hunting).[12] They continued to practice head-hunting even after it was outlawed by the Dutch in the nineteenth century. Until World War II, most of the head-hunters lived by the river. Now many Dayaks have been converted to Christianity and live in settlements.[13]

These riverside peoples lived in longhouse communities in crowded conditions with around hundred members. Dayak ancestry is traced through male and female lineages. The basic unit of society was the family, with children remaining with their parents until they are married. A male often looked for his bride in another village, and once married, the couple lived in the husband's community.[14]

Work and Business Life

For the Dayak tribe, farming is the norm, sometimes shifting from one plot of land to another, and it consists of the following activities: inspecting the land, determining the area, cleaning the tools (which has a spiritual

---

10 Amin Faisal, *Text and Paratext Study on the Construction of Islamic Dayak Identity in the Early 20th Century* (Jakarta: UIN Syarif Hidayatullah, 2020), 20–35.

11 King, *Essays on Borneo Societies*.

12 Headhunting was usually done in groups, both small and large. Dayaks used to behead their enemies alive because the heads of the dead were not considered valuable. After a head was cut off and brought home, the hair would be taken and used to decorate shields and sword hilts. The heads would be dried and hung in front of houses as symbols of courage, family pride, and magical power to repel enemies and spirits.

13 King, *Essays on Borneo Societies*.

14 King, *Essays on Borneo Societies*.

meaning), cutting, planting, harvesting, and giving thanks (known as *begawai*).[15] Besides farming, Dayaks engage in trading, hunting, and fishing. Equipment such as knives and pickaxes are tools for farming, while spears and knives are weapons for hunting in the forest. Fishing is still an activity carried out by the Dayak tribes today.[16]

Some Dayaks are involved in cultivating and producing traditional medicine using spices. No written knowledge or recipes for concocting these ingredients exist; they are based on oral knowledge passed on from their ancestors.[17] These Dayaks are environmentally conscious because the natural environment is their source of life.

Animistic Religious Practices

In Dayak society, all life, whether human, animal, or vegetable, is endowed with spirituality. Spirits and gods are rampant, and Dayaks are taught to consider, respect, and appease this pantheon of invisible beings. Spirits encounter individuals through dreams,[18] which are believed to be revelations sent by spirits and gods.

Dayaks believe that Jubata is the supreme being, which is like the concept of a supreme god in Hinduism.[19] As in Hinduism, animism has many gods; therefore, the notion of only one god is not established in Dayak thinking.

15 Masri Sareb Putra Suriansyah Murhaini, *Dayak Tribe Farming System* (Central Kalimantan: Dayak Literacy Institute, 2016).

16 Rizka S. Bella, Ahmad Ilham Gujali, Ratna Sari Dewi, and Eddy Lion, "Community System and Organization of the Dayak Ngaju Tribe (Case Study in Mandomai Village, Central Kalimantan)," *Jurnal Kewarganegaraan* 5, no. 2 (2021): 366.

17 M. Yatimin Abdullah, *Introduction to the Study of Ethics* (Jakarta: PT. Raja Grafindo Persada, n.d.).

18 Martin Baier, "The Development of the Hindu Kaharingan Religion: A New Dayak Religion in Central Kalimantan," *Anthropos* 102, no. 2 (2007): 566–570, doi:10.5771/0257-9774-2007-2-566

19 Herwig Zahorka, "Ethnohistory of the 'Tumon Dayak' in the Schwaner Mountains of Central Kalimantan," *Borneo Research Bulletin* 43, (2012): 245–254.

At birth, Dayaks are considered fulfilled beings with the gifts of mind, body, and several souls. Each of these aspects is necessary for them to live complete lives and to enter the afterlife.[20] The Dayak concept of heaven is a place filled with ancestors, spirits, gods, and the supreme being, Jubata. This divine realm is available for those who have respected the spirits and maintained the proper balance of life.[21]

The religion of the Dayak tribes is known as Kaharingan and is thought to have originated in Central Kalimantan and South Kalimantan.[22] Kaharingan also means "to grow or live," and when compounded as *danum kaharingan*, it means "living water."[23] Kaharingan teaches its adherents to respect the spirits of their ancestors. It is believed that the spirits of the ancestors continue to care for and protect their children and grandchildren.[24] People who believe in the Kaharingan religion also believe in the existence of supernatural powers in inanimate objects, such as stones, large logs, and jars.[25]

Animism in Borneo is generally characterized by certain supernatural or shamanic beliefs. Conley wrote that "the religion of all Kenyah [indigenous Austronesian] before Christianity came was called pieces of *tepun;* tepun means ancestors."[26] Everyone who lives in a longhouse has a supernatural guard called *bali um*, who acts as the guardian of the longhouse's inhabitants. Another spirit, *bali kamat*, is believed to give "courage to humans, especially in head-hunting."[27]

---

20 Baier, *The Development of the Hindu Kaharingan.*

21 Baier, *The Development of the Hindu Kaharingan.*

22 Budi Susanto, *Politics and Postcoloniality in Indonesia* (Yogyakarta: Kanisius, 2003).

23 Fridolin Ukur, *The Harvest Is Great: History of the Evangelical Kalimantan Church Since 1835* (Jakarta: Gunung Mulia, 2002).

24 Musni Umberan, *Kalimantan Cultural History* (Jakarta: National Historical Inventory and Documentation Project 1993), 25.

25 Umberan, *Kalimantan*, 3.

26 William W. Conley, *The Kalimantan Kenyah: A Study of Tribal Conversion in Terms of Dynamic Cultural Themes* (Ann Arbor, MI: School of World Mission, 1973), 520.

27 Conley, *The Kalimantan Kenyah*, 53–55.

The events of "death, illness, and bad attitudes, such as jealousy and doubt, are believed to be caused by evil spirits,"[28] and if a falcon flies from left to right, it is a good omen.[29] In addition to the above examples of spirit beings, I now highlight two rituals practiced by Dayaks: *naik dango* and *adat balala*.

Naik dango: This is a ritual undertaken during harvesting activities and is held once a year by the Dayak Kanayatn community, which is a subgroup among Dayaks. The *naik dango* tradition is also embodied in *gawai dayak*, a traditional ceremony usually held after the rice harvest in April. *Naik dango* aims to express gratitude to the creator, Jubata, for the blessings received in the form of crops. It is believed that when people offer gratitude and pray during the *dango*, the following year's harvest will be even more abundant. In addition, this prayer event is believed to ward off disasters and pest disturbances in the fields.

The day before *naik dango*, Dayak Kanayatn women and teenagers prepare for the spiritual event by pounding rice in a mortar. Traditional snacks will be cooked the next day and served to the spirits in conjunction with *nyangahatn*—reading a prayer to Jubata by a traditional priest who is called *panyangahatn*.

Adat balala: In Indonesian, this is a custom of abstinence. *Balala* means getting rid of bad luck, known as *badi*, and all kinds of diseases that have occurred during the previous year. It also serves as prevention for the year to come. The Dayak Kanayatn community still maintains this custom as a legacy from its ancestors. *Balala* is also done whenever an extraordinary event occurs, such as an outbreak of disease. For example, during the COVID-19 outbreak, *balala* was performed on several occasions.[30]

The *adat balala* tradition for the Dayak Kanayatn community is carried out over four days. On the first day, the ceremony is held in an open area. On the second and third days, fasting is restricted to the home

28 Conley, *The Kalimantan Kenyah*, 55.

29 Maunati, *Dayak Identity*, 79–80.

30 Some of the information in this chapter are from my field notes taken in various parts of Kalimantan and Central Java, Indonesia during the period 2010–2023.

dwelling, and on the fourth day, the traditional ceremony of releasing evil spirits and cleansing the community is carried out.

Evangelism and the Beginning of the Church in Kalimantan

Protestant churches in Europe and America first paid attention to Kalimantan after hearing about the journey of Pastor Walter Hendry Medhurst from the London Missionary Society, who visited South and West Kalimantan in 1829. Medhurst owned a printing business; therefore, he was able to disseminate his mission visit widely, claiming that a mission to the Dayak people was urgently needed.

In 1834, the general assembly of the Evangelical Council of Protestant Christians in Germany sent missionaries for the evangelization of Borneo, especially for the Dayak tribes. Two pioneer missionaries, Barnstein and Heyer,[31] arrived in Batavia on December 13, 1834.[32] Over several months of negotiations with the government, Heyer suffered health problems and was forced to return to Germany. However, Barnstein remained and proceeded on a boat from Jakarta to Banjarmasin, South Kalimantan for over fourteen days.[33]

Barnstein conducted surveys on the shores of the Barito, Kahayan, Katingan, Mentaya, and Pemburan rivers.[34] After these surveys, he decided to focus his outreach on the Dayak tribe and locate his evangelism post in Banjarmasin, the former capital of the province of South Kalimantan. Barnstein was a prolific missionary who opened missionary bases from Betabara to Tamiang Layang. However, after twenty-three years of intensive ministry, fewer than fifty converts had come to Christ at Barnstein's various mission bases.[35]

31 Records show that Missionary Barnstein had the first and second name initials of J and H; however, no initials could be found for Heyer.

32 Fridolin Ukur, *The Harvest Is Great.*

33 Ukur, *The Harvest Is Great.*

34 Ukur, *The Harvest Is Great.*

35 Ukur, *The Harvest Is Great.*

The Christian church continued in West Kalimantan with the evangelization efforts of Charles Worthington and U Chim Seng in 1906. In 1908, Worthington dedicated a church in the town of Singkawang and built an elementary and a high school, as well as two houses, which served as residences for the pastors and evangelists. His work still lives on in the form of an evangelical church known as the Greja Kristen Kalimantan Barat.

Presumably, the lack of success by the aforementioned missionaries was due to their lack of cultural knowledge and their theological mindset when it came to the issue of the supernatural in Christianity. On the latter, according to Arnold, some Western Christian scholars have denied "the real existence of evil spirits."[36] Arnold took seriously the existence of a spiritual realm of demons ruled by Satan and argued against attempts by scholars to demythologize these powers.[37] Arnold contended that Paul's conception of evil spiritual powers, as mentioned in Ephesians 6 and Colossians 1, served as an important source for formulating a Christian worldview on such spiritual powers.

Discipling Dayaks: A Contextual Model

From the explanation above about the various Dayak cultural and religious contexts, especially the animistic practices, it can be concluded that Kalimantan is a difficult mission field for the Christian church. The challenge is for the church to effectively teach Dayaks how to live after they become Christians.

Christianity came to Indonesia in an environment characterized by religious plurality, suffering, poverty, ecological damage, and social injustice.[38] Without considering the contexts and how the Bible fits the

---

36 Clinton E. Arnold, *Powers of Darkness: Principalities and Powers in Paul's Letters* (Downers Grove, IL: IVP, 1992), 192.

37 Arnold, *Powers of Darkness*.

38 Rijnardus A. van Kooij, Agus Patnaningsih, and Yam'ah Tsalatsa, *Revealing Facts, Arranging Real Work: Practical Theological Contributions in the Search for Contextual Congregational Development Models* (Jakarta: BPK Gunung Mulia, 2007), 50.

situations, Christian missionaries have made mistakes that have long-term consequences. For example, many of the early missionaries in Kalimantan in the 1900s were very happy to see Dayaks coming to Jesus and becoming members of their churches. However, these new Christians were still engaging in their past pagan practices while attending church, and many gave up their Christian faith when persecution came.[39]

Therefore, I propose a five-part contextual pastoral approach that can be used to disciple our community: pray and fast, understand the culture, develop a framework for discipleship, create a Christian community, and make regular pastoral visits.

Pray and Fast

Prayer is the communication of every believer with the "most high God" (Ps 57:2), a description that is relevant to cultures in which there are many gods and spirits in their belief systems.[40] Dayaks have a deep sense of spirituality that cannot be taken lightly or explained away. After Jesus successfully cast out a demon despite the disciples' failed attempts, Jesus told his disciples, "This kind cannot come out by anything except prayer" (Mark 9:29). In the same way, those who are involved in Dayak evangelism, discipleship, and training must give priority to a deep prayer ministry.

In Ephesians 6:11–13, the injunction is to "put on the full armor of God, so that you can stand against the wiles of the Devil; for our struggle is not against flesh and blood, but against the rulers of this dark world, against the evil spirits in the air." A disciplined life of prayer is a source of strength to defeat the power of Satan. Tjandra explained, "Prayer can restore human relationships with God and restore nations to God's will."[41] In my two decades of experience in Dayak ministry, I have participated in exorcisms, healings, and deliverance encounters, and these were all performed primarily through the means of prayer and fasting.

---

39 Jennifer Connolly, "Becoming a Christian and Dayak: A Study of Christian Conversion among Dayaks in East Kalimantan, Indonesia" (PhD diss., New School University, 2003).

40 In Hebrew the term "most high God," reserved for the God of the Bible, is *Elohim*.

41 Jimmy Tjandra, *Doa Yang Di Tolak Tuhan* (Jakarta: Anggota IKAPI, 2009), 209.

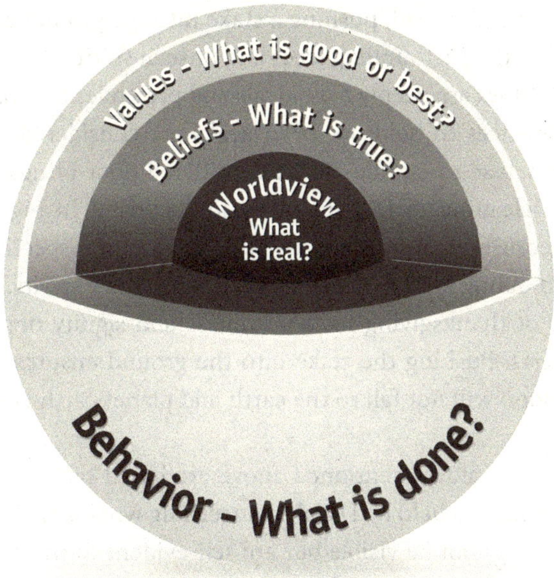

Figure 17.2. How to understand culture (Source: William Carey Publishing, used with permission).

Understand Culture

Missiologist Kwast developed a model to understand and unpack the deep interface of culture by starting with behavior, values, beliefs, and worldview.[42] Our discipleship and training must cater to each of these aspects of Dayak culture. I provide a few examples under each of the first three aspects, then share the fourth aspect, worldview, in more detail.

Behavior: This includes rituals and activities that are part of the shared experiences of the Dayak community.[43] Dayaks work from morning to night, and even their children are engaged in farming. They routinely perform five types of rituals: looking to the moon, cleaning all instruments,

42 Lloyd E. Kwast, "Understanding Culture," in *Perspectives on the World Christian Movement, ed.* Ralph D Winer and Steven C. Hawthorne (Littleton, CO: William Carey Publishing, 2009), 363.

43 Kwast, "Understanding Culture."

showering with pig's blood, pushing a stake into the ground at night, and offering food to the surrounding trees and unseen spirits.[44]

Values: Values are deeply held ideals and principles that have become positive preferences to hold on to.[45] Dayaks are considered workaholics because they refuse to be idle. To be considered poor brings shame to a Dayak.[46] The cleaning of instruments and "baptism" in pig's blood are performed because of the Dayaks' cherished value of respecting the land and the surrounding spirits by being acceptable to the spirits. Food offerings are acts of thanksgiving for fruitfulness and signify hope of future fruitful harvests. Pushing the stake into the ground ensures orderliness, so that the moon will not fall to the earth and planet earth will remain in place.[47]

Beliefs: The values mentioned above are based on a cultural belief system of convictions held by Dayaks concerning what is true and what is false.[48] Beliefs may not be visible but are self-evident to the people. From my examples listed above, it can be surmised that Dayaks see themselves as part of the unseen world of spirits and gods. Dayaks are convinced that they can control the events of everyday life, the orderliness of the planets, the harvest, and the fruitfulness of their lives through performance, appeasement, gift-giving, and respecting the unseen world of spirits.

Worldview: The deepest level of Dayak culture, which is the set of preconceptions and assumptions that pertain to existence, values, and beliefs, is their worldview.[49] Here is where prime reality is discovered: how Dayaks see the world, nature, human beings, the issue of death, the afterlife, and right and wrong. As mission workers, we are called to emulate the example of Jesus, who took on the flesh of the Jewish culture full of lost people (John 1:14). The apostle Paul became "all things to all men" to reach "some" (1 Cor 9:19–23). Our task is to convey the message of the gospel within the cultural framework of the respondents, and the starting point is to have a grip on the worldview of the culture.

44 Field notes, 2018.
45 Kwast, "Understanding Culture."
46 Field notes, 2018.
47 Field notes, 2018.
48 Kwast, "Understanding Culture."
49 Kwast, "Understanding Culture."

Table 17.1. Dayak worldview versus biblical worldview (adapted by Daliman 2023).

Dayak Worldview	Biblical Worldview
• There is a divine being, Jubata, but he is in many respects unknowable. • The universe is the result of collision (disordered power). • Man and woman were created from the ruins of the devastated tree of life.	• God is a sovereign. He created the world in an ordered way. • Jesus is Lord, creator, and ruler of the nations. • All other gods are powerless. God created man and woman in God's image.
• Man and nature are one (no dichotomy). • Dayaks can control nature.	• There is a distinction between creator and creation. • God controls every aspect of the universe.
• There is no distinction between evil spirits and good spirits. • Evil spirits influence and seek to control human life with the law of taboo, punishment, et cetera.	• God is omnipotent/ sovereign. There is a distinction between God and Satan; God owns and rules the universe, and God is holy.
• At death, the deceased will enter the prosperous village directly and there is no judgment of their sin. • The resurrection of the body is not a reality; only the soul is resurrected.	• The ultimate revelation of God is in Christ, proven by Jesus's resurrection from the dead. • Believers in Christ will escape hell and receive the inheritance of heaven through resurrection. Believers will have a glorified body united with the soul. • Jesus Christ will judge the world because of its sin.
• There is no concept of sin in the biblical sense. • Sin is not appeasing the spirits.	• Repentance is necessary because of sin and guilt. • The blood of Jesus cleanses sin. • Only Jesus saves from eternal condemnation.

(*Continued*)

Dayak Worldview	Biblical Worldview
• There is no concept of future judgment. • There is no concept of hell. The dead will travel to the village of their relatives in the Upper World.	• The reality of a future judgment (moral and spiritual accountability). • The teaching that God will righteously judge the world through Jesus Christ. • There is bodily resurrection.
• The present life is lived in fear of the deities (taboo, punishment, etc.) who need to be appeased.	• God has freed us from the bondage of sin and Satan's power. • There is the blessing of forgiveness of sin and God's grace in Christ's work on the cross. • At the cross, Jesus overcame Satan and his minions.

Develop a Framework for Discipleship

Table 17.1 depicts the Dayak worldview in contrast to the biblical worldview. I use the three-stage missiological model developed by James to teach Dayak Christian leaders how to frame and evaluate cultural aspects considering the Bible's teachings:[50]

- Keep the good cultural values/practices or use them as points of contact.
- Shun the cultural aspects that disagree with clear Bible teaching.
- Redeem the neutral or marginal aspects with fresh biblical input.

50 Jonathan D. James, "Culture and Christianity: How Asian Missions Can Be Modelled According to the Indigenous Principle," (Lecture, Kadesi Theological Seminary, September 18, 2017).

Keep the good/find contact points: A good contact point with Dayaks is their concept of a supreme being. Even though this borders on an unknowable God, I celebrate the fact that Dayaks have a concept of a supreme being. Tomatala shared how God works: "God . . . reveals Himself to the world through human culture."[51] Therefore, understanding and finding points of contact in the culture is crucial to bringing in new content in our discipleship ministry. Just as Paul testified to the Athenians, who had a shrine to the "unknown God," we can testify to Dayaks that their unknown God can be known because the God of the Bible has revealed himself though Jesus Christ (Acts 17:22–23).

Furthermore, the blood sacrifice of pigs used as a cleansing exercise by Dayaks can be used as a contact point to show the truth of the blood of Jesus in cleansing sinners from all sin: "It is impossible for the blood of bulls and goats to take away sins" and "How much more then will the blood of Christ . . . cleanse our consciences . . . from death" (Heb 10:4; 9:14).

Shun the unbiblical: Several Dayak rituals and practices are prohibited in the Bible, such as worshipping ancestors (although respect for parents is considered a biblical virtue with a promise of blessing[52]), offering food to the spirits, and using charms, magic, and the like. These practices must be shunned; however, they must be replaced by biblical practices. The book of Exodus 20:3 teaches, "You shall have no other gods before Me." This means that God is the only being that is worthy of worship. The Bible also teaches that heaven and earth were created by God. Therefore, everything in our universe, such as the sun, moon, stars, sea, and mountains, is subject to him and should not be worshipped by human beings.[53]

The Bible records God's view of nations who worshipped other gods. In Genesis, God, in love, called Abram, which was later changed to Abraham, meaning "father of nations," out of polytheism and animism to know the true God. With God's explicit instructions, Abram formed a nation that worshipped the true and living God. Thus God changed the animistic ways

51 Yakob Tomatala, *Teologi Kontekstualisasi* (Malang, Jawa Timur: Gandum Mas, 1996), 73.

52 See Exod. 20:12 and Eph. 6: 1–3 for both Old and New Testament renditions of honoring parents.

53 Johannes L.C., Abineno, *Aku Percaya Kepada Allah* (Jakarta: BPK Gunung Mulia, 1983), 19.

of Israel to a new way of worship. He taught Israel his sovereignty over all gods (Isa 43:10). He warned against the use of divination, magic, and sorcery (Deut 18:9–12).

As the nation Israel interacted with other nations and their gods and idols, the Lord showed his authority. He sent plagues to Egypt to confront Ra, the sun god (Exod 10:21–29). God also taught the Israelites that his sovereignty and power transcended geography and terrain. When the forces of Israel's enemy Ahab planned to attack Israel in the area that was under the influence of the enemy's gods, God sent a message to King Ahab through the prophet Elijah: "Because the Arameans think the Lord is a god of the hills and not a god of the valleys, I will deliver this vast army into your hands, and you will know that I am the Lord" (1 Kgs 20:28). The people of Israel slowly but surely realized that their God was omnipotent and omnipresent, and this helped them take their eyes off their own gods and submit to the God of the Bible. Both the Old and New Testaments contain records of the tension of seeking pragmatic associations with ancestral and territorial gods and completely trusting the Lord of the Bible.

Redeem the neutral and marginal aspects: Some aspects of Dayak culture may be deemed neutral or marginal, and these aspects can be analyzed and given new biblical meaning. For example, the thanksgiving festivals during harvest time can be infused with the many accounts of biblical celebrations, and a fresh liturgy can be produced for Dayak Christians.[54] Another aspect worth considering is the Dayaks' use of symbols and tattoos. Since Christianity is rich in symbols, such as bread, wine, the cross, and the dove, Dayak Christian leaders can consult and initiate acceptable symbols for the Dayak Christian community. Ancestor worship can be redeemed with meaningful events or ceremonies to honor parents, which is a basic biblical teaching in both the Old and New Testaments.

It is critical that the content of the preaching program at the church and the weekly Bible studies should address the Dayak worldview vis-à-vis the Christian worldview. Pastors and Christian leaders should have a systematic plan to disciple Dayaks through the expository preaching of

54 See 2 Chron. 7 for an account of the Temple dedication and celebration, and Neh. 12 for how the wall was dedicated to God.

selected passages in the Bible that speak to the Dayak context. In this way, knowledge is shared, and helpful discussions can take place during weekly Bible study times on how to practically resolve daily issues with a biblical framework.

Develop a Christian Habitus or Community

Whereas preaching the gospel is vital, so too is living the gospel through the daily routines and habits of Dayak Christians.[55] Effective culture-specific preaching must aim to produce a transformed people in a community where biblical concepts are put into practice. In this way, the gospel is transformed into a way of life in which Dayak believers can practice culture-specific Christian liturgies. For example, the communion service and baptism may incorporate appropriate Dayak symbols and traditions, with new biblical meanings infused into these sacraments. Thus the traditional *balala* cleansing ceremony may be replaced by dedication and consecration services wherein Dayak Christians dedicate their lives to God and his work.

Pastoral Visits

Apart from the strategies mentioned above, discipleship needs to be augmented by pastoral visits. The Dayak worldview gives much attention to this world rather than the afterworld. Daily existence and meeting the challenges of life in family and work situations consume the hearts and minds of Dayak Christians. Pastoral visits can help Christian leaders discover people's struggles, have biblical conversations, and pray. Since Dayak Christians struggle to understand the Christian worldview and the teaching of the Bible after years of involvement in their traditional practices, pastoral visits can help prevent attrition and the emergence of other problems.[56] Such visits may be carried out in the congregant's home or in public places where residents gather.

---

55 Omar Lizardo, "The Cognitive Origins of Bourdieu's Habitus," *Journal for the Theory of Social Behaviour* 34, no. 4 (2004), 375–448.

56 M. Bon-Storm, *Apakah Penggembalaan Itu?* (Jakarta: BPK Gunung Mulia, 1999), 52.

Conclusion

The discipleship of Christian believers in the Dayak community in Kalimantan is fraught with challenges on many levels. Christian leaders must be aware of the nature of animism and the traditional and ritualistic practices of the Dayak community. The Dayak worldview is based more on this world than the world to come. In such a context, pastors and leaders need to think about how the Bible can be made relevant to Dayaks in their day-to-day living. Based on this worldview, an all-embracing discipleship training must be designed for Dayaks.

Pastors must have both a comprehensive understanding of Dayak culture and a strong biblical foundation. Pastors and leaders also must possess the analytical and procedural skills to navigate the intricate balance between faith and Dayak culture. After decades of experience in Dayak ministry, I have formulated a contextual model based on prayer and fasting, cultural understanding, and developing a discipleship framework and a Christian community with sustained pastoral visits.

In essence, Dayak culture must be enhanced with biblical teaching and practices that make sense to Dayaks. While Christianity does not have rituals or formulas for controlling the weather, the Christian faith is replete with teachings on prayer about a gracious, sovereign, and holy God who will one day culminate world history and usher in his heavenly kingdom with majesty and true justice (Rev 19:1–12).

Bibliography

Abdullah, M.Yatiman. *Introduction to the Study of Ethics*. Jakarta: PT. Raja Grafindo Persada, 2006.

Amin, Faizal. *Text and Paratext Study on the Construction of Islamic Dayak Identity in the Early 20th Century*. Jakarta: UIN Syarif Hidayatullah, 2020.

Arnold, Clinton E. *Powers of Darkness: Principalities and Powers in Paul's Letters*. Downers Grove, IL: IVP, 1992.

Baier, Martin. "The Development of the Hindu Kaharingan Religion: A New Dayak Religion in Central Kalimantan." *Anthropos* 102, no. 2 (2007): 566–570. doi:10.5771/0257-9774-2007-2-566.

Bella, Riska, Ahmad I.Gujali, Ratna S. Dewi, Eddy Lion, and R.B Maryam. "Sistem Masyarakat Dan Organisasi Suki Dayak Ngaju (Studi Kasus Di Desa Mandomai Kalimantan Tengah)." *Jurnal Kewarganegaraan* 5 no. 2 (2021): 366.

Bon-Storm, M. *Apakah Penggembalaan Itu?* Jakarta: BPK Gunung Mulia, 1999.

Conley, William W. *The Kalimantan Kenyah: A Study of Tribal Conversion in Terms of Dynamic Cultural Themes*. Ann Arbor, MI: School of World Mission, 1973.

Connolly, Jennifer. "Becoming a Christian and Dayak: A Study of Christian conversion among Dayaks in East Kalimantan, Indonesia." PhD diss., New School University, 2003.

Johansen, Poltak. *Traditional Leadership in the Ngaju Dayak Province of Central Kalimantan. Pontianak*: STAIN Pontianak Press, 2014.

Joshi, Laxman, Kusuma Wijaya, Martua Sirait, and Elok Mulyoutami. "Indigenous systems and Ecological Knowledge among Dayak People in Kutai Barat, East Kalimantan—a Preliminary Report." *ICRAF Southeast Asia Working Paper* 3 (2004).

Jura, Dempsey, and Wellem Sairwona. "Deskripsi Praktik Okultisme Di Kalangan Remaja Suku Dayak Maanyan Di Gereja Sidang-Sidang Jemaat Allah (Gsja) Wilayah Kabupaten Barito Timur Kalimantan Tengah." *Jurnal Shanan* 2 no. 2 (2018): 1–35.

King, Victor T. *Essays on Borneo Societies.* Oxford: Oxford University Press, 1978.

Kwast, Lloyd E. *Understanding Culture*. In *Perspectives on the World Christian Movement,* edited by Ralph D. Winter and Steven C. Hawthorne. Littleton, CO: William Carey Publishing, 2009.

Lizardo, Omar. "The Cognitive Origins of Bourdieu's Habitus." *Journal for the Theory of Social Behaviour* 34, no. 4 (2004): 375–448.

Maunati, Yekti. *Dayak Identity*. Jakarta: Lkis Pelangi Aksara, 2003.

Putra, R. Masri Sareb and Suriansyah Murhaini, *Dayak Tribe Farming System*. Central Kalimantan: Dayak Literacy Institute, 2016.

Rijnardus A., Van Kooij, Agus Patnaningsih, and Yam'ah A. Tsalatsa, *Revealing Facts, Arranging Real Work: Practical Theological Contributions in the Search for Contextual Congregational Development Models*. Jakarta: BPK Gunung Mulia, 2007.

Singarimbun, Masri. "Beberapa aspek kehidupan masyarakat Dayak." *Humaniora*. 3, no. 2 (January 1991): 139–151.

Susanto, Budi. *Politics and Postcoloniality in Indonesia.* Yogyakarta: Kanisius, 2003.

Ukur, Fridolin. *The Harvest Is Great: History of the Evangelical Kalimantan Church Since 1835*. 3rd ed. Jakarta: Gunung Mulia, 2002.

Umberan, Musni. *Kalimantan Cultural History*. Jakarta: National Historical Inventory and Documentation Project, 1993.

Zahorka, H. "Ethnohistory of the 'Tumon Dayak' in the Schwaner Mountains of Central Kalimantan." Borneo Research Bulletin, 43, 245–254. *Kalimantan. Borneo Research Bulletin* 43 (2012): 245–254.

CONCLUSION
Whither Asianization?

by Jonathan D. James

Introduction

Unlike other religions, Christianity began with a great miracle: Jesus Christ became man, and "the Word became flesh and made his dwelling among us" (John 1:14).[1] Jesus was born into the Jewish culture and was true to his culture in every way. Jesus chose to identify with the Jews so that they, in turn, would share his message with all the cultures of the world (Isa 49:6).[2] Before Jesus ascended to heaven, he gave his Jewish disciples the Great Commission: to "go into all the world" (Matt 28:19) and be his witnesses to the "ends of the earth" (Acts 1:8). Therefore, from its very inception, Christianity has been a cross-cultural faith. It is equally true that all Christians have lived their faith in specific cultural contexts (Acts 2:1–12).

I commence this concluding piece with my observations on the state of Christianity in the twenty-first century, then I define and trace how the term "Asianization" fits in with this scenario. Next I reexamine the concept of Asianization and summarize its meaning and implications as argued by the authors in this book. Finally, I will introduce a new model of mission that I see emerging from the chapters in this book and conclude with a brief comparison between old and new models of mission and contextualization.

---

1 A portion of the introduction is adapted from my preface in the book: *Rethinking, Reforming and Renewal: Christianity in Myanmar* (Yangon: Rakhine Missions Band for Christ, 2020), 1.

2 "He says: 'It is too small a thing for you to be my servant to restore the tribes of Jacob and bring those of Israel I have kept. I will also make you a light for the Gentiles, that my salvation may reach to the ends of the earth.'"

World Christianity: Trends

Ching makes the astute observation in chapter 11 that Asianization signifies that the gospel has come full circle: originating in West Asia (the Middle East) and now returning to its origin. The great expansion of Christianity to Asia, however, came largely from the West.[3] But the West is currently undergoing a crisis of belief and, arguably, being overpowered by secularism. Bosch contended that the Judeo-Christian worldview, once the integrating arm of Western civilization, is being replaced by secularism and morphing into what he termed "dechristianization": "The West—traditionally not only the home of Catholic and Protestant Christianity but also the base of the entire modern missionary enterprise—is slowly but steadily being dechristianized. . . . Because of the dechristianization of the West and the multiple migrations of people of many faiths, we now live in a religiously pluralist world, in which Christians, Muslims, Buddhists, and adherents of many traditional religions rub shoulders daily."[4]

While the West (loosely encompassing the Northern Hemisphere) was struggling with its own issues, the center of gravity of Christianity shifted from the Northern Hemisphere, the traditional heartland of Christianity, to the Southern Hemisphere. This evolution from west/north to south has been well monitored and documented over the last forty years (see figure 1).[5] For example, in 1900, 82 percent of Christians lived in Europe and North America, but in 2020, this figure had declined dramatically to 33 percent. During that period, Christianity increased from 18 percent to 67 percent in the South, comprising Asia, Africa, and Latin America.

---

3 Although Christianity was birthed in the Middle East (or West Asia), the trajectory of its influence has been toward the nations in the Northern hemisphere, with some exceptions, one being India. There is strong historical support that it was the apostle Thomas who first brought the gospel to India.

4 David Bosch, *Transforming Mission: Paradigm Shifts in the Theology of Mission* (Maryknoll, Orbis, 2012), 3.

5 Todd M. Johnson of the Center for the Study of Global Christianity and the co-editor of the Atlas of Global Christianity, Edinburgh University Press, the Lausanne Congress on Evangelization, and several related agencies have been observing these trends since the mid-1970s. See Jonathan James, *A Moving Faith: Mega Churches Go South* (New Delhi: Sage, 2015), 1–5.

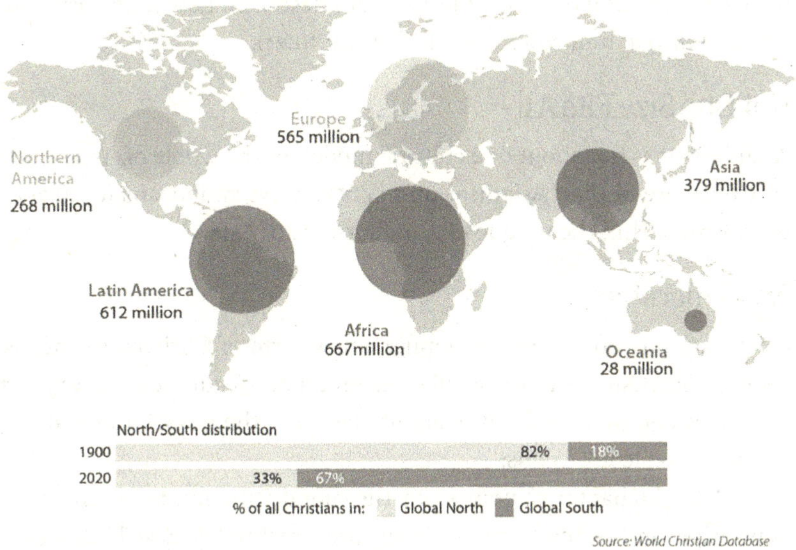

Figure C.1. State of Christianity in the North and South (Source: World Christian Database, used with permission).

Asianization Revisited

Asianization must be studied in this context of the unprecedented growth of Christianity in the nontraditional heartlands of Christianity. As described in the introductory chapter, I want this book to be a clarion call for the Asianization of Christianity. The term "Asianization" is synonymous with "indigenization" and "contextualization," but further definition is deemed necessary, as follows.

Not an Implication of Superiority

Asianization does not imply that any group's culture is superior. It is a recognition that missionary work is cross-cultural and that all missionaries must grapple with the important and demanding task of communicating across cultures. The motivation and power relations between the missionary and the nonbeliever is best portrayed by Jesus Christ as he encountered the rich young ruler in Mark's Gospel. When Jesus shared with the young ruler about the kingdom of God, the rich ruler went his own way, rejecting the way of Jesus. Mark described how Jesus responded: "Jesus looked at him and loved him" (Mark 10:21).

Not One Size Fits All

Asianization is not about one cultural model for the whole of Asia; it is the very opposite of that. Asianization refers to ways and means for adapting the gospel within the unique cultural formats of Asia.

Not Syncretism

Asianization is not about developing a new form of Christianity, nor is it about syncretism, "the reconciliation or union of different or opposing principles and practices."[6] It is about clarifying the gospel and making it understandable for Asians.

Rakhal (chapter 7) points out the fine distinction between contextualization and syncretism in Nepal, presumably because Hinduism in Nepal is quite different from that in India, and what worked in India for Hindus who came to Christ may not necessarily work in Nepal. Rakhal is concerned with the uncritical use of Hindu practices in Christianity, such as simply using Hindu practices to reveal Christian truth, and he contends that careful contextualization is helpful. The problem Rakhal alluded to is consistent with what the Jesuit Bulatao in the Philippines called split-level Christianity.[7] Bulatao, as cited by David, defined "split-level Christianity" as "the [uncritical] superimposition of imported Christian meanings upon native religious beliefs and practices. Priests took the place of our local shamans. And the sacred mountains, those ancient places of worship, were replaced by the colonial churches . . . scapulars replaced amulets. Images of saints displaced the wooden gods in our ancestors' homes. But the new forms did not erase the substantive spirituality."[8]

---

6 *Macquarie Compact Dictionary*, 8th edition (Sydney: Pan Macmillan Australia, 2020).

7 Jaime Bulatao, S.J. *Split-Level Christianity* (Manila: Ateneo de Manila University), 1966.

8 Randy David, "Split-level Spirituality," *Randy David*, 1997, accessed April 10, 2023, http://www.randydavid.com/1997/03/split-level-spirituality/#:~:-text=A%20long%20time%20ago%2C%20the%20Jesuit%20psychologist%20Fr.,Christian%20meanings%20upon%20native%20religious%20beliefs%20and%20practices

This is a term that Castillo (chapter 16) is familiar with because he and his team have endeavored to train and disciple village pastors in a country with a rich Roman Catholic background.

Notwithstanding the fears that many Christians have of contextualization turning into syncretism, the case for *not contextualizing* is just as dangerous, as pointed out by Trihandarkha (chapter 12) and Daliman (chapter 17). In these chapters, we read that insufficient contextualization coupled with inadequate rigorous discipleship in animistic societies can lead to "weak churches, whose members will cling to non-Christian, syncretistic explanations, follow non-biblical lifestyles, and engage in magical rituals."[9]

Amjad (chapters 9 and 10) argues from his experience that biblical contextualization engages with Muslim people at the level of their deepest needs and aspirations, and that this level of engagement is the secret of the flourishing of their new contextualized churches. The under-contextualization and over-contextualization continuum presented by Amjad is useful in the Muslim context and for the rest of Asia's diverse religious contexts.

In summary, the call to Asianization is a call for loving, respectful, contextualized expressions within the diversity of Asia's cultures so that the gospel is understood.

All the case studies in this book support Whitman's claim that when the gospel is truly contextualized, "the Gospel itself will be understood in ways the universal church has neither experienced nor understood before, thus expanding our understanding of the kingdom of God."[10] Hence we will see a fuller and richer picture of God and his heart for the nations through contextualization (Rev 7:9).

Past Mission Successes

We celebrate this moment in history, when Asia has come of age in terms of its contextualization of the gospel, but I hasten to remind the reader that the Asian church did not arrive at this point by itself. The seeds of the gospel were planted by Western missionaries despite the imperfection of

9 Whitman, "Contextualization: The Theory, the Gap, the Challenge," 1997, 8.

10 Whitman, 1997, 11.

their perspectives, strategies, and motivations regarding mission, as they were products of their time.

In chapter 2, Violet James gives us the benefit of her historiographical perspective on the successes and failures of indigenization and contextualization in Asia. In this vein, we celebrate missionaries like William Carey (1761–1834) and Adoniram Judson (1788–1850), who pioneered missionizing efforts in India and Myanmar, respectively, where the cultural and religious issues were formidable. While it is beyond the scope of this piece to list all the significant Western missionaries in Asia, the work of Robert Morrison, who came to China in 1807 and was one of the first to translate the Bible into Chinese, and James Hudson Taylor, who arrived in 1853 with an emphasis on reaching inland China, are noteworthy.[11]

Furthermore, we celebrate the contributions of Robert de Nobili (1541–1599) and Bartholomäus Ziegenbalg (1682–1719), who both brought the gospel and boldly contextualized the faith in India in groundbreaking ways.[12] To this list of notable Westerners who undertook contextualization, I add Coenrad Laurens Coolen (1775–1873), a government official from the Netherlands who pioneered the first indigenous church in Java, Indonesia.[13]

We also celebrate Asian missionaries Nehemiah Goreh (1825–1895), Sadhu Sundar Singh (1898–ca. 1929), and John Sung (1901–1944), who realized the importance of indigenization and contextualization. We celebrate Asian pioneer mission leaders David Cho of Korea (1924–2020), Theodore Williams of India (1935–2009), Petrus Octavianus of Indonesia (1928–2014), and G. D. James of Malaysia and Singapore (1920–2003), who collectively launched Asian mission societies and sodalities in their respective nations, a practice that put them ahead of their times.[14]

At this time, when new models of mission are emerging, Paul's depiction, "I planted the seed, Apollos watered it, but God has been making it

---

11 Charles H. Robinson, *History of Christian Missions* (Edinburgh: Clark,1915).

12 Cyril B. Firth, *An Introduction to Indian Church History* (Chennai: CLS, 1961).

13 Sostenis Nggebu, "Coenrad Laurens Coolen: Pioneer of Contextual Mission among Javanese Abangans," *Evangelikal: Jurnal Teologi Injili dan Pembinaan Warga Jemaat* 6, no. 94 (2022): 94–108.

14 Martin L. Nelson, *Readings in Third World Missions: A Collection of Essential Documents* (South Pasadena, CA: William Carey Library, 1976).

grow" (1 Cor 3:6), seems especially apt. Thus the mission story of the Bible unfolding in the Asian context continues.

New Model

The new mission model emerging from these chapters (see table conclusion 1 below) has eight features, which I have grouped under five rubrics: people, principles, structures, scope, and praxis.

Table C.1. Old model versus new model of mission (Source: James 2023).

Old Model	New Model
CONTEXTUALIZATION	**BEYOND CONTEXTUALIZATION**
Done by Westerners	Done by Asians
Static communication	Dynamic communication
Systematic theology	Narrative, devotional & encounter theology
3 Self churches	4 Self (Self-theologizing)
Western churches or denominational churches	Indigenous churches, satsangs, house churches, churches specific to cultures
Scope – limited	Scope – comprehensive: contextualization in church, evangelism, discipleship, and training
Location-centered	Global, diaspora targeted, and communication technology used
Doing – Make Christianity fit culture.	***Being*** – Communities practice contextualized faith and become Christlike as a community.

People

The people who are energizing the new paradigm are increasingly Asian missionaries. All the writers in this volume are Asians at the forefront of ministries to their own people. Many are using the "Asians reaching Asia" motto with great specificity. For example, we have Nyunt (chapters 5 and 6), a former Buddhist monk who is modeling Christianity to Myanmar Buddhists, and Amjad (chapters 9 and 10), a former Muslim who is creating a sacred space for Muslim believers in Christ.[15]

Rakhal (chapter 7) addresses the importance of employing both the national language and local dialects with Nepali people groups. Cortes (chapter 15) recounts how discipled Filipinos in Singapore are reaching their families back in the Philippines via the heart languages and social media, thus performing a full-circle mission but with greater intensity.

Fu (chapter 14) demonstrates the comprehensiveness of discipleship programs in China and how Chinese Christian leaders are replacing indiscriminate Western discipleship materials with local ones. For example, leaders are drawing anecdotes, fables, and myths from their own culture and history, enriching the Chinese understanding of Jesus's parables.

Ajith Fernando's prediction that Asian nationals evangelizing their people would do what they do best in partnership with foreign missionaries is now being fulfilled.[16] Based on anecdotal evidence I gathered in 2022, 80 to 90 percent of the worldwide mission force (i.e., foreign missionaries) had to leave their mission fields and return home during the COVID-19 pandemic. In contrast, indigenous missionaries stayed on to missionize as citizens of their respective countries.[17]

Principles

Nyunt (chapter 3) asserts that mission is communication, but this communication is not just conveying the gospel as a product to nonbelievers. In

---

15 Both Amjad and Thein are noted for initiating indigenized modalities and well as solidities in their approach to mission.

16 Ajith Fernando, "Missionaries Sill Needed: But of a Special Kind," *Evangelical Missions Quarterly* 24, no. 1 (January 1988): 18–25.

17 Personal communication in 2002 with Pioneers International, a USA-based missionary organization.

the new model of communication represented in these pages, communication is constructed for and with the recipients *in their cultural contexts*. For example, Nyunt identifies *nibbana* (i.e., release) as a major preoccupation of Buddhist theology. Communication of the gospel to Buddhists, therefore, must address this preoccupation.[18] Previously, Christianity was taught from a communication framework in which the sender's mindset was preeminent. In the new model, the focus is on the recipient's worldview and how they process the message.

In this respect, Park's insights (chapter 4) reveal how the Bible should be presented to East Asians who hold the shame-honor worldview. The presentation should open new vistas of their knowledge of God and his mercy to remove their shame and replace it with honor. In addition, the biblical habitus of a new community that Park presents is appealing when read with Asian eyes.

In my interview with Rakhal in 2005, I learned of a village pastor from an obscure village who attended the ACOM program in Nepal. After the village pastor completed the diploma program, he made the diploma course available to all sixty members of his church in remote Nepal, many of whom were unlettered, untraveled, and poor. Through the meaningful relationships he fostered with his congregation, the pastor knew how to make his teaching of the academic program dynamic and interactive. This underscores yet another aspect of this new model: the reframing of unfamiliar material so that it is within the grasp of all parties, even the illiterate.

Thaiwatcharamas (chapter 13) describes how Thai Buddhists come to know reality. Words are not their primary focus. Their truth/learning is attained via their concrete interactions with the Christian communicator, which is a finding that corresponds with Rakhal's in chapter 7.

Both Thaiwatcharamas (chapter 13) and Castillo (chapter 16) purport that the Asian value of collectivism must be recognized and incorporated so that the gospel is focused on the collectivist decision-making level instead of the individualistic level. In other words, family evangelism and discipleship are the way forward in these cultural contexts.

---

18 Daniel R. Shaw, "Beyond Contextualization: Toward a Twenty-first-Century Model for Enabling Mission," *International Bulletin of Missionary Research* 34, no.4 (2010):208–214.

The *satsang* approach used by Yesudas (chapter 8) advocates the use of narrative accounts of Christ from the four gospels. According to Yesudas, *satsang* speaks to the hearts of Hindus who come from an oral tradition. Narrative theology, introduced in the late twentieth century, postulated that a narrative presentation of the faith, rather than systematic theology, speaks to the hearts of contemporary people.[19] Yesudas's recommendation corresponds with a concern raised by African theologians that the doctrine of Christ they had inherited from the West "jumps far too quickly from the cradle to the cross" and overlooks the immense importance of the life and ministry of Christ.[20]

In many parts of Asia, where chronic illness and demon possession coupled with unaffordable medical care prevail, the narratives of Christ and his miracles can provide experiential, pastoral, and realistic resources for discipleship and growth in Christlikeness.[21] According to Fu (chapter 14), a deep understanding of the life of Christ may hold the critical key to unlocking the door to true gospel contextualization in China, where the government has stepped in to have its say on the contextualization of Christianity.

Yesudas (chapter 8) makes the striking observation that reaching Hindus is best done in the context of worship. Yesudas's understanding of worship includes the singing of *bhajans* with Indian instruments. This is remarkable because, while many churches have used contextualized principles previously for teaching, most churches are still attached to Westernized forms of worship.[22] Contextualized worship in the church makes sense because Jesus said he came to seek true worshippers (John 4:23–24),

19 Keith E. Yandell, "Introduction," *Faith and Narrative*, ed. Keith E Yandell (Oxford: Oxford University Press, 2001), 1–3.

20 David W. Smith, *Against the Stream: Christianity and Mission in an Age of Globalization* (Leicester, UK: IVP, 2003), 127–128.Smith (2003) is referring to the African theologian Kenneth Ennang, who mentioned this principle in his book *Salvation in a Nigerian Background: Its Concept and Articulation among the Annang Independent Churches* (Berlin: Verlag von Dietrich Reimer, 1979), 334.

21 Smith, *Against the Stream*.

22 In the 1970s, the charismatic movement that originated in the USA (and produced worship and praise songs in a prolific way) was responsible for

so worship in Asian churches needs to reflect the languages and cultures of the people of Asia rather than rely on Western worship and liturgy.

Another important aspect of this new model is what I term "encounter theology." Many people in Asia live in a world of spirits, and they need to encounter Jesus to break free and see his reality in the process. In both Amjad's and Thaiwatcharamas's chapters (9, 10, and 13), we were informed that most people have come to Christ through healing and deliverance from spirits, as well as through dreams and visions. This is similar to Acts 8:7–8: "For with shrieks, impure spirits came out of many, and many who were paralyzed or lame were healed. So there was great joy in that city."

The three-self principle advocated by John Nevius in the 1800s stipulated an indigenized church in three ways: self-governing, self-supporting, and self-propagating.[23] In the new model, the church takes on a fourth dimension, self-theologizing, because Asian mission agencies and churches are looking at the Bible with Asian eyes, as articulated by Park in chapter 4. That the initiative to contextualize is coming from within, and that Asian pastors and mission leaders are becoming theological thinkers, is propitious.

Structures

There were two structures in mission history and strategy: church (modality) and mission agency (sodality). American missiologist Winter[24] argued that the church was originally involved in mission as one integrated entity (i.e., sodality and modality).[25] However, after the reformation in 1517, when the church was split into Catholic and Protestant, the

---

influencing the worship of churches throughout the world. So in a sense, worship and liturgy escaped much of the contextualization process in Asia.

23 R. Pierce Beaver, "The History of Mission Strategy," *Perspectives on the World Christian Movement*, ed. Ralph D Winter and Steven C. Hawthorne (Pasadena, CA: William Carey Library, 1999), 191–205.

24 Winter indicates that the monasteries in the Roman Catholic Church were considered the sodality or early prototype of the mission structure of the church.

25 Ralph D. Winter, "The Two Structures of God's Redemptive Mission," in *Perspectives on the World Christian Movement*, ed. Ralph D Winter and Steven C. Hawthorne (Pasadena, CA: William Carey Library, 1999), 178–190.

Protestant church failed to use the power and infrastructure of sodality. As a result, the Protestant church was left without a suitable "mechanism for mission for almost three hundred years."[26] The mission mechanism of Protestantism was restored in an embryonic form in the 1600s and, later, in a more focused way, when William Carey (1761–1834) started the Baptist Missionary Society in 1792.[27]

In the new model of mission, we see a vital change in both sodality and modality.[28] New indigenous mission agencies have emerged (sodalities), with indigenous modalities or churches that are specific to various Asian cultural people groups. In chapter 8, Yesudas bypasses the politicized term "churches" to employ the contextualized term *satsangs*. In chapter 6, Nyunt advocates house churches for converts from Myanmar Buddhism, and in chapters 9 and 10, Amjad reiterates that mission to Muslims is not just about getting the terminology and theology for the gospel right; it is about setting up a substitute spiritual home for former Muslim believers. He also proposes showing radical Christian love to Muslims. I concur that the structures for mission and church that worked in the past may have to give way to newer, nimbler, and more effective structures.

Scope

While contextualization was previously discussed within the confines of the ivory towers of theological seminaries, our book shows that the scope of contextualization is far-reaching and comprehensive—that is, the church, mission, and theological centers are all involved in contextualization. Moreover, contextualized issues are all-encompassing: for church life, evangelism, discipleship, and training.

Thaiwatcharamas (chapter 13) argues that in Thailand, discipleship comes first because the gospel is difficult for Thai Buddhists, and it takes a long time for them to understand Christianity. Therefore, the starting point of evangelism is discipleship, which is drastically different from the

26 Winter, "The Two Structures of God's Redemptive Mission."

27 Winter, "The Two Structures of God's Redemptive Mission."

28 Many of the sodalities (mission agencies) are small and unknown, but they are playing a key role in ensuring that the church nurtures the flock while the mission embarks on ongoing outreach.

Western model. Thaiwatcharamas's treatment of identity in Thai society is eye-opening for Thai Christians, who have been bound up in the Western Christian mold for hundreds of years. Thaiwatcharamas honors the Thai value of meekness to affirm Thai culture and encourage believers to follow Jesus their way.

According to Cortes (chapter 15), the challenge of evangelism and discipleship is not restricted to one location but is wherever people groups are found. For example, the Filipino diaspora is being trained and discipled in Singapore and is likely to transport this mission experience to several countries worldwide. Similarly, Amjad (chapters 9 and 10) has focused his outreach among Muslims living in Western lands.

Ching (chapter 11) reveals how the Muslim community in Southeast Asia is using the internet to contact Christian websites, which is a safe and sustainable way to learn about Jesus and grow knowledge of the Bible in basic discipleship training. Castillo's approach to discipleship for village pastors in the Philippines (chapter 16) shows how, after years of neglect, these pastors are receiving systematic on-site training in their respective villages using relational learning.

Praxis

Part of the release that former Myanmar and Thai Buddhists experience in finding their new identities as Myanmar and Thai Christians (chapters 13 and 6) is that they now have the desire to share the message with their fellow people. The dynamism and ripple effect of this approach is unique because insiders instead of outsiders (i.e., mission practitioners from abroad) are now instigating the work of telling their fellow citizens what they ought to know.

As we saw in Amjad's example (chapter 10) and consistently throughout this book, Asian believers are living the gospel in their respective contexts while preaching it. The praxis of Christian mission was evident during the COVID-19 pandemic, when AEFI leaders in ten Asian countries suffered alongside their fellow citizens, and yet they actively shared food, clothing, and medicine.[29] The implications of this God-in-our-midst enactment

29 Based on reports received at the Asia Evangelistic Fellowship International office in Perth, Australia from various AEFI fields in Asia from 2020–2023.

made the gospel real to people of many faiths and changed the mission dynamic from one of merely doing to being. The Indonesian Missionary Foundation, an indigenous mission organized by Indonesians to reach Indonesians, shared their experiences of being Christ during COVID-19:[30]

> As the country tries to recover from the crisis, IMF together with the local government tried to navigate tricky questions about transforming society through mission for a better quality of living by providing shelter for those who are in need. IMF became a place for Covid-19 patients in Batu and for East Java area. . . .
>
> IMF . . . opened its area and provided buildings to care for the sick. The newly completed building which was previously facilitated by the government for school facilities was used for the purpose of accommodating and caring for sick people. . . . Our building became a place of healing since the year 2020 and has accommodated more than 1000 people[.] . . . [I]t became a good witness of God's work through the presence of the institution.

Conclusion

Since the work of contextualization has only just begun in Asia, this compendium of chapters may serve as a useful tool and a further impetus for taking the eternal gospel into the unique contexts of various Asian cultures. The contributors and I are excited about the prospect of Asian Christians taking all that is good and biblical in their cultures—the great art forms, ideologies, and rituals—and eschewing all that is not biblical, such as polygamy, corruption, child sacrifice, and spiritism. We also look forward to seeing how Asian Christians provide fresh biblical perspectives to aspects of their culture that are deemed marginal or neutral. But in noticing these new developments, we are not implying that Christianity needs to be transformed.

---

30 Roland Octavianus, and Theresya Leiwakabessy, "Partnership in Missions," *Asian Missions Advance* 74, no. 22 (2022): 8.

On the contrary, we uphold that at the heart of Christianity is a powerful and breathtaking love story: the story of the interaction between God and human beings, as seen and experienced through the eyes of Jesus Christ. The life, narrative, and influence of Jesus have proven to be the touchstone for all who call themselves believers. Christians of every age, culture, and tradition have come to terms with the ultimate question: "Who is Jesus?" They have found that to know Jesus Christ as Lord, savior, and brother is the key and integrating point in this matchless story of Christianity—a story that is well and truly being fleshed out in Asia.[31]

Bibliography

Beaver, R. Pierce. "The History of Mission Strategy." In *Perspectives on the World Christian Movement,* edited by Ralph D Winter and Steven C. Hawthorne, 191–205. Pasadena, CA: William Carey Library, 1999.

Bosch, David. *Transforming Mission: Paradigm Shifts in the Theology of Mission.* Maryknoll: Orbis, 2012.

Bulatao, Jaime, S.J. *Split-Level Christianity.* Manila: Ateneo de Manila University, 1966.

David, Randy. "Split-Level Spirituality." *Randy David,* 1997. Accessed April10, 2023. http://www.randydavid.com/1997/03/split-level-spirituality/#:~:text=A%20long%20time%20ago%2C%20the%20Jesuit%20psychologist%20Fr.,Christian%20meanings%20upon%20native%20religious%20beliefs%20and%20practices.

Ennang, Kenneth. *Salvation in a Nigerian Background: Its Concept and Articulation among the Annang Independent Churches.* Berlin: Verlag von Dietrich Reimer, 1979.

Fernando, Ajith. "Missionaries Still Needed: But of a Special Kind." *Evangelical Missions Quarterly* 24, no.1 (January 1988):18–25.

Firth, Cyril B. *An Introduction to Indian Church History.* Chennai: CLS, 1961.

James, Jonathan D. "Preface." In *Rethinking, Reforming, and Renewal: Christianity in Myanmar,* edited by Peter Thein Nyunt, 1. Yangon: Rakhine Missions Band for Christ, 2020.

James, Jonathan D. *A Moving Faith: Muga Churches go South.* New Delhi: Sage Publications, 2015.

31 This whole section is adapted from my preface in the book: *Rethinking, Reforming and Renewal: Christianity in Myanmar* (Yangon: Rakhine Missions Band for Christ, 2020).

Macquarie Compact Dictionary. 8th edition. Sydney: Pan Macmillan, 2020.

Neil, Stephen. *A History of Christianity in India, 1707–1858*. Cambridge: Cambridge University Press, 1985.

Nelson, Martin L. *Readings in Third World Missions: A Collection of essential documents.* South Pasadena, CA: William Carey University Libraries, 1976.

Nggebu, Sostenis. "Coenrad Laurens Coolen: Pioneer of Contextual Mission among Javanese Abangans." *Evangelikal: Jurnal Teologi Injili dan Pembinaan Warga Jemaat* 6, no. 94 (2022): 94–108.

Octavianus, Roland and Theresya Leiwakabessy. "Partnership in Missions." *Asian Missions Advance* 74, no.22: (2022): 1–8.

Shaw, Daniel R. "Beyond Contextualization: Toward a Twenty-First-Century Model for Enabling Mission." *International Bulletin of Missionary Research* 34, no. 4 (2010): 208–214.

Smith, David W. *Against the Stream: Christianity and Mission in An Age of Globalization*. Leicester, UK: IVP, 2003.

Sperber, Dan and Deirdre Wilson. *Relevance: Communication and Cognition.* Oxford: Blackwell, 1995.

Whiteman, Darrell L. "Contextualization: The Theory, the Gap, the Challenge." *International Bulletin of Missionary Research* 2, no.1 (1997): 2–11.

Winter, Ralph D. "The Two Structures of God's Redemptive Mission." In *Perspectives on the World Christian Movement,* edited by Ralph D. Winter and Steven C. Hawthorne, 178–190. Pasadena, CA: William Carey Library, 1999.

World Christian Database. *Center for the Study of Global Christianity*. Accessed April 2, 2023. https://www.worldchristiandatabase.org/.

Yandell, Keith E. "Introduction." In *Faith and Narrative,* edited by Keith E Yandell, 1–3. Oxford: Oxford University Press, 2001.

CONTRIBUTORS

M. T. Amjad

M. T. Amjad is the chairperson of Khushkhabri Fellowship, a charity registered in England and Wales that works among Pakistanis in the UK and beyond. He has been working among South Asians in West London and other cities of the UK since 1998. He helped plant a church among South Asians in West London and worked as a pastor for ten years. Previously, he was a research fellow and worked on marine botany and published several publications. After coming into the ministry, he conducted ethnographic research on Muslim believers and Muslim seekers between 1996 and 2022 in South and East Asia and the UK. He has helped many Pakistanis in the UK and beyond.

Metosalem Castillo

Metosalem, or "Met," is the president of AEF Destiny Ministry, Inc., the Filipino entity of Asia Evangelistic Fellowship International (AEFI). Concurrently, he is the international director of the East Asia region of AEFI. Met holds a doctorate in missiology and a master's in missiology from Fuller Theological Seminary, a master's in theology from Asbury Theological Seminary, and a bachelor's in divinity from Union Biblical Seminary (India). A missionary by calling, Met, together with his wife Ina, served in Mindanao, Philippines; India; and Singapore. He was the first director of the Asia Mission Commission, which put missions in the programs of the members of the Evangelical Fellowship of Asia. Met is referred to as "Mr. Missions" in the Philippines. He taught missiology in the Philippines, Singapore, and Indonesia. He founded and established the Alliance Graduate School of Missions and the Great Commission Missionary Training Center, both in the Philippines. Met has written several books, such as *The*

Church in Thy House, Let's Plant Churches, Get Involved, and *Evangelize or Fossilize.* Met and Ina have three children and seven grandchildren.

Markus Ching

Markus is the Asia international director for AVC-BTM, a global missions agency based in Europe, which covers over ten nations in Asia and beyond. He researches comparative religion and writes about multimedia, social media, and the impact of religious dialogues on sociopolitical culture and the public space. Markus holds a doctoral degree and serves as an adjunct lecturer at Tung Ling Seminary, Malaysia and has taught at the Malaysia Baptist Theological Seminary and the Sabah Theological Seminary. He is on the international faculty of Haggai Institute, a center promoting cutting-edge leadership in contemporary culture.

Jingle D. Cortes

Jingle is a lawyer by profession. Her budding political career was interrupted when she and her husband Jonathan obeyed the Lord's call to go into full-time ministry with Navigators Singapore in 1987. She then entered church ministry as a worship and music pastor and evangelism and migrant workers' pastor to follow her passion for the Lord in outreach, discipleship, and worship. She graduated from Singapore Bible College (SBC) with a master's in divinity and a doctorate in ministry. She pastors the growing Filipino congregation in Bethesda Bedok Tampines Church in Singapore. Her goal is to make disciples of potential Filipino leaders in Singapore.

Muner Daliman

Muner is the founding pastor of Jemaat Greja Kristus Tuhan in Yogyakarta, Indonesia. In 1995, he founded STT KADESI, a theological seminary where he currently serves as principal. He received his doctorate in theology from STT Berita Hidup in Solo, Indonesia in 2014. In 2018, he was appointed as the president of Asia College of Ministry (ACOM) Indonesia. Muner is a noted educator and preacher in Indonesia, and his passion is to start training centers throughout Indonesia to equip village workers.

Peter Fu

Peter is the founding pastor of a house church in China. Before that, he was a pastor of a Three-Self Church for many years. His ministry focus is disciple-making and mission. For the last three years, he has focused on making disciples. He is an avid student of the Bible, and his other passion is preaching and teaching.

Jonathan D. James

Jonathan is the executive president of Asia Evangelistic Fellowship International (AEFI), a mission agency with nearly three hundred national missionaries in Asia and beyond. Educated in Singapore, the US, and Australia (where he completed his PhD), he is a researcher and writer on media, religion, politics, and culture. Jonathan is currently an adjunct lecturer at Edith Cowan University and a senior lecturer at the Sheridan Institute of Higher Education, both located in Perth, Australia. He is the author of various books, including *Transnational Religious Movements: Faith's Flows* (Sage 2017).

Violet James

Violet is a retired church history professor from the Singapore Bible College (SBC), where she worked for over forty years. She is currently an adjunct lecturer at the Singapore Bible College and the Baptist Theological Seminary in Singapore. Her PhD dissertation for the University of Aberdeen, Scotland was on American Protestant missions and their response to the Vietnam War. She has contributed to various publications, such as *The Atlas of Global Christianity* (Edinburgh Press, 2010).

Peter Thein Nyunt

Peter is the executive director of Rakhine Missions Band for Christ (RMBC), an outreach ministry that now numbers over two thousand former Buddhists and Muslims in Rakhine State, Myanmar. A former Buddhist monk, Peter holds a PhD in missiology from SAIACS in Bengaluru, India. Currently, he is the director of the Theological Commission and board chairman of the Myanmar Evangelical Graduate School of Theology. He is the author of three books and various articles on contextualization, including *Missions amidst Pagodas: Contextual Communication of the Gospel in the Burmese Buddhist Context* (Langham Monographs 2014).

Esther Park

Esther is the research and development director of Glocal Leaders Institute in California. She earned her PhD at the University of Wales, Trinity Saint David, UK. She has worked as a missionary in the Philippines for fifteen years. She is currently serving as a missionary to the Asian diaspora with Global Partners USA and Global Resonate in the US. Esther also teaches at the Presbyterian Theological Seminary and Grace Mission University in California as an adjunct professor.

Indra B. Rakhal

Indra converted from animistic Hinduism in 1977. Persecuted by his family, he went on to obtain his Master of Philosophy degree in sociology and anthropology and is currently a PhD candidate at Tribhuvan University, Nepal. He also studied theology in Maharashtra, India at Yavatmal College for Mission Leadership (1989–1991) before being appointed as the Nepal director of Asia Evangelistic Fellowship International (AEFI) in 1992. At AEF Nepal, he and his team have planted eighty-five indigenous churches and 220 house churches. He also founded Grace Academy (preschool to high school) in 1999, which now has more than five hundred students.

Pracha Thaiwatcharamas

Pracha is the senior pastor of the Sajatharm Baptist Church in Udon Thani Province, Northeast Thailand. He served as the president of the Thailand Baptist Seminary in Bangkok and worked with the seminary for seventeen years. He also founded the Thailand Christian Sports Association, where he evangelized and mobilized Thai Christians in sports ministry from 1990 onward. He received his doctorate from the Baptist Graduate Theological Seminary in Baguio, Philippines. He is currently the national director of Asia Evangelistic Fellowship (AEF) Thailand.

Daniel Trihandarkha

Daniel is the current chairman of Churches of Christ in Indonesia, an evangelical denomination with more than 230 churches nationwide and a combined membership of around ten thousand people. He was the youngest chairman in the history of the church when he was elected. Daniel has been teaching Old Testament theology and Christian counseling for more than twelve years. He is married and loves to spend time with his son Judah and listen to arias from famous operas. He discovered his love and gift of teaching when he studied in Tasmania, Australia for three years.

Anil Yesudas

Anil was born and raised in Central India. He obtained his Bachelor of Pharmacy and MBA in Indore, India. He also has a master's in health law from Loyola University, Chicago and a master's in community development from North Park University, Chicago. After ten years of working in the pharmaceutical industry, he resigned to serve God and the community full-time. Anil is interested in interfaith and housing rights activism. For over twenty years, he has been conducting regular contextualized devotions. He is associated with Asia Evangelistic Fellowship International (AEFI) and is a Brethren Assembly worker commended from Woodside Bible Chapel, Maywood, Illinois. He lives in Chicago with his family.

